Vernon Bailey

INTEGRATIVE NATURAL HISTORY SERIES
Texas Research Institute for Environmental Studies
Sam Houston State University
William I. Lutterschmidt and Brian R. Chapman, Editors

Vernon Bailey

Writings of a Field Naturalist on the Frontier

DAVID J. SCHMIDLY

Foreword by William I. Lutterschmidt and Brian R. Chapman

TEXAS A&M UNIVERSITY PRESS | COLLEGE STATION

First edition

This paper meets the requirements
of ANSI/NISO Z39.48–1992 (Permanence of Paper).
Binding materials have been chosen for durability.
Manufactured in the United States of America

Library of Congress Cataloging-in-Publication Data

Names: Schmidly, David J., 1943– author. | Bailey, Vernon, 1864-1942, author.
Title: Vernon Bailey : writings of a field naturalist on the frontier / David J. Schmidly.
Other titles: Integrative natural history series.
Description: First edition. | College Station : Texas A&M University Press, [2018] | Series: Integrative natural history series | Includes bibliographical references and index.
Identifiers: LCCN 2018018132| ISBN 9781623496791 (book/cloth : alk. paper) | ISBN 1623496799 (cloth : alk. paper) | ISBN 9781623496807 (ebook)
Subjects: LCSH: Bailey, Vernon, 1864–1942--Correspondence. | Naturalists--United States--Biography. | Naturalists--United States--Correspondence. | Mammalogists--United States--Biography. | Mammalogists--United States--Correspondence. | Natural history--United States--History. | LCGFT: Biographies.
Classification: LCC QH31.B155 S35 2018 | DDC 508.092 [B] --dc23 LC record available at https://lccn.loc.gov/2018018132

Dedication

To Harriet Kofalk (biographer of Florence Merriam Bailey) and Betty Hone (niece of Vernon Bailey) who started this project but unfortunately did not live to see it completed.

And to my lovely wife and soul mate of fifty-two years, Janet, who was my constant companion as I explored the archives and files about Vernon Bailey's life, and who read and provided critical advice about early drafts of the manuscript.

Nat*u*ral*ist /-list/ *n* (1587) 1: one that advocates or practices naturalism 2: a student of natural history; *esp*.: a field biologist.

—*Merriam-Webster's Collegiate Dictionary, 11th ed.*

Nowadays the field naturalist—who is usually at all points superior to the more closet naturalist—follows a profession as full of hazard and interest as that of the explorer or of the big-game hunter in the remote wilderness.

—*Theodore Roosevelt*

I have done all of the hard things possible for a man, and am glad. If I had been a woman I would have done all of the hard things that my mother did and gloried in them.

—*Vernon Bailey*

Contents

Series Foreword

Not so many years ago, most university ecology and natural history courses began with several lectures describing the history of the discipline. Textbooks often opened with an introductory chapter devoted to the historical significance of contributions made by the pioneers who established the foundation that stimulated further research and spurred the expansion of knowledge. In almost every academic course related to natural history, Vernon Orlando Bailey was mentioned as one of the earliest biologists to describe the unique fauna of the western territories of the United States.

As a young man growing up on the frontier in Minnesota, Vernon Bailey acquired an enduring interest in mammals. He trapped mink, otters, and other animals and sold their pelts to augment the family's income, taught himself taxidermy, and began his path to becoming one of the most renowned mammalogists. When he could not identify some of the specimens—particularly shrews—in his collection, young Bailey began corresponding with C. Hart Merriam, the first director of the fledgling government agency, the US Bureau of Biological Survey (later renamed the US Fish and Wildlife Service). Merriam quickly established an appreciation for the young man's skills and, after coaching Bailey on ways to measure, label, and catalog his specimens, he began buying Bailey's specimens for the national collection in Washington, DC.

In 1887, Merriam hired Bailey as a field agent and sent him to the remote edges of the expanding United States, including Glacier National Park, Carlsbad Caverns, and the Black Hills of South Dakota. In 1889, Bailey made the first of seven collecting trips to Texas. Many of his early trips focused on the Trans-Pecos region, but he eventually crisscrossed the entire state. The field work focused on collecting and describing the mammalian fauna but was supplemented by observations of birds, reptiles, and plants. The results and observations from his wide-ranging efforts in Texas were published in 1905 as North American Fauna Number 25 titled, *Biological Survey of Texas*.

David J. Schmidly first became acquainted with Bailey's life and career through a course taken as an undergraduate student. In the years that followed, David traveled a career path somewhat paralleling that of Vernon Bailey. After completing his BS degree in zoology, David remained at

Texas Tech University for his MS degree to study with noted mammalogist, Dr. Robert L. Packard. While conducting research for his MS degree and later his PhD under Dr. Donald F. Hoffmeister at the University of Illinois, Urbana, David traveled widely across Texas visiting many areas that Vernon Bailey had trod nearly a century earlier. Schmidly collected small mammal specimens from some of the same locales as did Bailey and examined museum specimens prepared by Bailey. Over his more than forty-year career as mammologist, professor, and academic administrator, Schmidly authored or coauthored more than 140 research papers and 12 books on mammalian fauna, including the widely used reference, *The Mammals of Texas*. Additional volumes described the mammals of the Trans-Pecos, East Texas, Texas bats, and the marine mammals of the Gulf of Mexico. Schmidly has served as president of the Southwestern Association of Naturalists and the Texas Society of Mammalogists as well as holding leadership positions in the American Society of Mammalogists. Few biologists can match the field experience acquired by Vernon Bailey, but David Schmidly is undoubtedly a close second.

David's field experience and admiration for Vernon Bailey was especially evident in his book *Texas Natural History: A Century of Change*. In this award-winning volume, Schmidly compared the mammalian fauna and habitats described in Bailey's 1905 comprehensive survey of Texas mammals to conditions existing nearly 100 years later. To illustrate the book, Schmidly visited locations indicated in Bailey's writings and compared habitats shown in photographs taken then with modern images showing the same geographic reference points.

As editors of the Integrative Natural History Series, we cannot express enough our excitement about Dr. David Schmidly's contribution to this series. He is the perfect author for this project. As a renowned mammologist himself, Schmidly's passion for the work and achievements of Vernon Bailey will become most obvious. His presentation of the accounts, history, and life-long accomplishments of Vernon Orlando Bailey derived from Bailey's original correspondence with family members, will inspire all naturalists and anyone who reads this biography. These accounts of history, government, politics, and most importantly the culture of place and time, makes this scholarly work a truly valuable contribution to integrative natural history.

—William I. Lutterschmidt and Brian R. Chapman
Series Editors

Preface

I first became interested in Vernon Bailey while studying Texas mammals as a graduate student in the 1960s. I read his 1905 *North American Fauna* bulletin "Biological Survey of Texas"[1] because one of the Texas species I was studying had been described and named by him. When I joined the faculty of the Department of Wildlife and Fisheries Sciences at Texas A&M University (TAMU) in 1971, I was given a transcribed copy of Bailey's handwritten field notes and descriptions of Texas during the time he worked in the state at the end of the nineteenth and beginning of the twentieth century.

My research on Texas mammals took me all over the state, including many of the places where Bailey had worked almost a century earlier. I began to understand how Texas was changing and the impacts of those changes on its fauna and flora. Then, in the 1980s and 1990s, while conducting research for my book *Texas Natural History: A Century of Change,* I visited the Smithsonian Institution archives and explored firsthand the extensive archival holdings of Bailey—his field notes, trip reports, specimen catalogs, photographs, and correspondence—not only from Texas but from all over the United States.[2]

I began to envision writing about this remarkable man and started putting together a list of other archival holdings to explore. I discovered that the American Heritage Center at the University of Wyoming housed an extensive archive about Bailey. These materials, which included his professional and personal correspondence as well as articles, manuscripts, and reports that he and his wife had prepared, had been saved over the years by members of Bailey's extended family and donated to the university by his niece, Betty Hone. His letters and papers were squirreled away in ribbon-tied boxes in one attic or another, and to those "pack rats" in his family a debt of gratitude is owed for making this book possible.

Other major archives with material about Bailey include the Library of Congress, the National Personnel Records Center, and the C. Hart Merriam and Florence Merriam Bailey papers in the Bancroft Library at the University of California at Berkeley. I examined all of these archives as well.

This book actually began as a presentation ("The Life and Career of Vernon Bailey: One of America's Greatest Field Naturalists") that I gave at the annual meeting of the American Society of Mammalogists (ASM) in Philadelphia in 2013. After that presentation, several of my colleagues suggested that I should organize a symposium about Bailey and the other naturalists who worked with him at the Biological Survey. That symposium, "United States Biological Survey and North American Natural History," was held the following year at the 2014 meeting of the ASM in Oklahoma City, and the edited papers were published as a compendium in 2016.[3] The article I wrote about Bailey chronicled the major achievements in his life and career.[4]

As I started to explore Bailey, my admiration for his many and varied accomplishments soon became a passionate search to learn more about this fascinating man. I became engrossed in the many letters he wrote to his family as well as his back-and-forth correspondence with C. Hart Merriam, the chief of the Biological Survey. The letters to his family documented his descriptions of the interesting places he was visiting in the Great Plains and the western United States, while serving his apprenticeship under Merriam, along with his inner feelings and experiences as he was transforming from a farm boy to a professional field naturalist. His correspondence with Merriam included a regular exchange of reports, feedback, and revised itineraries that were essential to his education as a field naturalist. Accordingly, I chose to weave excerpts from these letters into the text of this biography to convey the extraordinary qualities that compelled me to undertake this work. I hope that by using Bailey's own words I succeeded in some small measure in giving life to a man who came alive to me as I read his words.

Biographies have been published about some of the men and women who played a prominent role in Bailey's life and career, and they became a good source of historical material. In 1974 Keir Sterling published a biography about C. Hart Merriam (revised in 1977) who was pivotal to Bailey's development as a scientific naturalist.[5] In 1989, Harriet Kofalk published a biography of Florence Merriam Bailey (Bailey's wife, the sister of C. Hart Merriam, and one of the leading women ornithologists of her times), which also included much information about Bailey.[6] Then, I came into possession of an undated, incomplete draft manuscript that Kofalk and Betty Hone, Bailey's niece, had written about Bailey's life primarily based on his personal and family correspondence. Unfortunately, both Kofalk and Hone passed away before they could complete or publish their work. A copy of their unreferenced, draft manuscript has now been placed in the archives of the Southwest Collection at Texas Tech University where it is available for study.[7]

Bailey's early career was studied by a well-known historian of science, Robert E. Kohler, who, in 2008, wrote a major article about his socialization and development as a scientist growing up on a family farm and then coming under the tutelage of Merriam.[8] Kohler based his paper on the extensive letter exchange between Bailey and Merriam (housed at the University of Wyoming) as Bailey began his career as a field agent for the US Biological Survey.[9] This publication, plus Kohler's 2006 book about field survey work and collectors, which includes considerable mention of Bailey, is a major source of information for this book.[10]

All of this material is brought together in this book to focus on five aspects of Vernon Bailey's life and career: (1) his early childhood years growing up in a log cabin on the western frontier in Minnesota; (2) his apprenticeship and mentorship under C. Hart Merriam while working for the US Biological Survey; (3) his marriage in 1899 to Florence Merriam (C. Hart's sister) who would become his beloved companion on field trips and trusted confidante for over forty years; (4) the remainder of his career at the US Biological Survey following the departure of Merriam as head of the agency in 1910; and (5) his retirement years until his death in 1942.

The book is not intended to be a critical biography. Rather, it is primarily a chronicle of Vernon Bailey's interesting life. As a young boy myself, who grew up on a working family farm, where I developed an interest in natural history and subsequently became a naturalist after formal academic training, I have written about his life in terms of its meaning to me. I will leave it to others to work out for themselves the meaning of his life and work. Having made this disclaimer, however, I have attempted to discuss some of the emergent themes that tie Bailey's work and life to larger societal issues that were part of his era in US history.

The book is organized into five sections with multiple chapters in each section. Section I includes a series of chapters about the history of Bailey's family that were originally written, at the urging of Bailey, by his father, Hiram. That information was later edited by Bailey himself in a manuscript "The Hiram Bailey Family—Pioneers of America and Early Settlers of the Middle West" and distributed to family members. An original handwritten copy is housed in the Vernon Bailey Papers at the University of Wyoming.[11] This family history is followed by a series of chapters, also taken from material compiled by Bailey, about his early boyhood experiences.

Section II contains the largest number of chapters that detail Bailey's career, field trips, and life while serving his apprenticeship under Merriam at the Biological Survey. Section III has ten chapters describing Bailey's transition from strictly a field collector into a scientific naturalist who was publishing original work. Section IV has a series of chapters about how Bailey's work at the Survey changed following Merriam's retirement. The chapters in Section V chronicle Bailey's life and work following his retirement from the Survey in 1933. A final chapter summarizes the significant events of Bailey's life and career, including a discussion of his legacy and scientific accomplishments.

One appendix has been included. It includes a brief biographic sketch of the many naturalist colleagues with whom Bailey trained and/or worked and who are mentioned somewhere in the text.

Acknowledgments

As a naturalist and scientist, I have learned that it is not easy to write biography and history! I am indebted to many people who encouraged me along the way when I became frustrated and wanted to stop. From the inception of the project, Shannon Davies, director of the Texas A&M University Press, was patient in waiting for the final product and encouraged me to keep after it. Stacy Eisenstark, acquisitions editor for Texas A&M University Press, was helpful throughout the process, and two reviewers of the first submitted draft provided critical comments and suggestions to improve the content and readability of the book.

Several people helped assemble the background materials necessary to complete this work. Christine Hice, who worked for me as a research assistant while I was president of the University of New Mexico (UNM), with limited time for scholarly work, spent countless hours putting together a complete bibliography of Vernon Bailey's scientific publications and articles. This was no easy task given that many of his papers were written more than a century ago and were published in outlets that no longer exist today. Lisa Bradley, research associate and production editor for publications at the Natural Science Research Laboratory, the Museum of Texas Tech University, provided critical assistance with locating bibliographic reference materials about the US Biological Survey and members of its staff. Finally, I especially thank my wife and life partner for more than fifty years, Janet Schmidly, who assisted me at the various archives with recording information and copying materials as well as commenting insightfully on my work and making it tremendous fun at the same time.

For financial assistance, I thank the office of University Research at the University of New Mexico. A sabbatical leave provided by UNM in 2012, after I had retired as president, provided me the time to explore archival holdings, and it allowed a year to write, free of teaching and committee work. Shareen Siegrist in the Department of Biology at UNM was especially helpful in acquiring photographic images and documentation, and Amanda Jones, a graduate assistant, helped with the early stages of manuscript preparation.

I did much of my work at the American Heritage Center at the University of Wyoming (UW), which houses the Vernon Bailey papers, the most extensive archival holdings about my subject. I thank the president of UW, Tom

Buchanon, for providing unlimited access to the archives as well as providing Janet and me a beautiful place to stay while in Laramie. Tom also was kind enough to cover a sizeable photocopying expense at the Center so that I could have critical materials and documents back home to work on at my leisure. I also thank the staff at the Center for facilitating my use of the archives and for assisting with the imaging of critical photographs to include in the publication. The following individuals were especially helpful: Charles E. Anderson, John R. Waggener, Richard G. Ewig, and Ginny Kilander.

Many other individuals helped with various parts of my work. Tad Bennicoff, archivist at the Smithsonian Institution Archives, was especially helpful in providing access to the archives and facilitating the acquisition of photographic images. William Godwin, curator of the Natural History Collections at Sam Houston State University, assisted with access to the Horace Burke Natural History Library and the papers of Rollin Baker and A. S. Jackson. Barbara Hodges, a volunteer at the Churchill County Museum in Fallon, Nevada, provided access to archival materials about Anna Bailey Mills, Vernon's beloved little sister, and her family. Randy Kimbro, the son of Harriet Kofalk (deceased), assisted with information about his mother's contacts with Vernon Bailey's extant family and encouraged me to complete what his mother was unable to do. Alfred L. Gardner, research wildlife biologist, USGS-Patuxent Wildlife Research Center, National Museum of Natural History, and kindred mammalogist interested in the history of our profession, provided content and photographic materials from the Biological Survey files at the Wildlife Center.

Others who helped and deserve mention include the Manuscript Division, Library of Congress; staff members of the Bancroft Library at the University of California, Berkeley; National Archives & Records Administration, Still Picture Reference; the Conservation Center at the Denver Public Library; and the National Records Personnel Center.

To all of these entities and people, I owe a tremendous amount of gratitude for helping a field naturalist at the end of his string bring to life in print the accomplishments of a long forgotten naturalist who led a remarkable life.

I am, of course, solely responsible for any errors in fact or interpretation.

Vernon Bailey

Introduction and Background

Bailey's life and career (1864–1942) spanned the period in US history from the end of the Civil War until the beginning of World War II—a period of almost eight decades that encompassed the Gilded Age in American life, Reconstruction and the Indian Wars, the Progressive Era, including World War I and the Roaring Twenties, and the Great Depression. It also was a period of enormous interest in natural history and the conservation of natural resources.

Although the Civil War had slowed the acceleration of western expansion in the United States, it had picked up again in the last three decades of the nineteenth century due to the successful struggle to contain the Plains Indians in reservations and the completion of the transcontinental railroad in 1869. The mass movement was driven by immigration pressure and western homesteading and facilitated first by railroads and later by the automobile.

Over a period of four or five decades, from the 1870s to the 1920s, the North American landscape took on a mosaic character of dense settlements mingled with lightly occupied areas. Demographic pressure and a commercial society's hunger for property and profit drowned islands of nature in a rising tide of development. What emerged from this tension was an unusual intimacy between settled and natural areas, creating what has been termed an "inner frontier."[1]

Areas of relatively undisturbed nature, with much of its original flora and fauna intact, became accessible to people who lived in towns and cities, and it was this combination of wildness and availability that defined the inner frontiers. Many of them were in biogeographic regions where western and eastern, or northern and southern, faunas mingled, rendering them of great interest to field naturalists. Among the most interesting of the inner frontier regions were the "badlands" of the Dakota Territory; the deserts and isolated mountain ranges of the Southwest and Southern California; the canyon country of the Colorado Plateau; and the mountains, basins, and canyons of western Texas.

People of all walks of life began to access vast stretches of nature that just a few years before had been the domain of Indian hunters and the most well-heeled and adventurous sportsmen—men like Theodore Roosevelt, the twenty-sixth president of the United States.[2] This caught the attention of the

American public, and interest in natural history spiked throughout the country.

Hunting and natural history collecting became popular activities. The inner frontiers became a landscape for nature goers and nature going, as well as for scientists and collectors.[3] Young boys and girls grew up with an abiding interest and experience with nature and the ambition to become naturalists. As the railroads pushed even deeper into remote areas of North America, and followed beginning around 1910 by the automobile, naturalists were never far behind to explore the remaining pockets of relatively undisturbed nature still teeming with wildlife. Survey collecting became a dominant mode of field science expeditions dispatched to collect specimens and map the biogeography of species. This era became known as the "Age of Natural History Survey."[4]

Easy access to a wide spread of land made this a unique period in field biology. Collectors could easily reach areas that only a few years before had been virtually inaccessible and largely unknown (in any scientific sense) and make large collections using guns and traps that could then be shipped or mailed to metropolitan areas. The combination of railroad, telegraph, and a national freight and mail system allowed something never before possible: the rapid, coordinated, national collection of specimens. Earlier collectors had worked without immediate direction, often devoting considerable effort to reaching an area and staying alive, and then had to trust their collections to the mercy of cargo ships or wagons.

Onto this scene in the 1880s the federal government literally stumbled into wildlife work.[5] In 1884 the American Ornithological Union (AOU), a professional association of scientists studying birds, asked Congress to set up a new office to study the economic relations of birds and mammals. The next year, influenced by the lobbying of Spencer Fullerton Baird, secretary of the Smithsonian Institution, Congress appropriated $5,000 for the Office of Economic Ornithology in the Division of Entomology of the Department of Agriculture. Its first leader, C. Hart Merriam, a Yale-educated medical doctor turned naturalist, developed the agency as the first public institution devoted to natural history on a continental scale. In its glory years under Merriam from 1885 to 1910, the agency was to taxonomy and biogeography what the US Geological Survey was to field geology and physiography under John Wesley Powell.

Eager to professionalize mammalogy, in 1886 Merriam elevated the Economic Ornithology section into the Division of Economic Ornithology and Mammalogy, and Congress doubled its appropriation to $10,000. In principle, the new division was economic as it sought to develop a precise map of the continent's biogeographical "life zones" to serve as a practical guide to farmers in selecting crops that would survive in the semiarid homesteading regions as well as control noxious pests from damaging their crops. But in practice, Merriam was interested in the distribution of mammals across the United States. Owing to the creation of the Audubon Society and the AOU, birds were starting to be properly studied. But nobody was publishing similarly high quality bulletins about shrews, bats, mice, chipmunks, squirrels, gophers, groundhogs, skunks, ferrets, or dozens of other American mammals.

Very few naturalists previously cared much for mammals because they were nocturnal and difficult to capture. All of that began to change with the introduction of the first mass produced mousetraps. One kind of trap, in particular, transformed the science of mammalogy: the Cyclone Trap that was patented in 1883. This new trap allowed Merriam, and other naturalists, to collect in sufficiently large numbers and study the tiniest of species of shrews and rodents for the first time.[6]

Merriam realized that he could not do all of the work himself, including administering a new division and handling the political environment in Washington along with the scientific work. It became clear that he would need some talented people to assist him.[7] He especially realized that a survey of the mammal fauna in the United States could not be achieved without full-time people to work in the field and execute his strategy of mapping life zones and obtaining specimens and detailed descriptions of habitats and physiography.

Since no college or university provided the kind of training required for fieldwork with the Survey, Merriam preferred to hire "the farmer's boy who knows the plants and animals of his own home than the highest graduate in biology of our leading university." He felt that farm boys could be developed into sound general naturalists after learning about the fauna and flora of several districts.[8] As we shall see, this mold fit young Vernon Bailey to a "T"!

Vernon Orlando Bailey, the focus of this book, became one of Merriam's greatest protégés. As the first field agent of the Biological Survey he collected a large proportion of the specimens for Merriam's work.[9] After a few years Bailey was designated chief field naturalist of the US government, a title he held throughout most of his career at the Survey. Merriam nurtured, trained, and mentored Bailey from a young man with potential but no experience, growing up on a farm on the western edge of the American frontier without any formal education, into a capable field naturalist/mammalogist. After he had gained Merriam's confidence, Bailey became the trainer for most of the subsequent field agents hired by the agency.

Bailey's connection with his family and his work on the family farm fostered a desire to know nature scientifically. His scientific skills and vocation were not rooted in youthful leisure—the common path to scientific careers in middle-class families—but in productive, physically skilled labor on his family farm.[10] This connection with family work is one of the novel features of Bailey's story, and it is told in his own narrative in Section I of the book.

The young field agents, like Bailey, who worked for the Biological Survey while Merriam was chief, constituted a remarkable group. With little formal training in biology, the field agents were generally able to handle their complex assignments competently. They typically traveled to their field sites alone using railroad vouchers issued by the government for their fares. Once in the field, an agent paid his day-to-day costs out of pocket, since in those days the government did not reimburse Department of Agriculture employees for per diem expenses.

The field agent's job was to collect typical plants and animals native to the area where he was working and determine the life zones encountered. He would usually set out traps in a systematic manner, remaining in one place long enough to be reasonably certain of getting a representative collection of each species of mammal, reptile, or other animal. He then had to prepare skins and other specimens for shipment to Washington, where they could be studied at leisure. He had to make thorough notes about the areas covered so that adequate biogeographic summaries could later be compiled. A field agent might cover part of a state in depth or cover several states during the course of a collecting season.

A few of the more capable field agents were brought to Washington for museum work to learn the scientific aspects of taxonomy and systematics. Under the tutelage of Merriam, these men would "work up" the material from the field agents in the form of a scientific report of the region including the descriptions of new forms and later generic revisions and biogeographic surveys.

Working for Merriam was not easy since he was known to be strong willed, opinionated, and a petty tyrant when it came to expenses.[11] Throughout his tenure, the Biological Survey staff remained small and their salaries modest because the budget was modest. Bailey's first salary was only forty dollars per month, and he did not become a full-time employee until 1895 at a salary of $1,800 per annum.

Although the Survey began with an emphasis on research, after Merriam's retirement, it began to de-emphasize taxonomy and mapping flora and fauna. It focused on programs devoted to protecting and managing wildlife such as predator extermination, fur farming, and wildlife education.[12] Many of these added activities, especially predator and rodent control, would prove to be controversial with many stakeholders. The Lacey Act passed in 1900 pulled the Survey in the direction of managing, rather than just studying, wildlife as well as enforcing state and federal game laws. The protection of wildlife further expanded as an important part of the Survey's mission after Congress passed migratory bird protection laws in 1913, 1918, and 1929. Each of these developments affected Bailey's work at the Survey, although his focus always remained in the field and the use of that information to support policy of the Biological Survey.

Bailey's career at the Survey spanned a period of five decades that saw major changes in natural history. His career started in an era when collecting was open to all, requiring no special training and was, particularly in areas newly settled by Europeans, an important activity for science. Taxonomy was hardly required, and when it was, it did not require specialized knowledge. This was a time before universities became the sole point of entry into learned occupations.

We value stories like Bailey's not because they are typical, but because they are not! His story takes us back to an era when formal schooling was not the sole means of socializing into a scientific career. It illustrates the crucial role of family and of family work that instilled in this young boy an interest and appreciation for nature that, when accompanied by the opportunity for an apprenticeship with one of the leading naturalists of the times, eventually produced a man of enormous capability and productivity. Vernon Bailey was among the last generation of naturalists to be made entirely in the field, and it was through working in the field, trapping animals and preparing specimens, that he acquired a competence that would lead to an unusual life and career. We are unlikely to encounter anyone like him again in the field of natural history, and that is the real reason to tell his story.

I

The Bailey Family History

Vernon Bailey encouraged members of his family to write their history as they remembered it. The chapters in this section depict the history of the Bailey family from three family sources.

Both of Bailey's grandmothers were well versed in family lore back for several generations and loved to tell the experiences of fathers and grandfathers, uncles and great uncles, in the Revolutionary War and Indian wars back to early colonial times. One of Bailey's cousins (Hattie Roberts), who was raised by Grandmother Bailey after her mother died, wrote out for him what she could remember from her grandmother's stories.

Bailey's father, Hiram Bailey, in 1895, wrote out at Bailey's request what he could remember of the early history of the family up to the time when his father, Charles Thomas Bailey, settled on a farm in the wilderness near Clinton, Michigan, in 1835. The account included some of his father's hunting experiences there while he and his two older brothers, Alvin and Orlando, were boys.[1] Finally, Bailey himself wrote about his remembrances of family life growing up in Minnesota on the edge of the prairie frontier where his family had moved in 1869.[2]

From these sources Bailey compiled a manuscript, "The Hiram Bailey Family—Pioneers of America and Settlers of the Middle West," in 1928. Bailey was well aware of the uniqueness of his own experience and the times in which he lived. As he says, it describes "a condition never again to return and worth recording for those who will never see its type again."

Bailey saw his life as interesting and worthy of documentation. After compiling his autobiographical manuscript in 1928, he wrote the following letter in 1940 to the *Life in America* editor of the Houghton Mifflin Company to gauge their interest in publishing a book about this life and that of his family:

Dear Sir:
I have a meaningful manuscript, about 100 pages, of historical records of my father's family, during my growing up period of 1869 to 1898 in south-central Minnesota where we built a log house in the woods, cleared and developed a good farm in new country. There were 8 in the family, 3 boys and 3 girls, and we were 6 miles from the nearest neighbors but were never lonesome.

There was much hard work and we had to start with only what we had brought from southern Michigan in two covered wagons with two teams of horses, a cow and some chickens but our lives were comfortable and soon luxurious in the abundant produce of the farm, the game and wild fruits about us and a big comfortable house.

I started to write this book because in Hamlin Garland's "Pioneers of the Middle West and Some of the Middle Border" the hard things of pioneer farm life were too much emphasized. I wanted to show the joys of hard work and the strenuous simple life and the wealth of interests all around us, and show it in the simple narrative of home life.

The soil was rich, there was abundance of game including deer and bear, ducks and geese, prairie chickens and millions of passenger pigeons. Father and my older brother were good hunters and our fare was such as millionaires cannot have now.

We were all naturalists and I soon took up natural history as a lifework and have followed it ever since all over North America and have thought of calling the book "The Making of a Naturalist," instead of "The History of a Pioneer Family."

I have given the government 50 years of faithful and joyous service and at 76 years am still young and vigorous tho retired from active duties. I am not unknown among modern naturalists of the country but outdate most of those now living. I have published much but have a few books uncompleted, this one and one on the "Beavers of North America" and one on "Humane Methods of Trapping Animals."

Would you care to see any of my manuscripts?

You have published several of Mrs. Bailey's books under her pen name of Florence Merriam Bailey.

Sincerely yours,
Vernon Bailey[3]

No recorded response to the letter has been located.

Bailey's vivid fifty-page autobiographical account describes his childhood experiences on the frontier farm with his family. The chapters in this section begin with the early history of the Bailey family in the United States and continue with his account of growing up as a young boy on the edge of the frontier, which centered on the old log house his family built in 1871 in the edge of the hardwood forest of south central Minnesota and the family life typical of that part of the country from 1869 to 1887.

As Bailey recalled,

> On the edge of the forest, six miles from our nearest neighbors, my father and older brother built a commodious log house, in which my youthful days were spent in much comfort and a wholesome out-door life of hard work and great enjoyment. Our family comprised, besides my father and mother, two brothers and three sisters. The youngest sister, Anna, was born there in 1872. On our arrival, in the autumn of 1869, my oldest brother, Charles, was seventeen years old, Florence (Flo) was fifteen, Mary (Mate) seven, I was five and Henry was three years old—a well-balanced family, neither too large nor too small. For some years both of my grandmothers lived with us. Father's mother Anna Bailey (nee Wakelee) up to her death in 1875, and later my mother's sister, Lydia Taylor (nee Ogden), up to 1886.[4]

As we shall see in the next few chapters, Bailey's family environment along with his frontier life and farmwork were crucial to his development as a naturalist.

1

Early Family History (1637–1864)[1]

From Blacksmithing to Bailey Station

The Bailey's were an old, widely distributed name, well represented among the early colonies of America. The first of the family history that his grandmother knew of were two brothers who settled from England at the Jamestown Colony in Virginia soon after or at its founding (1607). One of them was killed by the Indians in the massacre of 1623, and the other moved to New Haven, Connecticut, in 1637 where he made a living as a blacksmith. He would have been Bailey's father's grandfather's grandfather. A large, strong man, supposedly six British seamen caught him at night while he was going home and tried to make him prisoner to take aboard their ship, but he slipped out of his coat, knocked them all down and ran away. The next day they sent word that he could have his coat if he would come aboard and get it!

The next story is of two brothers who were soldiers in the French and Indian War. One of them went on an expedition against the French and Indians (1755) and never returned and was supposedly killed. The next generation of the Baileys was Hiram's father's great-grandfather who was a blacksmith in New Haven. He was a soldier in the Revolutionary War (1777) and died about 1800.

Hiram Bailey's grandfather, Thomas Bailey (b. 1767, d. 1830), also was a blacksmith although he left New Haven and moved to the town of Washington, Litchfield County, Connecticut, where he bought a farm and did custom work in his shop and in the winters made hoes and other tools to sell in New Haven. He was a Congregationalist, rather strict in regard to their morals, as the Connecticut people generally were in those days, but known to be kind and pleasant to his family.

Hiram's grandmother's maiden name was Morse. Born in 1762, she had two uncles who served in the Revolution. One was in the Battle of Bunker Hill and the other was in a fort besieged by the British and their Indian allies where he was killed. His grandmother died in 1841 at the age of seventy-nine.

Hiram's father (Vernon's grandfather), Charles Thomas Bailey, was born March 2, 1794, and died December 18, 1850. At the age of thirteen he learned the carpenter's trade at which he worked for several years. He too was a conscientious Christian. He was in the draft for the War of 1812, but was not drawn and subsequently moved to New York where he worked in a copper shop for his uncle, Shover Minor. Charles Bailey married Anna Wakelee (b. 1795, d. 1875) in 1816 and subsequently moved to the town of Mina, New York, where they bought eighty acres of land and lived for ten years in this new, heavily timbered country. In 1835 Charles Bailey sold his farm in Mina and bought 163 acres of government land four miles from Clinton in the newly organized state of Michigan, where two of his uncles had located five years earlier.

Hiram Bailey, the son of Charles and father of Vernon, was born in 1831. In 1850, at the age of nineteen while he was attending college and studying to be a doctor, Charles died and Hiram returned to the farm to care for his mother and sister Sophronie. That same year he married Emily Ann Taylor, the daughter of Sher and Lydia Taylor, who was a teacher at the local school near Manchester, Michigan. Hiram made a living working on the farm and doing masonry work—building brick and stone houses, stone walls, and doing plastering. The first of his three children, Charles, was born there.

In 1856 Hiram moved to Tuscola County, near Saginaw Bay, and took a claim in the big white pine forest where he built a log house and lived until 1863. With only his rifle and ax and a few farm tools he cleared the forest and raised a family on the borderline of the frontier. Indians were his only near neighbors and, while friendly and harmless, they were a terror to Emily, who was often left alone for a week at a time while Hiram worked at plastering and brick laying. Hiram walked back and forth between jobs and packed flour and sugar home on his back to last until he could get a little more land cleared and a few crops growing. Hunting supplied an abundance of meat, mostly venison and elk along with ruffed grouse, passenger pigeons, and rabbits.

Very slowly progress was made in building up this wilderness home. Chickens and a cow and team were added, and grain and abundant vegetables were raised, so that wholesome food and some of the comforts of the frontier were available. Hiram always spoke of this life in the wilderness with the greatest enthusiasm, and even Emily, a beautiful young girl when she went into these somber woods, had much to tell of the interests and happiness of these years and little to say of the hardships and terrors. While

Hiram was fearless and optimistic, Emily was timid and nervous, but with a strength of will and character to overcome all obstacles and eventually to overrule all opposition. It was her knowledge of medicine and dietetics, skill in nursing and caring for both well and sick children that helped them survive under the wholesome but difficult conditions of pioneer life.

With a wife and three small children to support with his own efforts, Hiram considered his duty to be first to his family, and when the final draft for the Civil War came in 1863 he left his farm, borrowed three hundred dollars for a substitute, took his little family of three children back to Manchester and started again at his trade of plastering and bricklaying. It took him three years to pay off the debt while supporting his family.

2

Iron Creek Baby (1864–1872)[1]

Vernon Orlando Bailey, the second oldest son of Hiram and Emily Bailey, was born on June 21, 1864, in a little log house near the sawmill of his Grandfather Taylor in Manchester, Tuscola County, Michigan. He was the fourth member of the family that now included two older sisters, Florence Roselia (Flora) and Mary Sophronia (Mate), and his older brother Charles Asher.

The Bailey family lived in various rented houses in or near the town of Manchester while Hiram worked at his trade for a wage of three dollars a day. His brother, eleven years old when the family returned to Manchester, and sixteen when they left for Minnesota in 1869, was large and strong, and helped his father while learning a trade.

In 1869 Hiram sold the farm in Tuscola County and, with the money from the sale and what he saved, bought two teams and one heavy and one light wagon, in which all the essential family belongings were packed and they began a memorable journey westward to the unsettled country of the upper Mississippi Valley. Hiram had visited his older brother, Orlando Bailey, a couple of years before, near Elk River, Minnesota, and was greatly impressed by the open, easily cultivated, and rich-soiled country, as well as the abundance of game, fish, berries, timber, and native hay of this bounteous region.

There was plenty of government land, and the settlements were just beginning to occupy the choice prairie strips that lay ready for the plow. Having sold his previous claim before proving up, Hiram kept his homestead right and was eager to take advantage of it for a home.

Emily, Bailey's mother, wanted a home for her increasing family, which now included another son, Henry Clement, who was four years old, making five children in all. Although it meant long separation from her father and mother and sister and all of her old friends, she was willing to make the sacrifice, great as it was.

The heartbreaking parting between Emily and her parents and sister, out in the barn where the two covered wagons were well loaded behind the harnessed horses, was quiet and words were few, but the drawn faces and streaming of tears that flowed as they embraced made a lasting impression on young Vernon.

For Bailey, at the age of six, the relocation was a thrilling adventure and included many exciting incidents along the way with new scenes and different country. They experienced muddy roads where the horses had desperate struggles to drag the loaded wagons through; miles of rumbling plank roads that made the journey possible across the swamp lands of Indians; and rainy days when the wagon covers were a grateful protection to the occupants, and the soft bed in the back of the big wagon where the smaller children, including Vernon, rested and slept when weary. His older brother, Charles, a man in size and strength and energy, drove the smaller team, while Hiram usually drove the heavy wagon team. Emily did much of the planning and arrangements of the loads and placing of the children, as well as the camp cooking, and she was the guiding and directing spirit in the camp life. Vernon's older sisters, Flora, then ten years, and Mate, eight, helped their mother in the camp with household duties, and Hiram and Charles handled the heavier tasks and any part of the work that required time and strength.

Along the journey, they traveled through Chicago with its sandy streets sandwiched between boarded sidewalks and unpainted wooden houses. A little over a year later in 1871 they read the thrilling accounts in a daily paper of the disastrous fire that all but wiped out of existence the vast area of pine board houses.

Much of their journey was through farming country and between fields of corn and grain stubble, interspersed with small towns and farmhouses, where they bought supplies, grain and hay for the horses, and milk, butter, eggs, and vegetables for meals. As they reached the less settled parts of Wisconsin, many of the small lakes and streams contained ducks, and Hiram and Charles often secured a good mess of these along the way. They generally camped early enough to allow for comfortable camping. Good meals were enjoyed around the campfires, and feather beds in the two wagons under the covers gave comfortable nights, though often frosty mornings made the breakfast fire at dawn a most attractive spot.

In late October their wagon with its weary occupants crossed over a partly frozen river near the city of Minneapolis, which at that time was made up mainly of big mills and enormous piles of lumber. The river crossing proved to be an adventure because the river was partly frozen over so the ferryboat could not come to shore, and reaching the other side required crossing a wide body of ice on planks late in the evening for fear the boats would be entirely blocked by ice before morning. But they managed the crossing and soon afterward reached the farm home of Sophronie Wakeley, Hiram's youngest sister, and her husband, Gleason Wakeley, on the prairie west of Champlain and Anoke about twenty miles north of Minneapolis.

The family rested there a few days to recover from their journey that had covered almost seven hundred miles in five weeks. The trip had been a hard strain for all participants, including their sturdy teams. After a few days, they hitched up and completed the journey of about twenty miles farther north to Hiram's brother Orlando's place at Bailey Station, a stage station and hotel kept by him since 1852 on the Red River road. Later the name was applied to the railroad station on the Great Northern near there and remains today as a sidetrack and flag station about five miles north of the town of Elk River.

For a part of that first winter the family lived with Orlando, and the spring and next summer with Hiram's oldest brother, Alvin Bailey, who lived a quarter of a mile down the road on an adjoining farm. Hiram and Charles found plenty of work at plastering and brick and stone laying, at what seemed enormous wages—three dollars a day—when ordinary labor brought about one dollar a day.

During their second fall at Elk River the family moved into a small, abandoned log house about a mile from the new homestead and about five miles from their nearest neighbors. Between other work during the winter, Hiram and Charles began to construct a new house by using cut and hewed logs and timbers purchased at the sawmill in Elk River. Shingles for roofing, floors, partitions, doors, and rough furniture also were purchased at the sawmill. When spring came they laid the foundations of the house, and the walls were rapidly built of great logs that were fitted tightly together and hewed smooth on the inner surface. The roof was framed of dry tamarack rafters, wide roof boards, and good pine shingles, and as soon as the floors were laid and the doors and windows in the family moved into their own home with great joy and pride, although there was still much to be done to complete the house. The final plastering and tightening-up of walls and cracks was left until fall. A big fireplace, constructed out of bricks hauled from the only brick kiln within reach, about a dozen miles away on the west side of the Mississippi River, was built during the summer. It was a glorious fireplace that took four-foot logs and roared and cracked and threw out heat on cold winter nights. A cellar for vegetables was dug under the house after the roof was on, and later an outside bank cellar was constructed in the side hill at one corner of the house, where milk and meat and vegetables and fruit could be kept cool in summer and from freezing in winter.

When the great log house, with four rooms below and four upstairs was far enough along to be comfortable, a clearing was made on the warm slope nearby and garden vegetables, potatoes, turnips, corn, peas, and beans were planted in the rich, mellow, wood soil. Before the summer was over an abundant supply of fresh vegetables yielded luxurious fare for the rest of the season and a substantial store to carry the family through the coming winter. Two cows supplied milk and butter, and a small flock of hens supplied eggs for consumption and to sell.

Before cold weather began in the fall a log stable was built for the horses, cows, and hens, and plenty of hay was cut to last through the winter. It was one busy season for everyone in the family and they all worked hard. Vernon was then eight years old and Henry six years old, and they did their share of clearing ground, burning brush, hoeing the garden, hunting cows, and doing chores. There was no school, so the whole time was spent working, and the days never seemed long enough. Berry picking, wild strawberries in June, blueberries in July, raspberries and blackberries in August, and wild cranberries in September, provided an abundance of fruit, not only for the season but also to can and dry and preserve for winter use.

After the first season on the new place, there seemed always to be an abundance of everything needed for comfort and many luxuries. The abundant supply of game and delicious meats were an important factor in their lives and undoubtedly had much to do with the strength and energy required to conquer and build in a new country. Few now realize the importance of game and fur to the early pioneers and how settling the country would have been so difficult without them.

3

Life around the Bailey Homestead[1]

The first winter in the log house proved the wisdom of Hiram's choice of a homestead. With the cold weather, deep snows, and howling storms, his family was well protected, and blizzards that kept those on the prairies storm bound for days were mild and little felt in their sheltered forest home. Abundance of good wood was stored up from the summer's clearing; house and stable were tight and warm; and hay and all sorts of provisions were stored for the winter. They did not get out for regular work, except in decent weather. The principle winter work, along with regular chores and obtaining firewood, involved cutting tamarack poles in the swamp for fencing and cutting and hewing timbers for next year's building and to sell as railroad ties.

The long evenings around the big fireplace were memorable for the entire family. Usually someone read aloud while the rest worked or played or curled up in the comfortable corners around the fire. Hiram and Flora, Bailey's oldest sister, were especially good readers, and there were plenty of books and magazines and papers, some old and some new, to hold the interest of all.

A small flock of a dozen sheep had been added to the livestock and proved useful in several ways. An occasional large fat lamb made a good change from poultry and fat pork in haying time, but the primary importance of these sheep was their wool. Emily usually had a large basket of mending or garments to make for the family and plied her needle swiftly and skillfully. Grandmother Bailey, then living with them, was always knitting, and she turned out warm woolen mittens and big warm socks for everyone.

As a young boy, Vernon learned to knit. At first his part of the work was holding the skein of yarn, with arms stretched and thumbs up, while his mother or grandmother wound it into balls of yarn. But eventually he learned all the crocheting stiches that his sisters used, including learning how to make tatting and to use a needle to make patchwork blocks for quilts. In adulthood, Bailey would recall that this "was perhaps the best early training

I ever had in mechanical skill and deft use of the fingers, that have been of the greatest use through all of my work" as a naturalist.

Bailey's oldest brother, Charles, had become a hunter and often spent the evening cleaning his and Hiram's guns, which included a three-barreled rifle and double-barreled shotgun, both muzzle loaders. Bullets were made for the rifle from lead melted on the coals in a ladle and poured into a steel mold to harden. Boots and shoes and snowshoes had to be mended and greased, and there were many little jobs left over for the evenings to save the working time of the days for the regular work.

Charles and Hiram became great chums out together at work or hunting or fishing, while Emily was much more a part of the lives of the rest of the younger children. Often tired and sometimes irritable, she was generally sweet and gentle with the younger kids and as sympathetic with a stubbed toe as she was patient and skillful as a nurse through all the various maladies of a large family. Bailey could not remember a doctor ever coming to the house while he lived there up to 1887. When his sister was born, only his grandmother was with his mother.

On rare occasions visitors came and, if possible, were persuaded to stay overnight, and the news from other families and other settlements was always a treat and made the evenings last longer. If any of his Uncle Orlando's family came there was always a musical treat, even without an organ or any musical instruments. At bedtime there were always prayers and sometimes a chapter read from the Bible, or Hiram's deep earnest voice would offer the songs of David and the lamentations of Job.

In 1872, their first year in the new log house, Vernon's little sister Anna was born, eight years younger than he, the sixth child of the family and balancing the number to three girls and three boys. Always she was the pet and most loved of the family, but never spoiled or made selfish by it. She was most like Hiram—quiet, thoughtful, earnest, and so full of interest in all around her that the entire family took delight in watching her develop and grow. As she grew up, she became Vernon's naturalist pupil and companion, insisting on knowing all that he knew and sometimes more, and the two of them would enjoy a close, lifelong bond.

During the first winter in the log house, school was held at home with regular hours for study. Hiram and Emily would help the older children and Bailey's oldest sister, Flora, would teach the younger ones to read and spell and write. Not many books were required and the study hours were not long, because there was always much to be done, the girls helping their mother with the housework, and Henry and Vernon doing certain chores at the barn besides bringing in great piles of wood for cold winter nights. All of this involved real work and enough of it so there was solid comfort and some pride in finishing the chores and pulling off the caps and mittens and comforters, stamping and brushing the snow from boots or moccasins and getting ready for the hot and savory evening meal, prepared by Emily's skillful hands.

And such meals for hungry boys and hard-working men! A fair sample would be a big dish of venison stew with gravy, a platter heaped with meaty boiled potatoes and beans, homemade bread or hot soda biscuits, pickles and stewed fruit, and pie or berries for dessert. There was always plenty of milk and rolls of yellow golden butter except for short times when most of the cows went dry. During the summer, fat pork served with baked beans and boiled cabbage, fried rice and brown or cream gravy was another favored dish. Honey served on hot biscuits was a favorite at most of the family meals.

There were plenty of play times, too, snowballing and sliding downhill, shooting with homemade bows and arrows, tumbling in the haymow, and often before bedtime, a game of "blind man's bluff" in the corner of the big room well back from the fireplace. Whittling was also a great evening pastime, and Vernon and his brothers made many crude toys and playthings out of soft wood during those long winter evenings before the fireplace and by the light of tallow candles made in the tin molds from deer's tallow.

The children were not always little angels. There were the usual petty quarrels and bickering among a lot of children cloistered together, but wise parental authority smoothed out most of the imaginary troubles. As they grew up together, the children adjusted themselves to one another with ever-growing affection.

The winters were long and spring was greeted with great joy. As the snow melted halfway down and a few bare spots of earth came through, the maple trees were tapped and maple syrup and sugar were made in the big brass kettle on the stove, a rare treat to all of the youngsters. Soon the ducks and geese arrived and added variety to the winter fare, and the pickerel came up the creek or out on the flooded marshes, in great numbers, and their delicious white meat was another feast. A little later the passenger pigeons arrived in vast flocks, millions of them, so that a few loads of fine shot into a flock brought down enough for huge pies, which Emily knew how to make to near perfection. But soon the pigeons and game birds were nesting, and there was no more hunting or fresh meat until August, when the young prairie chickens were big enough to shoot.

New land was cleared as rapidly as possible, and the children did a fair share of piling and burning the brush, limbs, and sticks to make the ground ready for plowing. In this manner a few acres were added each year, but no extensive farming area was opened up for many years. Food for the family and the livestock was the main object in farming. Much attention was given to the garden, and from the time the pieplant (rhubarb) became large enough to use in May, radishes, lettuce, onions, peas, and beans came on, one after another, and provided wholesome food until green corn and new potatoes, string beans, summer squashes, and melons were ready in July and August. Then the winter vegetables, potatoes, winter squashes, pumpkins, turnips, beets, carrots, parsnips, onions, and beans, were matured and ready for regular use and to be cured or stored. This was perhaps the busiest season of the year for everyone because digging potatoes and husking corn and pulling beans was difficult work.

About the age of twelve, locating the cows became one of young Vernon's regular tasks. About five o'clock in the afternoon, after work in the hay field was winding down, Hiram would shout, "Who's going to get cows tonight?" And young Vernon was generally the first volunteer. His brother Henry often accompanied him and the two of them would be off on long walks through wooded trails for half a mile or a mile distance, guided by the cowbells to where the herd would be found grazing on the best grass the cows could find. For years they had the run of all the country outside of the fences as far as they wanted to go, although they rarely strayed more than a mile away. Often they came home at the time for milking but more often had to be hurried up or brought in from some distance.

Later in life Bailey credited that "hunting the cows" taught the boys fundamental woodsmen and hunting skills, and that tramping in the woods helped him to develop a deep curiosity about nature and natural history. They became familiar with every family of partridges and prairie chickens, with every duck pond and muskrat house for miles around. They learned to read the tracks along the road and trails, to know the plants and bushes and berry patches, the flowers and trees and where the hazelnuts grew biggest, and to locate the butternut trees that were going to yield a crop of rich nuts later on. When the cows were found it was a simple matter to start them toward home, count up to see that they were all there and to keep them moving, slowly and steadily. The jangling bells made a pleasant sound, and the boys could loiter by the best berry patches or hunt for frogs in the ponds along the way.

A major part of the farmwork involved haying. By the time he was twelve young Bailey could do a man's work in haying, cocking up the dried swaths, stacking, to keep and the lighter part of the work. Most of the marsh land was too wet and soft for teams, and the tall native brown-top grass, as high as a man's head, was cut with scythes, cocked up in large haycocks, poled by two men to a central spot, and stacked up about a ton or two tons in a round pilt to be hauled on sleighs in winter.

Bailey learned to carry the lighter rear end of the long smooth "hay poles" and took great delight in this feat, more of skill and activity than strength. Charles, by then a well-muscled man, would pitch the hay onto the stack while Vernon, light and quick, pushed and pulled it into place, tramped it down and soon learned to build up a neat and shapely stack that would shed water during the harvest rains and in winter yield a ton or more of beautiful, well-cured, bright green hay.

The cattle, horses, and sheep now required much feed for the long cold winters, and Charles and Vernon would often put up by hand one hundred tons of hay (estimated) to last them through the winter. Later they were able to ditch and dry the meadows, dig out the old stumps, pick up and burn the scattered sticks and logs, and seed the dried-out meadow with redtop, timothy, and red clover, thereby greatly improving the quality and quantity of hay and enabling them to use a mowing machine and horse rake to harvest the crop. Although Bailey later recalled this to be a great luxury, he did not think it was half of the fun of poling and stacking the hay by hand using the primitive method.

Charles was six feet tall and much heavier and stronger than Hiram, and he always took the heaviest part of the work. Vernon was not so large but, by the age of eighteen, was fully grown and very strong and quick so that he could keep up with Charles in almost any of the farmwork, taking great pride in doing a full man's share, especially in raking and binding the grain after Charles or Hiram, as they swung the old-fashioned "cradle" and laid the ripe wheat and oats in even swaths. Cradling grain was considered the heaviest work on the farm, and raking and binding over a good cradler took the most energy and skill, and only a few could keep up in a good stand of heavy grain.

During haying there were plenty of rainy days when the hay could not dry, and the family would bundle into the big farm wagon with pails, baskets, and washtubs to go "blue-berrying." In a good blueberry year the low bushes bent under the load of great bunches of light blue fruit that could be picked with both hands at once, and a large pail soon filled. Often they would bring back several bushels of these berries and feast on them for days as well as fill long rows of glass jars until the shelves in the outdoor cellar were stacked with the load. When all the cans were full and everyone was full, bushels were spread on papers on the wide piazza roofs and dried in the sun for next winter's use. These made wonderful pies, especially if mixed with dried pieplant or a few cranberries, for a tart flavor, or worked into mince pies with venison neck meat, suet, and chopped cranberries.

After a day's work in the hayfield, from six to twelve in the morning and from one to six in the afternoon, as the regular hours ran in those days, everyone welcomed the sound of the long tin horn calling them to supper. With scythes and pitchforks over their shoulders, they hurried home, washed up on the bench near the rain barrel, and soon were seated around the long table where Emily and the girls served a large meal.

The food would not be served until Hiram had fervently invoked a blessing on the food and their lives. There was no autocrat at the supper table but all had contributions to the day's news and doings, and the meals were the most social occasions next to the evenings. Although they were tired, the heavy day's work was done. After supper there were only the chores and in the long summer days a whole hour to do them in. Two of them usually milked the cows, three or four apiece, but sometimes there were a dozen cows to be milked and then others helped. Vernon had strong hands and usually milked. Four cows did not take long, which was his usual number morning and evening. The calves had to be fed, the pigs and chickens fed and the eggs gathered, the horses fed and watered, and vegetables brought from the garden for the next day. Everyone pitched in—with mother Emily taking care of the milk, the girls usually doing the dishes and helping with the other work, and the youngest usually gathering the eggs.

Bedtime was soon after dark in summer, but sometimes when they worked fast at the chores, there was half an hour of twilight before bedtime for a game of "three old cat" or to practice baseball. They always went to bed tired but slept quite well from the minute their heads touched the pillow to the break of day. On awakening they would jump into loose shirts and overalls and head off again to do the daylight chores, hustling to get them all done before breakfast was ready at half past five, so they could start for the field by six.

But always after breakfast, even in the busiest season, there was a quick gathering of the family in the other room, a brief chapter was read from the Bible, and all knelt in prayer while Hiram, in a rich earnest voice, asked for the day's guidance and blessing. Ten minutes every morning was given to devotion, which proved to have a huge influence in all their lives.

A new day, a bright world, new energy for the old tasks, in that sparkling climate of the north, the entire family kept up to it with wonderful spirit. In a softer southern air they might not have been able to keep the pace, but wholesome food and thought, infinitely varied duties and interests and the joy of growth and progress in a beautiful fresh, clean, new country gave them all the stimulus and zest needed. Mother Emily was often tired and worn, but so happy in a home of her own with a growing family around her that made life seem rich and full.

4

Wildlife and Hunting around the Homestead[1]

There was always time for hunting, even in the busiest part of haying and harvest. At the age of ten Vernon acquired his first gun—an old-fashioned, long-barreled, sixteen-gauge, muzzle-loading shotgun—and he was thrilled to finally reach the age where he could hunt. Up until then his bow and arrow had been his hunting weapon, but it had produced nothing larger than a pickerel and a muskrat.

Vernon's earliest hunting was largely for partridges (ruffed grouse) using his muzzle-loaded shotgun. He knew the general location of numerous flocks, and there was no trouble going out and getting a mess when needed, generally after supper or before breakfast in the morning. To shoot the large weapon required that he rest it against the side of a tree before aiming and pulling the trigger. Then he would have to measure the powder from the old powder horn, ram down a wad of soft paper, measure out an ounce of shot and put a cut cardboard wad on top of it, clear the tube and place a percussion cap, and get ready for another shot. Sometimes the birds would wait for him to load and sometimes not, but if the dog barked at them or if he kept whistling he found they would generally wait so that he could get two or three birds from a load. Four made a good meal, and that was generally considered the bag limit for a day.

To hunt prairie chickens, young Vernon had to go farther away, generally half a mile to a mile onto the more open ground where the blueberries grew. It was not until he was about fifteen years old that he could handle a gun rapidly enough to shoot these splendid birds on the wing as they rose with a booming roar out of the tall grass or low bushes. His older brother, with his double-barreled shotgun, was an expert shot and often accompanied him to hunt them. Shep, the family's bobtailed collie, would scare up the prairie chickens along the road and scatter a flock so that they could easily be flushed and shot. A couple of these big meaty birds were a good meal for the family, but enough for two meals was generally sought.

Although there were no game laws in those days, it was important, just like the Indians had done, not to waste game or kill more than actually needed, and especially not to hunt any kind of game in the breeding season. When the young grouse reached half size, only a few would be killed and the remainder spared until later when they had reached full size and were in prime condition. Special care was always taken not to kill the old grouse so long as the flocks were together and the female was needed by the inexperienced young.

Wood ducks were common summer residents, and a pair routinely nested in the big hollow basswood just back of their barn. Also, there was generally one or more pairs around each of the numerous small ponds in the woods, and, when the young were full grown in late August and the acorns had begun to fall, they would gather in flocks of twenty to fifty on the oak-covered ridges and feast on the acorns. The ducks soon became fat, and a mess of full-grown, fat, young ducks always made a great meal. For the early part of the season before the wild rice was ripe and the migrating ducks came down from the north, wood ducks were the most abundant and delicious waterfowl on the Bailey farm.

A few mallards nested around the lakeshores, but not many were seen until the fall migration began. Then mallards, blue-winged and green-winged teal, gadwalls, hooded mergansers, and later, lesser and greater scaup came by the thousands to feast on wild rice in many of the nearby lakes and in the creek that ran through the meadows near their farm. The best hunting was along the creek, when small flocks flew up, but by walking a mile before daylight to the nearest lake a mess of ducks could be had any morning as they came in or went out of the lake. The number of ducks seemed beyond all computation and the supply inexhaustible.

Canada geese came spring and fall in large flocks, and a few pairs remained every spring to breed. Nearly every large lake had a pair of these great birds, and out in the middle of some big marsh they would build a wide flat nest on some old muskrat house or some dry spot safe from high water. Occasionally, Vernon would take a set of six eggs, hatch them under a hen, and raise the quaint, greenish-yellow goslings. They were generally the tamest, friendliest, and most talkative birds of the barnyard, a great delight and interest.

Occasionally in early spring or late autumn long lines of irregular flocks of snow geese or "wavies" high overhead passed north honking but rarely alighting or coming low enough for a shot. The speckled, belted, and blue geese rarely were seen, although they were plentiful on the big prairie to the west. The whistling swans, with their thrilling bugle notes, were seen and heard every spring and fall, but they were too high up to be visible, and rarely came down to the ground.

Sandhill cranes were among the early spring birds that came soon after the snow had disappeared, at first in flocks of six to a dozen to alight and feed in the middle of some large field or meadow well out of rifle range, although a little later they were found in pairs on their breeding grounds. One pair generally nested on the marshy flat half a mile north of the Bailey home, where their bugle calls could be heard morning and evening as they returned from their feeding grounds along the marshy shores of Mud Lake, a mile away. They were never shot or disturbed, and their calls provided pleasure to everyone.

From early April, when a few ravens and crows came north, to be followed by eagles, hawks, mergansers, goldeneyes, geese, swans, and ducks, there was the expectation and excitement of new arrivals such as passenger pigeons, robins, bluebirds, flickers, meadowlarks, blackbirds, and a host of sparrows. Then, later in May, the warblers, tanagers, orioles, thrashers, thrushes, catbirds, wrens, nighthawks, whippoorwills, swifts, and, last of all, the tiny ruby-throated hummingbirds would arrive.

Any new or unfamiliar sound of the woods or fields or meadows was a matter requiring immediate investigation and sometimes the collecting of specimens to verify a rare record. No bird among them aroused more friendly feelings in Vernon than the upland plover with its trembling wings and long, delicately bubbling trill as they circled low and slowly around his head while he plowed the fields. He often found their gray eggs on the bare ground and moved them to a safer place so they could not be disturbed. The quaint flight song of Wilson's snipe could be heard high overhead on still evenings, or just before a rain, and the drumming of the ruffed grouse, the booming of the prairie chickens, and the pumping of the bitterns all made seasonal music around the Bailey homestead.

In summer the number of birds was reduced to the breeding species but with no reduction of interest. Nests, eggs, and young were rich in possibilities and problems, some of practical everyday importance, as when a flock of yellow-headed blackbirds stopped to pull up a few rows of sprouting corn, or a Cooper's hawk found that tame chickens were easier to catch for her hungry young than were the ruffed grouse nearer to her nest. None of these problems distracted the Baileys, because they always expected to replant some of the corn, and not many chickens were lost in summer and none in winter.

Passenger pigeons were common on their farm when Vernon was a young boy, and he witnessed their demise, later writing this account about their disappearance:

> For many years the pigeons were with us in what seemed inexhaustible numbers, but by 1886 they were becoming scarce, and that year I collected six sets of eggs, which are still, as I write in 1928, all in my old egg collection. They were all sets of single eggs and were taken in April and May. In 1887 the pigeons rapidly decreased. In 1889 a few were seen by my Father and brothers and sisters, and in 1890 the few last birds were recorded by my people while I was in the west . . .
>
> People are still wondering what became of the passenger pigeon but there was nothing strange about it. For ten years before they went a half dozen of our neighbors were netting pigeons for the market, and of course hundreds of others over the state. One of our near neighbors, Jim Kite, gave up working his farm, as he could make from six to eight dollars a day all summer catching pigeons for the market. Every few days he hauled a load of crates full of live pigeons past our house, 25 or 30 dozen to a load to ship to St. Paul and Minneapolis, where the commission men took them at one dollar to a dollar and a quarter a dozen and sold them to "sportsmen" for trap shooting. Pigeon shooting was a great evening sport all around the edges of the cities and the men from Minneapolis who came to our place in autumn to hunt ducks did much bragging of their exploits at shooting a dozen pigeons every evening over the trap and how easy it was to catch them in the air before they got a fair start and kill every one.
>
> The trapping went on all summer, all through the breeding season and right among the nests. Eggs were left cold and young birds starved in the nests by thousands. There were no laws to protect them, and we could do nothing but occasionally scare the birds off the baited pigeon beds, at the risk of being shot for it.
>
> The pigeon beds were placed under the trees where the ground was scraped bare for about eight by sixteen feet and fresh wheat scattered over the clean sand. It would be quickly found by the pigeons and in [a] few days the bed would be crowded at feeding time with hungry birds. A long fishnet was then staked down at one end of the bed and folded and covered with leaves along one side so that a quick haul from the blind on a rope attached to the one free corner would throw it over the whole flock of birds. As many as ten dozen were

> caught at a single haul but more often two to six dozen. Twenty or thirty beds were kept going by one man and only those well used were netted, a few birds each day, and then these were kept baited until new birds came.
>
> Is it any wonder the pigeons disappeared![2]

There were also plenty of mammals to hold Vernon's attention, and the first winter in their new log house was full of interesting experiences. The long log barn, with an ample haymow above the cattle and horses, also included a warm corner for the flock of hens that roosted on slender poles. As the snow got deeper outside, the native deer mice were naturally attracted to shelter, food, and a comfortable place to live, but they were soon followed by a little white weasel, who took up quarters in the barn and was often seen running along the logs and over roosts among the chickens. At first Vernon was afraid he would kill them, but he soon found that the weasel was only hunting for mice. Not a chicken was lost all winter but the mice were kept down to harmless numbers by this bold and bountiful little ermine.

Muskrats were abundant in the creeks that wound through the meadows and in all the old beaver pounds that still held water through most of the summer. Vernon learned from Charles how to set and fasten his traps on the banks of the creek close to deep water so the muskrat would soon drown when caught. Around the edges of the lakes he set traps under the water at the bank burrows and staked them down so the muskrats could not reach the surface and were quickly drowned. But mink and skunks and coons and foxes could not be taken without the cruel torture of mangled feet, and he did very little trapping for such animals.

Indians were practically gone from the region around the Bailey farm, although an occasional Chippewa and his wife would come through with a canoe gathering wild rice and small game along the St. Francis River or Tibbett's Brook, both of which ran through great wild rice lakes. The buffalo and elk were all gone and the caribou never got down quite so far south in the state. Large northern white-tailed deer, however, were still abundant, and fat venison was a staple of winter meat.

When the first tracking snow came in the fall, Hiram and Charles always went out and got a deer, which would last until cold weather and deep snow came followed by freezing weather for the rest of the winter. Then they would go out and kill from four to six deer, bring them in and hang them up in the woodshed where they kept frozen all winter and furnished delicious meat as well as buckskin for clothes, mittens, and moccasins.

In hunting deer Vernon learned to follow their tracks in the snow. When he went with his father and brother, he would carry a cowbell, and when the deer entered a swamp or thicket, he would walk through and drive them, while Hiram and Charles would go on both sides. The deer were not much afraid of a cowbell but would run ahead of it and keep stopping so that one or the other of the two hunters would generally get a good shot. A shepherd dog was generally taken along but kept at heel unless a deer was wounded, when he would generally hold it by barking until the hunters came up and killed it. Dogs were never used for running deer or foxes but their dog, "old Carlo," would occasionally find a bear in the swamp and hold him until the hunters arrived.

There was no check on market hunting and sled loads of deer were sold in Minneapolis and St. Paul every winter from any part of the country where they were sufficiently abundant. A good hunter would average two or three deer a day and make good wages selling them at very low market prices in the cities. Not until deer became scarce was there any thought of game laws or legal protection, but by this time there was plenty of cattle, sheep, hogs, and poultry, and there was less need of wild game, except as a luxury and an interest.

There were many fur-bearing animals around the homestead, mostly muskrats, mink, raccoon, skunks, red foxes, and a few otter. The extensive beaver dams, which were responsible for most of the great hay meadows, were important features of the country. Several ponds remained back of the larger dams where water was held all summer, and these were always choice breeding grounds for water birds and muskrats.

Bears were still fairly common when Vernon was a boy, and a few were seen almost every year. He distinctly remembered the spring of 1872 while his family was in the little log house on the old Tibbett's place before their new home was built. Three black bears came out of the tamarack swamp not far from the house as the snow was disappearing and bare ground was showing through the marsh grass. They were evidently gathering cranberries, which had been frozen through the winter and were sweet and pleasant tasting. For an hour, while the bears searched the vines for berries, Vernon and his siblings watched them through the window, but his mother would not allow them out of doors because Hiram and Charles were away at work on the new house.

Later, about 1880, their hunting dog, "old Carlo," drove a bear out of the tamarack swamp near home while Vernon was after the cows on "old Bess," one of the farm horses. As the bear came past with "old Carlo" at its heels,

Vernon gave chase and, horse as well as dog entering into the spirit of the game, crowded the bear so closely that he climbed up a burr oak tree with great speed and agility. Vernon had only a light, single-barreled shotgun, but a well-placed load of buckshot brought the bear tumbling to the ground quite dead, fortunately for the dog. Vernon measured the tracks where the bear's claw struck the bark of the tree and found that the hind feet had made their first scratches just a little higher than Vernon could reach with the tips of his fingers. After this experience, Vernon and Charles killed several more bear on different years with "old Carlo" along. Most of the bears lived farther north in the heavy timber, but for ten or a dozen years came down every fall when the acorns were ripe and laid in a store of fat for their winter's sleep.

5
Schooling and the Making of a Naturalist[1]

In the fall of 1873, with the haying and the harvest over on this fourth summer in Minnesota, the question of better schooling became important and much discussed. About four or five families had settled within a radius of a mile of the Bailey farm, and a dozen children of school age were eagerly waiting for a chance to go to school. A general meeting was held to discuss the matter, and a school district was organized with immediate plans to build a log schoolhouse. Then the neighbors gathered and built a substantial structure. One of the neighbors gave an acre of ground and six or eight men made quick work of the building. All of the work was volunteered, and the actual cost of the lumber and glass for the whole building could not have been more than twenty-five dollars in those days' prices. The schoolhouse was done before winter set in and a teacher hired for fourteen dollars a month and her board. "Boarding around" was the term used, staying at one house for a week then for a week at the next, or a part of the time proportionate to the number of children in the different families.

Fortunately, the Baileys had the largest family in the neighborhood, so they had the teacher for the greatest share of the time. Her name was Amanda Snow, and she was the daughter of the county surveyor from Big Lake, the next little town north of Elk River, and a friend of Hiram's. At eighteen, she was also near the age of Vernon's two oldest sisters and soon became fast friends with them. It was her first school as a teacher, and her education was not so far ahead of Vernon's older sisters. She had a strong, pleasing personality, refinement and a womanly poise, and she was important in awakening an interest and ambition to learn in young Vernon. After a dose of formal schooling, young Vernon soon became an avid reader and developed a flair for self-expression, self-teaching, and learning.

Vernon, his two older sisters, and his younger brother never missed a day during the winter term and, though blizzards often filled the trail with snow a few minutes after they had passed along, they were hungry for the schooling and took advantage of every moment for study. The winter term lasted only three months but it gave them a good start, and books were kept where they could continue some of their schoolwork after the term was over.

Three of the subsequent teachers were inspiring young women from the family of a Mr. Hill, fresh from the normal school at St. Cloud. They taught in sequence, and were followed by their brother, Chester Hill, who took the school for two additional terms. In many ways he was an inspiration for young Vernon and gave him a start in real knowledge. Without regard to any course of curriculum, he brought to school the books that Vernon wanted to study and gave him the free use of them and all the assistance he could ask. Aside from the regular routine he offered lessons in physics, physical geography, geology, chemistry, and astronomy.

At the same time, young Vernon was getting all he could hold of natural history in its broadest fields. Because of his work on the farm, he became attracted to the outdoors and developed an interest in natural history early in his life. By the time he was a teenager he began to collect birds, mammals, reptiles, and skeletons and plants. He picked up various lines of taxidermy by himself with the help of a little book by Oliver Davie.[2] He began to mount all of the specimens of birds and mammals he could and soon had a room full of these, besides doing occasional mounting for other people.

Through some correspondents in Canada, he had learned of a firm in Germany that supplied museums with specimens of birds and mammals and wrote to ask if they needed any specimens from his location. In reply, he received a very promising letter from Wilhelm Schneider at Halle von Salle, Germany, offering what seemed to him very large prices for the common mammals around his farm.[3] Soon he filled a considerable order for skunks, weasels, mink, raccoons, foxes, muskrats, and some of the smaller mammal skins accompanied by cleaned skulls and full data as to the scientific (taxonomic) and the common names.

With this success in his natural history work, which had become an absorbing interest, he began to devote all his spare time outside of a full day's work on the farm to collecting specimens of mammals and preparing them to the best of his knowledge. Although he seems to have been the one of his family most involved in naturalizing, his parents and siblings were interested in his work and eager to help. His youngest sister, Anna, now thirteen years old, was his constant companion in trapping, hunting, and making up specimens, and soon learned to skin and prepare birds and mammals as rapidly and skillfully as he could. Her help was a constant advantage and encouragement. For hunting and collecting he was now using a double-barreled shotgun, and Anna took little Stephen's single-barreled, 16-gauge shotgun that he had previously carried. She soon became an expert hunter with good wing shot and could bring down a prairie chicken or a duck with the certainty of an experienced marksman.

Even during the summer season, when work on the farm required almost all of his time between daylight and dark, young Vernon found it possible to keep lines of little traps out in the woods and meadows. In winter the farmwork was less pressing, and he devoted more time to collecting specimens, including many of the fur-bearing animals, squirrels, flying squirrels, rabbits, and many of the mice that did not hibernate, as well as several species of small shrews.

The shrews interested him especially because he could ascertain that there were more different kinds than he had supposed or that anyone seemed to know about. Using a few small traps he made himself, he started catching a considerable number of shrews in the day by keeping out food such as meat, fat, and bones for them to gnaw at under the old logs and other places in the woods. Since all of these little animals were active throughout the winter and soon gathered around any food supply, he was able to catch two or three a day in each trap by visiting the traps at frequent intervals. So, with half a dozen traps and many baited places he caught all of the shrews he wanted or could prepare for specimens. But the names of these little animals were a mystery to him. The differences were evident, but what to call them was beyond his comprehension.

Since he did not know of any book that could help him, Vernon wrote to a taxidermist, John Mordan, in London, Canada, asking if he knew of any way to identify these little animals. Mordan replied that he did not know of any book that would help him out, but he had heard of a man who was studying mammals and gave Bailey the name of Dr. C. Hart Merriam, a physician at Locust Grove, Lewis County, New York, and suggested that Dr. Merriam might be able to assist him with identifying specimens.

Vernon wrote to Merriam and received a prompt and courteous reply, offering to identify any specimens that he could send and also asking if he would collect certain things for him that he wanted. Vernon was more than glad to do this, and he began to supply Dr. Merriam with series of specimens of each of the different kinds of shrews, mice, and small mammals that he was finding, and the prices he was offered seemed fabulous to the young farm boy. For example, Merriam paid him $268.55 in 1886, equivalent to

$4,056 in today's currency, for a specimen allotment of 495 skins, 575 skulls, and 10 pickled specimens.[4]

Merriam was particularly interested in the shrews Bailey had sent to him. In obvious response to a query on how he had managed to capture so many shrews, Bailey told him about his trapping methods. Merriam admitted that he had never had much luck in catching them except in jars sunk in their runways, and he requested that Bailey send him a trap or a sketch of a trap that he had used. Merriam delighted in the trap, after seeing it, and commented on its simplicity and stated that he intended to make one just like it for himself.

At first Merriam wanted to purchase all the shrews Bailey could get, but when the number ran into the hundreds he put a limit on the number of each kind that he would need. He also wanted to buy skulls of many of the larger mammals including those trapped for fur, such as muskrat, mink, otter, and foxes. Of these he wanted all he could get, but when Bailey sent him the first lot, including a hundred muskrat skulls nicely cleaned and labeled, Merriam said that would be enough muskrats for the present, but he continued to take other species in moderate numbers. Young Bailey's greatest interest soon became hearing from Dr. Merriam and getting names of different animals that he was sending him, and, more important, getting his criticism and suggestions in regard to preparing specimens.

Dr. Merriam took the greatest pains in correcting errors in his methods, giving careful directions for taking measurements, labeling, cataloging, and keeping notes on all mammals collected. He wanted information on habits and abundance and many factors relating to the lives of all mammals, and Bailey furnished him useful information in exchange for providing the training needed for natural history work.

In 1884 Merriam sent Bailey a copy of his *Mammals of the Adirondack Region*, which had been published that year.[5] This book inspired young Vernon and led him to believe he could have a future career as a naturalist. Without books or any association with other naturalists, he was somewhat handicapped, but the enthusiasm now developed carried him over all obstacles and energetically forward in the delights of discovery. His farmwork had given him strong muscles, health, and endurance, and with eight hours of sleep at night, the rest of his time was eagerly filled with energetic efforts. New opportunities opened faster than he could meet them, mostly through the interest taken in his work by Dr. Merriam, but gradually he came in touch with other naturalists interested in both mammals and birds.

In 1885, with Dr. Merriam's assistance, he was elected a member of the

American Ornithologists Union and soon became acquainted with men who were interested in bird study. Professor W. W. Cook wrote him from Oklahoma, asking if he would be willing to keep notes on the migration of birds. This he was glad to do but soon found that his knowledge of species was very limited. He had no book and had never seen a book on birds, but, at Professor Cook's suggestion, he invested a dollar in Wheaton's *Birds of Ohio*, which included most of the species in his part of the country.[6]

Now with his time more than filled by study, correspondence, and collecting specimens, Hiram said never mind the farmwork as long as he needed the time for collecting specimens and learning what he needed to know. However, in the summer season he did not shirk any of the farm duties, but in the winter, when the rest of the family could easily carry the work, most of his time was devoted to collecting and study. For the next few years he kept full notes on the arrival and departure of birds during the fall and spring migrations and, besides filling out the regular schedule, listed the resident species with notes on habits and abundance.

Although these were busy and happy years, his schoolwork had been neglected except for what could be done at home in the long winter evenings. He felt the need for improvement in reading, grammar, and mathematics. In the autumn of 1886 he gave up some of his work for the sake of study and entered the high school in the village of Elk River. Fortunately the principal of the school, Mr. J. C. E. King, a medical student at the University of Minnesota taking alternate years off to teach and pay his way through school, became his teacher and mentor. He gave Bailey freedom in selecting what studies he needed most and all the help and encouragement he could in carrying them through. His knowledge of anatomy, physiology, and medicine were a great stimulus to Bailey, and he got a great deal out of the courses in anatomy, physiology, hygiene as well as physical geography, history, and mathematics.

Both of his older sisters were now married. Florence and her husband Chester Hill, Vernon's previous teacher in the log schoolhouse and now county superintendent of schools, were living in the village of Elk River. Vernon lived with them during the school week, but every Friday night walked home seven miles if he could not catch a ride with some of the farmers, and spent the weekend collecting and preparing specimens. Occasionally a deep snow or blizzard would cut off all traffic, but on skis or snowshoes the deep snow did not interfere with his trips, and toward spring, when the snow was well crusted and the skiing good, he could make good time and shorten the distance by cutting across a big swamp. The winter went all too rapidly, and the interests of his life were filling every waking moment.

By this time, in 1886, young Bailey clearly had his sights on a career as a commercial natural history collector, and he saw this as a way to contribute to his family's well-being. He did not yet see himself as a scientific naturalist nor understand what such a career might entail. Education in the frontier setting where he grew up was rudimentary, and he had only completed seven years of public school and two years of high school. He dropped out before the end of the school year in 1887 to go west for Merriam (see below) and again in 1888, for good, just before his graduation exams. Most of his education had been embedded in family and community life, but his early education, haphazard as it was, gave him a respect for learning and teaching that would inspire all his subsequent work as a naturalist.[7]

And now, he had met a man—a noted and respected naturalist—who recognized his potential and would provide him with the necessary instruction and training to become a career naturalist. Meeting and coming under the tutelage of C. Hart Merriam at the Biological Survey at a time when a career in natural history was fully possible without a formal education was the second major factor in Bailey's life and career.[8]

6

Specimens and Trapping Talk (1886–1887)

Merriam, who had just taken on the job of heading the federal government's first foray into natural history, could see the potential of Bailey and wanted to groom him as a collector. After receiving the early shipment of specimens from young Vernon, Merriam began to instruct him in the Linnean system for naming species that Bailey knew only by local common names. Merriam wrote out precise instructions for bringing the quality of his specimens up to his own standards and mailed Bailey one of his specimens as a model.

To Bailey, the attention was flattering and, thankful for the professional help, he saved the letter. Most of it is included here to illustrate the level of detail that Merriam used to train Bailey in his methods of specimen preparation.

US Dept of Agriculture
Economic Ornithology
Dr. C. Hart Merriam, Agent
Washington, DC
January 13, 1886

Mr. Vernon Bailey

Dear Sir:
Since receiving your box the other day I have been sick in bed with a severe bronchitis—hence please excuse the delay in writing.

Your work, while not quite up to my standard of excellence, shows very well that you are capable of making the best of skins; hence I will take the trouble to call your attention to several little points which will help you on the road to perfect skin making.

1st. Remove all *fat from skins. A number of yours are greasy and will become worse of course. Grease rots skins in time so that they fall to pieces.*

2nd. The fore legs should be placed close to or under the sides—never out an angle.

3rd. Always sew up the belly.

4th. Use a longer wire in the tail so that it will extend up further in the body.

5th. Take a little more pains in stuffing the heads and in arranging the feet—hind as well as fore.

6th. Always write out the month *on your labels instead of using numbers. One of your striped spermophiles is dated: "12.11.85 [male symbol]" but the skin does not look as if it was made in Dec. last. It is a poor skin and looks old. Two of the Shrews are dated respectively "12.9" and "12.11." Were they taken in Dec.? A Chipmunk is marked May 24, 1885, "[circle with +* above *it]." Is it a [male symbol] or a [female symbol]?*

7th. Use better paper and stronger thread for labels, and tie same on very firmly.

8th. Tie a tag onto each skull as soon as taken from the skin and number it with the same number on the skin. This is the only safe *way. I use small parchment paper tags (a few of which are enclosed) and tie one firmly to each skull as soon as removed from the skin. In this way (and in only this way) can a large number of specimens of the same species be handled at the same time without danger of getting the skulls mixed. In the Gray Squirrels sent, you have the skull marked "1" attached to the skin marked "2." But what is much worse and what I don't understand at all is this: You have a skull tied to a striped Spermophile which has another skull inside the skin. Now one beast cannot well have 2 skulls and as this second skull has no data—either as to sex, locality or date, I am totally at a loss to know what to do with it.*

I see that you do not keep a catalogue of your specimens. This is a great mistake. Every collector should keep a catalogue so that the data concerning any particular specimen can be found if necessary at any future time. I enclose sample page of a good form to adopt. The numbers should be consecutive and run from one to two and the skull and skin of the same individual should invariably bear the same number. A skin without a skull, or a skull without a skin, should be numbered independently and consecutively with the rest . . .

Some of your skulls, particularly those of the mice, are somewhat injured. This is most apt to happen about the base of the skull, where the delicate pterygoid processes are easily broken. This you can easily avoid by exercising a little more care in cleaning. In fact, you show such cleverness in this work that I am tempted to make you a proposition which I never made any other of my 20 collectors, namely, to clean the skulls entirely, ready for the cabinet. I think that with a very little practice you will be able to do this without injuring the skulls. If you will undertake the job, . . . I will, of course, pay you for the extra work.

Enclosed you will find a statement of the material recd. and prices I will pay for the same. If satisfactory I will send my check by return mail on hearing from you; if not, I will return the specimens according to the original agreement.

I would like 4 more badger skins and skulls and 2 "roughed out" skeletons. Also: 1 adult *fox in handsome pelage; 1* adult *coon d[itt]o; half a dozen large and half a dozen small weasles* [sic]*; 10 gray squirrels; 5 red squirrels and a lot more mice and shrews of all kinds—as well as chipmunks and spermophiles. The "black-backed shrew" wh[ich] you sent is an American race of Sorex vulgaris. (*?) The little one is probably Sorex palustris.*

I will send you, either in time or in a day or two, a schedule of prices wh[ich] I will pay for first class specimens in quantity with perfect cleaned skulls. I will take any number of good skulls of Badger, Otter, Skunk, Coon, Bear, Mink, Marten, Fisher, Wolverine, Beaver, Weasel, Muskrat, Pocket Gopher, Franklin's Gopher, Shrews, and a few foxes and wolves, without *skins at fair prices if accompanied by data.*

You are evidently a good hunter and trapper, and if you can get other mammals than those already mentioned, please let me know.

Hoping to hear from you soon, I am

Very truly yours,

/s/C. Hart Merriam[1]

Arsenic was the main ingredient in preserving specimens, and those using it often learned the hard way how to handle it. With his sudden increase in business, Bailey overdid his use of the product, writing Merriam that he had poisoned himself, a common hazard of the trade. Merriam, a physician who chose to focus on nature rather than people, responded in his best professional manner that he too had been poisoned and was very susceptible to its effects. He explained that arsenic was a local poison that operated by contacting skin, not through the blood or lungs. It was important not to get it on your hands or beneath your fingernails and then avoid contact with the face as well as cuts or scratches on your hands. He offered Bailey a few practical solutions to avoid the problem, writing to him on March 28, 1886,

I find that mixing alum into arsenic in the proportion of 1 part alum to 4 of arsenic lessens the liability to poison . . . I find that washing my hands often in cold water, and brushing out under my nails with a nail brush, helps immensely when using arsenic. Sal-Ammoniac is good to rub on a surface which is inflamed and painful from arsenic. Just moisten a chunk of it and rub it on 2 or 3 times a day.[2]

The remedy apparently worked and soon he was back to his preserving work and sent another shipment to Merriam. By June Merriam was eager for more. "I will take all the skins with skulls you have. In great haste, C. Hart Merriam."[3] In July, he had run up another account of $123, adding more to the income of the Bailey family farm. Ever the teacher to his young protégé, by August Merriam offered more advice on preparing specimens and then proposed a life-changing opportunity, so scantily mentioned at first that it must have seemed like a dream or vision to young Bailey: "Aside from the above mentioned defects, your specimens are very satisfactory,—so much so indeed that if agreeable to you I would like to have you make a special trip for me into the Great Plains after I have paid you for these specimens and have enough cash ahead to meet the cost."[4]

Their correspondence continued into August with Merriam instructing Bailey on specimen preparation and labeling. He inquired about skins that lacked matching skulls and was especially critical of the skull for a red squirrel that was marked "substituted" commenting,

I infer from this that the skull belonging to the skin was lost and that this, being of the same sex and date, was substituted for it. This must never be done. The original skull or none should accompany the skin in all cases. It often happens that a person is in doubt as to the age of a given specimen and not being able to tell them the skin goes to the skull which is always reliable. Hence if the skull came out of some other skin you can see what hole a man would be in.[5]

Merriam expressed pleasure that Bailey seemed agreeable to go on a collecting trip, promising him that it would be interesting. By October, Merriam had a secretary, to whom he dictated a very formal letter to Bailey, thanking the young naturalist for his comments and notes on a circular "Economic Relations of Mammals" that Merriam had provided him.[6]

In January 1887, Bailey heard from another ornithologist, S. O. Widmann, in St. Louis, Missouri, about some winter records of birds that Bailey had observed around his home, including the snow bunting, the northern waxwing, the Canada jay, evening grosbeak, and the pine grosbeak. Widmann encouraged him to publish the information, "Your winter notes give one a good idea what birds occur at your place during the depths of winter, & I think they would make an interesting article for the 'Ornithologist & Oologist.'"[7] Bailey's reputation was spreading. Additional orders for specimens came from Germany, with one correspondent noting that he could not order anymore because of an imminent war between Germany and France.[8]

With the turn of seasons, Bailey heard again from Merriam, adding more intrigue, "When do you expect to leave school? I have just thought of a scheme by which you may be able to take a little trip into Dakota in May if you would like to."[9] Clearly, the relationship between Bailey and Merriam was ready for another step—a new dimension of the apprenticeship between collector and mentor. This also would prove to be the beginning of a new life and career for Bailey.

Hiram Bailey, twenty-seven years old. Daguerreotype. Courtesy of the Vernon Bailey Papers, Box 18, American Heritage Center, University of Wyoming.

Emily Ann (nee Taylor) Bailey with son Charles Asher Bailey, Vernon's oldest brother. Daguerreotype from 1858. Courtesy of the Vernon Bailey Papers, Box 18, American Heritage Center, University of Wyoming.

Vernon Bailey's maternal grandfather Asher Taylor, 1858. Courtesy of the Vernon Bailey Papers, Box 18, American Heritage Center, University of Wyoming.

Vernon Bailey's father Hiram Bailey. Courtesy of the Vernon Bailey Papers, Box 18, American Heritage Center, University of Wyoming.

Vernon Bailey's three sisters, Flo (left, Florence Rosalia), Mate (right, Mary Sophronia), and Anna (center, Anna Laura) in 1884. Courtesy of the Vernon Bailey Papers, Box 18, American Heritage Center, University of Wyoming.

Vernon Bailey's younger brother, Henry. n.d. Courtesy of the Vernon Bailey Papers, Box 18, American Heritage Center, University of Wyoming.

II

Working for Merriam and the US Government

After discovering Vernon Bailey, and seeing his response and improvement with criticism and instruction, Merriam began to see that the young farm boy had exceptional promise as a collector and naturalist, but felt that he needed to be "tested" with a field trip of his own to see how he would adapt to the rigors of the work.

Bailey was thrilled at the prospect of travel. He had been no farther from home than the prairies just to the northwest of Elk River, and he was finding that wildlife in his home area was becoming scarce as the country got more settled. He was young (twenty-two years old) and unmarried, and he could go anywhere and stay as long as he liked. "I have plenty of good steady work at home on our farm," he wrote Merriam, "but I like collecting better as I then have a chance to study a little and I like to collect for you as I get much besides money for my work."[1]

So, in 1887, although he had never personally met Merriam, Bailey received an appointment as the first special field agent of the US Department of Agriculture at a starting salary of forty dollars per month, supplemented by an additional ten dollars per month provided by Merriam himself. Merriam planned the itinerary of Bailey's first trip to take him through a biogeographically most interesting region—where eastern fauna gave way to western—from Minnesota through Dakota Territory to the Black Hills.[2]

The chapters in this section are based on letters, mostly between Bailey and Merriam, documenting in detail his first experiences as a career collector and naturalist, traveling across the American West from 1887 to 1892. These letters contain Bailey's detailed reports of what he was finding and Merriam's scientific analysis of the new material and his revised directives for the next leg of Bailey's fieldwork. Most of Merriam's letters to Bailey survive, as well as a good many of Bailey's to Merriam.

There are almost weekly, and sometimes daily, letters between Bailey in the field and Merriam back in Washington. When Bailey's shipments and reports arrived at Washington, Merriam would immediately identify specimens and correct his species lists and maps. This knowledge would then be returned to Bailey in letters identifying and naming his specimens, with instructions on the species that Merriam expected Bailey to find at his next stop. Merriam urged Bailey to reread his letters (like a reference book) and would occasionally return identified specimens for Bailey's education.[3]

Much effort went into keeping this communication system working smoothly. Itineraries were carefully designed so that Bailey could stop regularly at places with post offices. He was expected to telegraph his whereabouts and plans regularly to home base. Merriam would occasionally send duplicate directions to several places, enjoining Bailey to check for telegrams wherever he was near a Western Union office. Lapses in communication caused agitation on both sides.

Bailey's work often involved strenuous, unrelenting labor in trying circumstances. Just the routine hazards of moving cross-country with gear and boxes of specimens could be trying. And Bailey had to do most of this by himself because he was alone for a year or more on his first trips for Merriam in the late 1880s. His work involved an unrelenting cycle of trapping, preparing specimens, packing, and shipping. Typically, he liked to hunt and clear his traps in the morning, skin and prepare specimens in the afternoon, and then go hunting again after supper. This routine was punctuated by visits to the nearest railroad station and post office to send out boxes of specimens and receive letters of praise or chastisement, plus instructions for the next leg of the trip.

Bailey had to rely on local infrastructure for logistic support: railroads and wagon tracks, river and coastal steamers, logging and mining camps, military posts, and tourist resorts. It was important to stay within the network of railroads, telegraphs, post offices, and rural towns to receive directives and send back crates of specimens.

How did young Vernon Bailey handle being away from home and experiencing field survey work for the first time? We get a glimpse into his inner thoughts and feelings from the letters that he wrote to his family, back home on their frontier farm near Elk River, Minnesota. Following the tradition of his family, devout Methodists who kept the Sabbath, Bailey kept Sundays free for letter writing, and his weekly letters are a vivid record of his experiences and feelings during his first sustained work as a career naturalist. His letters to his parents and five siblings are free of literary artifice, and his language is frequently revealing about the inner experiences of his transformation from farm boy and would-be commercial collector to professional field naturalist.[4]

Bailey's ritual of Sunday letter writing also sustained his ties to home. The Sabbath was a day of reflection and communion with family. As he once observed, the act of writing was to him like actual conversation, "There is nothing I enjoy so much as a nice Sunday morning, with nothing to bother me and a quiet day ahead to get some letters from home. Then to sit down and write to you seems almost like talking to you."[5] However far afield, for one day a week, at least he felt close to the folks at home. We have lost touch with letter writing as an art in our culture, but Vernon Bailey practiced it well and often throughout his life and career.

7
Employment and a Field Trip

May 4, 1887, was a red-letter day for young Bailey. The mail brought his official appointment, effective that date, from the US Commissioner of Agriculture as "a special Field Agent of the Division of Economic Ornithology and Mammalogy of this Department, at a salary of forty dollars ($40) per month."[1] It must have been a red-letter day for Merriam as well—the first trip of his first field agent in what would become a lifelong association. Bailey was to work for the federal agency for the next forty-six years. Bailey described the situation as follows,

> In the spring of 1887 I had a letter from Dr. Merriam, asking if I would consider a collecting trip into Dakota and Montana when the snow had gone and the spring migration had begun. I wrote him at once that I would be glad to do so, and on May 9 received my first appointment as a field agent of the newly created Division of Economic Ornithology and Mammalogy of the United States Department of Agriculture. This was signed by Secretary Norman K. Coleman and was followed by detailed instructions from Dr. Merriam as to the nature of the fieldwork desired. I was at school when the letters came, and, closing my desk, said goodbye to my teachers, and went home that night, made all the preparations for the trip the next day, and the following morning, May 11, took the train at Elk River for Washington, Minnesota.[2]

Along with the official itinerary from the commissioner for his upcoming trip, Merriam described his own idea of what the journey would include and agreed to bump his salary with his own funds. Merriam's letter lays out in great detail the expectations for how Bailey was to conduct fieldwork:

> *You must keep a careful daily journal of this trip, to be sent to me on your return. Before leaving any locality at which you have stopped a few days, give*

a brief account of the more important physical features of the place. This will help explain any peculiarities which the species found there may suggest. . . .

When in localities where letters may be mailed frequently, you will write to the Ornithologist at least twice each week, reporting progress, and asking any questions which may suggest themselves. . . .

In addition to the $40 per month which you will receive from the Department, I will pay you $10 per month personally so you will receive in all $50.00 per month besides your expense, which I think you will find profitable as well as agreeable.

I have planned for you a remarkably interesting trip and envy you in it. Would give almost anything if I could go myself. . . . You will find new mammals and new birds constantly after entering Dakota. . . .

You understand, of course, that the idea is to keep in fruitful localities as much of the time as possible. I have so worded your instructions as to give you entire liberty to stop off wherever and whenever you find promising places, and to pass over places which prove unfruitful. I have so planned the trip, also, as to take you into the most interesting faunal regions of Dakota, and at the same time the regions characterized by most diverse physical conditions, as you will see later.

What sort of a collecting gun have you? You will of course take plenty of arsenic and alum (for preserving specimens) and a good outfit of traps. You can send all the specimens you collect direct to the Dept. from the field. You had better ship a box on leaving each locality. . . . I particularly want things that you have not already sent me from Elk River. . . .

A large part of your journey will be made by stage and wagon, and some trips on horseback and by boat. In all of these, as in everything else, be very particular *about getting sub-vouchers properly signed. . . .*

Heretofore, you have not kept—or at least have not sent me—much in the way of field notes. On the trip it is essential *that you keep full notes on the habits, food, etc. of all species, both of mammals and birds. . . .*

Since the principal object of this trip is to determine the geographical distribution of species, you had better make a list of all *the mammals found at each locality you visit, and of all the birds found* breeding. *Determine with as much precision as possible the boundary line between the Eastern and Plains faunas. . . .*

If you conduct this expedition in a manner satisfactory to both of us, it is not likely to be your last.

Now in regard to funds: I imagine you may not have enough money in hand to give you a fair start. If this is the case, telegraph me and I will send you some to Round Lake by registered mail.

You will draw your salary the first of each month, but must sign duplicate vouchers first. You had better sign the enclosed now *and forward them to me so that I can draw and send you your salary promptly on each pay day.*

You had better, also, send in vouchers for your expense account at the end of each month. With this voucher (find sample enclosed) you must send the accompanying sub-vouchers or bills which need not *be in duplicate. The large vouchers must always be in duplicate, and must be receipted at the bottom before sent. With each must be sent an affidavit (blanks sent to Round Lake) which you must swear to before a notary.*

Write in full about anything you don't understand. Hastily, /s/C. Hart Merriam[3]

Bailey's response, written on May 10, showed both his excitement and trepidation about the trip ahead:

I received your letter containing my appointment, yesterday at noon and I tried my best to get off today but found I could not and be well prepared, so will start at 6 oclock tomorrow morning (the 11th) for Round Lake.

I have taken the oath & will send it & the vouchers by next mail, with this.

I have my outfit all packed and am quite well satisfied with it. I have about 15 traps, No. 0 and larger; a good single barrel breech loading T. Stevens shot gun, & a repeating rifle. It seems doubtful whether the transfer order will take me from here to St. Paul as it seems necessary to take it to a general passenger agent or the superintendent of the road before transportation can be had. And I can not see these persons until arriving at St. Paul but I will go some how. I now have about $12.00 which will last me for some time. But, if you will, please advance me $10.00 when you receive this if I do not draw any pay until the first of next month.

Your instructions are so full & plain that I do not think I will have any trouble in understanding what is wanted.

The appointment was a most agreeable surprise to me & the route you have chosen is exactly to my liking. I do not feel well qualified for the work but shall do my level best to make the trip a success and if hard work & study can bring anything out of it I am not afraid of it either. Will write you as soon as I get to Round Lake & take a look.

Yours very gratefully,
Vernon Bailey[4]

8

Dear Folks at Home (1887)

By mid-May, young Bailey was well on his way west, following the instructions he'd been sent. He dutifully sent his first report to Merriam from Heron Lake, Minnesota. It brought back a request from his boss for more specimens—a lifelong desire that was to frustrate Bailey at times when he wanted to send special skins home to his fledgling naturalist sister. Although Bailey had trepidations about what his new boss would think of his work, Merriam encouraged his young charge with one brief sentence at the end of his response: "Your report from Heron Lake is entirely satisfactory." Bailey had other questions, which Merriam answered in good faith, as he was to do throughout their lifetimes,

> *You say you do not understand exactly what is expected in the way of notes on mammals. Under this head you should record all you learn in each locality visited concerning the distribution, abundance, food-habits, breeding-habits, etc. of all the species found there. In cases where mammals are scarce, and you learn that the reason may be because of large freshets or spring floods, you will of course record the fact.*[1]

Merriam's letters to Bailey, especially when he was still learning the ropes of survey work, are full of injunctions to keep more complete and precise records and notes of his observations.

In what was to become a long-term, weekly pattern, Bailey worked six long days and took Sunday in quiet, going to church if a nearby one appealed to him, otherwise spending the day reading letters from home and any magazines they forwarded to him, such as the popular tabloid *Youth's Companion* or *The Auk* from the American Ornithologists Union. Sunday was also his day to write letters, most often generically to the "Folks at Home." His letters home were treasured and passed from hand to hand so all in the family could share in his adventures. He included lengthy descriptions of the land he saw and the natural wonders that awed him all of his life and which he worked so hard to conserve.

Bailey's first letter written from the field is quoted in its entirety to set the stage for what was to come:

Heron Lake, Minnesota
May 15, 1887
To all the Dear folks at home,
It is Sunday and so I have time to write a long letter.

The weather is beautiful. I couldn't improve it any if I had the handling of it myself, and I have very pleasant quarters in a small but neat hotel.

I have no adventures to relate yet, haven't killed any Indians nor seen very many buffalo, but just wait till I get farther west, at present I am taking it easy.

I did not write sooner because I was not settled, hadn't much time, but principally because I wanted something to write about.

Leaving Elk River Wednesday morning at 6 I went to St. Paul and then back to Minneapolis and struck off on the C. St. P. & Omaha [rail]road and go into Worthington in time for supper, staid there all night and took the train for Round Lake in the morning. Merriam said I would find letter, blanks, vouchers, catalogues, supplies, and instructions waiting me there; I found one small envelope of tags and nothing else. Have not heard a word from him yet. I had instructions to return at once to Heron Lake if I found corn was not up at Round Lake; it was not up and not much planted yet so I took the next train back, but had to wait all day for the return train which gave me plenty of time to look over the country. . . . I will try and describe some of the country as I go along. Along the R. R. from Minn. to Chaska it is mostly timber and very hilly, at Chaska we struck the Minnesota R. and followed the river bottoms until past Mankato. These river bottoms are about 2 or 3 miles wide, very level and not much above the river. Large tracts of it are marshy but it seems to be good farming land. The valley is skirted by high hills—I have seen nothing but clay soil since leaving Minneapolis—covered with timber; they are so high and steep they can't be farmed. The timber on the hills is much like ours—thick, brushy and of mixed kinds but in the valley is mostly box elder, soft maple, willow and cottonwood. Some of the cottonwoods are very large. Between Leres[—?] and St. Peters there is a region of clay barrens—high steep hills, bare of vegetation except a very short fine and scattering grass. . . .*

At St. Peters there is a large sandstone quarry and another at Mankato. Between these places there are ledges cropping out and in one place the wall of the valley is solid sandstone, worn into strange shapes and creases by the water.

Soon after leaving Mankato the timber region is passed out of and it begins to be more open. Prairie—slightly rolling, in long gradual swells, with a good many lakes and sloughs is the general characteristic of the rest of the journey; though at Round Lake it is more uneven, the hills are higher and steeper and the sloughs and lakes more depressed. None of the prairie is treeless but there are no original trees, only groves that have been planted.

Every farm has a grove of cottonwoods—tall and from 2 to 6 in. in diameter. Most of the groves are about an acre in extent and set in straight rows and the house in middle. I stood on a high place in the prairie at Round Lake and counted 60 groves, none of them less than a mile off and some were probably 10 mi.

The country isn't thickly settled. Not a tenth of the land is farmed, though it seems rich. Wheat, oats and flax are the crops mostly raised. Flax is the staple. They say it is too far north for corn. Hardly any is raised, but they could not raise it if ever so warm without holding the seed in the ground and covering the ears with tin; the blackbirds are so thick. I think the ground is too cold and damp for corn, . . . The wind blows nearly all the time and it never seems hot like the sandy land and in the woods, or has not been since I have been here.

This is my last sheet of paper and I have not said a word about the birds yet. I have been here 2 days and looked around some. It is about a mile to Heron Lake, which is 7 or 8 miles wide and around the south end is a vast marshy, reedy tract where the birds nest. I went down to the lake yesterday and near the lake saw a man out in the garden weeding cabbages. He was a rustic looking fellow so I passed that way for a talk and as we were talking of the weather, crops and cabbages he asked me where I was from. When I told him I was from Elk River he wanted to know if I knew a Vernon Bailey there. He was greatly surprised to see me and we were friends right at once. It was Thomas Miller. I found him a very pleasant and intelligent Scotchman and an ardent naturalist and geologist. He has promised me his assistance and I expect much help from him in my work, as he lives near the lake and is familiar with all the water birds. The lake absolutely swarms with Yellowheads and other blackbirds. Night Herons and Cormorants are nesting there by thousands, Gulls and Terns that I never saw abound and Mudhens, Divers, King Rails, Teal, Canvasbacks, Redheads, Shovelers, Widgeons are common and lots of other birds which I have not yet seen are said to be here. I wish Anna was here, I would keep her at work for a while. If it wasn't for the game law I would send home a ton of birds for her to skin, but Miller will get me some next fall I guess.

I went to church today but the sermon was not first class. Guess I will go to the Catholic next time.

I was at the post office last night and there was no mail but as I was going to church the postmaster came out and told me there was a letter for me. It was from

Flo and had a money order for $6.50 which makes me feel better as I was almost out of money, only had $2.50 left. I had to pay my fare from St. P[aul] here and with other expenses was running low. I telegraphed, from Worthington, to Merriam for money but have not got it yet, but I am all right now.

This is my last sheet of paper so guess I will direct it so all hands reach it and save writing another letter to Flo and Chet [Chester Hill]. I am nearly to the end so goodbye to all. Write soon and very long. All write.

Anna, you don't have anything to do, write me a letter a mile long. I will probably be here more than a week, maybe two weeks.

Your loving Son and Brother,
Vernon Bailey[2]

The next week's mail to Bailey in the field brought him more verification that he could show to local authorities in case of questions about his authority to collect. Officially typed on USDA letterhead and signed by Merriam, it certified that he was a "Special Field Agent of the US Department of Agriculture" and that birds killed by him are shot in the interest of science and for the use of the department.[3]

Two postcards he sent on May 23 from Heron Lake attest to the pattern he was already setting for his life. One mentioned to his father that he'd already "been writing all day and it is bedtime now so goodbye." Completing reports for the Washington headquarters took an enormous amount of his time and he always grated at this a bit, preferring to be out in the field than behind a desk. He sent a postcard to his older brother Charles asking him to find an ad for Coues's *Key to North American Birds*.[4] He was finding so many species new to him and he needed help to identify them. He often sent specimen skins to Washington for identification, but his innate curiosity made him eager to learn them for himself.

Each day brought its own directions, rarely from official sources in Washington but more often determined by weather, plant and animal life, and the vagaries of the stagecoach and train schedules or availability of horses and wagons.

By the following week he had made his way out of Minnesota and into Flandreau in the Dakota Territory, and a "Hurrah!" opened his next letter home written on May 29:

I am in Dakota, on the plains of the mighty west, among the wild Sioux.

I am seven long miles from Minn. It seems like leaving friends to leave Heron Lake and I haven't found so agreeable a place to stay here though it is not bad. The people are the roughest lot I ever struck but good natured and friendly. There are lots of Indians in town, they are regular dudes wear stand up collars & silk hats, carry watches & cut quite a swell.

Flandreau is about the size of Monticello, quite a busy little place but rather bare and desolate as there are almost no trees, and very few anywhere around. . . .

The Sioux R. runs near the town. Along its banks are scattering trees and brush and the sides of the river valley rise in high steep hills but back from those the prairie is quite level, treeless, and there are no sloughs. The land seems good: tis a loose gravelly clay. Wheat, oats, and flax are the crops, no corn is raised.

The wind is blowing a perfect gale now. As I was going to church my hat blew clear over a high store. . . . I went to the memorial service at the Methodist church but it was not good. . . .

Merriam sent me a 2 gal. can of alcohol and a dandy little gun, a J. Stevens 15 in. barrel, 32 cal. breech loading shot gun, pistol stock, with tools, a can of wood powder and half a thousand shells.

I had to stay all night and half a day at Pipestone, waiting for a train, but was not sorry. It is a very interesting place, guess it's worth describing. . . . Of course it is all prairie. Along the east side of a valley, for two or three miles, the ledge is exposed. The west edge is broken down. In some places it is perpendicular and others slope gradually down into the valley where it shows in places. Most of the stone is a dark red color and very hard, much like flint. The soft stone is only found in small quantities.[5]

It didn't take long for homesickness to set in, despite the long, hard, working days and the joys of new discoveries. Perhaps he had no one at hand to talk to or perhaps he was always this open with his family, but his clarity and ease of talking about his feelings are admirable even today. On stationery of the Merchants Hotel in Orionville, Minnesota, "leading hotel in big stone country, terms one dollar per day," he wrote in early June [specific date omitted]:

I have nothing to write about today that would be of interest to anyone and what is the use of describing things. I forget them myself as soon as out of sight. I have been traveling half the week, to get from Flandreau to here. To save time and money I came across lots and lost both by it for it would have been cheaper and quicker to have gone to Minneapolis and from there to here.

I only got here yesterday morning so have not done much yet but find that there are plenty of mice of some kind and will begin work in the morning.

I feel somewhat lost about my work, not having heard from headquarters for so long but will probably get my mail soon as I have written back to all of my old stopping places to have the mail forwarded.

School is out I suppose, and the scholars feel greatly relieved. I wish you would send me the Star, just the home part, and send me the O[rnithologist] and O[ologist] when you get through with them.

My place here isn't anything extra though I manage to get enough to eat and try not to see the flies and dirt but I have plenty of room and that is quite an item. Guess I can stand the rest. . . .

Please write occasionally and I would like to hear from anyone there I am acquainted with too.[6]

Certainly his frustration must have deepened at the next official communication he received from Merriam. Not only did it take him to task for not reporting more regularly, but pointed out that two of his expenses were "disallowed because no sub-vouchers were taken from them (i.e., paper and bottles); and the telegram was disallowed because it was personal. Telegrams stating change of address are official and may be sent *collect*."[7]

On arriving at Ortonville on June 5, he immediately wrote to Merriam expressing frustrations about the transportation situation:

As you see I am now at Ortonville on Bigstone Lake. I have spent much time & seem to have accomplished almost nothing. When I reached Flandreau, Dakota, I decided to wait there until I heard from you or the general passenger agent, at St. Paul, to whom I wrote about using the transportation orders. I waited a week but not hearing from either you or the agent decided to move on though I suppose I am traveling at my own expenses. I have asked you twice about using the orders but have received no information on it yet.

The agent at Elk River looked them over carefully and advised me to simply hand the order to the conductor and say nothing which I did on the train to Minneapolis & he told me to fill it out and accepted it, but on the road from Minneapolis to Heron Lake the conductor said he knew nothing about it & I had to pay my fare & have had to in several cases since. I don't think they are to give to the conductors but cannot find out what to do with them. Please do not neglect giving me the desired information longer.

While staying at Flandreau I tried to make as much of the time as possible but did not get many specimens but sent what I got by express, on leaving that place.

I wish you would give me as much advice & information about my work as possible for I am not accomplishing much as yet and if I can not do better the trip will not be of much use.

Please answer soon. I telegraphed my address this morning. I have only one transportation order left.[8]

After another week in Ortonville, he once again wrote home, describing the landscape and also his first church experience there.

Went into a church where I saw the people going early but when it commenced it was all Norwegian so I did not stay & and was too late for Sunday school in the next church but staid to meeting & heard quite a good sermon; guess I will go again this evening.

I would [give] my shirt for a letter from home today. I have not had a letter from anywhere for a week & feel as if I was all alone in the world "with silence speechless as the grave & people all around." I don't suppose you have missed me yet but it seems to me as if I had been away from home for ages & ages; and I have almost forgotten where I used to live & who the people are that I used to know.[9]

Merriam was a hard taskmaster and determined to set his young charge on the right path early on. Although Bailey had responded to the earlier message, it wasn't enough as he made clear:

It is the first and only letter we have received from you since the one you mailed at Heron Lake May 23rd.

Either you have written letters that have miscarried (your instructions call for two letters per week), or you must be absent minded at times. How could I write you at Flandreau, Dakota, when I not only did not know you were going there, but did not even know that there was such a place?

In regard to the transportation orders: On bonded roads the ticket agents are obliged by law to accept them. The agent should take the transportation order instead of cash, and give you a regular ticket in exchange for it.

On roads not bonded, the agents are not obliged to accept these orders, but many of them will do so as an accommodation. Sometime the agent of a bonded road will give a person a through ticket (over several other roads) in exchange for a transportation order.

Cash expended by you in fare on roads not bonded will be refunded to you by the Dept. as a matter of course.[10]

Fortunately, at this same time came a letter from an old friend, his teacher when he and Anna had briefly shared the joys of schooling together. Mr. King wrote to him from Elk River about how pleased he was,

> *to know you are so well started and are finding something new and of interest to you all the time.*
>
> *The world is full of wonderful and curious things but the trouble with most of us we do not see what is so plain to one who has trained himself to observe. With the great majority of mankind it seems to be literally true that "having eyes they see not." The truest and best education a man can get, it seems to me, is a training which makes him observe things about him. . . .*
>
> *Book learning alone won't do at all. There must be something in the man himself, something to develop, and more than all he must have some definite aim, some fixed purpose, if he would make the best success in life.*
>
> *Now it seems to me that your former habits of observation have peculiarly fitted you to fill the position which you hold and to make a success of it too. I would not undervalue the study of books nor the gaining of a culture as broad and as deep as possible, but still in my opinion you ought not to feel diffident entering upon your work; but plunge into it as boldly as may be, and you will be sure to succeed.*[11]

Bailey's mother began a campaign to get her son to have his picture taken. She was sure he would be too far away to find a photographer, but he assured her—the first of many times in the weeks to come:

> *I expect to stay here a few days yet & then don't know where I will go. I have been very busy all the week & have got a lot of specimens, though nothing rare or wonderful. I will get my picture taken before long ma. Don't worry about my getting so far away that I can't. The towns out here are not so small [as] you many think. There are two photograph galleries here but not very good I guess.*[12]

He occasionally addressed letters to other family members, although they all shared all his letters. His other letters were most often to Anna or to his nature-mentor sister Flo, now married to a schoolteacher and interested in educational topics as well.

9
Grand Collecting Country—Dakota Territory (1887)

By mid-June, Bailey had made his way to Fort Sisseton in the Dakota Territory. His enthusiastic reports won not only the heart but also the envy of his boss: "As I sit here at my desk [in Washington, DC] with the thermometer way up nearly to 90, and no chance to get out into the fields & woods for a little fresh air, I envy you from the bottom of my heart, and wish I could drop everything and take the first train to join you."[1]

Bailey provided this lively description of the territory in his weekly letter home from Fort Sisseton written on June 20:

> *Sunday again! How the time goes! I have about lost the past week both in reckoning and in regard to work for there seems to be nothing here to collect or else I have failed to find it.*
>
> *I have had to stop twice since beginning this to watch the soldiers parading and listen to the band. The soldiers are all gentlemen of color and consequently they have lots of music and good music too, both singing and by the band. Altogether they are a very jolly set of fellows. They spend most of their time shooting at targets, drilling, playing billiards, and drinking beer, though they do a little work, hoeing in the garden, cutting hay and the like. The officers are all white and put on lots of style. They have their families here and live in very nice houses, have nice horses and carriages and everything as civilized as possible. . . . The grounds around the fort buildings and officers houses are mixed up very nice with sidewalks, drives and shade trees, making a very pleasant place of it. . . .*
>
> *I am boarding with the trader and have a room over the store. If it wasn't for the bedbugs I would be very agreeably settled but they are so thick that I can not sleep half the night and feel rather used up for want of sleep, but it is only one more night.*

The trader and his family are perfect types of the upper class of French, highly educated, refined, and intelligent, but lacking the substantial, honest sincerity of some plainer people; still there is something almost charming about their manner that I have seldom met with.

I have met a few acquaintances here and they all seem interested in helping me, especially Mr. Belt, the hospital steward, who is quite a naturalist and a very pleasant gentleman. He took one long tramp with me, showing me some nests that he had found, pointing out breeding grounds of various birds; and gave me much information in regard to the natural history and features of the country that I could not have gained myself.

He took me to some Indian grounds and we picked up some bones and studied ostology [sic] *a little and compared ideas. He shot at a Jack Rabbit but missed it and it was too far off for my shot gun. He seems a good deal like Doctor Robberts.*

Just been to dinner, or lunch as they call it. We will have dinner at five.

I sit between a lieutenant and a pretty little French girl at meals, so don't imagine that I am not enjoying myself.

Perhaps you would like a description of the country here. Well, just shut your eyes and imagine you can see long, high hills, in some places very steep and sprinkled over with boulders. The soil is rich and grass grows high and thick but in the distance the hills look as though covered with velvet. There are lots of sloughs, some are clear grass bordered lakes but they are mostly full of rushes and cattails and are all very strong of alkalie [sic]*. Along some of the sloughs and even on some hills there is a scattering growth of small timber and brush that makes the country seem more home like and less barren. The Ft. is 25 miles from Webster, the nearest point on the R[ailroad], and the stage brings the mail from there every day. I never rode a stage before and was expecting lots of fun. Thought I would ride on top so as to see everything but was somewhat disappointed for it was only a little old wagon without springs drawn by a pair of hidebound, crippled mustangs that could hardly stand alone. . . .*

I expect to catch it when M[erriam] finds out what I have not done here. He is all the time telling how he envies me but I envy the men that shovel sand on the R. R. because they know just what to do and when they have got it done. So is life![2]

The next day, with a little spare time before the next trip and "nothing here to collect or else I have failed to find it," he starts to write another letter home, trying to write "on the installment plan." He soon thinks better of that or has less time, for the pattern of weekly letters on Sundays becomes almost exclusively his habit:

> *It is not long since I sent you a letter but when Sunday comes I feel like writing home so here goes another.*
>
> *I have changed my plans a little. The Post trader here has offered to take me across to Browns Valley tomorrow with a team for $4.00 which is less than it will cost to go around and I will get there as soon besides seeing new country and a chance to get some specimens on the road. It is about 40 miles.*
>
> *Wish you would send me my colored glasses by mail. I need them when riding, on clear days, and to keep the sand out of my eyes.*
>
> *I have not been here [Browns Valley] long enough to find out much yet but think it will be a pretty good place to collect. It is near the end of Lake Traverse and 4 miles from Bigstone L. in a valley that connects the two. It seems nice to get back among the springs after drinking rain water for a week. They use nothing else at the Ft.*
>
> *I have the best place to stay that I have had yet. Everything is clean and good, no bugs, and the folks are pleasant. Intended to get my picture taken here if I could but guess there is no photographer here.*[3]

There's nothing like a package from home to set one right. Young Bailey is no exception. His birthday was on June 21. He had been away from home for a month for the first time when he wrote home from Browns Valley thanking everyone for his package and providing more details about where he was and what he was experiencing and complaining about his transportation woes:

> *I got your letters and the papers yesterday and day before and feel more contented and more like enjoying myself than I have before since leaving home. . . .*
>
> *I expect to stay here, or someplace along these lakes, a week or two, at any rate until I hear from M[erriam] in regard to traveling for the transportation orders are of no use to me and they have got to furnish me some other means of traveling. I sent one to General passenger agent at St. Paul and he says they cannot be accepted for travel. I sent his letter to Merriam and told him to fix it some other way.*
>
> *The land lays much the same here as it does at Ortonville; in fact Bigstone and Traverse lakes occupy one long, deep valley and are only separated by four miles of bottom land that is but little above the lakes and is called Browns Valley. Probably the Red R[iver] once flowed through these lakes and*

down the Minnesota R. but the slopes have changed and the river broke in two here and flowed both ways. They intend to put a canal through between the lakes this summer if the people will give the required bonds ($20,000), but if they do not it is only a matter of time. . . .

Browns Valley is a small town in about the middle of the valley, a very quiet, social community of mostly yankees; all are acquainted and a stranger among them is an object of curiosity and interest.

I have just been to church and heard a good solid sermon by an honest man. There is a Sunday school concert tonight. Guess I will take that in too. Wish I could have been at Ortonville today but it would have cost me two or three dollars to go on the [railroad] cars and it is about 40 miles by the lake. I thought some of getting a boat and rowing down last night but it's so far I hardly dared undertake it and must not lose any time. . . .

There seems to be a marriage epidemic around there. Glad I came away. I am afraid there is something catching about it. . . .

It is possible that I may be at Wahpeton the fourth [of July] and if so guess I will go over to Fergus, but the chances are against it. I hope to be at Pembina by that time but may get orders to stop at points along the road for a few days. I have not killed much yet with the little gun. It shoots strong but carries so small a load that it will not be sure for more than two or three rods, is better adapted to the woods than to open country. When I see anything that I want to kill I want it bad and so to be sure generally use the old gun. I have seen quite a number of Jack Rabbits here but haven't had a shot yet. . . .

How are you going to manage about haying? I think you had better hire some help. Perhaps you can get someone to work for stock and I will soon be able to draw some money beyond what I need for expenses and will send it to you. I was in hopes that we could get along without using much of my salary for other things and that it would amount to enough when we come to settle up, so we could build [a new house at home] this fall but don't know as it is best to try it while there are so many other debts. I shall not use any more of it than is necessary.

I wish you could all enjoy my chance for travel and seeing new things. It seems like dull living to work in the same old place and way all the time and I feel mad at myself for not enjoying it more when I have such a chance; but really I believe the enjoyment is in us and not in our surroundings.

Don't forget to write.[4]

10
Full of Sharp Points (1887)

It was as difficult for young Bailey to know what was expected of him as it was for Merriam to tell him what he wanted. Neither man knew the territory; both were eager to know more about everything natural; and the "rules" for collecting were being created on the job. Bailey peppered Merriam with questions, but the responses were general at best, leaving wide room for the interpretation that Bailey did not yet know how to do.

Most difficult and emotionally wracking to Bailey was learning to find and catch animals unfamiliar to him. This became a problem as soon as he crossed the biogeographical boundary between eastern and western faunas, in western Minnesota and eastern Dakota Territory. He knew from Merriam's detailed instructions, and from what local residents told him, the kinds of animals he should find at each collecting station. So when he did not find and catch them, he did not know if his lack of experience and skill was to blame or if the animals were simply not abundant just then. When hunting or trapping was poor, should he cut his losses and move on to the next stop, or should he stay put and keep trying until he learned the habits of the species Merriam told him should be there? It was hard to know. All this made waiting for Merriam's weekly letters rather a trial, and it left him unsure if he should linger, risking his itinerary, or move on.[1]

Despite these mixed feelings, Bailey knew that the long-distance dialogue was invaluable. Without Merriam's deep knowledge of fauna and biogeography, Bailey would have had to learn everything on his own, from scratch and under time pressure. In fact, Bailey was a quick study and soon showed that he could not just meet but surpass expectations. With Merriam's tips he was soon able to recognize and catch species new to him. The first, on the Dakota-Minnesota border, was especially welcome, as he wrote to Merriam on July 1:

> *While out to my traps tonight after supper, I caught a not full grown Cricetodipus flavus which is the first mammal really new to me that I have found. . . . Did you ever get a specimen that you had been hunting for*

weeks and never had seen? I think I never felt more pleasure in making the acquaintance of a species. I have it laying on the paper as I write and spend more time with it than with my pen.[2]

Some of the deepest and most sustaining pleasures of fieldwork were those that attended the successful exercise of scientific skills, and Bailey's knowledge was expanding to become cosmopolitan and professional.[3] Newly confident, he caught three more species new to him the very next day. From Merriam's description he recognized them easily, one at a distance of ten feet, just from its tail and hind feet sticking out of the trap.

Now that he had been away for a few months, Bailey began to get some pressure from his family to return home. On June 28, 1887, his mother, Emily, had sent him a letter expressing concerns about his health and encouraging him to come home as soon as possible.

I hope you will try to keep your health, try not to let anything worry you and don't overwork brain or hands. This world is quite large, and if you fall once in your plans there is room for more to try but if you lose your health you lose your chance for doing and enjoying. . . . I wish you could come home the 4th [of July], it will be lonesome without you. I do want you to enjoy yourself but don't want you to be gone so long you will get weaned from home or want to spend all your life tramping round for we want you at home.[4]

But in the course of traveling on his own, Bailey was beginning to discover himself as well. A quiet sense of humor appears in his letters that was to be a hallmark throughout his life. Writing to his folks on July 10, he told them:

I am glad Sunday comes once a week. If there was no Sunday I would not know that I existed, for the time seems to go by like the wind until Sunday comes & then I can stop & take a look back & ahead. Both ways look pleasant: it is only the present that is full of sharp points.

It is 9 oclock & promises to be a hot day but there is a stiff breeze & that makes it some better. Papers, boards, boxes & a cloud of dust are travelling the street past my window and a fine stream of clean air is going through my room, making it quite agreeable.

I celebrated [the 4th] the same as I do every other day & guess I enjoyed it more than lots of others who tried harder. It was a splendid day here, fresh & cool after the rain & a pleasure just to breathe. . . . I think I will enjoy the trip most after I get home. Then I can only remember the pleasant part but I want to get as much out of it to remember as possible.[5]

The paperwork part of his job was already grating at him, as it would continue to do. But he learned to accept it as part of the process and always looked forward to the next outing for relief from it. "I have not done much but write for a day or two & begin to feel like getting out again, think it will be an interesting trip up the Red R. Valley. If I had a chum it would be much more agreeable."[6]

Bailey quickly learned about fast friends and easy money. His insights seem poignant today, and are a telling part of his powers of observation and the depth of his own character. "The people here seem like old friends but I will soon forget them I suppose. The landlord endorsed a check for $40.00 with me yesterday so I could get it cashed, which I would not like to do for a stranger."[7]

Merriam continued to encourage his young assistant and began to find in him the kind of support he needed in order to meet his own obligation to help farmers across the country. "We are particularly pleased with your notes on the food habits of gophers, and hope you will make a study of food habits wherever you go."[8]

In another week, Bailey was in Grand Forks, Dakota. He only went to church once that Sunday, in order to have a "good long time" to write his weekly letter home and "to read some." The resulting description of this new locale is more detailed than usual:

Grand Forks is a large place but I have found a good hotel near one corner and don't have to go far to get into the woods or on the prairie. I was surprised to find several large sawmills here and the river full of pine logs, but the Red Lake R. comes in to from the pine district and that is where the logs come from. The river is no wider here than Elk River, but is deep; and there are lots of large flat boats and some steamers here waiting for higher water they say, but one steamer runs from here to Fargo. If they run to Pembina I would go down on one but don't suppose I will get a chance. . . .

Don't worry about my health Ma, I am getting fat and too lazy to hurt myself at work. I think there is more danger of your hurting yourself walking after berries in this hot weather.

I am glad you are getting along so well with the haying and suppose you will soon have to go at harvesting. Sorry I can't help you but you must get some one else in my place. I am afraid I am going to run out of money before the end of the month. Traveling so far has taken it faster than I had counted on. If you can spare ten dollars of that I sent I think you had better save it awhile to see if I need it for I do not like to ask Merriam for more now because he has sent me more than enough for present expenses; and if I need it I will write for it. There is another month's salary due now and probably he will send that before I am out and then I can send you some more. . . .

In coming from B's Valley we entered the Red R. valley just north of Lake Traverse. There it had quite high banks, was about 4 or 5 miles wide, and mostly coarse grass, reeds and rushes; but in going north we soon came to drier land and some grain fields. Before reaching Wahpeton it has become almost solid grain (wheat, oats and barley) and was so until ten miles north of Fargo, and I never saw better grain. Much of it will go 25 to 30 bushels to the acre. . . .

The timber begins at Wahpeton and so far down has been an unbroken line along the river, from a mile wide to less. The trees are large and thrifty. There are a good many bur-oaks much more soft wood, as elm, hackberry, cottonwood and boxelder.

Five o'clock. I got so sleepy and stupid that I had to go out for some exercise and so went to the young men's meeting at the free reading rooms. There was no sermon but most all talked who would and some of them talked well; when through a lot of them went to the jail to read and sing for the fellows there.

They are the kind of men the world needs but while there are a dozen of them there, there are a thousand others in the saloons and on the streets.[9]

Health was rarely an issue for Bailey, but on those few occasions when it was he had the ready help of his physician/boss, who continued to encourage him on both professional and personal matters. On July 20, Merriam wrote to compliment Bailey on his work, especially balancing the conveniences and comforts of towns against the direct experience of staying in the country, and to offer some health advice:

Your reports are entirely satisfactory. . . . Of course you will not find it profitable to put up at large hotels in large towns. Keep in the country all you can, where you will be handy to your work. Be as economical as you can, but always get plenty of good food, and never give up a chance to do good field work because the expenses may be a little higher than somewhere else. . . .

I am sorry you are suffering from diarrhea. I was troubled greatly by it when west 15 years ago. You had better "drink easy" for awhile. Don't take long walks right after meals, and avoid greasy and other indigestible food. Also, avoid getting overheated. *Never mind if you don't accomplish quite a much as you meant to for a week or two. Don't drink too cold water, or too much water at a time—better drink often & only a little at once.*[10]

Keeping Bailey on his toes, Merriam wrote to him a few days later chastising him for not collecting more bird stomachs, and specifically instructing him to send at least "fifty or more gizzards of each species of blackbird" as well as large series of all birds that he found feeding on grasshoppers.[11] Even though his personal goal was to verify life zones and distributions of mammals, Merriam's official charge was still to help farmers, and he expected Bailey to pay attention to it.

On to his next adventure, Bailey traveled to Pembina, Dakota, which he described as:

a queer old town it is too, with old log houses on main street and various signs of age showing in many ways; but on the whole it is rather a pleasant place, half on the prairie and half in the bush, and at the forks of the Pembina and Red rivers. There are some nice buildings too. A large hotel, a court house and 4 churches, and some nice residences among the trees, near the river. The town is about as large as Elk River. A large part of the people are French Canadian and there are some halfbreeds and Indians.

It is a mile and a half to Canada. I took a walk just over the line to see how it would seem to be out of the US, but couldn't see any difference; in fact I couldn't find any line. There is a military post of a hundred men about a mile up the river that I will have to visit if I can get time.

I got here Thursday at 2 o'clock and located myself in a small, French hotel that is half saloon. I don't like the company that I am in very well but it is the best I could do and I have a good room to myself.

The cooks are halfbreeds (or more) and some things are not as nice as might be but I have a splendid appetite and am feeling first rate. The weather has been delightful. There was a light frost the first night I was here and it seems just like early fall weather. They have had frost every month this year and say that is generally the case, but crops are looking fine and have not been injured any yet. . . .

I have not found much that is new in animal life yet, except for a new species of Pocket Gopher, about half as large as ours, but hope to make some more discoveries.

I will probably stay here a week or two and then go to the Devil's Lake region. I am enjoying myself here better than at any place before. I have not a thing to worry about, no one grumbles as what I am doing and the prospect looks good for success here. I haven't enough money to pay my board bill but don't care for that. They will keep me as long as I want to stay and if Merriam doesn't send me some in time to settle up and leave I will write home for it and guess you can raise enough for me in some way.

I am sorry the crops are a failure but sorrier for some others than for ourselves, for it will go hard with some who have nothing but their grain to depend on, though most of them around there have hay and that will help them some. Lucky my pay doesn't depend on the weather. I suppose we will have to give up building this fall, unless Uncle Sam decides to send me south and keep me at work all winter; but if I do all that is planned for me now it will keep me busy for some time.

I hope you will get rain in time to save the corn and potatoes. Then there will be something to eat and feed the horses.[12]

Clearly the money from his government job had become an important source of income for the entire family.

On to Devil's Lake, DT [Dakota Territory], which was to become one of his more popular stopping places. On first view, it already had that appeal, as he described to his "Dear folks at home" on August 7:

The prairie is rolling & hilly with marshes & sloughs, & alkalie everywhere.

There are lots of new plants here (new to me) & a good many that I found at Ft. Sisseton & Browns & and have not seen since. Crops are generally good but some pieces of grain are not worth cutting & all is very weedy. In some places the alkalie [sic] *is so strong that nothing grows & the ground is bare & baked. It is quite thickly settled near here & seems a very good farming country generally. . . .*

My hotel is the Tower House & I am clear to the top. From the windows I can see for miles in all directions. If the scenery is not grand it is large & across the lake southward there are high hills mostly covered with heavy timber which relieves the monotonous stretch of prairie, lake & meadow, & promises a good field for collecting.[13]

The next Sunday he fulfilled his promise of a more descriptive letter, and the intrigue of the place shows in his enthusiasm about the name of Devil's Lake itself:

There is nothing especially Satanic about the place or about the lake if you don't want to drink from it; but the water is not very bad, even to drink. It isn't all salt as I supposed. You can hardly taste the salt but it gives it a slightly sickish taste, which is not so bad as that of weeds and birds feet. The water is clear & the beach generally sandy or stony, & this is where the salt appears, in a crust over the stones & everything that the water washes. . . .

There is no large body of water near here but two arms of the lake come around from different sides and nearly surround a large tract of heavy timber, and good timber too. . . . The woods are full of raspberries, wild currants and plums, and there is occasionally a log house or choppers shanty, but they are not much settled except near the edge.

I have been only two or three miles back in the woods but didn't find much game, no squirrels or chipmunks, but lots of birds and found an empty eagle's nest.

But the most wonderful thing here is the numbers of waterbirds. Gulls, Terns, Ducks and snipe fairly swarm. There are three kinds of white gulls, Franklin's Gull, Ring billed Gull (the largest) and Forsters Tern, and when sitting on the water or a sandy point, they look like acres of snow, but just crawl through the reeds to some favorite resting spot and shoot and the air is alive with wings in an instant, and such a squacking and yelping as they keep up. Instead of flying away they will circle round and round your head as if crazy and I have shot so fast that my gun barrel got hot enough to burn my hands and I would have to hold it in the water to cool, then bang away till out of ammunition. The two handsomest gulls are the most numerous (Franklins Gull and Forsters Tern) and a thousand in a flock is not uncommon.

There are at least eight species of the snipe kind here, from the smallest Sandpipers up to Willets and Great Marbled Godwits and some of them almost as numerous as the gulls. The ducks are shy and try to keep out of sight at this time of year but some sheltered bays and sloughs are fairly covered with Mallards, Bluewing Teal and some Redheads, but I have not spent much time with the ducks yet and will probably find several other species if I get time to look for them.

I am now in the land of sagebrush, Antelope, Blacktailed Deer and Cinnamon Bear, but haven't seen any of them yet. . . . This seems a good place for the smaller animals and I have found two species entirely new to me, the Red Bat and a gopher with a long name and short tail (Spermophilus richardsonii).

I have caught five of the bats hanging in bushes. They are little beauties, with the softest, silkiest fur of a bright yellowish red color.

I think this about the most inhabitable part of Dakota that I have found yet; though of course not so productive as the Red. R. Valley it is pleasanter and crops are good. . . .

I am glad you have got up so much good hay and think you had better hold on to the cattle as long as possible for they will not be worth much this fall. Men are talking, here, of going to Iowa to buy cattle because people there have no feed and must sell. They will surely be higher next year and perhaps I can earn enough to keep us through the winter. We have had some pretty warm days here but the weather is generally more pleasant and I am feeling first rate, never was healthier or able to stand more than at present. If my appetite don't kill me there is nothing to be afraid of.[14]

Bailey's letter home the next week is not only a travelogue of the land journey, but it also shows the maturity and confidence that is growing inside his mind.

It is Sunday and cold and raining. While you have to go out and milk and do chores in the rain, I put on some extra clothes to keep comfortable and sit down to write you a good long letter.

I have got done here, made out my report, and expect to start for Bottineau at 4 o'clock tomorrow. Shall try and get through there as soon as possible and go on to Ft. Buford and then I will be working towards home. It is almost September now and October will surely bring me home if I just follow out the plans that have been laid; and time slips away so fast that it will not seem very long to me and I hope to see the best part of my trip yet.

Merriam is still in North Carolina and I seldom hear from him, so have no one to bother me and can do just as I please and go where I please. His assistant sends me money and identified a lot of bird skins that I sent to him, and returned them so I could have them to compare with others.

I only got six of the new kind of gophers here and five Red Bats which will not be enough of either for M[erriam]. Wish I could have got more so I could have some for myself, for Merriam says I can have a pair of skins of all but the rare kinds. I saved a pair of the new Pocket Gopher at Pembina and will soon have enough trash of my own to fill a box and send home. . . .

I got your letter last night that was mailed the day before, and got a money order from the department for $38.00. I was nearly out of cash and wrote to Chet [Chester Hill] the day before for $15.00 which will probably be here tomorrow. This is the third time that I have sent to him for money and every time a supply has reached me from Washington before his. After this guess I will depend on them and not scare so soon.

It cleared up and looked pleasant so I got ready and was going to church but it has begun to rain again so I can't go, will go this evening if it don't rain then. I go to meetings as often as I can for I will probably not have as good a chance always, especially to hear so many different ministers and compare different denominations. I went to the Episcopal church last Sunday and to the Methodists Sunday before. I like the Methodist minister much, and would like to hear him again though he is not so eloquent or polished in manners, and evidently not as highly educated, as the Episcopal Bishop; but would not give much to hear him again. He is sound, but nothing but sound.

Don't worry about my health, Ma. I wish you was a hundredth part as strong and healthy as I am. You must take some time to rest, and I have a prescription for you that you must *follow. "Sit down and* rest *after every meal, at least 20 minutes and if possible an hour."*

I believe steady work and no time for digestion is largely what ails you, for digestion cannot proceed with half its power when the muscles are in action.

When I first started out on this trip I tried to make every minute count and would start for a long tramp right after a hearty meal and consequently was sick half the time for several weeks and lost more time than I gained by extra work. If I had kept it up I would not be at Devil's Lake today, but I knew what the trouble was and wrote to Merriam about it and he said no matter how much of a hurry, never go to work directly after a full meal.

It is still raining and I may as well keep writing for dinner won't be ready for most an hour yet. They are good cooks here and I have nothing to complain of except the size of my appetite and I guess I can stand that if the landlord can.

I don't get up mornings till breakfast is ready for it is too far to go where there is anything to hunt before breakfast, and I keep all of my habits as regular as clock work, sleep 8 hours every night, and generally hunt in the forenoon, skin and prepare my specimens in the afternoon and then go for another hunt or to my traps, after supper. Occasionally I take my dinner and go for an all day's tramp, or else hook a salt cup from the breakfast table and when I get hungry kill something and cook it.

It always takes me two or three days to make out my lists and report and pack and send off the specimens when I get ready to leave a place, so I always feel fresh and anxious for work when I get to the next place. There is enough change, hard work, and travel mixed up together to make them all agreeable.

You must get a lot of rice *and crackers, Ma, and use them all you can, and you ought to have lean meat too. I am making a special study of food*

> *habits you know and my advice is valuable. In fact I have made quite a discovery here, find thousands of the handsomest of gulls feeding on grasshoppers. I expect a gold medal for the discovery.*[15]

This last comment could be taken out of context to be egotistical, but in light of all his correspondence, it is simply a reflection of his comfort that rainy, chilly night, feeling "very comfortable and well satisfied for the present."

11

Get All the Mammals You Can (1887)

Bailey continued to build confidence in his work, encouraged by Merriam, who wrote to him on August 26, "I have no changes to suggest in your mode of working up a locality; hence operate at Buford & Berthold as you have been in the habit of doing elsewhere. Get all the mammals you can and all the information possible about them."[1]

Bailey wrote home two days later from Bottineau, Dakota Territory, describing it as:

> *a nice little place but only two years old and the gophers haven't moved out of the streets yet. The town covers about 4 acres. Is on the level prairie 2 or 3 miles from the hills, or Turtle Mts. which are only hills covered with brush. I have been up on the hills several times. They are the highest that I have ever seen, probably a thousand feet above the prairie. The view from them is large but nothing very grand, just a limitless extent of level prairie dotted over with towns. Sunday is the only day that I can spare a minute's time for anything but my work. It is getting to be cool weather now and if I don't hurry I won't get done before the animals are all froze in the ground.*[2]

Anna was growing up and headed away to school for the first time, so he began to write her separately and personally. On August 30 he wrote:

> *Probably you will be going to school when you get this & you must write to me every week at least, and I will write to you so you won't get homesick. When you feel lonesome think of me out here on the prairie a thousand miles from shore. But I haven't been much homesick this summer—just felt a little blue at first when everything bothered me. I value my chance too much.*
>
> *I feel more interest in the old log house at home than all the fine buildings in Dakota. Even the new animals & birds get common in a little while, but I*

keep finding out something about them that is new to me & that keeps my interest alive.[3]

He was having mixed results with his fieldwork and was starting to show frustration. On September 18 he wrote to the folks at home:

I am still at Buford but wish I wasn't. I am getting tired of the place and want to get away but can't until I hear from Merriam for I don't know where to go. I am not having much success collecting and have got the ground about all looked over within tramping distance. Can't get a horse to ride for love or money; not because horses are not plenty but people are afraid of strangers here and I don't blame them. I left my door unlocked the other day while I went to dinner (a door that opens outside) and when I came back found it open and the Winchester gone. I can't get any clue to who took it and guess it is gone for good. It is only a few rods to the brush—a regular jungle—and it is a regular nest for moonshiners and whiskey peddlers, but I am inclined to think someone took it who is familiar with the place. I have no use for the gun and it was quite a bother but I didn't care to dispose of it in that way.

The river is very low now, half the bottom is above water and I guess I will not get a steamboat ride after all. A boat was stuck in the mud near here about a week ago all night and half a day.

There are a good many Deer here but the brush along the river, where they stay, is so thick and high you couldn't find an elephant, but I did see about six inches of one and shot at it but it wasn't there long enough. I would like to kill one to find out what kind they are.

Don't know when they will let me come home. They have sent vouchers to sign for my salary for Sep. and Oct. which looks as though there was still work to be done.[4]

By October, Bailey was in Montana, staying at Tilyous Ranch, feeling chipper, and having acquired a pet grasshopper mouse. "I never felt better than I do now or could stand more tramping. It would kill anyone not used to it to follow me. I get all the mellons I want here & everything else that grows in a garden. . . . My grasshopper mouse is alive yet & is coming home with me if possible."[5]

From Glendive, Montana, he wrote to Anna on October 9 encouraging her in school and adding a bit of his own philosophy for her to ponder. He also completed the story of his pet mouse, along with a few other tales:

I am glad you enjoy your studies. If it is "heart-work" it will not seem hard. Who has not felt the impatient throb—The longing of a heart that pants and reaches after distant good. But many in reaching after distant good lose the present good and so lose all.

I have been among people lately who are honest and good hearted as any you will find but rough and care nothing for Sunday or anything else good. I am sorry for them and especially for the children who are growing up in the same way without the possibility of being different and it makes me appreciate our advantages more than ever before.

My Grasshopper Mouse died the other day so I am alone again. Expect I gave it meat that had arsenic on while I was skinning things for it acted like the cats did that I poisoned so.

I don't suppose Merriam will let me have one of their skins nor of the Pocket Mice and if I don't get more Prairie Dogs I can't have one of them, have only got 3 [this] year. They are very hard to get in any way and it is so late now that they are all the harder. I got two good Porcupines at Tilyous Ranch, the first I ever saw of the kind. Wish I could keep one but of course I can't, saved a good lot of quills though and one got stuck in my finger, while skinning them, so tight I had to cut it out. They go in awfully easy and come out awfully hard. I killed a Deer but all the good it did me was the sport and some nice venison to eat for a few days. It was a spike buck and very fat but I suppose you would rather have fried Bear. You must be careful or the bear skin will spoil before it dries.[6]

Three days later he wrote to Anna again, describing a prairie dog village he had visited near town:

I saw several dogs but couldn't get a shot at any, didn't try much for it is little use shooting them. I shot a lot while at the dog town I told you of before and only got one of them. I could crawl like a snake for a long way and get to within 3 or 4 rods of a dog and shoot him full of shot but he would fall back into the hole and slide down. A few kicks would take him far beyond sight and reach. The holes run down very steep and a long way, 10 or 15 feet so there is no chance to dig one out. When one sees you ever so far off it will run to a hole and sit in the mouth of it and bark at you. They sound like little dogs barking very fast, but it is really a chipper instead of a bark. They are larger than I supposed, are as large as a small woodchuck and just the color of the yellow gophers that I sent home. I set some traps for them today and think I can get some that way. Everyone says that they cannot be caught in traps but I caught one and believe that I can catch more.[7]

He still had no definite time to complete his work, although home was much on his mind. He wrote to his folks, "Have no idea of when I will come home but hope it will be soon."[8] His next destination, by stage, was the Black Hills.

In his next letter home, he talked about his feelings regarding education with the family at large. He was proud that Anna was doing so well in school but noted that he had learned "more this summer than I could have done at any school in the same time and have enjoyed it too, but I do want to get home again."[9]

By then he was in Deadwood, Dakota Territory, where the ten inches of snow had dried up in a few days, although the thermometer reached twelve degrees below zero. He described it as,

> the queerest old town I ever saw and quite a large town too and very busy. I don't know what time the sun rises but it doesn't show itself here till about 9 o'clock, then it takes a scoot across to the top of a mountain the other side and disappears sometime in the afternoon. The town is built in a deep, narrow, crooked gulch. Most of the way it has but one street and that is so narrow you could kick a cat across it. The houses are built very high and close together—no danger of cyclones—and are crowded as far up the hills as possible. The gulch is so crooked that you can only see a little piece of the town at a time when you are in it but from the tops of the hills you can look right down it all. The Black Hills is a very modest name for they are really a part of the Rocky Mt. system and as high or higher than any mountains in the eastern states. The highest point is 7,000 ft. To me they seem immense mountains but I am only a tenderfoot. Anyway it's a good hour's climb to get to the top of one of the hills and hard work at that. The hills are mostly covered with pine and spruce, or were until much of it was cut down, and have been dug full of holes by prospectors. There are old mines in nearly every hill but none that are at work now very near here, though I can hear blasting a little way up the gulch.[10]

But, in Deadwood he saw little he could identify, much less collect, noting, "I haven't had much success in collecting either, as the animals seem scarce and birds are few. Mountain Rats and Magpies are about all that is new to me here."[11]

In spite of the scarcity of collectibles, young Bailey continued to put his mind to new adventures, trying out whatever church appealed to him in each town he visited: "Have been to Catholic church today but was not much pleased with it. There are several other churches here and guess I will go to the Congregationalist this evening. I have a splendid chance to go to different churches and hear different ministers."[12]

But home was uppermost on his mind, and he kept his itinerary with that in mind. Meanwhile, his boss held out the proverbial carrot of new adventure to his young apprentice, including in a letter written on November 1, 1887, an offer to go south to Texas and New Mexico for the winter. If he was interested, Merriam explained he would begin making the necessary arrangements. Merriam also warned Bailey to make sure his vouchers and sub-vouchers were properly signed and dated, noting that by this time he certainly knew what the law required. Apparently, Merriam had had to "tinker" with a few of them so they would pass. Merriam's letter also told him to visit the Badlands to the southeast before the ground was covered with snow which would prohibit his collecting spermophiles and mice.[13]

In spite of the pull to travel farther west, Bailey was set on getting home. He even had a hard time writing to his family from Rapid City the next Sunday (November 6). The routine had perhaps caught up with him, as he wrote, "I am tired of describing places & things & have not killed or found anything worth telling about. Have killed two Jack Rabbits, two Prairie Dogs & a few small things, nothing new. Guess my brains have dried up so I will not worry them longer."[14]

And so it came to pass that the following week's mail from Washington was addressed to Mr. Vernon Bailey at Elk River, Minnesota. Yet Merriam wasn't about to give up. He explained that Bailey's suggestion to make the trip to the Southwest the following spring wasn't feasible once hot weather set in and needed to be made during winter. He implied that after Bailey had been home a few weeks that perhaps he would feel like setting out again.

Bailey's response, explaining his plans, and his feelings about his first year at work, was sent to Merriam from Elk River on November 19, 1887, and explained:

> *I want to go to school this winter so will have to give up the trip to Texas, though, for many reasons I should like to make it.*

Probably I will be at your service again about the first of next June if you have use for me. My trip has been pleasant and profitable to me in many ways and I hope my service has been worth all it cost. I have tried to do my best but wish that had been better.

I feel more interest in the work now than ever before and shall take pleasure in collecting for you what specimens and information I may be able. . . . I am afraid you will be dissatisfied in my journal for I could not seem to get anything of interest in it. If among my notes there is anything that you wish to ask about, the sooner you do so the fresher they will be in my memory and I will be glad to correct any mistakes or give any information possible. Grateful for many favors, I remain. Yours truly, Vernon Bailey[15]

The pressure from Washington continued. Bailey had his own agenda, but then so did Merriam, who informed him that he was still under pay until the end of the month and could put in the time collecting around Elk River and preparing a list of the mammals, with relative abundance, in that area. He also reminded Bailey that he was entitled to two weeks of vacation. Ever the teacher, he complimented Bailey on his skins, which are almost perfect, except for the way that you "have lately taken to turning the hind feet down flat in a way I do not like." He closed with a comment that he hoped to hear from him soon in regard to the Texas trip.[16] But Bailey did not take the bait. He complied with the list of mammals but made no commitment to go to Texas.

Bailey's official leave of absence without pay was effective from December 1 to the following June 1. As Merriam explained, this method does away with the trouble and uncertainty of getting a fresh appointment when the time comes. He couldn't resist a pinprick at the same time, admonishing Bailey for not going to Texas in the winter, commenting that he would have to send someone else who was not nearly as qualified or experienced![17]

By mid-December, Merriam had another bit of work—or excuse to contact Bailey while he was chomping at the bit. He wanted him to solve a problem with gray squirrels and determine "what relation the white bellies have to the dark bellied form." He also inquired when he wanted to start south for the region, "which promises to be full of new species."[18]

As the year ended, Bailey received a letter from the department's assistant ornithologist, Walter B. Barrows, thanking him for the information in regard to the breeding of the English sparrow in Elk River. Barrow explained that this was the most northern point in the United States for any record of the sparrow and that he was very pleased to get his notes on the subject.[19]

The notes were timely, for the department's first bulletin was about to go to press. Bailey asked Merriam about it and was told that the publication, which was to be Bulletin 1 of the Division, was devoted wholly to the English Sparrow and would be sent to him when issued.[20] Period. End of letter. Perhaps it was just the year-end cleanup of correspondence, or a busy work week, but the short, formal, uncharacteristic response seems geared to show a hint of disfavor that Bailey wasn't ready yet to go to Texas.

All in all Bailey's maiden trip in 1887 had continued the apprenticeship that began with Merriam's response to his first shipment from the farm. The directives were meant to continue Bailey's education, but they were also a normal part of expeditionary collecting. A regular exchange of reports, feedback, and revised itineraries was essential to efficient fieldwork, and Bailey had come to understand their importance.

It also is clear he had learned that on-the-road learning was profoundly different from the way he had learned as a local collector—and more stressful. At home, Bailey's success had depended on his intimate knowledge of local fauna, acquired gradually by long residence in that one place. But outside his familiar home range, Bailey had had to find, recognize, and catch animals that he had never seen before and whose habits and habitats he did not know. And he had had to learn fast, because he had to keep to a full and relentless itinerary, moving from one collecting station to another, often on a weekly basis.[21]

Travel was crucial to the apprenticeship of a professional naturalist. As a local collector, Bailey perfected his trapping and taxidermy techniques. But only by traveling did he begin to acquire the cosmopolitan knowledge required for modern taxonomy and biogeography. Likewise, managing the logistics of cross-country fieldwork and an ever-changing itinerary were skills that could be learned only on the move. It was these new aspects of professional work that Bailey—who was a skilled trapper and preparator before he ever left home—found most difficult in his early trips. But by the end of his first full season of fieldwork, he clearly had mastered the "logistics" of fieldwork.[22]

Clearly, Merriam seemed very pleased with Bailey's overall progress. That Merriam was pushing Bailey so hard to continue working and travel to Texas is evidence he was satisfied with Bailey's progress as a collector. Merriam had never ceased to correct Bailey's species identification and to blame him for leaving a place too quickly when Bailey failed to get species he especially wanted. But Merriam's tone had gradually softened as his protégé began to learn and improve. Bailey was making progress and was well on his way to becoming a promising naturalist.

But now it was holiday time at home, a cause for great celebration with his homecoming, no longer the "little Verny" who left some months before, but a man with a bearded face and with his feet set firmly toward the west. Texas, yes, but in his own time. Now it was time to rest, relax, reflect, and share the storytelling that keeps a family alive and well.

12
On the Road Again (1888)

Through a stream of letters to Elk River, Merriam eagerly continued to encourage his young assistant to return to the field as soon as possible, writing to him on March 10:

> *In regard to your coming trip, I would suggest that it would be preferable to work on a basis different from last summer's. I think it would be better to pay you a certain amount per month, including travelling and all other expenses, instead of paying you a salary and other expenses extra. I think we could pay you $120 per month, all told. How does this strike you?*[1]

It must have sounded good because by May, Bailey was once again on the road. His self-confidence shows through, as he begins his second season in the field. Writing home from East Pierre, Dakota, on May 20, he told his folks at home,

> *I didn't go to Ft. Pierre to stay because it is only just across the river, there is no fort there, and it is a miserable little shanty town stuck down on a patch of gumbo. I crossed the river in a skiff while it was raining to get my mail and pulled the soles of both shoes loose in the gumbo and kicked my legs most off just walking through town. Didn't get any mail either and haven't had any yet, but it doesn't scare me so bad as it used to.*
>
> *It seems quite natural to be in a little room all by myself again, with my traps scattered around, with birds and plants to study and work at and half a dozen notebooks already filling up. There are lots of birds and plants and flowers here and there is lots of work to do, so I am as contented and happy as possible away from home.*
>
> *I am once more in the land of gumbo, cactus, sagebrush, and Jack Rabbits. It looks here very much like it does at Buford only the Badlands don't show so plain, and the river is wider—over a mile. They say it is a splendid farming country, but just the same they don't farm it much, it's too dry.*

Wish you would send me one of the histories of Greece and Rome, send it by mail, but guess you had better send it to Valentine. I don't care which one, but if anyone is reading one send me the other and then we can trade when we get through them. I find that I want something to read at odd spells. I got a good Bible at Huron and a box of revolver cartridges, so completing my outfit.

There is a paper that I forgot and wish you would send. It is an official statement that birds killed by me are for the Department, is typewriting and in a bunch of envelopes and papers in my paper drawer.[2]

But Bailey's self-confidence is tempered with humility, as he continues to learn from Merriam. By June he was in Valentine, Nebraska, where Merriam informed him that his request for an assistant could not be granted as "the Department never employs but one field agent in the same region at the same time."[3] As we shall see, Merriam later changes his tune about this issue!

Writing from "Among the Sand Hills, Nebraska," the next week (June 10) Bailey described the new territory to his family:

The trip down the river was not so much fun as I expected. There were two steamers together bringing down 500 soldiers from the forts in Dakota and Montana. The soldiers were going to Texas, and there was just about enough room to stand up straight. Of course the officers and their wives had all of the cabins and I had to camp on deck with only a blanket. There was lots of fun in it though altogether. Some days we would stick half a day on a sand bar or else the other boat would and we would tie up to shore and wait for it to work off. Then we would all go ashore and do as we pleased till the whistle blew. Some of the men got left and I came near it once.

Ma, you needn't worry about my getting stuck in the sand or ponds here. They drive right through the ponds and brooks and it is as solid as anywhere.

I always hated the cactus but never will again. You have no idea what splendid *flowers they have.*

I came near getting a farm in Nebraska and must tell you about that. I could have taken a true claim and left it in care of Mr. King, where I staid; and would not have had to bother with or see it again for eight years. It is a 160 acres of valley land and as good as any in that part of the country. It would have cost me about $30.00 to file on it and pay for the chance and five acres of breaking and I would have had to lose two days of time. Then it would not have cost a cent of any taxes until 8 years from date, when I *could pay the expenses of plowing, putting out trees, and fencing, which are required by law, and prove up on the claim. Mr. King would warrant that all expenses would not exceed $400 and said that they would probably not be above $200.*

I think it was a rare chance to clear $500 or a thousand dollars in 8 years with an investment of about $30 now, and with but little risk; but there will be use for all the money we have to spare at present and speculation seems out of place.

I had a birthday party the other day, all alone, and worked like sixty all day.

I got the Graduating Class Programme and wish my name could have been on it too. I got a cowboy to sing the "Class Song" for me, and think it first rate. . . .

[P.S.] It will take some squeezing to get this letter through for two cents.[4]

To his own surprise, Bailey discovered a new talent for art in himself. Describing his apprehension as well as his success, he wrote home from Valentine on June 17, 1888:

I have been trying to get Merriam to let me have an assistant but he won't; though he says that if I can recommend someone else to do the same work that I am doing they would send them out in some other place. If you was a boy, Anna, you could have the place. I don't know of anyone else that could fill it. It requires a good taxidermist as well as a naturalist.

I forgot to tell you that I have turned artist. Merriam wants me to send sketches of all the animals possible and I have begun practicing. Sent him some the other day and perhaps when he sees them he won't want any more.[5]

Bailey wasn't the only one to be surprised. Merriam encouraged him with this response to the first sketches he sent. Writing on May 19, he told him,

The outline sketches you have sent surprise me very much, because they are very good indeed. I had no idea that you could do such satisfactory work in this direction. If you get a chance to see Dipodomys, Perognathus, and Cricetodipus alive I wish you would make sketches of them in natural attitudes, since, never having seen them alive, I do not know what positions they assume.[6]

The routine quickly set in again, and Bailey continued to write home as best he could. His next stop was Buffalo Gap, Dakota, as he wrote home on July 1:

> *Not much has happened in the past week. . . . I caught a Rattlesnake and put it in alcohol but it spoiled and I had to throw it away but the head and rattles. I have lost all respect for rattlesnakes. They are dull, stupid things and haven't a bit of fun in them. This one wouldn't bite at a stick and wouldn't even rattle till I stood on its head and poked its back with a stick. I tied a string around its neck and carried it home. They ain't half so gamey as a bullsnake.*
>
> *If I had had spunk enough I might have had a little adventure the other day, but extreme caution—if nothing else—spoiled it all. I was going to some traps up among the hills and down in a ravine saw a couple of young Panthers, about as big as Foxes: they were not more than twenty rods away and didn't see me, and I could have got close to them. . . . I could have killed one of them and probably both with what I had but would have nothing but no. 10 shot left for the old one, if she happened to be near. Well, I watched them till they went up a deep rocky canon and then went home.*
>
> *I got some buckshot and a dog and a fellow to go with me and we hunted for them most half a day but couldn't start them. I felt awfully mean about it; but, under the circumstances, would do the same thing over again.*
>
> *The next day, about sundown, the old Panther came by in plain sight about 80 rods from the house. She walked along a side hill, with head and tail low, until she came to the top; then she stopped, raised her head and took a good look at us. When she went over the hill I took the gun and ran around, but she had too much the start and was nearly to the hills when I got sight of her again. Perhaps you think I didn't run very fast but I did; for there wasn't the least chance of catching her.*
>
> *I wish Chas. and Carlo were here. Guess we would celebrate the 4th. It is a mean place to hunt such things (alone) in the canons and gorges of the hills. Anyway, it would take more nerve than I have got.*[7]

After receiving his information from Buffalo Gap, which contained scanty information, Merriam sent Bailey instructions at Custer telling him to make changes in his itinerary in order to reach Idaho before winter set in. Specifically, he was told to finish his work in the Black Hills around Custer and then proceed to Fort Fetterman where he would provide further instructions.[8]

In the meantime, Bailey answered Anna's letter from Custer where he already had arrived. Writing to her on July 8, he told her,

> *I haven't drawn any lately but will have to some here. M[erriam] said he was much pleased with the sketches that I sent. He has some drawings in the report, that he took from gophers that I sent him in alcohol last year. I think they could be more natural. He has a piece in the report, that I wrote about gophers, 3 or 4 years ago. He puts in all of the pieces just as I wrote them and they are about as chopped up and jerky as his letter. If I had known they were to be printed, I would have made it a little smoother.*[9]

Bailey described Custer to the family in his weekly letter home written the next day (July 8):

> *on the summit of the Black Hills—away up close to the clouds. Am at a little ranch about a mile from Custer. The place is in a narrow, grassy valley and the pine covered mountains run away up on all sides. They are high, broken peaks of granite; some of them bare, gray rock, but wherever there is any soil, they are covered with heavy pine timber. There are lots of holes and caves among the rocks and the woods are full of Mountain Chipmunks, Red Squirrels, Mt. Rats, Yellow Woodchucks, and birds. Narrow, grassy valleys with little tumbling brooks of cold spring water wind around among the hills; and, on the whole, it is just the garden for a naturalist.*
>
> *Probably I will stay here two weeks or more, and it will be just the place to spend the hot weather. It is cool nights and hasn't been very warm days yet. They had a frost two weeks ago.*
>
> *It is but eight miles to Harneys Peak and that is the highest point in the hills—9700 ft.—so am near the top. Probably this is over 7000 ft.*
>
> *I picked out the place myself; for Merriam wouldn't give me any more definite instructions than to get high up in the hills. He won't complain though, if I do good work here, and there seems to be every chance.*
>
> *I have a good place to stay though not very stylish. Have my office, workshop, bedroom in a granery. It is a first-rate place for my work. The people are neat and quiet—just an old man and his wife.*
>
> *I guess it rains most every day, but they are only short thundershowers. When the clouds run low they get all snarled up with the hills and trees. I wish you all could come up here for a week. Guess you would enjoy it. It's so healthy here they have no use for graveyards except for fellows who shoot each other. There, guess I have told you enough about the country.*[10]

Bailey's memory for physical places and scenes was vivid and unerring, even those he knew only fleetingly. Formal learning clearly was never the same viscerally engaging experience for him. As he wrote his mother, on September 16, 1888,

> *No, Ma. I don't think that I will go to school anymore, though I would like to; but I seem to fit the corner that I now occupy and like the work and all the time learning something of use, perhaps more than I could at school, and if I wanted to work for a higher position could probably gain it quicker in the field than in school or office. But I am not aiming high, only to do well what I am doing and don't know as I want to follow this always.*[11]

His feelings about his vocation were always mixed; he could never quite convince himself that a practical apprenticeship was superior to formal education, but he knew that for him it was the better way to a career. Although he regretted his lack of formal credentials, Bailey knew himself well enough to realize that he learned more effectively from doing than from reading. He was happier with objects than with words and remembered better what he learned by doing than what he read in books.[12]

13

The West Beckons—On to Utah (1888)

In October, Bailey continued on to Ogden, Utah, where his letters home take on a distinctive western flavor as he picked up the local lingo. On October 10, he wrote to his folks:

> *There is oceans of good fruit lying all around and it don't hurt me to eat all I want of it now. I don't drink any water but when I get thirsty just eat an apple. The water is* bad. *I haven't been down to the lake yet but saw it from the mountains. It is full of mountain islands and the other side hits the sky. The sun goes plumb down into the water but he seems to get out all right for he comes up and looks over the top of the mountains every morning about 8 o'clock.*[1]

Writing to his sister Anna, still away at school, on the same day, he teased her with the traditional role he secretly admires—staying at home—even though he encouraged her in a naturalist's career:

> *I am glad you don't approve of flirting; so don't I. There is enough to think of that is better worth thinking of, but you need not be in a great hurry about learning a trade, or profession. Why not stay on the farm & make butter & cook & boss around all you please? I think there is no place like home & would like to stay there all my life if I could.*[2]

Settling in to his routine and finding much to study in this new country, he notes the "rare occurrence" of writing for a third Sunday in a row from the same place. Although he is excited about the prospects for a visit from one of them, his anticipation turns out to be short-lived. Meanwhile, he finally meets Merriam for the first time. His boss arranged to spend a day with him, and they talked nonstop. He described the interaction to his family in great detail in his next letter home written on October 14:

First, I suppose you want to hear what kind of a fellow he is and how I like him and all of that. Well, Wednesday morning at 9 o'clock I was at the depo when the train came in, had my gun and hunting outfit so he would know me if I didn't know him, and when the people got off from the cars I looked them over without seeing my man and was just climbing over the cars to see those on the other side when someone behind me said "Vernon Bailey." I turned around and there he was, had just crawled out of a sleeping car and picked me out the first thing. I wouldn't have known him, for he is a big, plump fellow—weighs 180 lbs. and says he is poor now, and has beard all over his face; but he is really a very fine looking man, has handsome big brown eyes that look square at you and a fine head and features, but you don't think of his looks when you get acquainted. He is a perfect gentlemen and so jolly and good natured, though as severe a critic as ever. He had his gun and collecting outfit with him, and we went to a livery stable and got a rig and lit out for the hills to hunt and visit, but we talked more than we hunted. I killed a gopher, and he killed a chipmunk which were all we got besides birds, but we talked as fast as possible most of the time, or Dr. Merriam did; for we couldn't be together half long enough. Then we came back to Mr. Stakers for dinner and measured a lot of specimens and looked at the things I had collected and talked and laid plans till we had to go back to the train at 5:30.

It seemed like a very short day and we didn't get many specimens, but we laid lots of plans, and I learned some things and enjoyed the visit ever-so-much.

He told me about his trip of 10,000 miles in the last two months and about other trips and adventures and about scientific men at Washington who I know only from their fame. But what concerns me most is the change which he made in my plans. Instead of spending the winter shivering in the rain along the coast, I am to work south from Utah in about a month and cover as much as possible of New Mexico, Arizona, and southern California before spring.

He was very anxious to have me work through Idaho this fall, but it is now too late to make that trip a success and he plans to have me go from southern Cal. in the spring, to Puget Sound and then work east through Idaho. This outline will not give me a chance to come home before next summer or fall, but he says I may get a team and camp outfit and travel in a go-as-I-please-way this winter. That is just what I have been hoping and planning all along, because it won't cost any more to have someone with me, and the way of traveling will be so cheap that I can save enough more in a five months trip to pay someone's fare out here and back besides sinking something on the outfit.

And now I will tell you what my plans are for I have been laying a lot of them.

I have yet two places to visit in Utah and that will take till about Nov. first. Then I want to go to some place in S. E. Utah, buy a pair of broncos for about $50.00, a light wagon for about $20, and the rest of the outfit within the hundred dollars. Then to have some of you meet me, which will cost about $40 and the return fare from southern Cal. next spring will be about $60.

I think I can fit up for a hundred dollars and sell out next spring for half that, so there will be a loss of $150.00, which I think we can about save by the greater economy of that way of traveling.

Now the question is, can any of you come and who. I think Pa is about the only one who could be spared to waste his time for the winter and perhaps a winter where there is no winter would do him good. If Henry was skillful with his fingers and would ever make a good collector and naturalist, I would have him and try to get him a place, but it is not the work he is calculated for and I want someone this winter who can kind of take care of me. If Charles wasn't married (don't let Myra see that) I would have him along and make a collector of him, and then when I go to Washington would leave him in my place, but he has a home to look after now and probably wouldn't want to wander in the Rockies all of his life and probably couldn't afford to work all winter for nothing.

I think Henry is perfectly capable of managing the farm this winter and Charles will be a near neighbor and I know Pa would enjoy a trip through the mountains with me, and I will agree to send him back next spring perfectly satisfied to live in Minnesota. The worst of it is that Ma would have a, more than ever, lonesome winter of it.

When you have all talked these plans over thoroughly let me know what you think of them.

It is not a sure thing yet that I will go in this way but the plan has great advantages and Dr. Merriam approves of it. The trip will be through a region of few railroads or stage lines and much of it in an almost unexplored region and among villainous Mexicans, but two of us together could have a glorious time and expenses would be small. . . .

I want someone along who can drive team and cook and hunt and set mouse traps and learn to skin things, but most of all someone from home for company.

It may be that Merriam will get someone of his young collectors who needs experience and send him with me, and in that case I suppose the hundred dollars would be worth saving, but I would hate to give up the prospect of having one of you with me. Merriam said if I only was married now I could take my wife along. He is going to take his wife on a camping trip next summer and says if he can manage it so we will camp together for a few weeks.

He wanted me to work in Texas this winter but says the Mexicans will kill a fellow for two dollars and if they didn't kill me the fever would and he can't spare me just yet. He says he will want me in Washington one of these winters to work up my reports, but at present he can't spare me from the field work, even for a visit home. He has work planned away ahead for me and it seems likely to last a good while.

I have an idea that our wagon trip this winter will be so profitable that he will want me to go that way most of the time hereafter and then perhaps I will have some of you with me all of the time.[3]

He hears back from Merriam on October 21 about the upcoming wagon trip with a promise to send official instructions soon. He also received the good news that Merriam had made up his mind to send "a man whom you can instruct so that he will be able to start off on his own account as soon as he leaves you. We want another *good man* in the field, but don't know just where to find him—so perhaps we had better *make* him."[4]

At Salt Lake City, Bailey extended his religious education by visiting the Mormon Tabernacle. Afterward, he wrote home, on October 28, from "The Valley, Only House Opposite Temple and Tabernacle."

It is an immense building and there were about 5000 people present and room for as many more. The service lasted about 2 hours and consisted of the Sacrament, singing and music, and speeches by two men. One of them is a very smart man and the finest speaker I have ever heard. The sermons contained a good deal of doctrine and were not very good, but I learned some things from them.

The music was grand. The great pipe organ is as large as a house and just fills the building with its music, which rolls and tumbles and even shakes the house like distant thunder. There were about a hundred singers and lots of small instruments.

My statement of the size of the organ is not very definite and perhaps you

> *will get a better idea of its size if I tell you it is about 20 feet high and about as wide and long. The pipes are of different sizes, the largest six are about 15 ft. long and 6 or 8 inches in diameter and look like gold. It is said to be one of the finest organs in the world.*[5]

Vernon Bailey had been on his own for a year or more in his first trips for Merriam in the late 1880s. Although Merriam now wanted him to have a companion for the trip from Utah to California, partly for company but also because the Biological Survey was desperately short of expert collectors, Merriam found that the budget stood in his way. Bailey had suggested a young man from Ogden with an interest in natural history and a person he thought would make a good fieldworker. Merriam offered to pay him $5 per month out of his own pocket to cover expenses so that he gained experience in case they had the funds to hire him in the future. He told Bailey to "please communicate with him, and let me know the result at your earliest convenience. What we want is a young man who has the right sort of stuff in him, who will profit by your experience and example, and be able to make trips independently after the present season's field work with you."[6] Apparently in this particular case it did not work out and Bailey soldiered on alone.

Writing home from Provo the next month, November 11, Bailey's lack of companionship begins to tell on him:

> *It may be that Merriam will send Herb Keys if he will come, but it takes such an everlasting while for letters to go and come from Washington that I will not be likely to hear from M.[erriam] about it for a week yet. One fellow that I wrote to first couldn't go and that hindered some. Merriam can't seem to find anyone to go with me and wants me to pick out someone, but I don't know any naturalists that would go, unless Herb might. I proposed him and am now waiting for M.[erriam] to decide.*
>
> *I haven't been doing much collecting lately, for it has been so cold there was no use trying to find the small things. It freezes hard every night but the snow is mostly gone in the valley. The mountains are covered yet to the bottoms and it is mountains clear around me.*
>
> *I am staying with an old bachelor a mile from town and close to the mountains. It is a rather hard place to board but has some advantages; there are no children to bother and I can scatter my things around and make all the dirt I please and it don't trouble anybody. Things are not* extra *clean and we live mostly on pancakes, but I will soon be camping out and doing my own cooking and will keep things so clean.*

If I had stuck to the first plan of having Pa with me we would have been camping now, but this new bother has come up.

I haven't bought my outfit yet but have got it most all in sight. Know where I can get one good pony for 25 dollars and another for 30, I guess, and have a wagon picked out for about 30 and a harness for 15. . . .

I have about decided to fit up and start south the last of this week alone and then go to some farm house and camp where I can have my things taken care of while I am hunting. This will be cheaper and better than boarding around and then I can wait till I get someone to go along before I go farther.

This don't seem a bit like Sunday, but perhaps I will go to church this evening, or to the Salvation Army meeting. I went to their meeting last Sunday night, but it was hardly a meeting. The army seemed like some little kittens fighting a lot of bad dogs, and was composed of three women with an audience of about 50 ruffians who made all the noise and trouble they could. I felt like fighting, myself, and guess I will go again tonight, just to help keep 'em straight.

I caught a mouse alive yesterday and have been taking its picture. It is an Ochetodon longicaudus, a kind that I have only found in Utah and I have a lot of traps set for them now and hope to get more in the morning.

I have been eating apples till my teeth are all on edge. I eat about a dozen a day now.[7]

The day after Thanksgiving, while back in the field at Nephi, Utah, Bailey gets a new lease on life. This is the way he best pictures himself, and his enthusiasm crossed the miles along with the words written on November 25:

I am all alone, sitting on a box in my tent with my trunk still on my lap to write on, and it makes a firstrate writing table. There is a good fire burning just outside the tent door and that keeps me warm. I forgot to chop any wood for Sunday and had to chop some to get breakfast with, but the wood is only willow brush and don't take much chopping anyway, will burn just as good without. I am camped in the middle of a big valley where there is a little feed for the ponies and plenty of willow brush. Am about 3 miles from town and about half a mile from some houses. It is a good camping ground but a poor place to collect. There is nothing around but mice and plenty of coyotes. They howl all around every night and yesterday two of them kept looking around in plain sight all the morning, but too far for a shot. . . .

Last Sunday I was at Provo. The next day I hitched my fiery steeds together and then it took me all day to get my things together and ready to migrate, so I only got out of Provo a few miles before dark and had to camp. The next morning the horses' shoulders were sore and they wouldn't pull the wagon, so I had to go back to town and get some collar pads and didn't get started till most noon and then didn't get to Nephi till 3 o'clock the next day. I camped along the road most anywhere and as soon as I got here made a tent. It isn't very large, 6 × 6, but is big enough and is a home of my own.

My outfit is now complete, all but a companion. The ponies are not very rapid travelers, but are good for 30 or 40 miles a day and are improving. I feed them about 2 quarts of oats apiece a day and let them pick dead grass for the rest of it.

The country here is about like at Provo and all along the basin, rough mountains and sagebrush valleys. I have to take care of my horses and keep house and cook and there isn't much time left for collecting, have caught a few mice and that's all.

The cooking isn't very elaborate though. I fry some bacon and make some pancakes for breakfast and make a pancake sandwich to keep for dinner; and then when it gets too dark for anything else, I build a fire and bake some pancakes and fry some bacon and eat it while the Coyotes howl around. Everything tastes good, but I am going to get something else for a change before long, because it may be healthier. I have a tame mouse, an Ochetodon longicaudus, and with this and the ponies for company I won't get very lonesome; but hope Merriam will send someone to go with me soon so we can be moving south. Haven't heard from him at all for a week.[8]

December arrives along with a letter from Hiram in Elk River, written on the first of the month, cautioning Vernon to take better care of himself and bemoaning the economic conditions back on the family farm.

Ma and Anna are making you a little cake to send you by mail. I guess it will be good and I hope you will get it. You should get some dried fruit to take with you and some rice to cook with your rabbits etc., and a barrel of hard bread or crackers. They would be handy and healthier than pancakes. Don't try to live on nothing while we are having so many good things and are warm every night. You know I don't worry much over what I can't help but I am afraid your route lays through so high and mountainous a country that you may get snowed in and lose your ponies unless you get south pretty fast. . . .

Our corn crop was not very large, I guess we have 200 baskets yet but it is going off pretty fast. We are feeding our hogs yet and they are pretty nice but not quite fat enough. I don't know how we will get enough to keep our horses

> *unless we sell the pack. Hogs on foot are worth about $5.30 a hundred and corn 25 cts. a bushel. Uncle Alvin hadn't any flour and no money to get any and I took him 50 lbs this morning. It was bought with your money so if you want the recording Angel to give you credit for it it will be about $1.85.*[9]

Mother Emily appended a brief addition to the letter, expressing concern about his health over the winter and urging him to acquire comfortable clothes and good wholesome food to eat. She also opined that Merriam should have been able to find someone to accompany him so that he did not have to venture out alone.[10]

As he traveled in Utah, Bailey continued to learn about Mormonism and wrote home his impressions from Manti, Utah, on December 2:

> *I have been to Mormon church & listened to 3 sermons, good, bad, & indifferent. They preach "Mormonism" more than gospel, & I think that one reason why so many of them are not very good. I have heard bishops & lots of church members use very bad language, & the greatest fault that I find with them is, they are not good Mormons; that is, lots of them are not. One bishop remarked, in his sermon today, that "the devil had driven them to Salt Lake Valley & all Hell couldn't drive them away." Think I will go to Presbyterian church this evening. I am getting so I don't consider all sects but one or two as heathens, so much as I used to, & don't care much what people are if they are only good themselves, or try to be.*[11]

The routine becomes a whole new adventure when Bailey's new assistant, Herb Keys,[12] arrives at Manti in preparation for the upcoming trip to Arizona. Bailey informed his family that the weather is fine and the trip promises to be rapid and pleasant with a stop at Kanab, Utah, before pushing as far as possible to the Colorado canyon country in Arizona.[13]

14

It Takes Grit (December 1888 and 1889)

All seems well as the year comes to a close. Bailey was entering new territory, with a companion for the first time, preparing for more collecting and another adventure. Merriam caught up with him by letter at Kanab, Utah, on December 17, reminding him of the uncharted territory they were about to enter and informing him that after leaving Kanab the first post office address would be St. George. After leaving there, he was told to notify the department of his post office address a number of weeks in advance because the mail would be slow and the post offices few and far between in penetrating the region he was about to enter.[1]

The next day, December 18, Merriam wrote again, giving him detailed advice after talking with members of the US Geological Survey. The advice concerned the best place to enter the Grand Canyon, which Merriam had been told was by way of Kanab Wash and Kanab Canyon where you could take pack animals all the way into the canyon. Merriam went on to explain:

> *This is likely to prove the most interesting part of your canon work, and I wish you would make a special effort to accomplish as much as possible while there. In addition to your work on mammals and birds, I wish you would collect and put into alcohol any small reptiles or batrachians you may find, and if you see any shells, by all means save them. It would also be worth the while to preserve as many plants as possible. . . . The matter of other side trips from Kanab I leave entirely to your own judgment, as being on the ground you are much better able to judge than I. I fear the time of year is against you for any work in the mountains. . . . I am told that there is an old man at Kanab by the name of Adams, who has been to the Grand Canon several times by way of Kanab Wash and Canon, and who knows all about the country and the best methods of navigation there. You had better make it a point to see him.*

St. George is very much lower in altitude than Kanab, and proportionally more southern in its fauna and flora. From St. George you will again visit the Grand Canon by way of the Grand Wash. By this route you will be able to take your wagon nearly if not quite into the canon, and can camp there as long as you find it profitable. Theoretically the locality does not promise so much as Kanab, so I hope you will make the greatest effort at Kanab Canyon.[2]

But because of deep snow, Bailey was unable to go into the Grand Canyon from Kanab. Instead he and Keys headed east where he wrote home from Fort Defiance, near the border with New Mexico, on December 30, 1888, as the year ended:

Don't look for Ft. Defiance on the map for you wouldn't find it. I am not sure whether it is in Utah or Arizona, anyway it is 24 miles from here to St. George. The fort is an old pile of rocks that was built to keep the Indians away but no one lives here or anywhere near. It is Sunday and we are still on the road to St. George. We had to camp last night where there was no water and so came about 5 miles this forenoon and found an old deserted house at Ft. Defiance and good water, so we camped here to spend Sunday. It don't seem a bit like Sunday and I would not feel as though it was if I didn't write home. The first thing I did this morning was to pepper a Coyote with fine shot while I was in bed. It came up to within a few rods of our bed and I just turned my gun around and gave him some fine shot but didn't hurt him much. Then we hitched up and traveled the same as other days and now are boiling some meat and making bread in a fireplace for supper.

We see Coyotes every day & at night they make lots of music for us to sleep by, but we haven't seen any signs of large game. The ground makes a first rate bedstead & with a few weeds or cedar boughs under our blankets, we sleep as well as if on feathers. I never slept better than I have lately & I don't take cold at all. It is rather bracing to crawl out of a warm bed & put on frozen shoes, but that is all the clothes we have to put on in the morning.[3]

There was no hint, as the new year opened, of the distress that was to come. Merriam continued to address Bailey at Kanab, as he moved forward in validating his "life zone" theory. His letter instructed that while Bailey was in the Colorado River canyon he was to take pains to notice the effect of slope exposure on both vegetable and animal life. He explained that "where there are shelves of sufficient extent above the reach of freshets there ought to be a marked difference on the two sides of the canon, and I shall be glad to receive a full account of such differences as you notice which can be attributed solely to slope exposure."[4]

But because he couldn't get onto the Colorado Plateau, Bailey had left Kanab early, failing to obtain some of the species that Merriam wanted. This drew a sharp rebuke from his boss, writing on January 10, 1889,

> *Your letters of Dec. 24 and 25 from Kanab gave me the bitterest disappointment I've had in many a day. You must have forgotten your instructions from the Commissioner (sent you at Salt Lake or Provo) or you would not have hurried through the Kanab country where we* particularly *wanted you to stay long enough to secure all of the evidences obtainable of the northward extension of the southern fauna there.*[5]

Just as puzzling is why he headed east to Fort Defiance instead of going west to St. George according to his instructions.

Nor do Bailey's letters home give any clue. With no complete record, the gaps in the narrative can only be filled in by intuition and speculation. But, by January 20, 1889, Bailey and Keys had returned to St. George, Utah, where he wrote to Anna:

> *There isn't anything worth writing about, for the birds and animals that I find are all strange to you and you can't get any idea of them from my description. But I haven't found anything here of any special interest. There are lots of queer plants that are new to me and that I can't identify because my botany doesn't describe them. I am very anxious to get to St. Thomas and get some letters from you and expect a lot of them, then I won't get any more for a long time, but you must write me some good long ones to Mineral Park, Arizona.*[6]

And so he headed south, writing home from Dolans Spring, Arizona, on February 2:

> *We were lucky in finding a good sized, stone house with thatched roof & a fireplace to camp in. It is more roomy & convenient to work in than a 6 × 6 tent, & then the fireplace beats a campfire all hollow to cook by. I can bake first rate bread in the fireplace & we get up lots of new dishes for variety. We got some Quails & lots of Rabbits for fresh meat & killed some Snow Geese at the river, & they lasted a good while.*
>
> *There is no wood, or even brush, around here except pine away up the*

mountains, so we burn the dry stems of Spanish Bayonets. These grow as large as trees & have trunks often a foot through & 10 or 15 feet high, but are kind of oily & the wood is soft, spongy stuff.

There is no big game here except Coyotes but they are thick enough to make up for small size. They howl around on all sides at night & often in daytime too.[7]

Merriam's tone seemed to soften when he sent a handwritten note on February 12 to Bailey urging him to slow down and be more thorough in his work:

Was much pleased with the last lot of specimens though they were not as numerous as expected. Some of them suffered from being packed green. Now drive slow! *You are in a mighty interesting region and I want you to appreciate the fact before you get out of it. You are on the ground a man must be on in order to solve several problems of distribution and of the interrelations of species, and I hope you will not move too hastily. . . . How is Keys panning out?*[8]

On the same day, Merriam sent a more formal, and somewhat terse, letter to him at Mineral Park, requesting that he return all of the map sheets of the Grand Canyon region in his possession with his exact route traced on the maps including all of his camps and his dates of movements. This letter also provided some specific instructions for Bailey to follow in the future:

In future please be particularly careful in your notes under the different species to indicate the altitude and general character of the country where they were found in cases in which this information will be of importance to us in determining their distribution. Of course you have found out that altitude has more to do with limiting the distribution of species than any other single cause. Therefore I wish you would take special pains in writing your report to indicate the limits of altitude between which the species treated are found. This you can do with considerable precision when traveling, as at present, in a country of which you have Geological Survey map sheets.

You speak of dry regions as particularly objectionable, and seem to pass through them as rapidly as possible. This you should not do without first demonstrating the absence of animal life.[9]

Five days later he wrote home from Mineral Park, happy to be closer to civilization, at least to railroads and in "a less deserted country" where he would "get mail more regularly." He continued:

> *Ma, you seem to think we have a hard, disagreeable time but I don't see why. I wouldn't take a thousand dollars for this winter's experience; but then, I am not sorry it is most over.*
>
> *I read what you said, Pa, about there being more stuff produced than there was demand for and everything so cheap, and then I bought 75 pounds of barley for $2.50 and paid a dollar for a can of butter, about a pound and a half, and 5c for a pound for potatoes and 10c for oatmeal. We are still using bacon that I paid 19c a pound for at St. George, so you can see we don't feel the effects of overproduction out here. There is nothing produced here at all but gold and silver, though there is plenty of copper and iron.*
>
> *The mountains are full of mines (and old holes that didn't pay) and there are lots of quartz mills around. I was at a mine yesterday and a fellow gave me some good specimens of ore, some with free gold in it and some with native and ruby silver. The miners are a different class of men from the Mormons but are good natured, rough fellows and always accommodating if you are civil with them.*
>
> *Our horses have been gone for 3 or 4 days and everybody around has promised to let us know if they see or hear of them. I hope we will find them soon for I want to leave here now as soon as possible.*
>
> *All that people come here for is to dig up a fortune & that takes so long that some of them don't get away.*[10]

He continued to encourage Anna in her taxidermy, writing her the same day:

> *Why didn't you say something about that Great Gray Owl. Chas. said you had mounted one and he supposed you had told me all about it. You don't know how excited I feel about it. It is probably the first that has ever been taken, and saved, in the state. They are extremely rare.*
>
> *Get this one if you can possibly. Get it as cheap as you can but do not stop at less than five dollars. Whose is it? Get all the notes you can about it, especially as to date, sex, if shot, etc. Its stomach would be of importance if saved in alcohol. Write me about it.*
>
> *They are not in market but a good specimen is easily worth 25 dollars, or more. The only one I ever saw was the one I found dead about 8 years ago and I never felt very sure of that one.*

If whomever it belongs to won't let you have it then charge them $5.00 for mounting it.

I am glad you get some work to do and like it. You will make a first class taxidermist if you have practice and I don't know of a better proposition for a girl of your tastes; but you must study just as much as if for a lawyer. A taxidermist that isn't a naturalist isn't worth shucks.

You can make more in a week as a taxidermist than in a month as a teacher, and it is pleasant work, only teaching gives you a chance to study more.[11]

Letters home continued to tell the tales of the West, and to show his eagerness to return home. He wrote his family on February 24 about the coyotes at Mud Spring, Arizona, who "came within 20 feet of the tent last night and took two jack rabbits and a lot of gophers and mice that we had skinned and thrown out."[12] As he described it, they howled all night and day but were hardly ever seen.

From Harpers he wrote to Anna on March 3, talking about his and her future careers as naturalists:

Hope you do not yet get very tired of school, for I want you to keep going till you know more than the teachers anyway. I believe you & I are destined to be naturalists & a naturalist needs a good education, which I have not got & can't seem to get; but you can learn enough to help me out & we can work together sometime. Who knows but we may publish books & be famous yet! But school isn't the only place to learn & I expect you will enjoy a vacation thoroughly, all the more that you are getting tired of school! We are never quite happy. How I would enjoy being at home & how you would enjoy being out here; but it takes grit to hang on till we accomplish what we are at.[13]

He also wrote home that day, describing what they were doing and offering some advice to his father:

There are lots of Bats around evenings but we can't seem to kill them. I made a lot of little hooks & baited them with flies & hung them in the old house for Bats but they wouldn't bite.

Pa, I don't think you had better go to Montana to keep stock. That has broke more men than farming has. Stock business in the west is as much overdone as farming, & you would find feed short & cattle cheap & lots of bigger men ahead of you. Just wait till we get out of debt & we can live on the farm without any money.

We are both pretty [worn] out of shoes too but expect to find some at the fort. Had to keep our old ones mended up to make them hold out till we can get more. Mine have lasted 3 months with the help of two old pairs & that is better than most of them do.

Three men just came along here & stopped for a talk, were horseback & looking for stock. They are the first men I have seen for nearly two weeks. Of course they had a bottle of whiskey along but we declined the treat.[14]

While he discouraged his father from raising stock, he found an alternative to be enthusiastic about, writing home from Fort Mohave, Arizona, on March 17:

believe I have found a place that would suit you, at last, Pa. There is no winter here. I asked an old Indian if it ever snows here and he said, "What you callim snow?" "Me no sava snow." He is one of my nearest neighbors and a daily visitor about meal time. Keeps 10 hens and last Friday had saved 6 eggs and took them to the fort and sold them for 25c. How would it suit you to raise chickens here? They could live on "mesquite beans" and so could you. The Indians live on them mostly. They are wild—grow on thorn trees and there are any amount of them here. The Indians gather them and store in big willow baskets on platforms and grind them between two stones. They are said to make good whisky too.[15]

Bailey's assistant, Herb Keys, left to seek work in Prescott. Bailey continued, alone again, and wrote home from Needles, California, on March 21, describing plans for his forthcoming boat trip down the Colorado River:

I have reached the R. R. and sold my outfit for $55.00 and bought a boat for $15.00 and am ready to start down the river in the morning for Ft. Yuma. It will probably take 6 days to run down but the river is said to be smooth and I think the trip will be safe and not unpleasant. Have a good steady boat and the weather is fine. Hastily written but with love, Captain Bailey[16]

15
Down the Colorado (1889)

Merriam wrote to him again on March 12 with further instructions to proceed to Fort Yuma, California, either by boat or by driving along the west side of the river, using his own judgment. The letter also chastised him for sending in a report with ink so pale that Merriam could hardly read it. He was told to be careful and always use permanent black ink.[1] Bailey seemed thrilled with the thought of a boat trip and shortly after receiving Merriam's letter he set out in that manner.

Typically underplaying his adventures, Bailey composed this essay and the journal that follows, found penciled in his field notes of the year, describing his descent down the Colorado River by boat.[2]

Down the Colorado; March 1889

It was early in March and in the valley of the Colorado R. summer had arrived. The days were not yet too hot and the nights were warm enough for comfortable sleeping on the ground. Birds were singing and building their nests in the mesquite bushes. Ground squirrels were scampering among the creosote bushes. Flowers were blooming everywhere, big white evening primrose, great scarlet and yellow cactus flowers and over all the valley a rich robe of yellow flowers of the creosote bush.

Half an hour before sunrise I pushed my boat out from the willowy bank of the river near Needles and felt a thrill of delight as it was caught by the rushing current and swept along almost without the aid of oars. The shores were soon racing backwards at the rate of 5 miles an hour. The yellow, muddy water gurgled and surged and swirled along and broke into cross channels on the sandbars.

Ten miles of smooth running and the face of the country begins to change. The low, sandy shores jut out here and there in rocky points, and right across the river in front rises a jagged mass of black, sunbaked rocks two thousand feet above me.

The river seems to run slow against these mountains. There is not a visible break through them. A big rock rises in the middle of the river and tears the water apart and sends it foaming on both sides. The strength of the current is increasing. I know there is a canon ahead, but, inspite of the fact that Indians frequently run through it with row boats, I begin to feel a little solemn. If I only had a companion to help manage the boat, or just someone to talk to, I should enter the canon with a lighter heart, or if I knew just what to expect or what dangers to look out for. . . .

March 22—*Packed things in boat & started down river at daylight. Found I couldn't row at all, just steered & paddled to keep it straight. Stuck on bar, and had to get a push. Ran under A. P. R. R. bridge. Passed a steamer on the Mohave, went on board. . . . Ran through Mohave Canon, got into some rough whirls, camped at lower end of canon, at 2 P. M. Set 34 traps, 3 Indians went by in boat, was glad to see them. Found some beautiful cactus blossums [sic], larger than roses, very delicate, and brightest crimson. Shot at bats in evening. Made the canon fairly roar. Killed one bat, a little thing, new to me. My potatoes burned while I watched bats. Have got a lame back from paddling.*

March 23—*Caught 2 Perognathus and 4 Hesperomys. Started at sunrise, passed Snyders ranch. Country open and low. Cottonwood along river. At 2 PM entered rocky country again. Stopped at Ringon (*?) Mine No. 10 deserted. A fine mill of 10 stamps. Picked up some ores, found a Beaver skull. Passed the mouth of Bill Williams Creek, entered a deep canon. Water rough in canon. Saw the first Giant cactus. Stopped at a gold mine and got ores. A little 5 stamp mill. Had a good talk with the men. Ran about 5 miles farther and camped on island. Could row pretty good. Came about 50 miles today, have blistered my hands and got a lame arm.*

March 24—*Sunday. Stayed all day on island, read, wrote, rested. Island flat, sandy and brush. Heard bells at Agency below.*

March 25—*Started before sunrise. Soon came to agency. Sent a half naked savage to P. O. with letters. Gave him a quarter. Took 6 eggs in change for 50c. Ran steadily and rapidly till 3 PM. Camped on W. side, set 27 traps. Have been all day in a broad valley between ragged mountains. Much cottonwood on river flats. Indians and wood piles all along river. A warm day. Could row all night.*

March 26—*Caught 2 kinds of Hesperomys and 4 Perognathus. Started early, reached Ehrenberg at noon. Sent letters, got Beaver trap and a supply of provision. Ran till 2 PM. Camped in E. side, set traps, made 6 skins in evening. In cotton-wood valley all day. Beaver tracks and slides common all along bank. Valley sandy. Clear and warm.*

March 27—*Caught a Perognathus, a Dipodomys deserti, and a D. agilis. No beaver. Started after sunrise, ran till 3 PM. Camped on E. side 15 miles above Nortons. Stopped at Paymaster Mine—silver—and had a talk with a white man. Passed a big steamer stuck on bar. Took a run over the hills at noon but found nothing of account. Set traps. Made skins in evening. Baked bread for tomorrow. The timbered valley that I entered above Colorado Agency ends here in a rocky canon.*

March 28—*Caught 3 Perognathus and 2 Dipidomys agilis. Reached Nortons silver mine a little before noon. Mailed letters and got some butter and fruit. Saw a white woman. All the hands in mine were Mexicans. Ran till 2 PM. Camped on east side in Canebreak Canon. Fine scenery, bare rocks. Caves along each bank. Set traps. Made 5 skins in evening by candlelight. Shot at bats, made the canon roar, only killed one. The rocks are black lava, granite, schist, quartz. Mountains not very high, perfectly bare, very rough. Camped near a giant Cactus—20 feet high and 18 inches through at middle, 26 Woodpecker holes in it. Donkey tracks in the gulches. Beaver, Coon, Skunk, and Wildcat tracks common.*

March 29—*Caught two Neotoma, 2 Hesperomys and a Perognathus. Started about 8 o'clock. Ran steadily till 5 PM and camped near Ft. Yuma. Ran about 50 miles in 9 hours. The river is wider and current slower. Valley wide and covered with cottonwood and willows after leaving Canebreak Canon to Yuma, bare mountains in the distance. Saw a few Indians along the bank. Some Beaver tracks.*

After the Colorado River trip was completed, Merriam sent Bailey a rather terse letter in early May about the specimens he had sent to Washington from the Arizona trip, including some direct advise for improving his work:

> *I was very much pleased with the contents of the box of specimens sent us from Yuma, but regret that it did not contain a single Hesperomys eremicus, although you state in your report that you found the species common at Fort Yuma on the California side. Having previously written you to collect both sides of the river and to get more Hesperomys, I thought you would be sure to send a good series. In skinning over the head of this species of Hesperomys you will have to look out for the cheek bones, which are thinner than in any of the other species, and are almost certain to be broken unless special care is taken. Also in removing the tongue and cleaning the base of the skull of small mammals of various kinds, particularly Spermophiles, you sometimes scrape off the pterygoid bones. Please take pains to avoid this injury in future. It is much better to leave more flesh on than to run the risk of injuring the bone.*
>
> *One of the Spermophilus tereticaudus collected at Yuma is remarkable for the shortness of the skull and the fact that the nasal bones are turned up slightly at the tip. It is an adult female. On first looking at this skull I thought it was another species, and it is still difficult for me to believe that it came out of the skin whose number it bears, the departure from the ordinary type of skull of this species is so great. At the same time I do not think it could possibly be anything else, and undoubtedly it really belongs to this species.*
>
> *Two of the specimens sent had no labels at all, one a Badger and the other*

> *a Fox. Please give me full data concerning both Badgers and both Foxes, so that I may get the correct labels by elimination.*
>
> *There is a short-tailed, light colored small Spermophile which I hope you will encounter before long.*[3]

An overly sensitive person might take such criticisms harshly and get discouraged, but it didn't seem to bother Bailey. He had such respect and trust that Merriam was trying to teach him the proper methods for field natural history that for the most part he accepted criticisms such as this in stride and as part of his apprenticeship.[4]

16
The Promise of Plenty of Company (1889)

Once at Yuma, Bailey continued his work unabated, writing to his folks on April 3 that he was looking forward to joining a Geological Survey party in Texas and encouraging them to begin thinking about constructing a new house:

> *Now at work in the valley of the Rio Grande near El Paso. If I do, I will have plenty of company then and there are several other advantages. It is not decided yet.*
>
> *I find by balancing my accounts for last year that I cleared 70 dollars a month for the 7 1/2 months of 1888. That includes what M[erriam] still owes me and will pay the 15th of May, about 100 dollars. For Jan., Feb., and March I have averaged 96 dollars a month, but that average will have to come down before long. Probably you can count on about 70 a month this summer.*
>
> *Now, Pa, I wish you would make out a statement of all our debts; who to, when due, how much, rate of int. and cet[era]. Are you planning to build a house this summer? If you can do the work and there are no debts that I have got to be paid this summer—or large ones, there is nothing to hinder building. The old log house won't do for another winter anyway.*
>
> *I would not build a very large house, but have it well planned. Leave a room upstairs for my museum, 10 × 8 or 12, or somewhere near that will do. I want you to get it planned soon enough so I can see the plans before you build. Want to kind of have a finger in the pie myself. Write me all about where you are going to build and send plans. Lay plans for the yard, and fence and gate and road and trees and flowerbeds and all such things. Then make them* good *and let them* stay.[1]

Descriptions of life in southern Arizona must have seemed otherworldly to the "Dear folks at home." Writing a few days later, he described some of his observations from around Yuma, Arizona:

There are a good many Beaver here but I can't catch them. An old trapper came by the other day with 20 Beaver skins & a Mountain Lion skin.

There is a lizard sunning itself on the roof of my tent. It is about 6 inches long. They keep sunning over the tent all day. There are at least 8 or 10 kinds here from 6 in. to a foot & a half long. I have to send specimens of all of them. I generally have to shoot them or kill them with stones. They can run faster than I can anyway, & climb trees too.

Yesterday while I was out to my traps I found two little rattle snakes, nice little brown fellows about 18 inches long with 11 rattles. I was bringing them home and coming along a path through the brush thinking what a dull stupid thing a rattlesnake was when whiz *went a great racket and an old brute, 49 inches long and as big as my arm rared up about two steps ahead of me in the path. I did not screech nor jump, but I stopped so quick I nearly fell over backwards. This was another kind. He was too big to carry home alive, besides he had a disposition of his own, so I pecked a load of shot from the auxiliary through his neck and now his skin lays on a box drying. I can get along with rattlers all right but I do hate scorpions and tarantulas. . . .*

Yuma isn't much of a town anyway. There is a prison and R. R. hotel and one street with a row of adobe stores and saloons along one side of it. Most of the people are Mexicans and of course there is a row of Indians from one end of town to the other.

Merriam says the Geological Survey will let him send a man with one of their parties now in the valley of the Rio Grande. He says they will carry my chest and feed me free but I will have to buy a horse to ride. Says the country is one of the most important to study up. He didn't say much about it but wanted to know what I thought of going. I told him it would suit me. I don't altogether like staying down here all summer, but that region is rather high and not so hot, besides I would have good company all the time and my expenses would be small. It used to be a dream of my ambition to go with a Geol. Survey party. I would be with men who know something.[2]

On May 1 Bailey received a long letter from Merriam critiquing his recent work and offering advice that clearly indicates his confidence in Bailey is growing. Also, he provides more advice about how to cope with arsenic poisoning and what to do about scorpion, tarantula, and rattlesnake bites:

Your letters of April 20 and 22 reached me day before yesterday, together with your report from Yuma. This morning's mail brought your letters of the 23rd and 24th from Texas Hill. The specimens sent from Yuma have not yet arrived. Your report from Yuma is very full and satisfactory.

I regret that you did not spend a week or ten days on the California side of the river below Fort Yuma. I supposed you had done this, or should not have written you to proceed eastward so soon. In such cases you must always use your own judgment as to the time of leaving, it being impossible for me to know exactly what you are doing or how well a locality is panning out. In a good locality like Yuma it is desirable to stay much longer than in most localities which you have visited. At any time in the future when you receive instructions to move on as soon as practicable, you will consider yourself at liberty to stay a week or two weeks longer if you deem it best. We do not wish to hamper you by detailed instructions. You know the objects for which you are working, and are much better able to judge of the details of your movements than we are at this distance. . . .

I am sorry to learn that you are suffering from arsenic poisoning. I think you had better adopt the method I employed so successfully last summer. . . . Cover your arsenic with alcohol and put it on the skins with a brush. I use no dry arsenic at all, and in this way avoid finger sores.

I hope that you will find the temperature lower as you proceed eastward. Whenever practicable you should do as much work as you can on the very tops of high mountains. This you have not done heretofore for various reasons, and unquestionable you have left many new species unobserved.

You ask what you had better do in case you are unfortunate enough to be bitten by a rattlesnake, scorpion, or tarantula. In this case it is easier to advise you what not to do than what to do. First, do not get drunk. Second, ligate the arm or leg above the bite in order to prevent the blood containing the poison from returning immediately to the heart. Then incise the wound so as to make it bleed freely, and suck out the wound if you can get at it. You had better carry a small vial of spirits of ammonia with you; in case you are bitten pour a little full strength into the wound; also take a few drops (not more than ten) in water about every quarter or half hour if much depressed, to keep the action of the heart. In case you are bitten and use the ligature, you must slacken up on the ligature gradually in order to let the blood return to the heart slowly. The great danger from bites is fright; the bites themselves as a rule are comparatively harmless, particularly those of scorpions and tarantulas.

In a few days I shall mail you, addressed to Phoenix, instructions for your movements after leaving this region. Possibly we shall want you to stop over at Tucson in order to visit the high mountains near that place.[3]

Bailey's growing understanding of the West is apparent, and he made note of the fact in describing a copy of *Youth Companion* he bought in Phoenix in which he read "about Utes & Navajos in Utah & cattle thieves in Texas. I often get stories now that describe things & places familiar to me." This letter, written on April 28, also pointed out his growing familiarity with facets of life elsewhere, because he met a young fellow from Australia who had never been out of a little province near Victoria until he started out two months ago for a tour of the world. According to Bailey, "He was a jolly fellow & thoroughly alive. Wanted to learn all he could. I was willing to tell him all I knew in exchange for what he knew of Australian life, & for five hours we talked most of the time."[4]

After receiving his father's ideas on building the new house, Bailey gave his advice on how to proceed. Although young, he was already taking on the parenting role to his family, as the son out in the world looking back to keep his family comfortable at home. The plan suited him well. From Phoenix he wrote home on the May 27:

There are more debts to pay this summer than I expected, but if all goes well we can pay them when due and build a house too. . . .

I think the best plan is to build the upright, 16 × 24, as you have planned this fall, make it warm and snug to live in through the winter. . . . I have no change to propose in the plan. It seems to me very good. I advise you to lay plans to build some time before next winter. If you wait until towards fall we will know nearer how we are coming out financially. Probably you could do such things as digging the cellar and laying the foundation between jobs through the summer.

That is business enough for today and too much, but I had it all thought out and it rests my head to get rid of it.

It is 2 PM now. I went to church at 10 o'clock and stayed until 12:30. There was Sunday school and communion and preaching. It was all very good and not too long. It is a Methodist church. There is no other place where a stranger can be so much at home as in a good live Methodist congregation. . . . I enjoyed the meeting very much but I think it is a good thing to be alone sometimes and get acquainted with yourself. I believe it would do lots of folks good. A fellow told me once that he didn't like to be alone, he wanted better company. . . .

This seems to be quite a decent country to live in. It isn't near so hot as down at Texas Hill and Yuma. 102 degrees is as high as it has been here yet and 95 is about the common limit. The nights and mornings are cool and pleasant. There are no mosquitoes and the scorpions don't scare me any more. I haven't seen any rattlers lately either. The water is good and pure and there is lots of shade. These are blessings that I don't believe you can appreciate. . . .

I have not found anything of much account here yet, have been trying to catch a Beaver but haven't yet. There are lots of birds and several kinds new to me, but birds are not my specialty. They are so well known that I have little hopes of finding any new ones, while I have already brought to light some 6 or 8 species of mammals before unknown. That would make me famous if I was doing it all by myself so as to have all the credit. As it is I get all the credit that I earn.[5]

Extending his descriptions of local fauna, he wrote to Anna the same day:

There are a lot of new birds here, and I will save some skins for our own collection. I got one nice [male] Cardinal Grosbeak. There are some Blue Grosbeaks and Vermillion Flycatchers—like a Phoebe dressed like a Tanager—Then there are lots of Bullocks Orioles and a kind of little dove about as big as a Fox Sparrow, and a large dove with white wings. Mocking birds are common and I have heard a few of them sing nice. The Night Hawks are the Texas species, a little different from ours. I haven't found any new mammals here.[6]

Fieldwork next took Bailey farther south still, to Tucson, which he found a

queer old city. I imagine it is not very different from the cities of Mexico, only the public buildings a few houses of American design. I will send a picture of part of the town so you can see what an adobe house is like. It is a good deal like the pictures of Jerusalem and those old cities in the quarterly. There are few two story buildings. I am in the second story of a large hotel and can look all over the tops of the houses clear across town. The hotel is of adobe too and the back part only one story high, so you can go out for a walk on the roof, and can look down into the square courts of the Mexican houses around. A large Mexican house is generally built square with an open space in the center. That is so they can sleep outdoors and have the house all around them. Most everyone sleeps outdoors here in summer.

Dr. Merriam told me to call on a Mr. Brown here and present his compliments. I did so yesterday and found Mr. Brown a very pleasant gentleman with a fine collection of birds and eggs. He is Editor of the Daily Citizen and a member of the A. O. U. and is well posted on birds of Arizona. I spent most of the day with him yesterday and all of a long evening. He gave me much information about the country here and on his recommendation I am going to Mammoth, a small place up in the mountains north of here. I expect to start in the morning on the stage. Don't know how far it is but guess it is about 60 or 80 miles. Probably will stay up there 2 or 3 weeks. Merriam says he thinks this will be my last stop before joining the survey party and I hope so.

These adobe houses are cool. Tucson streets are so narrow that not much heat gets to the ground, and they are so crooked that the sun can't shine length ways of them. I suppose if this was home I would think it is paradise, but it isn't. . . .

I think the mountains will agree with me firstrate though. I can see black, pine covered ranges from my window and they look cool.[7]

A few days later Bailey sent an inquiry to his boss about the Gila monster, and Merriam responded with caution about the well-known beast and suggested that he not permit himself "to be bitten by one in order to show the natives that it is not poisonous."[8] He had come to understand the brashness and adventuresome nature of his young protégé!

17

On the Very Border (1889)

Merriam wrote to Bailey on May 25 about the importance of his work at El Paso but again left the itinerary details to him. Merriam regarded El Paso as one of the most important places in the whole United States because a number of species had been described from there and the type specimens for them subsequently had been lost or so injured by age that they no longer served the purpose of comparison.[1] But Merriam cautioned Bailey about the heat in that part of the country in June and told him to head to the mountains of north-central New Mexico and return to El Paso in the fall if necessary.

Sure enough, the trip to El Paso took more energy than Bailey anticipated. June in that part of the country was not his idea of heaven, nor was the city. In his weekly letter home, written on June 21 following a very brief foray into Mexico, he expressed himself as having been on the very border of civilization:

> *It isn't Sunday but I have nothing else to do but write, rather I don't feel like doing anything harder.*
>
> *I have been in El Paso 3 days & have not been well since I came. Intend to leave tomorrow for Albuquerque. The water is bad here & the weather is hot. Together they undo me, as I was afraid of before coming, but hoped to stand it awhile. Today is cooler, scarce a hundred; yesterday it was 106; day before 105.*
>
> *El Paso is not a loveable place. It is quite a large town & does a good deal of business, but it is bare & dusty & hot. The country around it is barer & dustier & hotter & stonier. There are more trees & green things & some farms lower down the valley "where the Rio Grande's flowin." The river doesn't inspire my poetical nature. It—the river—is a stream of yellow mud, very much like the Colorado but smaller. The banks are low & brushy & it is full of sand bars.*[2]

Albuquerque, two hundred miles north, brought Bailey the promise of better health from some recent illness that had slowed him down. Writing on June 26, he told his folks:

I am not very well yet. The doctor said I was bilious. Then my eyes turned yellow & he said I had the jaundice. He doctored me for that & said I was all right but I am still weak & can't eat. I have a good place to stay & if I should be sick would be taken care of. There is a hospital here too, but I hope I am not going to be sick. It is claimed to be a healthy place & is about 6000 feet high. I will write often. Have nothing else to do. I have plenty of money & that makes friends anywhere.[3]

A week later he wrote home that he had had time to do lots of thinking:

It would be very hard to stay away from home a year with nothing to keep busy at. I thought for awhile that perhaps I would have to come home but now I am feeling right again, only can't stand so much tramping as I could without getting tired. The yellow has about all left me eyes, my appetite is good, and nothing seems to hurt me if I don't eat too much. I sent some pictures yesterday. One is of Flagstaff, in the San Francisco Mts. That is where Merriam and I are planning to get off and camp for a month. Not right there by the R. R. track, but in some canon over behind the first row of mountains probably. I look forward to that spot with much pleasure. It is keeping me from the survey party and keeps my expenses pretty high, but a month with Merriam will be worth much to me.[4]

Still encouraging Anna, he looked forward to being home with her. Writing on July 7, he told her:

You must learn to ride horseback and ride fast. When I come back I will want to go all over my old stamping ground and if you can ride, you can go too. . . . There is nothing to hinder your being a naturalist as well as a taxidermist and they ought to go together. A taxidermist has a good chance to study birds and generally does more hunting than just a naturalist. You will need to study and practice drawing more than anything else, for taxidermy is an art and you must be an artist.[5]

His letter to her the next week, written on July 13, contained some teasing language:

> *I believe you are getting misanthropic. You don't seem to care for anybody and say the boys are the worst things you can think of. Glad I ain't a boy. I don't believe you are naturally very charitable, or else you are unnaturally uncharitable. If you don't give people credit for all the good they possess, the world will seem pretty bad. Sometimes I hope you can travel with me and see more of the world than Meadow Vale. If you could see everyone at work here today as much as on any weekday you would think our quiet neighborhood quite a respectable place.*[6]

After a brief stay at the ghost town of San Pedro (near Socorro), he returned to Albuquerque, writing to the family once again on July 21, with encouraging news:

> *My health has been good and I have felt quite strong until yesterday, when I got 5c worth of cherries and eat half of them and that upset my digestion again. Am all right this morning and ate a good breakfast, but find I have got [to] stick to plain food.*
>
> *Last Sunday I told you I would have to pay $5.00 to come down from San Pedro on the stage, but I didn't. The stage didn't come down Monday, but I found an express wagon just ready to start for Albuquerque and the fellow brought me down for $3.00 and it was a good easy spring wagon too. I would rather pay that much than had my things shook up in a freight wagon without springs, so I did not lose by not coming down Sunday after all. Besides that I got some specimens along the road and got a bath free. When we were out on the plain between the mountains and Albuquerque, a big cloud came up and looked green and wet. The driver hurried his mules and thought he could get to the first house before the rain came but when we were within about a mile of the house the storm struck and the mules could hardly stand up and just swung around tail to the wind and stopped. I never saw rain come down faster or pelt harder. It came in streams and great splashes and the wind blew a small gale. In half a minute there wasn't a dry thing about us and for about 10 minutes we had to stand and hump our backs up to it without any shelter and the ground was all a river. We were well washed, but it was clean water and not cold and we soon got to town and changed our clothes.*
>
> *It rains a little every few days. July and August are the rainy season here.*

No one tries to farm though without irrigating. There are good farms on the river flats but the high ground is not much use, except to make the country large.

There was a letter from M[erriam] and he thinks he will be at Flagstaff the 25th. That leaves me here four days yet, but I have use for the 4 days. Yesterday I found holes and tracks of Dipodomys deserti back about 3 miles on the mesa and am very anxious to catch some. They were only known in southern California until I caught them clear across Arizona and now to get them here will extend their range still farther.[7]

18

A Splendid Trip—In the Field with Merriam (1889)

Now that he was comfortable with Bailey's development as a field naturalist, Merriam planned a major expedition into northern Arizona to begin testing his life zone theory. The primary field party consisted of his wife, Virginia Elizabeth, Vernon Bailey, and two other government scientists (Frank H. Knowlton, paleobotanist of the Geological Survey and the United States National Museum; and Leonard Stejneger of the Smithsonian Institution). They began work in the last several days of July 1889, and continued until the end of September. Their work of specimen collecting and mapping life zones included the region around San Francisco Mountain and neighboring peaks (around Flagstaff, Arizona) as well as the Grand Canyon and Painted Desert areas. When their work was completed, they had identified seven life zones, each of which had distinctive animal and plant forms, and documented that the different combinations of plants and animals found on the mountain's slopes were the same combinations of plants and animals that one would expect to encounter in traveling from the arctic regions of Canada to the American Southwest.

Bailey could hardly contain his excitement about a lengthy field opportunity with his boss, and he wrote home on July 28 from Flagstaff after they had met there:

> *There is much to write about today, for I am with Dr. Merriam and his wife and in one of the grandest mountain countries in the world.*
>
> *First I want to tell you what I have been doing today. It is Sunday—a beautiful day—and I have been buying a horse. It seemed very necessary to get a horse before tomorrow morning, as other preparations are all made for starting out in the mountains in the morning. A fellow came along with a horse and saddle to sell and I bought it. It don't seem right [to buy it on Sunday], but I couldn't seem to help it.*

I have been here since yesterday morning and M.[erriam] came the day before. It takes him a long time to get things all ready to leave but expect to start in the morning for a spring about 18 miles north; there we will camp for probably two months but make lots of side trips and excursions.

He hired a man and team and takes a good supply of provisions, has 3 tents and lots of baggage. It is going to be a splendid trip and pleasant, too, I think.

The Dr. don't look so old as he did last summer, I suppose because his wife makes him shave, don't look much older than I do. His wife is a very pleasant little woman with yellow hair and big blue eyes. I did not suppose she was coming with him till I got here. . . .

Now I must tell you something about the country here. It is high, over 8000 feet here at Flagstaff and our camp is to be higher and near a mountain that is nearly 13000, so it is not very hot. The mountains are all covered with big yellow pine—Pinus ponderosa, except open, grassy parks in the valleys. These pines are giants and make splendid timber. That makes Flagstaff a pretty busy little town. It is a young town though and not fixed up very nice but I like to see the big pines all among the houses and along the streets. . . .

I saw the Zuni Indian village of Laguna as I came along. Guess I sent a picture of that. It is a queer town. The Zunis are the smartest looking Indians I have seen yet and they have little farms and raise lots of wheat and corn and melons and fruit. They are neat and clean and some are good looking.

Yes Charl, if you was here you could keep camp for us. That was the hardest thing to find, a man to cook and take care of horses and camp; but the Dr. has one engaged now at 45 dollars a month, pays him 2 dollars a day for his team besides. Uncle Sam has to pay all his expenses—Merriam's—so he takes care of me along with the rest. Only I have to buy my own horse. Gave 75 dollars for a horse and saddle and bridle. It is high but a good outfit and ought to sell well when I am done with it. . . . The horse is very gentle, Ma, so don't be afraid of his eating me up. He isn't a bronco.

Probably I won't be alone any more this fall and perhaps not any more. Don't know as I can stand that. Perhaps I can't send letters every week but you won't worry now that there is someone to take care of me. Merriam is out hunting now but I ain't and won't hunt Sunday for anyone. He is gentleman enough to respect other peoples ideas though.

Hope you won't all dry up before it rains. It's nice to live in a country where you can't raise anything, then it don't make any difference whether it rains or not.[1]

A week passed and Bailey, still euphoric over his good fortune both of place and of company, wrote home from San Francisco Mountain, just north of Flagstaff:

I am not lonesome tonight for I can hear the fire crackling over at the Dr's tent and hear them talking. I am in my own little tent again and sitting on the ground on a saddle blanket. It is evening and cool.

We are camped at Little Spring among big pines and spruces and firs. It is a grand place and such cold, pure water. I feel like my old self and eat a piece of pie an inch and a half thick and big as a quarter of my pot for supper, just to hold down a lot of pork and beans and squirrel and biscuits. Can eat and work as hard as I want to now, and enjoy it.

The Dr. is not very healthy now, but works all he can stand and the past week has been a busy one for us both. We have got a lot of skins of birds and mammals and some extra fine ones, but haven't gone far from camp yet.

Dr. Merriam and his wife are both very pleasant and to have such company after so long alone seems too good to last. Probably it will last for two months though and we intend to make several quite long trips from here and return, one of them to the Grand Canon.

We haven't been up on the mountain yet but can see lots of snow up there, expect we will try the climb in a few days.

We have three good horses and saddles and take some good long rides, expect to take longer ones soon. Mrs. M.[erriam] is a good rider, a good cook too when she takes a notion. Our cook is rather slow and not a professional, so she goes down and stirs him up once in awhile and shows him how. We have 4 tents up, one for a kitchen and the cook, one for the Dr. and his wife, one for skinning our specimens, and my little tent for myself. It is quite a camp for only 4 small people.

This letter is short, but I have done so much talking in the past week that my ideas seem all used up.[2]

On August 30, Bailey wrote the folks back home to inform them he had sent some money and to describe some of his experiences with Dr. and Mrs. Merriam:

My salary has come at last and I will send it as soon as possible. Sent 100 dollars the other day.

Let me know as soon as you get these as I have to send them to town by the cook.

I will write again soon but haven't much time now. Put up 24 skins today. Have been living up on the mountain most of the week above 11000 feet.

Am feeling first rate. . . .

Last Monday morning M.[erriam] & I went up the mountain to the edge of timber line & took my blankets & a bag of biscuits & some bacon. Then M.[erriam] came down & I staid up there until Friday, but only staid two nights alone. M.[erriam] & his wife came up—staid one night—the cook came up to hunt sheep and staid one night.

It was a nice place to live up there at 11000 feet. I wore a coat most of the time. There was frost one night. The spring water was 33 degrees, and there is a little snow. . . . We went up to the summit & had a good look over the country with M's glass. Didn't see any more sheep & killed a big golden eagle. It measured 7 feet & 2 inches across. M.[erriam] & I fried the breast on a stove & made two good meals on it. It wasn't bad eating.

They brought me up a letter from Ma and Anna & I read it on the mountain. Am glad to know you are intending to build this fall. I ought not to spend the money for a trip home, but it will be only a months wages lost; for my salary for the month will about pay my fare home & back.

Dr. Merriam sent to Washington for some medicine . . . he says will cure me entirely. There goes the breakfast whistle & my time is up. Will have something to write about when we get back from the Canon I hope. Good bye, with much love, V.B.[3]

The San Francisco Mountain expedition produced many arduous adventures involving Bailey, Merriam, and other members of the field party. Two, in particular, proved to be very challenging, as documented by Keir Sterling in his 1977 biography of Merriam.[4] The first involved a week-long trip from their San Francisco Peak camp eastward through the Painted Desert region, with Merriam, his wife Elizabeth, and Bailey along. They ran out of water after a few days and for three days they went without water, nearly dying of thirst. They searched for several springs indicated on their map, all of which proved to be dry. They met an elderly Hopi Indian, who spoke no English, but who understood their problem and led them to a dirty mudhole where he proceeded to use an old rubber hose as a siphon to suck out the water with his mouth. Although the water did not look very appealing, Merriam made some coffee with it, which while tasting strange, was palatable. The travelers continued on to the ancient pueblo of Oraibi where they came on a group of Hopi children eating melons who willingly shared some with them.

Then, things got very interesting. A terrific thundershower suddenly came up, which brought the chief out with a blanket, which he placed around Elizabeth's shoulders. He drew her into his house, where they were joined by Bailey and Merriam, who noticed for the first time that the old chief had no clothes on under his blanket. No one commented on this fact, and presently they were brought some kernels of blue corn, which they found delicious, as well as some goat's milk in a dirty cup with dirt and insect remains at the bottom. Merriam arose out of curiosity to look around and glanced into a back room. He took one look, said that Elizabeth had probably had enough of the corn, then suggested that she take a look for herself. There sat an old Indian woman, shucking the corn with her teeth. After getting some water from the Indians, the group returned to their base camp near San Francisco Mountain.

The second adventure, which included Merriam, his wife, Bailey, Knowlton, Stejneger and the cook, involved a fifty-five-mile trip to the Grand Canyon from September 9 to 16. On this trip, Merriam and Bailey left Elizabeth and Stejneger with Knowlton and the cook and took some traps, a bag of pancakes, their guns and started down to the bottom of the canyon. Finding a spring halfway from the trail to the river, they camped and set their traps. Merriam had such a lame knee that he couldn't walk next morning; he stayed behind while Bailey continued down in the company of an old man working on the trail. He was the only one of the party to see the river from the canyon's bottom and to camp there for the night, returning to the rim next day. Merriam in the meantime waited until one the next morning, then returned to the rim by moonlight. His knee recovered within a day or two, and the group returned to their base camp.

The expedition broke up on October 1, and the Merriams returned to Washington, while Knowlton traveled to San Francisco, and Stejneger went off for a brief trip to Prescott. Bailey later met Stejneger in Prescott and the two then spent some time in the field together.

Although he was homesick and wanted to go home, Bailey gave in to Merriam's entreaties and agreed to work straight through the end of the year because it afforded him time to spend with Leonard Stejneger, a naturalist he particularly admired and learned much from. As he explained to his family, "I like Dr. Stejneger much. He is a quiet, pleasant gentleman and knows a great deal—has traveled in Asia besides all over Europe and the Pacific Ocean and knows the languages of most of the people he has seen. I could not ask for better company."[5]

Thirteen years older than Bailey and broadly educated, Stejneger embodied the all-round naturalist that Bailey wished to become. He wrote to his family that in time he believed Stejneger would become one of the greatest naturalists of our time.[6] Bailey was beginning to understand that one of the best ways for him to acquire a broad education was by working side by side with trained naturalists like Stejneger.

Bailey departed San Francisco Mountain when it was getting wintery and snow was already on the mountain. He headed for the warmer southern part of the state, writing next from Phoenix on October 13, using letterhead with a picture of the Commercial Hotel, billing itself as the "leading business and family hotel of Arizona."[7] It was a long trip south and he detailed the picture, including the flavor of the journey and of Prescott, a midway stop between Flagstaff and Phoenix:

> *S[up]pose I must tell you about my trip from Flagstaff. Down to Prescott it was by rail and not specially interesting. The branch R. R. from the A. P. to Prescott deserves mention because it is the worst railroad I ever saw and charges 10c a mile. It is 74 miles long and about as straight as our creek. It runs uphill and down and goes around all the trees and mud holes, and the train is made up of old thrown away cars and an old engine that leaks and is lame in its hind legs. Fortunately it was 18 hours late, owing to the water having all leaked out of the boiler on its way up, and that saved my having to stay at the junction all night. As it was I got into Prescott the same day that I left Flagstaff, but not till after dark.*
>
> *Dr. Stejneger had gone and Herb [probably Keys] was out at a mine about 15 miles from town, so I didn't see anyone that I knew. Prescott is a mining town with lots of rush and bustle and noise. The saloons are like palaces and are generally crowded, but I could only find one little church. It isn't a very big town, but there are some nice houses, and I s[up]pose lots of fortunes have been made there and more lost. It is in mountains and there are pines and cedars around town, but it is awfully rocky.*
>
> *I didn't stay long in Prescott. Took the stage for Phoenix at 8 in the morning and had for company a bar tender and a gambler and a bookkeeper and a lawyer. It is 110 miles to Phoenix from Prescott, and takes 24 hours, took us 25, so we rode all day and all night. The road is awfully rough and rocky most of the way, but we had good spring coaches and it wasn't a bad trip. The country is pretty bare of life, but of course there is a great change in coming down from 5500 feet to 900. It was a nice, moonlight night and I could see pretty good all night. I didn't sleep much, just caught a few little naps. We got into Phoenix at 9 o'clock the next morning and I found Dr. Stejneger waiting for me. . . .*
>
> *I got my hair cut and had a shave at Flagstaff and was surprised to find*

> *a dimple in my chin. I weighed 137, which is two pounds above my average. Believe I told you I sold my horse and saddle for 50 dollars.*[8]

The old wistful homesickness tone returned briefly, because he closed the letter with "S[up]pose I will have to keep thanksgiving alone again this year."[9]

Regaining his composure, he penned another letter that day to Anna, continuing to encourage her in school—the education he never had in books, but more than most of his contemporaries had in the outdoors:

> *I am glad you will have botany in school. Yes, it will do good to study it in school and you must study it hard and learn all you can of the science of it. It is not impossible that I may be able to choose an assistant botanist sometime and then it might be to your advantage to be a good botanist. You know you have to get an education for me too. Learn everything as thoroughly as you can; for I have plans to use more knowledge than my small head can hold. It is nice to be with Dr. Stejneger, who knows about all there is known, so I can ask him about things.*[10]

Northern Arizona had been the perfect place to study and substantiate Merriam's life zone theory of plant and animal distributions, for all the zones were available within a short distance of one another. For Bailey, it also was the perfect opportunity to spend time in the field honing his naturalist skills with his boss, and mentor.

19
A Great Place for Cactus (1889–1890)

As Bailey continued working his way south in the Arizona Territory, he discovered one of the landmarks still popular with tourists today, although few would consider reaching it on foot as he did. He described it in this letter to his family written on October 20, 1889:

I have been to church today. That is why I haven't begun my letter till evening. It was quite a walk and we didn't get back very early. It is 10 miles from here and I think we did pretty well to walk 20 miles for the sake of going to church. We didn't know it was so far though. A fellow told us it was 7 miles; but, as usual, he lied. Perhaps you wonder why we were so anxious to go to church. Well, it is the nearest one for one reason, and for another reason it is an old Spanish Mission Church and some 300 years old and now in ruins. It is the "Mission de San Juan Tumacacori," the finest pile of old ruins I ever saw. The buildings cover an acre, or so, and are in a tumble-down condition, but the main part is mostly standing.

It is built of adobe bricks and some of burnt bricks and plastered inside and out. The walls are 3 or 4 feet thick with abutments, arches, domes, and towers. . . . There are vaults and cells and queer rooms that I don't know the use of and winding stairs; then in the yard back of the church is a round tower about 20 feet across and 15 high that Dr. Stejneger says must have been a Baptistera. . . . Most of the outbuildings have fallen down and so we cannot tell what they are. The whole thing has been very strong and must have been built for protection as well as for a church. It is a fine old ruin and worth a 20 mile tramp to see, though we would hardly have started out today if we had known it was so far.

We were in Phoenix when I wrote last Sunday. The next day we came to Tucson and stopped overnight to see to a little business. I had to deposit five dollars with the express agent as guarantee of express charges on a box I sent from there in June. The agent forgot to send me the money so I stopped to remind him of it. Then we came down to Benson and took the train for Nogales, on the Mexican line. That was not a good country for collecting and we decided to take the next train back to Calabasas, 10 miles N. of Nogales, but on hearing that there was to be a bull fight in Nogales that day we changed our plans enough to stay over another day. We didn't want to waste a day, so we went out hunting and killed some birds and a couple of gophers and a lot of lizards.

Came near getting into a bull fight too. We met a greaser driving a big long horned cow. He yelled and swung his hands at us, and we thought the fellow was crazy; but when we got pretty close to the cow, we saw she had a chain around her neck and a bloody nose. She seemed to take a special interest in us, which we thought quite natural until she made a charge at us. Then we skipped. I went for a telegraph pole and Dr. S. ran for a tree, but the cow couldn't decide which one to follow and so stopped between us and tried to look both ways at once. She finally concluded to annihilate the Dr. first and went for his tree and pawed up the stones under it without getting any of his gore.

Then she thought she wanted me, but I had got up a tree too and she couldn't climb it. The greaser tried to drive her away and she came near getting him, horse and all, but finally she chased him far away that we got down and skulked over the hill. That is all the bull fight we had. . . .

The next day we came up here to Calabasas, which is not a town, but a depot. We got rooms in a large house that was built for a hotel and get our meals at a Spanish woman's nearby. She can't talk English any more than we can Spanish, but we have to learn some Spanish on that account and take our books to our meals.

Dr. Stejneger learns quicker than I do. When we were hunting for the church we went to a Mexican's ranch and the Dr. said "Donde eglasia" [sic] *(where is the church) and the Mexican said "Just across the river behind those trees."*[1]

As Bailey's youthful high energy and self-confidence grew, occasionally he was caught in his own cockiness. Even without other details, this note from Merriam to him tells it all: "So long as you will persist in drinking grease and eating things unfit for human stomachs I don't see how you can hope to remain well for any length of time. Both you and Dr. Stejneger need guardians."[2]

Such eating often may not have been Bailey's choice, but what was available where he was working around Calabasas. He described the fare to his family in this letter written on October 27:

> *Beans and red peppers are their principal crops and principal food. We have beans 3 times a day but can't stand the peppers. These Mexicans eat red peppers stewed up like tomatoes and hot enough to kill a mule. We get enough to eat without the peppers though, but everything has a queer taste, sort of an onion and grease flavor. We have to pay $6.00 a week for our meals and $3.00 for rooms apiece and that makes living rather expensive. If camping out, I could furnish better board that we get at a cost of $3.00 a week. Guess we will hire a team and camp out in the Santa Rita Mts.*
>
> *I wouldn't object to having some of Ma's butter and some of that honey, even if I am not camping out, but I get enough to eat. What I long for most is good plain, healthy food. I eat too much that is rich and indigestible and abominable.*
>
> *No, I haven't forgotten the old home. . . . I suppose things will not look just the same when I come back. The trees will be two years larger and some things will be gone and new ones in their places, but I think I would know the place.*
>
> *My memory is better for holding places and scenes than facts heard and read. . . . I remember the places that I visited in Dakota and Montana two years ago as plainly as those I passed through two weeks ago. I don't know how long my memory will hold out, but hope it will for a good while.*
>
> *We don't make much progress with our Spanish lately, don't have time to study it and forget about as much as we learn. Dr. Stejneger learns more than I do because he knows Latin and Italian and French, and lots of the words are the same. If he lives long I believe he will be one of our greatest naturalists, in fact he is now, but his work is only begun.*[3]

The opportunity to cross the border and experience Mexico was too good to be missed. Dr. Stejneger couldn't accompany him because he was traveling on government per diem and his expenses could not be covered outside of United States. Since Bailey was paying his own expenses, he was free to go. Although he traveled only 60 miles into Mexico from the US border, he felt the distance in more than miles. "I used to think Arizona was away out west, but now it seems like away back towards home. . . . I suppose you would like to know what I have seen that is strange and new in Mexico. There is nothing new, but lots that is old."[4]

Dealing with customs, especially carrying alcohol for pickling his specimens, was a whole new adventure for the young naturalist, as he wrote home on November 3:

At Nogales, where the US and Mexico line runs through the depo, I took my trunk to the custom house to be examined. Only one of the officials could talk English and he not enough to do any good. They pulled everything out of my trunk and tore open bundles and mixed things up generally. When they came to my alcohol tank they made me open it and then took a sniff. The fellow said "whisky" and looked at me as though he had caught a smuggler, but when I fished up some snakes in it he let it pass. Then they said I would have to pay a duty of 10c a pound on my traps. I had about 20 pounds of traps and would have paid the duty but the office was closed for the day and they said I would have to wait till the next day. I objected to that and finally, after a good deal of bother and jabbering and hunting up new offices they said I might go through if I would not sell any of my traps.

I left Nogales at 7 PM and reached Magdalena at 12 at night. It is a true Mexican town. All the buildings are adobe, one story high with flat roofs; the streets are narrow and not very straight.

The adobe houses are built solid along the streets, but are built in small blocks so as to all open to a court in the back. Some larger houses have each a court of its own, and are better furnished and fixed up, but most of the people seem to be about as primitive and poor as Indians, and are, if anything, blacker and dirtier.

There are lots of little stores all along the streets where they keep red peppers, beans, squashes, cheese, sugar cane and corn stalks, and a shelf full of bottles of whisky, and cigarette papers and tobacco. Whisky and tobacco seem to be cheap necessities and are kept in all the stores. No canned goods are to be found except a few sardines; which, owing to the duty, cost 1 1/2 times as much as in Arizona. There is one quite large store in town kept by some Jews. I wanted a tin pail and went to them for it, but found a small pail cost $2.50 so concluded I didn't want it.

Then I went to a native store and bought an "ore" [olla] (which is an earthen jar that the people make for holding water) for 12c and a wash basin of the same stuff for the same price. I am losing faith in protective tariff. They try to protect home industry, which isn't, never was, and never will be. The only thing in town of much interest is the old church. It is probably very old and is still quite a fine building, is much like the one we went to see near Calabasas but is not so much of a ruin. It is kept in repair and is used constantly. . . .

I couldn't find a place in town to get any meals and lodging in the same house, so I rented a room and got my meals for the first day at a place they called a hotel. One day was all I could stand there. They gave me stewed peppers, meat fried with onions, boiled beans, and bitter coffee. Everything was dirty and greasy and I would have to wait an hour or so for each meal. I just bought some provision and lived at home . . . with enough wholesome food that is better than such stuff and not so much danger of its killing me.

The Rio Sonora runs almost through town. It is a small stream but furnishes water for irrigating the little farms along the valley and it might be a good farming country if the people would work. There are a good many oranges growing in town and a few grape vines, but pomegranates are the principal fruit. They are just ripe now and very cheap. I just bought 7 for a nickel and eat two of them with my lunch. They look like apples, but are just a great berry. They have a rough rind full of red grains that look like red corn and are sweet and juicy. They are very good and I can eat all I want of them.

This is a great place for cactus. Besides the Giant Cactus and a smaller species of the same genus, there is a flat stemmed, branching cactus that grows 20 feet high and as big as a tree. Of smaller kinds there is a great variety.

I bought 26 dollars of Mexican money at Nogales for 20 of US money. Of course the dollar passes for its face value here so I get things 30% cheaper than the price of them.

I have found several species of mammals new to me, one a Skunk with black back and a white stripe along each side and one a large Perognathus.

Then there are some birds I never saw before. The Caricray [caracara] is common and is a queer, half vulture, half hawk. I have one hanging on my wall that I shot last night.[5]

Bailey had not heard from Merriam in some time and was beginning to feel neglected. He decided that the way to get him to write was to make him fret: "I haven't heard from Dr. M[erriam] for a month," Bailey wrote his family. "Now I am going to punish him by not writing to him. When he doesn't hear from me for about a week I will begin to get letters every day. He seems to think I don't need any looking after."[6] The flow of letters soon picked up!

Following his Mexican adventure, Bailey headed east once again, greeting December in Deming, New Mexico, where the weather typically froze nearly every night but was warm enough through the day. In writing home, he pontificated that "it is too bad that such nice weather has to be wasted on such barren countries as Arizona and New Mexico; but, as it is all they have that is good, let them have it."

He also bragged that he had put up 103 mammal skins, besides a good many other specimens, while traveling over 800 miles and that his expenses for the month only totaled $75.00![7]

On December 5, Merriam wrote to him with further instructions about his work in West Texas, suggesting he take the Southern Pacific Railroad out of El Paso, stropping first at Sierra Blanca and then going to Marfa. But Merriam was adamant that he not leave El Paso until he had secured a good series of *Perognathus flavus*, Geomys, *Dipodomys ordii* (the small species), *Tamias harrisi*, and as many other species as occur in that region.[8] Merriam did not want a repeat of what had happened in the Grand Canyon.

As Christmas approached, homesickness returned. Spending the holidays alone was never his preference, nor his family's, but it was the reality in 1889. He began to be aware of it—or at least to write home about his lack of friends and the importance of staying on the road, a turn-of-the-century version of nonattachment. He was also becoming aware of the value of his own version of education, no doubt influenced by his companionship with Dr. Stejneger. He wrote to Anna from Sierra Blanca, Texas, on December 22: "I don't like the idea of going to school to learn. I think it would be better to have a teacher and study while at work. It's too bad that you are not a boy. Then we could work together as soon as you was out of school."[9]

To the family, he poured out his heart in a letter written on the same day: "Everyone but me seems to be acquainted, but I don't stay anywhere long enough to get acquainted, am slow at making friends anyway unless I find someone who cares for the same things that I do, which is not often. Still I like to be among agreeable people."[10] Christmas came and went and he wrote to his family again five days later, "There was a dance here but I didn't go. They celebrate Christmas with firecrackers out here."[11]

Then it was on to other news of the day and the realization of how different his world view was from that of the Texans he was among. He continued his letter of December 27, reflecting his northern views:

> *Was there much fuss made over the death of Jeff Davis up there? I was in El Paso when he died and it was the first thing that made me think of being in a rebel state. About half the business houses there were closed & people were lamenting their dead hero. The papers were full of his virtues. It seems strange to talk with men who were rebels & still think the south oppressed.*[12]

Among the memorabilia from that holiday is a deerskin-bound notebook tied with faded grosgrain ribbon. Inked onto the cover are the words, "Christmas 1889." Inside he penned, "received Christmas 1889, Sierra Blanca, Texas, Vernon Bailey." The notebook contains favorite poems by and from his mother, as well as from Anna, Flo, and perhaps others as there are several different handwritings. Still treasured in the family boxes, it remains as mute testimony to a Christmas away from home of a young man with a sensitive heart and a loving family.[13]

South of Marfa, Texas, Bailey searched out Mr. Lloyd, a naturalist and fellow member of the AOU. Merriam had suggested a collecting trip with Mr. Lloyd as a protégé and prospective field agent. He explained to his family that Merriam "says Lloyd can't make good skins and can't trap but wants me to show him all I can and get him started at it."[14]

Not all good field naturalists made good survey collectors. Some were just too slow or ham-handed in making specimens; others lacked the desire or discipline to keep up the relentless pace of survey work.[15] Apparently, that was the case with William Lloyd who previously had collected for the British Museum in Mexico (where he had also spent a year in jail for killing a man). Bailey tried to teach him to trap and make good skins but concluded that it was hopeless. "He is slow and not skillful though a thorough naturalist," he told his folks.[16]

Except for a brief reference to another bout with biliousness, Bailey's next step is unexplained but understandable in light of the length of time he had been away from home. Merriam's letter of February 8, 1890, addressed to him at Del Rio, Texas, was forwarded to his home in Elk River, Minnesota:

> *Hope your biliousness was only a temporary result of an overdose of grease. But if it should be otherwise you must go home at once. I don't want you to get sick in Texas. On the other hand, if you are well, it would be a great pity to leave now just as you are entering a region we know next to nothing about. It would be much better to wait a month or six weeks longer anyway before turning back.*
>
> *In regard to plans for the summer it is impossible for me to answer your questions. It is too early yet. The appropriation bills have not even come up in committee yet. I hope and expect to go somewhere myself and work up a large area. Of course I want you with me, and shall try to have a better equipped outfit in every way than last year.*
>
> *I cannot do anything until our appropriations bill passes. We have asked for more money now (i.e., to be made immediately available) and if we get it we can do much. It is my intention to give you an assistant, but I cannot do anything until we have more money. Moreover, I intend to try to raise your salary to $150 per month after July 1st.*[17]

A week later, Merriam was still unaware that Bailey had "defected." The next letter, written on February 15 and marked "Personal," was also mailed to Texas, then forwarded to Elk River. It leaves little doubt what his boss thinks of Bailey's sudden journey back home:

> *I never thought you would run away unless you were sick, and I don't believe you have the faintest idea of what you have done, looked at "officially." You seem to have lost your head suddenly, and I can't account for it at all.*
>
> *Your letter of Feb. 8 from Del Rio announcing your intention to start for Elk River the same day reached me on the 12th and fairly paralyzed me. After about an hour I recovered my senses sufficiently to rush downtown to a telegraph office and telegraph Attwater at San Antonio to hold you if true—but too late, as appears from your letter from Ft. Worth which has just arrived.*
>
> *When the time came, I expected to make out and send you for signature the necessary formal blanks for leave. Now I don't know what to do. The official aspect of the case is simply this: You have abandoned work without authority. If I report this in the Dept. the natural result would be your dismissal. If I withhold the information and it ever leaks out, the natural result would be my dismissal. I don't know at all what to do, but for the present shall simply keep still and see if I can think of any way out of this scrape.*
>
> *But this is only one aspect of the affair. The other disappointment is the loss of Texas. I had believed that we were getting into this great field at last and would get our share of the new things. Now we are cut off right in the doorway. It is fearful. I haven't felt so badly over anything since somebody died.*[18]

There is nothing in the written record to indicate why Bailey left Texas so suddenly, but the most likely reason is that he was homesick and literally exhausted. Survey collecting involves exacting, skilled labor—strenuous, unrelenting labor often in trying circumstances. The daily routine involved an unrelenting cycle of trapping, preparing specimens, packing, and shipping. Just the routine hazards of moving cross-country with gear and boxes of specimens could be trying. It seems that he had had enough for a while and needed to get away.

20

Sagebrush, Alkali, and Mountain Magic (1890)

Peace was quickly made between the two men. Bailey and Merriam needed each other and both knew it. Merriam appreciated Bailey's dogged determination, willingness to accept instruction and criticism, and consistent improvement. As he progressed through his apprenticeship with Merriam, it became evident that Bailey had the knack for fieldwork and that he enjoyed and took pleasure in it. Merriam quickly realized how vital Bailey could be to his idea of a systematic survey of mammals. He could see that young Bailey potentially could bring those dreams into the realm of the possible. And, at the same time, although at first he didn't know it, Bailey was training for the grand vision that had taken shape in Merriam's mind. His inner transformation from a farmer and commercial collector into a full-fledged field naturalist was gradually and haltingly underway.[1]

On March 8, Bailey received formal orders from Washington that his travel was to include northern Minnesota, western Nebraska, the neighborhood of Bridger's Pass in southwestern Wyoming, the basin west of Utah Lake, and finally northward into Idaho.[2] A more detailed letter from Merriam arrived two days later. It included instructions about the first part of his itinerary. He was to spend two to three weeks in northern Minnesota learning as much as possible concerning the range and abundance of fur-bearing animals, deer, and as many smaller species that he could find. Merriam especially wanted exact information about the distribution of the five members of the deer tribe known from northern Minnesota—moose, elk, caribou, Virginia (white-tailed) deer, and black-tailed deer. After leaving northern Minnesota, he was told to proceed directly to western Nebraska and secure specimens as well as information about *Spermophilus obsoletus*.[3]

Merriam wrote to him again on April 7 with further travel instructions and details about what to collect, stressing the need for additional information and specimens documenting the distribution of *Spermophilus obsoletus, Perognathus fasciatus flavescens*, and the pale yellow *Geomys* from the neighborhood of Valentine and Kennedy, Nebraska. From there he was instructed to work westward, following the railroad, in the hope of finding the western limits of distribution of these species. Merriam stressed that he was not to tarry so that he could reach Bridger's Pass as early as possible, collecting at Bridger's Pass, Fort Bridger, and the Uintah Mountains south of Fort Bridger in order to secure specimens in spring pelage of *Spermophilus*.[4]

In sharp contrast to the homesick boy of the previous Christmas, a new wave of self-sufficiency appeared in the spring, as he wrote home from Valentine, Nebraska, on April 13, where he was staying with a family:

> *This is Sunday and I can think of nothing better to do than write to you again. It is a poor way to visit but is the best we can do now. The people around here are rough and coarse and I don't care to get acquainted. It is more lonesome to be among people that you don't care for than to be alone, but I don't care to get acquainted with anyone yet. It seems natural to be among strangers again but I haven't forgotten home enough yet to feel at home anywhere. We will soon fall into old ways though. . . .*
>
> *It never seemed harder to leave home than when I started out this time, though the prospects for a pleasant trip are better than ever before. I don't believe I will always wander around this way. I am not the right kind to enjoy it for a whole lifetime. . . .*
>
> *The folks have most all gone off visiting and it is more quiet than usual in the house. The house is built of logs, has but 2 rooms and no chamber and a leaky board roof. There are six children, and the nine of us make quite a house full.*[5]

Freedom is one thing, responsibility another. Merriam reminded him that handling live animals is a job for the zoo, not his department, writing on April 15:

> *The live Porcupines reached here in good condition, and were turned over at once to the Zoological Garden. Hereafter be careful to send living animals addressed to the US National Museum, not to this Department. In the present instance we had to pay express charges, which of course we cannot afford to do. The same is true of skins of large game, such as Deer or Sheep, which should always be sent direct to the National Museum so that they will pay charges.*[6]

At Kennedy, Nebraska, Bailey stayed at Mr. King's place "right in the sand hills," as he had done two years before, getting reacquainted with his school teacher from childhood days:

> *Things haven't changed here much in the past two years. The same people are here & doing about the same things. I thought I had forgotten most of them but the faces are familiar & I even know where to look for the same old Gopher holes where I caught gophers then.*
>
> *The folks here use a drink made of the shells of Cocoa beans. It is about like chocolate, or better. They send to Montgomery Ward & Co., Chicago, for it. Freight & all, it costs them about 5c a pound. It is much better & healthier & cheaper than coffee. Why don't you send for some? I like it better than chocolate.*[7]

King tried unsuccessfully to convince Bailey to take up a tree claim, noting that even if he couldn't put enough trees on it "there would be a fine chance to raise sheep here."[8] Bailey was impressed with Mrs. King, who could speak five languages and quote from any author or write an eloquent essay, although he noted that he could beat her at cooking![9]

Arriving in Douglas, Wyoming, at the end of April, Bailey found himself

> *once more in the land of sagebrush and alkalie. The first man I saw here was the postmaster of two years ago at Ft. Fetterman—the one whose cat I poisoned. He keeps the best hotel in Douglas now & I am his guest again. We don't mention the cat. I found out a funny thing about him though. Another man was telling me that this Postmaster believed me to be a detective when I was there at Fetterman. I did believe him to be a villain but I wasn't after him. He seems quite at ease now though. Fetterman was one of the few places where I was ever afraid of men and slept with my revolver under my head. It is funny to find that they were afraid of me too.*[10]

On May 17 he was at eight thousand feet, high in the Rockies at Bridger's Pass, writing once again to his "Dear folks at home":

> *It is a first rate place to stay and for collecting. The ranch is in a canon among high hills. A little stream of pure water runs down the canon and there is timber—mostly popple [Bailey is referring to aspen here]—along the sides higher up. It is hardly mountainous but the hills are steep and rocky*

and probably 1000 feet high from the valley. The valley is about 7000 feet, so we are high enough for mountains, it is cold enough for mountains too. Snow lies on the north sides of the hills yet, often 50 feet deep of solid hard snow and sometimes much deeper. Each snow bank makes a creek so there is plenty of water everywhere around. The north side of a hill will be covered with snow and the south side with flowers.[11]

His heart and his words sang as he explored the high country, on May 25 he wrote to his family about the possibility of Anna joining him for part of the trip:

I put up my tent in the yard and sleep and work in it, so am at home all the time. Have a nice grassy place for the tent and a deers hair mattress to sleep on, and everything is as convenient as if I had a room in a first class hotel. . . .

I hear spurs jingling, guess the boys are going out for an Antelope hunt. . . .

By the time you get this I s[up]pose Anna's school will be out. If you can spare her at home, she can come out here as soon as she gets ready. I think we can manage it so as to get along all right, and it will be pleasant for her and me too, though I know her help is needed at home. The expense will be considerable but if she proves to be useful M[erriam] may arrange it so as to pay her expenses at least, after awhile. I will be going away from here about a week from tomorrow, I think, and will send her money for the trip and her outfit then, also instructions about coming. Probably she can meet me at Provo, Utah, and if so she can come over the D&RGRR from Cheyenne. That is the "scenic line of the world" and one that I always wanted to go over. Then we will go through Salt Lake C[ity] on our way north and of course stop over Sunday there and go to church. Perhaps we will get a team and camp outfit at Ogden and travel that way up through Idaho but I don't know yet. Haven't heard from M.[erriam] about it.

She ought to start before the 10th of June to meet me at Provo. She will need some time to get ready and I can tell her something about what she will want for an outfit. From 5 to 8 dollars ought to get a strong all iron bound trunk, not so large as wide but long enough to take in the barrel of her shotgun.

For clothes a soft gray traveling dress, a best dress, and one or two stout dresses for the brush. A night dress of something soft made so it will do to wear anytime. It was very convenient for Mrs. M.[erriam] to come to breakfast in her night dress I noticed when we were in camp. Don't bring a large supply of clothing. More can be had when it is needed.[12]

He continued discussing the plans and instructions in the next week's letter home:

> *Merriam thinks snow is rather an advantage to working in the Mts., so tomorrow I start for a trip up into the Uintahs. Will take a horse and probably stay 4 or 6 days. This will put off my leaving here for another week. I will send Anna the money and directions for coming when I leave here. Don't want her to start till I can tell where I will be to meet her. M.[erriam] wants me to stop awhile at Park City, Utah, so I will not be down into the valley for a couple of weeks yet at least.*
>
> *Anna will have plenty of time to get ready. She might make a little pillow like mine and a woolen night-cap. My old knit cap and the little pillow make sleeping on the ground a luxury. Get a little valise, Anna, one of those little leather ones just big enough to carry a notebook and some handkerchiefs and a couple of lunches in. If you can't get a good one there, wait till you get to Minneapolis. Don't bring anything that you don't need as we will be for awhile where we can get anything we want. I will get you some hunting shoes and hat out there. Will make a list of things you need to bring and send when I send the money but tell you of a few things now so you can get them ready. . . .*
>
> *M.[erriam] may not come out west this summer. I don't know how that will be now. If not he will have all the more money to spare for Field Agents. I won't let him alone till he gives me a chance to do more and better work. I am writing a book now.*[13]

He could have been writing a book of his adventures at the same time, but that was not to happen. He worked on his comments among the more formal descriptions of animals in the *North American Fauna* monographs he would later write of several states. That was the closest he came—until now.

On June 8, 1890, from Fort Bridger, Wyoming, he wrote home catching them up on the happenings of the past week:

> *Last Sunday I told you I was going up in the Mts. I did. I took a horse and a bag of bread and some bacon and oatmeal and a little frypan and a couple of blankets and overcoat, and Monday morning started up the trail. Went 30 miles up to where there used to be an old mill and camped. Found an old log cabin, without any roof or door or chinking, but it kept off some wind. It is about the middle of the timber, there is about 10 miles of solid pine and spruce this side and about as far the other side before reaching the bare snow*

covered peaks that rise above timberline. The camp is at alt. of 10,000 feet, the peaks rise to 13,694 feet.

No one lives in the timber, and my nearest neighbors were at least 20 miles away, we didn't quarrel any. I got back Friday night, didn't see a person while gone.

I never saw Deer thicker. There was no use trying to follow a track. I wanted to kill one. They were out of meat down at the ranch but a Chipmunk gun is no good for game. . . .

I made two trips from camp up to timberline on the mountains 10 miles beyond and caught two Lagomys princeps, *an animal that I have never taken before. It is like a Rabbit, as big as a Rat, without any tail, and lives among rocks only above timberline. They cost me two days of hard work but work well paid for.*

I strained my eyes watching for Bears but never saw a bear, though there were lots of tracks and some big ones. One measured 6 1/2 inches wide across the ball of its foot on solid ground in the road. There was one big Wolf track and some Lynx tracks but it is thick timber and I didn't see any of these animals. I did want to see a Grizzly but not too close up and I wouldn't have shot at one, unless I had had the advantage in some way. I don't think it would be political economy.

I never read Natural Laws in the Spiritual World. If it is long and dry don't send it. Give me a review of it when you have read it.[14]

Moving from the high mountains of Wyoming into the mining country near Park City, Utah, Bailey was deppressed by his failure to get Anna out west to join him. His weekly letter, written on Sunday, June 15, begins with "it hardly seems like Sunday," although he looked at his calendar and the people told him that it was:

It hardly seems like Sunday with a dozen or more great ore mills running, smelters, and stamps, and lines of heavy teams hauling ore through the street, and every kind of business going on as usual. I have a very quiet place though, a pleasant room in a little hotel with the sun shining in the window.

The way I had to disappoint Anna after she had got almost ready to come was too bad, but I hope she can come to me yet before long.

Park City is a mining town, is larger than I supposed and a very lively, busy place. They claim about 4000 inhabitants. It is high up in the Mts. and is built in a gulch. It has only one street which follows the gulch—the houses along both sides, just like Deadwood. The street is narrow and isn't straight

> *and doesn't run in any particular direction. There are 4 or 5 big ore mills in town and a lot more all up through the gulches. One big mill with all its buildings and people makes quite a town by itself.*
>
> *The people here are most all Irish. I have not seen or heard of any Mormons here. The Irish are never Mormons. Polygamy among the Irish would not work. There was a fight between a couple of Irish wimmen just across the street the other day and one of them laid the other out with a poker.*[15]

Merriam had written to him on June 6 detailing the plan for the trip into Idaho, which made him realize that it would not be seemly to include a young girl on such a trip. The letter, which addressed him as "Dear Bailey" was another sign that their working relationship was strengthening as was their mutual respect. Merriam began the letter by bragging about his beautiful specimen collection made at Bridger and the Uintas. Then he outlined the plans for Idaho. Two young men would be joining him and he was told to hire or buy a good wagon team as well as someone to cook and tend camp. Also, he was to buy all the provisions as well as a saddle horse for himself and for the boys. In dividing the costs, Merriam suggested that Bailey buy the wagon, mule team, and saddle; the boys buy their own saddle horse or horses and the "grub" for the party; and that the three of them share the cost of the camp man. Merriam recognized that the plan put most of the expenses on Bailey but noted that he was getting $150 per month while the boys only got $75. Moreover, he would be joining the group in August and would relieve Bailey of the heaviest expenses as well as pay him for the use of the wagon and mules. He suggested that when it came time to sell out at the end of the trip that Bailey should recover half of his cost. Merriam also made it clear that Bailey would have total control of the party and that while he was not expected to work Sundays, he was not to put any obstacle in the way of the boys if they wanted to work on the Sabbath.[16]

Basil Hicks Dutcher, n.d., a close friend of Bailey's who he also trained for the Survey. Courtesy of the Library of Congress, MSS 35428, T. S. Palmer papers.

Clark Streator, 1930. Courtesy of the National Photographic Archives, Records of the US Fish and Wildlife Service, RG 22-WB-46.

E. W. Nelson in Baja California, 1895. Courtesy of USGS-PWRC, Biological Survey files.

Ned Hollister, 1922. Courtesy of USGS-PWRC, Biological Survey files.

Arthur Holmes Howell, 1903. Courtesy of USGS-PWRC, Biological Survey files.

Harry Church Oberholser examining bird specimens at the US National Museum in 1937. Courtesy of USGS-PWRC, Biological Survey files.

A. Brazier Howell, 1916, with his hunting dog. Courtesy of SIA, Jackson files, RU 7172, SIA 2013–08282.

21
All Hurry and Change (1890)

Soon it was time to travel on, and the mountains were left behind—at least briefly—for the lowlands of Fairfield, Utah, where it was "quite a change, coming down from the snowy peaks of the Wasatch into the warm valley, just a jump from the middle of spring to the middle of summer."[1]

Within a week Bailey took time to "get close to some mountains" at Cedar Fort, adding to his account for the "Dear folks at home" on June 29:

> *Cedar Fort is a nice little village of Mormons. There is a big spring that waters a dozen or 20 farms and the people all live above the farms in a little bunch. There is a PO and store and school and church house. . . . A great big desert-valley lies in front and the mountains rise behind the town. . . . I am staying with Bro. Bennett, the bishop. He and his wife are a nice old couple and it is a good quiet place to stay.*
>
> *Probably a young fellow will come to me here in a day or two from Washington. His name is Dutcher and that is all I know about him. He will probably stay with me all summer. Another fellow will probably meet me at Ogden or in Idaho and stay with us a month or so and then go to Washington State to collect the rest of the season. If he does, I will not go to Wash.[ington] and Oregon as I expected but will stay in Idaho most of the season. M.[erriam] says I can go to Blackfoot, SE Idaho, and get up an outfit and then strike across the Idaho desert north of here.*[2]

That's the unofficial word. Officially, Merriam wrote to him at Blackfoot, Idaho, informing him that Basil Hicks Dutcher and Clark P. Streator would be accompanying him for the upcoming trip. His instructions called for him to teach both the details of labeling, trapping, making reports, preparing specimens, and all other matters connected with the work. Merriam was very specific about what he wanted to accomplish: "I wish to publish a biological map of the area traversed, showing the boundaries of the several life zones as accurately as possible."[3] So, he was told to pay particular attention to the fauna of the lava beds, Camas Prairie, and the Snake River Plain between

Blackfoot and Big Lost River. Merriam's letter explained that there were no collections extant from this region, and full series of everything collected would be important. He urged Bailey not to hurry across the region between Blackfoot and the mountains so that he could make a reasonably full collection of the mammals occurring there, including chipmunks, squirrels, spermophiles, arvicolas, *Hesperomys, Arctomys,* or anything else from the region. He also was informed that the Geological Survey had never mapped any part of Idaho, and the only good map available was the Land Office map of 1888.

A few days later, Bailey received a letter from the secretary of the Department of Agriculture, dated July 1, 1890, that "your salary is hereby increased from $125 to $150 per month. You will pay your own traveling and other expenses as heretofore."[4] Evidently, Merriam and the department continued to be satisfied with his work!

Bailey's stay in Salt Lake City was quite different from his first, when he had experienced the Mormon Tabernacle. This time it was a chipmunk that enticed him. Writing on letterhead from a local hotel, the "White House, rates $2 per day," on July 6 he shared his new find with his family, as well as the now-expected local description:

> *M.[erriam] wrote me that a Chipmunk which I got at Park City was a brand new species, and that he wanted about 50 more skins of them, so I went up there again and staid part of three days and got 36. That will have to do. With what I got before it makes 44 specimens which is a fairly good series to describe from. . . .*
>
> *There is not much news to write. The little things that happen along the way don't seem to be worth writing about. I see lots of funny and interesting things, meet lots of queer people, some pleasant and some not; but these things are not worth writing about, not for me. . . .*
>
> *It is hot down here at Salt Lake. The flies are fearfully thick, so are the people. . . . It is expensive and not very pleasant staying here. Most of the hotels are over full, and here I can only get a cot in a big room with 20 others. The board is no better than at a poor dollar-a-day house. The Hotel is in the center of town and close to the temple. Electric cars run all over town now. It is as good as fireworks to watch the lightning fly from the wheels and wire after dark. They light them by electricity too, with incandescent lights.*[5]

Once his two assistants arrived, Bailey found himself supervising for the first time. Never his forte, he preferred joining with them in a group effort and characteristically described their first meetings from that perspective:

It is Sunday and we are camped down by the river in a sagebrush valley here in Idaho. We are quite a party. A young fellow by the name of Streater was here when Dutcher and I arrived. He has collected and traveled a good deal but I don't like him so well as I do Dutcher. He is a kind of rough fellow and not of the best of morals, still a good natured, jolly fellow and ambitious. I like Dutcher very much. He knows a great deal that I do not and is pleasant and refined, there is good stuff in him too, is ready for hard work or any kind of roughing it. Both the boys are with me to help and to learn what I know about the work. Streater will probably stay with us about a month and then go to Oregon. Dutcher will stay till October. M.[erriam] expects to be with us early in August and to stay a month or two. His wife will not come out this time.

As soon as we got here, we took our things down to the river about a mile from town and camped in the brush. Put up my little tent and got some provisions and a few dishes. We soon got tired of cooking and have hired a man to cook and keep camp. He is not a very agreeable fellow and we will ship him as soon as we can find another. He wants to boss and do all the talking and we have to shut him up so often that it is not agreeable. He is a pretty good camp cook though. We pay him 20 dollars a month.

I furnish a team and wagon and camp outfit and help pay the cook. D. and S. furnish the provision and each stand a third of the cook's wages. Dutcher has got him a good pony and saddle and I have got part of my outfit. Bought a heavy 4 spring wagon that is just the thing for our use for 30 dollars, and bought a team of solid, 1000 pound, young horses for 40 dollars apiece. Have not got a harness yet and will have to take a day or two to get all of the outfit together.

. . . Probably we will leave here in about 5 days and start across the desert. Will probably make one trip of 40 miles without water, but with a good team and good roads it will be no trouble. After we get across the desert and over on Big Last River, it will be all in a fertile country and in mountains and Mt. valleys. The country is said to be full of game and the streams full of fish. It must be a splendid region.

Everyone in town knows all about us and our history, and it is easy to get all of the advice we want. Some of the people are very agreeable but I don't care as much to make wayside friends as I did when alone. . . .

Dutcher and I went to church at the tabernacle last Sunday. They have improved the organ by putting in a tenor bass since I was there. We took a bath in Salt Lake Monday, too. It was funny to float around on top of the water like a duck but not funny to get salt water in our eyes. . . .

M.[erriam] says that it will hardly do to take Anna on this trip, and I agree

> *with him. With the crew we have at present it would not do for a girl to be along. There are times when we have to be off, one in a place, and many hard trips. I have just ridden 50 miles with some rough fellows, staid at this ranch all night and slept with them on the floor of their shanty. It was a hard trip and all I wanted to stand myself. It would not have been sensible to have taken a girl on such a trip nor would it have been any better for her at camp. You will have to give it up Anna for this trip, but I hope it will come around to suit us yet. Now that I am in charge of a party, I have to keep myself and all the rest busy. . . .*
>
> *I wonder what you are all doing in the quiet old home and in the new homes that have branched off from it. What a difference in our lives? All quiet and steady work with you till you long for change, with me all hurry and change and something new every day till I wish I could settle down to something more peaceful. Still it is all well if we only take hold of it right and do what seems best.*[6]

On leaving Ohio, Bailey received instructions from Merriam on October 27 to go to Nevada and then move in the direction of Death Valley to begin preliminary work on a forthcoming expedition into that region. His itinerary called for him to proceed slowly from Battle Mountain south, following the valley of Owen River, to Owen Lake, spending an entire month in the area that was virtually unknown biologically. He was told that an assistant would meet him at Owen Lake and that E. W. Nelson would join him enroute. Merriam suggested that he employ a competent man as cook and general camp hand with the cost to be shared by his assistants and him.[7]

The operative words here were "to proceed slowly," and after receiving his telegraph from Battle Mountain, Merriam fired off another letter a week later chastising him for moving too rapidly. Apparently, he had already left Battle Mountain, prompting Merriam to write, "at your present rate of speed you will skim over the country without securing any substantial information from any part of it which will be possible to make use of in the region we hope to map next summer."[8] For collectors in the field, deciding to park in place and when to move to another locality was a fretful experience; it was a constant challenge for Bailey.

Feeling the urgency to slow Bailey down, Merriam wrote him once again on December 3, further stressing the crucial importance of this trip, and explaining that Nelson and Dykeman were at Keeler waiting to meet up with him. His instructions called for him to take Nelson in hand at once and teach him about trapping and making better skins. Bailey was informed that the small

Dipodops (=*Dipodomys*) that he had sent in the last lot of specimens was possibly a new subgenus, and he was charged with securing a large series of the animal. Merriam closed the letter by explaining he was eager to hear from him in regard to the price of mules, burros, and feed in the Owen Valley country, and he informed him that his friend Coville would be accompanying the forthcoming expedition as botanist.[9] Merriam also asked for a telegraph address where he could be reached from December 18 to 20 so that T. S. Palmer, who was headed out from San Bernardino, would know where to join the expedition.

The reason for Bailey's fieldwork in Nevada, and arranging to meet up with E. W. Nelson and T. S. Palmer on the trip, was to make advance preparations for the large expedition that Merriam had planned in Death Valley the following field season. Following the preliminary work in Death Valley, Bailey returned home for the holidays, but soon after Christmas he was at work again, in a completely different part of the country—in Renovo, Pennsylvania—apparently dispatched at the last minute to check on the status of a small shrew that had been collected there a half century earlier.

On letterhead of the "Renovo Hotel, Philadelphia and Erie Division Pennsylvania RR, among the Allegeny Mountains, 1200 feet above ocean level," on New Year's Eve he described another part of the country unknown to his family:

> *It is Sunday up here in the hills of northern Penn., just as it is at home, I suppose, and I must write you about a part of the country that is new and interesting to me. They call 'em mountains here, but I am in doubt whether to call them little mountains or big hills, either would do.*
>
> *The town and hotel are at the bottom of the valley of the west branch of the Susquehanna River. The valley is so narrow and steep that it is almost a canon. The tops of the hills are 1000 feet above and on opposite side of the river are scarce a mile apart. The railroad is blasted out of the sides of the rocks part of the way along the river. Here and there a little flat is found large enough for a narrow farm. Lots of side streams come in and back towards the heads of these the country is not so rough and farms are perched along the side hills and in all sorts of nooks and corners among the rocks.*
>
> *Tuesday I went up one of these side streams about 10 miles and staid 3 days at a farm—a typical hill farm—[with a] man [who has lived] there all his life. . . . He has about 30 or 40 acres of poor, stony land under cultivation, lives in a little, unpainted, board house, has a wife and 2 children and a few cows and a pair of fat horses, and seems perfectly contented and happy. His*

boy (10 years old) had seen a railroad but had never seen the cars. He came with us when his father brought me to town and saw his first train, only a freight train then. That is the sort of people who live here, mostly dull, ignorant and unambitious. . . .

Still the country, and even people, are not without interest to me. All is different from anything that I have come across before, and I find that I am constantly comparing different people, different parts of the country and all the comparable objects that come to notice. . . .

So far as the real object of my trip is concerned—getting the little shrew described from here 50 years ago by Bachman—it is a failure. Still I have partly redeemed the time and saved my reputation by getting a lot of small mammals that are of some interest and by catching a lot of Wood Rats (Neotoma) that were not supposed to occur in the part of the country.

By the way, Father, I think you have mentioned a native rat that used to live in Mich., or somewhere, that was driven out before the wharf-rat. This is it, I suppose. Can you remember anything about it now? I should be glad to get every bit of information possible on its range and when it was known to occur at any place where not now found.[10]

Bailey's interest in and knowledge about small mammals was growing. He was also becoming aware how little was known and also how quickly information can disappear unless memories are tapped.

Now he prepared for the first of a lifetime of winters in Washington, DC. While home, he wrote a holiday letter to his childhood teacher, who had mentored him in life and continued the role with a philosophical outlook on what his education in life can mean. Mr. Jenkins replied to him at Elk River, and the letter was forwarded on to Washington. The change had already begun.

Dear Brother Vernon, I was glad indeed to get your letter of Dec. 27th, for I have long felt a deep interest in you and your chosen work. I rejoice that you are to have the advantages for improvement which your stay in the national capitol is to give you. One's surroundings have a marked influence on habits of thought and ideas. Then you will have time to visit the Senate and House, and the Supreme Court. I advise you to carefully study all of our distinguished men, so you will be able to carry them in your mind always. It will be worth a vast amount to you. Fix their names and their faces, and . . . you never will lack for material for interesting and profitable conversation. Your society will always be sought, to your advantage . . . /s/ W. W. Jenkins[11]

22 Into Death Valley (1891)

Bailey's first stay in Washington was brief, for there was more work to be done in the West. Merriam had done a lot of advance planning for the study of Death Valley, but a last minute request from the president to serve on the Alaska Fur Seal Commission prevented him from joining the field party right away. In addition to Bailey, the team Merriam put together included Nelson and Palmer, with the latter placed in charge while Merriam was away; A. K. Fisher, as expedition ornithologist; Frederick Coville and his assistant, Frederick Funston, as botanists; and Albert Koebele as entomologist. The US Weather Bureau and the Geological Survey detailed people to accompany the party, and a Chinese cook, Tie Sing, handled the camp and cooking duties. In all 20 men participated in the fieldwork.[1]

The fieldwork began in December of 1890 and continued on into the fall of 1891. The expedition, which acquired its own mystique because of the hardships endured by the naturalists, covered some 100,000 square miles of territory in the southern part of California and adjoining portions of Nevada, southwestern Utah, and northwestern Arizona. The Mohave Desert, both slopes of the Sierra Nevada, parts of the Tejon Mountains to the west, and the coastal areas of Monterey and San Luis Obispo Counties were explored in some detail. The region ranged in elevation from 282 feet below sea level at Inyo, California, to the peak of Mt. Whitney, nearly 15,000 feet above sea level.

While the weather in the valley in winter was generally pleasant and the nights often cool, the temperature in unprotected parts of the valley floor often shot up to between 117 and 126 degrees in the shade in spring and summer. The field agents had to be especially careful with their horses. Dr. Palmer allowed his team of horses to wander off one day while en route to the town of Daggett, California, which left him at a dry camp some forty miles from the railroad. When he came into Daggett on foot a couple of days later he was so near the limits of his endurance that he required several weeks of hospital care to get back on his feet.

Bailey once made the mistake of dismounting to shoot a rattlesnake. His horse took fright when the gun went off and hightailed it for camp, leaving Bailey to walk six miles. One another occasion, Bailey was 150 miles from his base of supplies with a horse weakened because of inadequate food. He headed for his objective, leading the horse over several mountain ranges and several low-lying areas, including Death Valley. Part way across the valley, Bailey discovered that his canteen had sprung a leak, and it was thirty hours before he and the horse could climb up the steep 8,000 foot slope of the Panamint Range, down the other side, and on to Panamint Hot Springs, where warm alkaline water was available. A. K. Fisher remarked on a trip their group made one day from the thick alkaline dust on the valley floor, with the temperature near 126, to Telescope Peak, over 8,000 feet high in the Panamints, where he and Bailey threw snowballs at each other in twenty-foot snowdrifts.

After the conclusion of the trip, when Merriam and his expeditionary team returned to Washington, they had brought back 6,000 specimens of mammals, 4,500 insects, a thousand birds, the same number of reptiles and amphibians, a number of fish and mollusks from some of the hot springs encountered in the desert, and some 25,000 plants! Among the important scientific discoveries were a new kind of desert mountain sheep, later named for Nelson (*Ovis nelsoni*); a new species of desert fish named after Merriam (*Empetrichthys merriami*); and another fish named after Bailey (*Cyprinodon macularius baileyi*).

Some 50 years after the expedition, Bailey was asked if he wouldn't like to go over Death Valley today the modern way—by air—to which he responded, "Such a trip does not appeal to me. When I do go back I want to travel over the Valley floor so that I may see all the things that live there and recognize old friends in plants and animals. I hope to return once more to the Valley on a camping expedition and, just as I did fifty years ago, make my bed at night on the good, warm earth."[2]

Because no one had penetrated its depths scientifically before, Bailey took special care to report to his family in detail about both the people and places he experienced. This chapter includes several letters he sent to his family beginning with his arrival in Death Valley in late January:

At last we are in *Death Valley, right in the middle of it too. Have been here 5 days and are not dead yet. I must write fast for I want to write a lot.*

First I will tell you about our new outfit and the men who have joined us. The men are all first rate fellows, but I like Palmer and Coville the best. They are quiet, thoughtful men, well educated and know a great deal that I don't. Another thing is, they are not always swearing. The amount of profanity in camp is fearful. The men seem to get worse the longer they are out here. I have had a chance to get more acquainted with Coville than any of the others. I go with him when I can go as to learn the plants. He can identify most of the plants out here, and I learn them from him. He is good about always telling me when he finds a new plant and telling me the name and all about it. It is a nice way to learn botany but will not stay by me so long as if I had to work harder for what I got.

He and I went across the valley the other day. Each took a blanket and grub and a gallon canteen of water and what other things we needed. Went afoot. A horse can't cross the valley because it is muddy. We went over into the Funeral Mts. and staid all night. I set traps and Coville collected plants till dark. Then we spread our blankets on the soft sand and slept till we got so cold we had to get up and hunt wood and build a fire. It wasn't very cold though—only down to 39 degrees. The next day we tramped back to camp—about 10 miles and got in at 11 o'clock. He is a splendid walker, is 6 feet, 2 1/2 inches in stockings, and weighs 175, is splendidly built and very strong.

We had several long tramps together. No one else in the party cares to go with us on foot. He makes me hurry over level ground but on the mountains I can keep up with him easily. He is 23 years old, graduated from Cornell College when 20. He is reckoned among the few best botanists in the country.

Palmer is a quiet, pleasant fellow. Has a very good classical education, is clear headed and has a talent for managing men—is better at that than at managing horses. He is a good worker but does hate to get up in the morning. He is a little younger than I am, I don't know just how old. Is just beginning to raise a moustache and has a boyish look.

Dr. Fisher is about 35. He is always joking till his face has settled down to a funny, dry smile, except when he rides horseback. Then it wears an expression of painful endurance. He is about my size, light complexioned, and is, all round, a jolly fellow to be with.

Funston is Coville's assistant. Not because Coville needed an assistant not because he is a botanist but because he is a "Senator's son." He has very little to do and draws good pay. That makes one senator solid with the division and helps in getting appropriations. Fortunately Funston is not a disagreeable fellow but takes what comes in a philosophical manner. He is obliging and good natured, has a shammy kind of education (I think) but has seen a good deal of the country and is fairly well posted. Writes some for papers, Saint Nicholas for one. He is about my age, I guess, is a short, thick-set fellow, and is especially noted for funny, dry remarks, and for adapting his profanity to the occasion, for which they call him the "parson."

Our other men—teamsters, cooks, packers etc., 4 in all—are not specially noted. The man that drives the big team gets $60.00 a month, but it is a mean job. I wouldn't do it for twice that. All of the men have more work than they can do in 16 hours a day and are hustled about by one and then another. Tie does first rate since he has nothing to do but cook. The big wagon ran over his toe and took a nail off the other day. He is with Palmer now. Our man is going to leave soon, can't stand the work. I don't blame him.

The big wagon with 4 horses has gone back to Daggett for a supply of grub and horse feed. We will get around in the valleys with my little wagon, 2 buckboards and pack animals. Will spend about a month more in the general region before working west to Owen Valley again.

Death Valley

Now I will try and tell you something of what the valley is like. It lies nearly N. and S. is about 40 miles long and 10 wide. That is between the bottoms of the mountains. You might say 20 mile wide between the tops of the mountains and by counting in Amargosa and Mesquite Valleys you might call it 100 miles long.

We entered the valley at the SW corner and followed it along the edge of the flat bottom to about the middle at Bennetts Wells, where we camped Jan. 20. This is a little to the west of the center of the valley and is said to be 8 1/4 feet below sea level. The greatest depression is about 4 miles east of Bennetts Wells—100 feet below sea level, according to Wheeler's survey. As we came through Long Valley, back about 16 miles, we saw a signboard with "16 miles to Hell" in big letters. Several graves along the road (3 or 4) of men who had died of heat and thirst made it seem rather a gloomy prospect, but we had plenty of water and it was not too warm for comfort. The 40 miles drive with only what water we could carry was not difficult. We made it in two days on 20 gallons of water. Palmer's party came through in 3 days with the big team and carried 170 gallons of water. He had 12 animals. We had 4. Along the middle of the valley is a bare, flat strip of salt, soda, and borax crusted land about 4 miles wide. Nothing grows on it and most of the surface is white as snow with salt and borax. Part of it has a hard crust, formed by the salt, and part is soft, damp and muddy. We crossed it on foot easily but could not get a horse across. This is the "sink" where all the water from the surrounding country, when there is any, flows and evaporates, leaving its deposit of mineral. The reason things do not grow on it is its salt and minerals. Along the sides of the flat where there is less salt are lots of plants, salt grass, a coarse bunch grass, grease bush, Sueda, Sphyrotachis, Atriplex, and Mesquite. Farther back along the sides of the valley there are few plants. The ground is covered with small, dark colored stones that must get fearfully hot when the temperature is up to 140 in the shade. The Funeral Mountains on the east side of valley are over 6000 feet high. They are very rough and jagged, are striped and spotted with bright colors, black, brown, red, blue, yellow, white, and a hundred shades between. There is not a thing to be seen growing on them till you get near enough to see some little dry plants in niches and shaded places. They rise abruptly from the lowest part of Death Valley and are so steep that Coville and I had to try 3 canons before we could get up.

The Panamint Mountains run along the west side of the valley. They are over 10,000 feet high and have cedars and pinon on the tops and snow comes down 2000 feet on them. Lower down they are bare and rough like all the other mountains around. There is some water on them from the snow and the springs along the base come from the canons.

Instead of being a "terrible region of death" this is the pleasantest camping place we have had this winter. Here at Bennett Wells we get plenty of good water, splendid grass for the horses, and good wood. The weather, for the past 5 days, has been as near to my liking as it could be. The coldest has been 30 degrees and the hottest only 75 degrees. Clear and pleasant all the time. That is all right for January but I don't want any of it in August. It must be terrible then. Men do stay here and work all summer but the graves scattered over the valley are an evidence of what it is in summer. The stories of deadly gases and poison water are all bosh. It is pure heat and dense air that kills people. The dense air becomes heated and conducts heat rapidly. A person cannot live long without water in hot weather. Now I can go 2 days without water here and not suffer, though I don't propose to try it.

The mountains around here are rich in gold and silver and lead and antimony and borax and other minerals. The whole low part of the valley would be valuable for salt and soda and borax if it was not so far from RR. There have been large borax works here and they hauled their supplies 125 miles, and their borax the same to market. Most of them have been abandoned now. The region will be valuable sometime.[3]

After two months in Death Valley, Bailey felt more comfortable with himself and with his surroundings. Yet home continued to draw his thoughts, writing to his family on April 5:

Today is quiet enough, for I am all alone. . . . The rest of the fellows are scattered all around, some in camp in the Panamint Mts., some up the valley farther, and Palmer gone to Daggett to meet M[erriam]. I am staying at Bennett Wells to watch our things here and meet Palmer and M.[erriam] when they return. . . .

You all seem willing that I should come home next fall. I rather think I shall, but still there is a chance that I may keep at it a little longer. M.[erriam] will probably want me to stay and I may stick to it awhile longer, but I am tired of being away from home. I am not a Spartan. M.[erriam] ought to be able to spare me, as he is getting other good collectors at work.

Palmer's management doesn't suit me very well, but I hope M.[erriam] will make some changes when he comes. Palmer would make a good school teacher, but he don't know much about horses and does some foolish things for the sake of economy.[4]

In April Dr. Merriam had joined the party at Bennetts Well on his return from the Bering Sea and Pribilof Islands. He reorganized the expedition party and sent small groups of two or three in different directions to work over a wider field. Merriam and Bailey formed one team and they took off on a month and a half reconnaissance stopping at 20 different localities. During this time, the two men covered on horseback 960 miles (measured by the odometer on the wagon wheel), collected 249 mammals and a considerable number of birds, reptiles, and plants; and, most important, noted every change of life zone limits on every slope traversed.

Then, while he and Merriam were camped at St. George, Utah, on the edge of Death Valley, he wrote his parents on May 13 about returning to:

my old camping ground among the Mormons. The country looks very natural and it is nice to be in a good fertile region again after living on the desert so long. There are great fields of grain and alfalfa and orchards and vineyards. It is a pretty good farming country and St. George is a rather nice town—probably has 800 or 1000 people. One of the 5 temples is here. They have 2 good stores, several churches and no saloon. . . .

This is not Sunday and I am writing in the tent by a poor lantern in the evening. Am afraid it will hurt my eyes to write long. We have been shooting bats and that hurts my eyes trying to see when it is too dark. . . . I put in about 14 to 16 hours in a day, but it is all interesting work and we get new things every day.

The weather is nice and cool here. It was pretty warm down along the Colorado River. 100 degrees and 102 degrees were common in the shade. M[erriam] kept his thermometer out in the sun in a little bag one morning at 9 o'clock and it went up to the top—116 degrees and broke the bulb. Now he borrows mine and keeps it in a cool place.

M.[erriam] talks about my going to Washington next fall to work on some of my field notes and perhaps do some work on mammals—working out species and describing. Of course it would be a great thing for me. It would be a start on scientific work—at least a chance to tell whether there is the stuff for a Naturalist in me. To collect summers and do such work in winter would be a great deal better than being out all the time. I will not stay in the field all the time hereafter anyway—would rather give it all up and come home. Probably it would be the pleasantest for me to give up the work entirely and come home to the farm, but now that I have got so much of a start it seems too bad to let go just as I begin to do work that is of some use.

If I should go to Washington it would give me a chance to study some and most of my work would be study itself and that is what I need. There is probably a chance to work up if I was capable of it, as others have done, and be able to do some work worth doing. Home is between here and Washington anyway, so I will be at home first. Then we can talk it over.

It is 10 o'clock now and I am sleepy. Have a long string of traps to go to before breakfast—53.[5]

In June, Bailey and Dr. Fisher returned to the heart of the valley to list the summer birds that remained to breed and in the process experienced some of the hottest weather on the trip, ranging upwards of 136 degrees. The party then traveled on to California, but local descriptions took second place to money matters at home. Writing from Lone Pine, California, on June 14 Bailey talked about his father's request that he provide money for a school back home:

I hardly know what to say about advancing money for the school house, Pa. It would be a good, safe investment I think, but I might want to get at my money to use it before it would come back. My plans are now so unsettled that I hardly think it best. If I keep at this work and go to Washington there will not be much chance to use my money myself, but I might find some way to invest it to advantage.

M.[erriam] proposes to pay me about $200 for the use of my money in the outfit this summer and then I will have the stock left. Likely there will be such chances to use money at times if I stay in the business. Guess I can send you some money now to use on the house and for what you need at present. Money is coming in again but I keep lending it about as fast as I get. Have nearly 600 dollars on hand now but M.[erriam] wants some and I have to keep enough to run an outfit on for a month or so.[6]

Merriam departed, and the others returned to Death Valley, camping at Furnace Creek, where Bailey wrote his family on June 20:

There is one other point in the valley that we have to work—the old Eagle Borax works. I will ride down there tonight after sundown (it is 20 miles) and stay and watch for birds tomorrow and ride back the next night. Then we will be ready to leave the valley the next morning. Will probably never come back to Death Valley again.

It has been up to 116 degrees here this month, but that is cool. It sometimes goes to 136 degrees in the shade. . . . We sweat and keep fairly comfortable, but I don't care to stay longer in the valley than is necessary. We have found quite a lot of birds breeding here. One that is new to me—the California Cuckoo.

You all seem anxious to have me come home to stay, and there is no way that I can think of that I could enjoy life so much as on the old farm, situated as we now are to make a comfortable living. I think it over every day, and it seems so pleasant that I can hardly give it up. Then I think of this work that is in many respects so rich and full of interest, that is lifting me up among men of great knowledge and that I am helping along a good work and something to be of use to thousands after I have got all I can from it, and it is hard to decide—not between two evils, but between two goods. But I don't need to decide yet, and time may decide it for me. At any rate I think I had better go to Washington this winter if there is a chance. That will add so much to my education and in ways that I have especial need for.

One thing I often think of is the quiet Sundays at home and everyone around caring for what is good, while out here I am almost the only one who cares for Sunday and I have hard work to hold my own. But then what is the good of being good when it is easy? We are apt to value what we have to fight for. It is often hard to tell just what ought and what ought not to be done.[7]

Rarely did Bailey take time, throughout his life, to write as philosophically as that. Most often, it was tidbits like this that kept his family in touch:

We just got into Keeler [California] today from our Death Valley trip. The next day we left the valley and came up to the top of the Panamint Mts. where it was cool enough. Went to top of Telescope Peak (10,957 feet) and back to our camp at 7200 feet the next day. That was a hard day's work. As

Dr. Fisher remarked, "not many people have been below sea level one day and 11,000 feet above the next." It was quite a change of climate from 114 degrees to the great snow banks around the peak.[8]

Or this from Kern River in early July:

The mountains rise abruptly all around and are covered with pines and shrub-oak. There seems to be a good deal here to trap for, coons and foxes and skunks and coyotes and small things. I caught one skunk. Shot a coyote the other day with my rifle, that makes 3 coyotes I have killed with it and 2 rabbits and 1 hawk. Haven't missed many things either. Am gaining confidence in the rifle. Very truly Your Wanderer, VB[9]

Bailey continued to work in California, traveling down the San Joaquin Valley, trapping as he went, finding it, as he wrote to his folks on July 26:

nice country, a great level plain where they can raise one poor crop or wheat or barley a year without irrigating, but 12 or 15 bushels to the acre is a fair yield with irrigating. With plenty of water they can raise almost anything, and they have splendid farms along the streams.

A large area in the valley is covered with splendid oak trees, trees 4 to 9 feet in diameter but low—50 to 75 feet high. These are the famous oaks of California and they are a nice tree and make a nice open forest with the ground smooth and grassy under them. I think there are just as pretty places around home though.

Lots of fruit is getting ripe now—peaches and apples and apricots and plums and nectarines and melons. We have had all the fruit we wanted for a few days, now we will not see any more for months, maybe, but we have 40 pounds of good raisins along, guess that will do. . . .

I sent a lizard—a Crotophytes baileyi*—from Bakersfield a week ago and forgot to write you to put it in alcohol and keep in a dark place so the colors won't fade. It is my namesake.*[10]

In August, he wrote to Anna from Mineral King describing the giant redwood trees that he had seen for the first time:

But the greatest wonder we have seen is the giant Redwoods (Sequoia gigantea). We have not seen the largest ones yet, but the small ones are large. I measured one that had fallen. It was 10 feet through, 20 feet from the butt and 260 feet long to where the top had broken off where it was 14 inches through. We saw larger ones standing that we did not measure. From 10 to 12 feet through above the swelled butt is the general size of the large ones. It is a magnificent tree, straight and smooth as an arrow, bright brown bark and leaves like a cedar and cones somewhat like a pine. It is no use telling you how big they are. They must be seen close by to appreciate their size and then they are too big to seem like a tree.[11]

Mineral King proved to be a good stopover study place. Even the food was good, as he described in his weekly letter home on August 9:

It is Sunday and we have just been to dinner—had a potato and dried beef stew and fried rice, bakebattle bread and stewed raisins, a very good Sunday lunch. We have had plenty of fresh beef till today and real milk too. Now we are camped higher up in the Mts. and cannot get things so handy.

We are up at about 10,000 feet now. We are so close to timberline that lots of Arctic plants and animals come down to us. Yesterday I caught a Zapus, our own Jumping Mouse. I believe it is the first ever taken in California. There are lots of great big yellow Woodchucks here. They keep getting in my Marten traps, but the Martens don't. I can't seem to catch a Marten anywhere. They are said to be common up here. I caught one big Weasel yesterday. It ate 2 young Blue Grouse that I left by a tree and paid for them with its skin. There are not many Grouse here, we have had some twice, and no fish yet. Tomorrow we intend to go over onto Kern River where there are lots of fish. . . .

This has been a very quiet Sunday. Coville is cataloguing plants, Mrs. C.[oville] has been reading to us from Longfellow and Scot. Now she is reading the paper while we write. She often reads us a chapter in the Bible, and other books as we work. She never shot a gun much but the other day borrowed my gun and 4 aux. cartridges and killed 2 Chipmunks and 2 birds. Yesterday she beat Coville shooting his rifle. Now she wants to kill a Bear.[12]

Between the new sheep and the native trout, life continued to be interesting both for Bailey and for the folks at home who read about it. At Kern Lake, a week later, he wrote:

Our grub stake is getting low and we may have to send a pack train to Lone Pine before long. It will depend some on how many fish we get. So far we have had about all the trout we wanted for the 4 days we have been here.

There are any amount of trout in the streams and lakes but they don't bite well. . . . Lots of them weigh 2 pounds and the average is about a pound. . . .

Sheep have eaten the country up. Have cleaned out the grass and killed the bushes. The dry ground is like a desert under the trees. . . . Are there any sheep in the country around there now? I wish we could get a flock started. . . .

PS 8/19. We arrived at Whitney Meadows day before yesterday. Are camped in a pretty good place at about 9600 feet. . . . The streams are full of trout. Coville and I caught 103 yesterday morning before breakfast. One of our men caught 130 today. They are small—6 to 10 inches long, but so easy to catch we get all we want. Eat about 6 to 10 apiece at a meal.[13]

Visalia brought civilization's return, for better or worse. He wrote to his folks at the end of August about the bed and not the camp being the novelty:

I am once more in a hotel and don't own a horse or frying pan or tent. Last night I slept in a bed the first time for a long while, the first bed up above the ground I mean. The change is quite agreeable. I have been camping steadily for over 14 months. Have got pretty well used to it but guess I can break myself in to living in houses again. I did not fall out of bed last night nor throw any bones on the dining room floor. I want to come [home] over the D&RG through Colorado. That is the one line I have not been over and the best line of the through routes for scenery. After going over that I will have a pretty good idea of the geography of the western states except Washington and Oregon.[14]

The long trip through Death Valley, in Nevada and California, was over, and home was on the horizon, although not for long.

23
Farmer or Naturalist?

Bailey had reached the end of his apprenticeship with Merriam, and he was conflicted by the decision of returning to the family farm or continuing to pursue a career as a naturalist. The following narrative about the difficulty of his transition is adapted from Robert Kohler's excellent article about Bailey's socialization as a naturalist.[1]

Bailey's correspondence suggests that his transformation from a farmer and aspiring commercial collector into a full-fledged field naturalist took place gradually and haltingly but with serious internal conflict along the way. At first, when he went to work for the Survey, Bailey did not consciously fashion himself as a career naturalist. Rather, he worked his way into the role, acquiring a new identity while serving his apprenticeship under Merriam. Merriam almost certainly had a clearer idea of Bailey's future as a career naturalist than the young man had himself because Merriam could see firsthand Bailey's value to his grand project of a national faunal survey.

Throughout his apprenticeship, Bailey remained close to his family and their farm. Returning to the farm always remained an option for him. While his fieldwork was interesting and educational, it also made a contribution to his family's household income. Because he watched his nickels and dimes, he seldom spent all his salary and regularly sent money home to be saved or used to improve the farm.

Although he was deeply confident in his ability to perform skilled work, Bailey had little social experience outside his family circle, and he felt his lack of formal education. Socially, he was a local farm boy operating in unfamiliar territory, and it took him some time to see himself as a professional naturalist. For example, when residents of the Nebraska sand hills described him as a "U.S. Ornithologist" and "a Prof. Bailey of the U.S. Dept. of Science or some such place," Bailey was bemused—though not unpleased.[2] He was gratified when Merriam used part of his field report in his annual report to the secretary of agriculture, as he wrote to his family: "It sounds very familiar and is quite interesting to me, more so than it will be to anyone else." He seemed surprised, as well as honored, when Merriam casually revealed how vital Bailey's work was to his own scholarship. "I asked the Dr. last night when he was going to publish his book on mammals," Vernon wrote home, "and he said when I got done getting new species for it."[3]

He felt proud of Merriam's monograph on their joint work on life zones in the San Francisco Mountains; yet the literary effort seemed forever beyond his reach, "It is a book that interests him and me probably more than anyone else, but I think it is a pretty nice book. M.[erriam] is the only man since Humboldt died that could carry on such a work."[4]

The thought of being a professional naturalist himself always came mixed with self-doubt. Collecting with Leonhard Stejneger in West Texas on December 29, Bailey wrote of his longing to learn more about botany and allowed himself a moment's dream of being a real naturalist—but just a moment:

> *Here is an ocean of plants all around that I don't know anything about and can't stop to look at, though most of them I never saw before, and no one knows anything about many of them. Lots of them have no names and probably all that have are not named correctly. If I could be a Naturalist on my own hook and do just as I pleased—probably I wouldn't do anything.*[5]

Bailey's letters do not reveal a single moment of conscious commitment to a professional career, or even of realizing that he had become an accomplished field naturalist and Merriam's right-hand man. He wrote often about the educational value of his travels, but almost never of the career implications of what he had learned. If Bailey saw his trips for Merriam as a prologue to a scientific career at the Survey, he never said so. In the beginning of his work for Merriam most likely he saw his travels as an interlude in a life of family farming. Or, perhaps, he wanted both. He wrote often of a yearning to return home and resume his former life—but just as often about staying with science a while longer.

Traveling through agricultural regions and observing local farmers at work also reminded him of what he was missing at home. "Sometimes I almost forgot how things look around home, and then a little thing will make it all come up so plain that it seems as though I had not been away a week."[6]

Bailey was a constant and critical observer of local farming practices. Ever curious and interested in different kinds of people, he judged their worth principally by the quality of their farming practices. He especially admired the astonishing productivity of Mormon farms and the compact and well-ordered

Mormon settlements, which dispelled his former prejudice against their religion and custom of polygamy. He admired the Zuni Indians for the same reason.

Bailey's most uncompromising statement in favor of a farming life came toward the end of his work in Death Valley in 1891, in a letter to his family:

> *I am tired of writing about country and places and people. It all doesn't amount to shucks. I am tired of being bossed around and having to boss others around, tired of being alone and tired of company that I don't like. The more I think of quiet farm life with a few people around that I care for and a few common comforts, the more I feel disgusted with this sort of life. If I come out with a few dollars ahead next fall, I believe I will come home to stay, settle down to work on the farm along side of the rest of you. I think we can make a living and all enjoy ourselves better that way. It has been a great advantage for me to have been over the country I have and seen and learned something of different places, but if I keep going it doesnt do me or anyone else any good. The country out here is full of interesting things, but so is our own part of the country, as much, or more so. Some of you know lots that I ought to know and do not, while I may have found out things that some of you would like to know. Why shouldn't we be together and help each other. To be sure I earn more money than I can on a farm, still I go ragged and dirty and live on coarse grub—bacon and boiled beans and camp bread and black coffee and dried apples.*[7]

Bailey had expressed such sentiments before, especially toward the end of overlong stints of fieldwork, when he was physically worn and sore, as he was just then. But never before had he portrayed the advantages of farm life quite so vehemently. Most likely he was just letting off steam from a very difficult and trying stretch of fieldwork.

Perhaps Bailey thought that he might be fortunate to live in both worlds—be a career naturalist and also enjoy the life of farm and family—without having to choose one or the other. He seemed to reflect most openly on his future hopes and fears when he was with professional naturalists—when his reflections were usually mixed with thoughts of farm and family. With Merriam in the Idaho mountains, he had written to his family about his desire to bring Anna out to be his assistant and his fears of being passed over in favor of men with credentials:

> *Anna is young and can learn. My head is getting hard, and though I can fill this place fairly well, men with good educations are stepping over me.*[8] *Merriam is educating men to carry out his plans, why shouldn't I do the same. Unless I see some way to make it practicable for her to be with me, I think Anna had better go to school this winter and make the most of the course. I need an artist, a chemist, a botanist, and a Latin scholar.*[9]

Here, mixed together in just a few lines, are Bailey's confidence in his practical skills; his fear that these skills, without formal education, might not bring him the rewards of a professional career; and his reflexive trust in the cooperative work and mutual instruction of family farming. Together he and Anna, the better scholar, could do what he alone could not. He wanted the best of both worlds and still hoped to manage it.

The company of well-educated men who had established careers and reputations seemed always to have set Bailey thinking about his own aspirations and prospects. He instinctively regarded Merriam, Stejneger, and Coville as teachers and to see in them the qualities that he most admired and wished to have himself, most notably formal education and broad learning. At the same time, with the latter two, he saw himself less as a student than as a colleague, and he seemed to measure his own ability by what he saw them do. As a practical field naturalist he was, after all, as capable as any of them. In forming bonds of friendships and sharing field experience with career naturalists, Bailey had, consciously or not, become part of a social world of professional science, bound together by communal work and interests, much as was his smaller world of farm and family.[10]

It was fieldwork with professional naturalists such as the aforementioned men that made Bailey see that he too could become a naturalist—indeed, that he already was one. Bailey relished the company of well-educated scientists, because he felt he could learn a lot from them that he could not learn on his own from books.

At the same time, what he liked most about farmwork—its egalitarianism, unspoken harmony of purpose, and certainty that hard work would produce abundance and home comforts—was precisely what he could not count on in his scientific work. It was the residential qualities of family farming that he missed and that he did not want to give up. This is apparently why thoughts of a future as a full-time employee of the US Biological Survey came always mixed with thoughts of home—and why he dreamed of having his younger siblings or his father with him on his travels, as companions or assistants; it was a way of doing professional work without giving up the pleasures of farm and family.

But as Bailey's work was drawing him into a professional community, changes at home were making a return to farm and family less likely. By 1890 his older sisters were nearly thirty, Charles and his wife had a farm of their own, and his parents—now around sixty—were planning for a partial retirement in their new frame house and a farm operation reduced to what they needed and could handle themselves. The communal unit of the frontier family farm was dispersing.[11]

At about the same time, Congress had given formal approval to Merriam's faunal survey (July 1891) and that for the first time would have made it clear to him that his work for Merriam was not just a temporary episode but the prologue to a job as full-time Survey naturalist. It must also have been clear to Bailey that the life of a frontier family, bound together by the communal work of subsistence farming, was no longer a real option but an inevitable casualty of time and human life cycles. There really was no choice but to be what he had already become: a career naturalist. Family remained important to him, but not because family farming was a viable option for his life's work.[12]

His wide-ranging trips for Merriam had given him a broad and deep understanding of the fauna of the American West and the ability to master new regions and faunas quickly. By 1890 Bailey was appointed to train new recruits, and within a few years he was overseeing all the Survey's fieldwork, under Merriam's general supervision. By then the exchange of information and directives was just the routine business of survey work, without the deferential tone of master and apprentice. Bailey's education was over; he was in practice, if not yet consciously, a career naturalist.[13]

He continued to have a strong relationship with his family but his letters home began to change from those of his early travels.

Clinton Hart Merriam, 1887, shortly after assuming the role of Chief of the Division of Economic Ornithology and Mammalogy in the Department of Agriculture. Courtesy of the Vernon Bailey Papers, Box 18, American Heritage Center, University of Wyoming.

Vernon Bailey as a young man, 1887, just after going to work for the Biological Survey. Courtesy of the Vernon Bailey Papers, Box 18, American Heritage Center, University of Wyoming.

US Biological Survey personnel in the San Francisco Mountains, Arizona, November 30, 1889. Front row (*L to R*): Virginia Elizabeth Gosnell (Mrs. C. Hart Merriam); C. Hart Merriam; Vernon Bailey. Back row: Leonard Stejneger (*L*) and Fred Knowlton (*R*). Courtesy of the Smithsonian Institution Archives (SIA), Jackson files, Record Unit (RU) 7172, SIA 2013-07580.

(*L to R*) A. K. Fisher, E. W. Nelson, W. H. Osgood, and Vernon Bailey working at the National Museum of Natural History in Washington, DC, 1900. Courtesy of the Vernon Bailey Papers, Box 18, American Heritage Center, University of Wyoming.

Vernon Bailey on horseback in the Rabbit Hole Basin of Nevada, 1898. Courtesy SIA, Vernon Bailey Papers, RU 7267, SIA 2011-1382.

Vernon Bailey and field agents in the Big Bend region of Texas, 1901. (*L to R*): Harry Oberholser, Louis Agassiz Fuertes, Vernon Bailey, McClure Surber. Courtesy of the National Photographic Archives, Records of the US Fish and Wildlife Service, RG 22-WB-B5502.

Vernon Bailey, 1903, shortly after his marriage to Florence Merriam, the sister of C. Hart Merriam. Courtesy of the Vernon Bailey Papers, Box 18, American Heritage Center, University of Wyoming.

Vernon Bailey in the field as a young man in 1905. Courtesy of the USGS-PWRC, Biological Survey files.

Vernon Bailey, 1910, a few years after having been promoted to be in charge of Field Investigations at the Biological Survey. Courtesy of the Vernon Bailey Papers, Box 18, American Heritage Center, University of Wyoming.

Tent where Hiram (*L*) and Emily (*R*) Bailey lived in Fallon, Nevada, 1908. Courtesy of the Churchill County Museum, Fallon, Nevada.

Grave of Hiram and Emily Bailey, July 6, 1916. Courtesy of the Vernon Bailey Papers, Box 18, American Heritage Center, University of Wyoming.

C. Hart Merriam (*L*) and Vernon Bailey (*R*) on horseback at Adler Springs, California, September 5, 1916. Courtesy of the National Photographic Archives, Records of the US Fish and Wildlife Service, RG 22-WB-0613.

First meeting of the America Society of Mammalogists, Washington, DC, April 4, 1919. Courtesy SIA, American Society of Mammalogists file, SIA 2013-08280.

Vernon Bailey holding a wild beaver just removed from a live trap in Conrad, Pennsylvania, 1921. Courtesy of the Vernon Bailey Papers, Box 18, American Heritage Center, University of Wyoming.

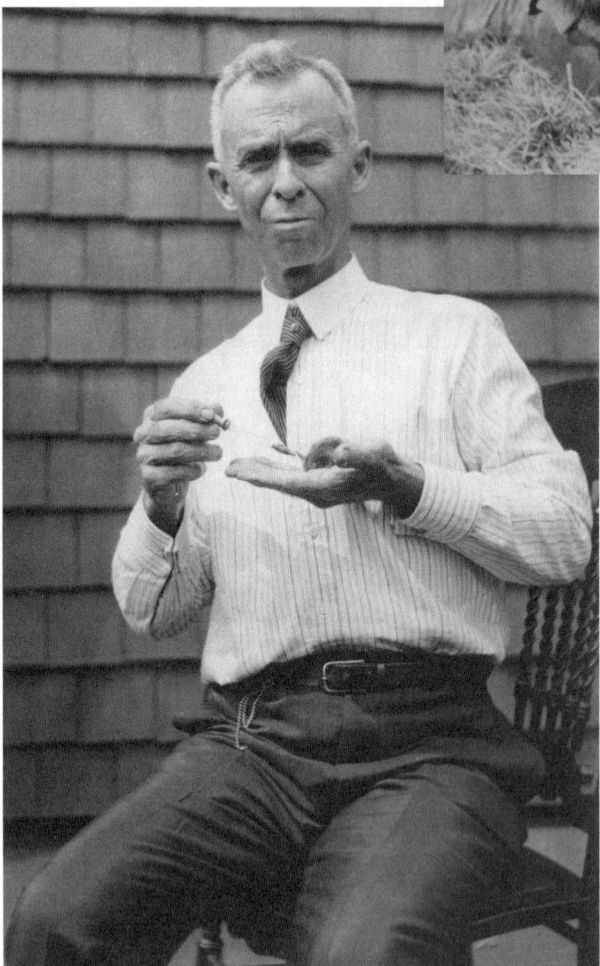

Vernon Bailey feeding a young vole, July 4, 1924. Courtesy of the Vernon Bailey Papers, Box 18, American Heritage Center, University of Wyoming.

Vernon Bailey, inventor of Verbail Traps, holding muskrat cage trap. Courtesy of the Vernon Bailey Papers, Box 18, American Heritage Center, University of Wyoming.

Vernon Bailey coloring life zone map of the Grand Canyon. Courtesy of the Vernon Bailey Papers, Box 18, American Heritage Center, University of Wyoming.

T. S. Palmer getting a haircut from a Native American woman during the Death Valley expedition, 1891. Courtesy of the Smithsonian Institution Archives, RU 7172, SIA 2013-07579.

Edward W. Nelson as a young man, 1890s. Courtesy SIA, Nelson and Goldman collection, RU 7364, SIA 2008-6031

E. A. Goldman, Major, Sanitary Corps, US Army, WWI. Courtesy of US Geological Survey–Patuxent Wildlife Research Center, Biological Survey files.

E. A. Preble, colleague of Vernon Bailey's at the Biological Survey and editor of Nature Magazine. Courtesy of USGS-PWRC, Biological Survey files.

III

Becoming a Scientific Naturalist

In the five years between May 1887 and April 1892, Bailey was in the field for almost four years (forty-seven months, give or take). One trip kept him on the move and away from home for twenty-two months straight. His travels had taken him to just about every part of the American West. Although the living conditions on these trips were harsh and austere, Bailey thrived for the most part on the work. He was a quick study, not just meeting but exceeding expectations. With Merriam's tips, and his skill, he soon learned how to recognize and catch species new to him. He was sending in thousands of specimens and information about the fauna of the southwestern and western states that were contributing to the taxonomic and faunal surveys being published in the new journal of the Survey, the *North American Fauna*. By 1891 he was a salaried government naturalist and was himself training green recruits for the Survey.

From 1892 on for several years, Bailey's fieldwork was confined to the customary season of six or seven months, from snowmelt to the first snowfalls. And thereafter, Merriam regularly brought him to Washington for instruction in taxonomy, as well as to improve his writing and editorial skills. By now, Bailey had become a close friend, and he stayed at the Merriam home on many occasions when he was in Washington. Bailey enjoyed living in a big city, which as a young farm boy he had never experienced before. He continued his development as a naturalist, publishing more and achieving election to the Biological Society of Washington where he regularly attended seminars and social events. And, with the same zeal and enthusiasm he showed in the field, Bailey learned and excelled at every turn, although he was much happier in the field.

Bailey's apprenticeship with Merriam came at the end of an era when field-trained naturalists could still find new opportunities as scientists. But in the space of a few years around the beginning of the twentieth century that road to upward mobility was abruptly closed, as those with formal academic credentials began to corner the market. By the early 1900s the usual path to a career in scientific natural history involved some combination of field experience and academic study.[1] Bailey was fortunate to squeeze in his training in field survey work before this abrupt change took hold, and luckily for him he was uncommonly skilled and worked for a man who put his trust in graduates of the school of hard knocks.[2]

The chapters in this section chronicle Bailey's continued development into a scientific naturalist producing publications from the material he had collected and joining scientific societies, while at the same time continuing his work in the field. Also, he finds a lifelong companion when he marries Merriam's sister, Florence, which also provides a boost to his scientific career. He continues to have a strong relationship with his family but his letters home begin to change from those of his early travels.

24

Country Boy in the City (1892)

One can only imagine the joy of homecoming after eighteen months of exploring the unknown West. The holidays were very special that year, with "Verny" at home once again. Yet by New Year's 1892, he was ensconced in Washington, absorbed in his work, and writing to his parents on January 3:

> *On New Year Eve I was sitting in my room writing and had both windows open at 12 o'clock. Had forgotten the time of year and time of day. Was somewhat surprised when all the steam whistles and bells and cannon and guns and firecrackers in tin horns began a chorus. At first I thought it was a fire but looked at my watch and concluded they were just welcoming the new year—1892.*
>
> *Of course New Years is a holiday in the department, so is half the day before. I intended to work at home on my notes all day but as usual it mostly resulted in intentions only. Perhaps Dr. Merriam's remark the other day that "he was paved like Hell with good intentions" would apply to others beside himself. It was mostly his fault though that I did not work all day. He advised me to go to the President's reception which I did and am very glad that I did. Then afterwards he took me around to call on Secretary Rusk and on Mr. Willits.*
>
> *Besides the President and Mrs. Harrison I met quite a number of noted people. At Secretary Rusk's I was introduced to Mrs. Stanley Brown, daughter of President Garfield. She is an uncommonly pleasant and sociable little woman but not specially pretty.*
>
> *Will have to tell you something about the President's reception. I was not a distinguished guest, or one of a few who called on his excellency, but was one of a double breasted line some miles long. For an hour and a half a column of people, 2 abreast, filed in at one side of the White House, around through several rooms to the Blue Room where Mr. Harrison shook hands with each one, including 2 or 3 in a cordial "how do you do gentlemen" or a "Happy New Year gentlemen." There were some distinguished men with*

the President and besides Mrs. Harrison there were a good many of the wives of Cabinet officers present. Of course with such a crowd we could not stop long and I did not know many of the people anyway. We passed on to the next large room where we wandered around a short time, looked at the flowers and pictures or talked with anyone you happened to know, which in my case was no one. Then we passed out into the large grounds surrounding the house. The Marine Band played in the front room. I had too much else to think of and see to appreciate the music.

Mr. Harrison is a plain, sensible looking man. Is about as tall as I am and not a man you would pick out of a crowd as looking like a President. I like his looks though.[1]

After growing up with grandmothers as part of the family, the death of his mother's mother was especially meaningful. In his letter home on January 3, he wrote, "No death has ever seemed to come so close home to me. I was young and did not feel it so much when Grandma Bailey died. It seems wonderful how we have all been spared so long."[2]

Life in the big city of Washington was full of its own explorations. With the same zeal and enthusiasm he showed in the field, Bailey learned at every turn. He wrote home on January 10:

There is so much around me all the time that is new, that I can hardly pick out anything to write about. . . . I get 4 good lectures a week now—2 on geology by WJ McGee at the Columbian University, one on biology at the Biological Society (of which I am a member) and one at the Geographic Society. With the lectures and what I learn in other ways I can pick up some knowledge if I stay here long enough. M.[erriam] talks about my coming back next winter. Probably that will depend on whether I am of much use here this winter. . . . There is about 2 inches of snow here. Came 3 days ago. The weather is just cool and nice, freezes nights and thaws through the day. Walking to office and back gives me plenty of exercise.[3]

The cultural discoveries must have seemed awesome not only to young Bailey but also to his family in Elk River, Minnesota. The following week, when he told them about attending both the opera and the theater, he fell back on familiar metaphors of the open spaces he knew much better:

Christine Nielson and Mary Howe sang in it as the central attraction. I liked Mme. Howe's singing better than Nielson's. She has a stronger and clearer and sweeter voice than Nielson though not as pathetic. The other soloists were Ivan Morawski and William Lavin. They were the best men singers I ever heard. I can't describe such music. It was grand, was like some great mountain standing up alone that you cannot imagine anything like until you see it.

Last night Palmer and I went to the theater and saw Sarah Bernhardt play La Tosca. It is a French play and very tragic. Sarah is considered the best actress living. I could not imagine anything acted better than La Tosca. Now that I have seen some of the stars in both theater and opera I will take a rest and not go again for some time. Am getting interested in my work, or in parts of it, especially writing up what I know of the habits of mammals.[4]

In seeking ways to help his family, Bailey struck on the idea of their raising sheep to supplement their cash crops. He had definite ideas about how this was to be done, no doubt from his own observations in the West. This was all new territory to his family, and they were willing to learn from the peripatetic son. The correspondence went on for months before decisions could be affirmed by all. After all, they were in this together. One letter on January 22 breifly sketches their family process. With the consistent regard for holding Sunday apart from business, he wrote:

It is not Sunday so I am going to talk over our plans some. I don't want to fence for sheep. Unless we can get up a drove large enough to pay to herd them I do not want any. Our timber land ought to be fenced and pastured so the fire would never run in it. It would be a good plan to finish fencing in Charl's, Henry's and my 3 southeast forties for cattle pasture. It would keep out the fire and help clear the land. I will furnish the wire for it if the boys will build the fence. Don't put up any but good, solid fences.

Now about sheep: Chet [Chester Hill] is afraid Marinos won't stand our climate. I have seen them in a good many different climates and under different conditions and have no use for any other kind of sheep.

You suggested taking some sheep on share, Pa. I did not propose it before as I thought if you could buy the sheep in any way you would have all you could make on them. I would be glad to buy several hundred and let you and Charles and Henry take them on shares. Would want them herded so the Coyotes could not kill them and so they would be taken good care of.

I don't know much about terms for letting sheep but will make you an offer.

I will furnish the sheep, you furnish everything else and take care of them and do all the work, and we will divide the profits evenly. You take half the

> *wool and half the increase, or all the wool and I all the increase, or you all the increase and I all the wool. This seems to me fair. It would make no difference to me which terms you choose. I would get 300, which would be as small a flock as it would pay to herd. If Chet gets some too I would rather not get over 200 to start with. A flock will soon grow.*
>
> *Now I want to hear what you think of these plans of sheep in general. Want to hear from Pa and Charl and Henry and Chet, and all the rest. Let's decide on something.*[5]

With only a month under his belt in the nation's capital, Bailey took another big step, attending the Botanical Club for the first time. He liked it well enough to write home that he planned to join. And, more importantly, he spoke out in public at the meeting about diamond willows for about ten minutes, a sure sign of his growing confidence.[6]

Meanwhile Anna continued to step out into the world as well, as she continued her education at the state university in Minneapolis. He envied her ability to work spiritually with the "heathen Bohemians," as he explained in his letter to her on February 18:

> *If you can get their confidence and love you may be able to help them. It is well worth trying and you shall have my earnest prayers and sympathy for the work. It seems impossible for me ever to help anyone to see things as I see them. There are always young fellows with me that I would be glad to help and perhaps they need just a word, or a little sympathy to turn them to better lives, and I would be so glad to give it if I only know how or what to say. It is not like helping the poor and ignorant. They are bright fellows, brighter than I am and better educated and how can I help them. I have talked with Dr. Fisher some. He seems fairly hungry for some hope, and still does not believe there is any truth [in] the Bible and doubts if there is a God.*
>
> *Young men all around me are growing up in the same way—doubting. What can I do to help such ones. "Not many wise, not many noble are called." It is easier to teach those who look up to you than those who look down at you. I hope you may do good among your little Bohemian arabs. I have often noticed that little shanty town down on the flats. The people must be poor.*[7]

He goes on to tell her of his upcoming first visit to New York City, planned with Dr. Merriam, to stay with the Dutcher family, whose son had assisted him in the West the previous year. Obviously not aware of how much the city had to offer, he planned to arrive Saturday morning and return to Washington Monday night "so as to lose no time" at work, noting "that will give me time to see a good deal of the city and for a good visit with Dutcher. Wish you were going with me."[8]

On his return, he wrote to Anna again on February 28, reporting on the trip:

> *One of the best little trips I ever took, and was well worth what it cost. I staid at Dutchers all the time I was there. They are as pleasant a family as I ever met. Wm. Dutcher is a splendid fellow. He is probably 40 years old but as much a boy as Basil or I. He is a self educated man, but seems as well informed as any college man. Is a very accurate and careful Naturalist and a good business man. Is Secretary of the Brooklyn Life Insurance Co. Mrs. Dutcher is a pleasant woman and Mary would make a good country girl. She is 12 years old, is very bright and seems old for her age but is as much of a tomboy as you used to be—I daren't say as you are. I never saw a family who all seemed so much in love with each other as they do. As they have a nice house and very pleasant surroundings you can imagine that it is a pleasant home.*
>
> *It rained half the time I was there but that did not prevent our going around. Basil and I went to St. Patricks Cathedral, the finest church in America I guess, is Catholic, went into Grace Church, a splendid Episcopal church. Then he took me all through Columbia College and School of Mines, where he is in the last year of his course. Then to the Lenox Library and looked at old books and at letters of famous men, most of which I could not read. Then we went to Central Park and spent most of the afternoon in the Metropolitan Museum of Art, which has the reputation of being the best art collection in this country. There were a great many famous pictures and statues. The original Rosa Bonheur's "Horse Fair" which was bought by A. T. Stewart for $53,500. Another—Friedland—was bought by Stewart for $66,000, but there were others that I liked better. One could spend a good deal of time there to advantage. We looked at the obelisk, which is not pretty but with the history about and on it together with the work of making such a column from a single piece of granite makes it very interesting.*
>
> *Saturday evening Mr. Dutcher took me to a theater—Basil was not well that night and could not go out. It was the best theater in the city—Dalry's. We saw Ada Rhean act "Live in a Landeau." It was good but even I could see that she does not compare with Sarah Bernhardt.*
>
> *We went over to Mr. Allen's [Sunday] evening and had a pleasant visit*

with the great Naturalist and his wife. Allen and Dutcher are the two men among all of my Naturalist friends who are openly Christians, I mean of Naturalists with fixed reputations. I believe that many others are in reality if they do not acknowledge it. The law of a Naturalist is to believe the truth and reject what is false. Some reject the evidence but not the truth, if they cannot believe positively, they need not disbelieve.

Monday we went through the Zoological gardens and saw a great collection of live animals. The director, Mr. Conklin, showed us all through the rooms where they kept things not on exhibition. I won't try to tell you what we saw. It would take a month and spoil all the paper in the division. Next we went through the American Museum of Nat. History of which Mr. Allen is Curator. Their collection of mounted birds and animals is nearly as good as that in the National Museum, and will probably be improved a great deal before long.

We met Dr. Merriam's father and Miss Florence Merriam by accident, had but a few minutes to talk to them, but I was very glad to see them at all. Mr. Merriam is a fine looking, tall man with white hair and beard. Miss Merriam is not striking in appearance but like the Dr. is very pleasant. Wish I had had more time to be with them.

I told you that Basil had an ideal girl picked out for me. Well, like all the rest she has gone and got married. That is the way they all do except the old maids and they would like to.

I saw Grant's tomb on the bank of the Hudson River opposite the famous Palisades. Went down to Castle Garden where the immigrants land, saw hundreds of big ships, looked at the magnificent business buildings along Broadway. The Jewish synagogue is one of the finest buildings I ever saw. The architecture is different from anything else I have seen. Would have liked to go inside but did not. Of course I walked over the Brooklyn Bridge. It is one of our seven wonders. Did not go out to the Statue of Liberty but saw it plainly from shore.

The trip cost me 15 dollars including all expenses, would have cost a good deal more but for the Dutchers. As I have to get my education by seeing things—sort of a kindergarten—I consider this one of my best courses and very cheap schooling. You have to study dry books. I am helping to make still dryer books. . . .

I have had some good work on my group of Kangaroo Rats for the World's Fair. They are now about done. I have been to the taxidermist's every few days while he worked on them and have learned more of the art that I ever learned of anyone before. They are mounting lots of large things there and I see every stage of the work. If I ever do any more mounting it will be a great help to me. Of course they have no idea that I am interested in taxidermy. Perhaps I will get time to write out all I have learned so you can make use of it too.

Miss Stejneger said a lady wanted to know the names and addresses of all the lady Naturalists in the country, wanted to form some society. I gave her your address and referred her to the list of AOU members for others.[9]

Anna responded in kind to his inquiry about spiritual help, as well as about her schoolwork in chemistry, botany, and the like:

I know how very much easier it is to help those beneath you than those above, but if you watch you may have the opportunity to give even Dr. Fisher just the help he needs sometime. We can't tell what the influence of a work or an example will be. Only keep your own faith clear and your life true, little brother, and God will show you what to do or say for him. My prayers are always with you. I have found my own Christian life strengthened by my interest and work among the children on the flats.[10]

By now Bailey's family was used to his work but still needed some help on what to do with items like wolf skulls that turned up at home. In this letter home, written at the end of February, he advised them:

Label them and put them away and keep all such things till you get enough to send quite a lot at a time. I have not asked M.[erriam] if he wants them but know he does all such things. It is a bother to send a few little things at a time to get acquisitions for small payments. M.[erriam] hates to bother with little items. A great many of the specimens sent in are stacked away and not looked at for years if ever. I have lost some of my enthusiasm for collecting miscellaneous specimens for them. They are not often appreciated.

I have begun work on the Gopher Bulletin, which has been worked on by several members of the division and never finished. I hope to get it ready for publication before starting out on my next trip. It is interesting work. Am mapping the range of Pocket Gophers and Striped and Gray, and getting together all of our reports on their habits. It is very interesting work for me as I have to hunt out all the records of their occurrence and of their habits from a lot of books, look up the places on maps and mark them in red ink. As I have been over a good deal of the country where they range, I have the advantage of knowing many of the places and just how located. Then I have to include all of my own notes and write all I can of their habits. The bulletin will be of greater interest to me than anyone else—that is if we ever get it done. . . .

I was at a meeting of the Phylosophic Society last night and listened to a paper on the climate of Death Valley by Mark Harrington, Chief of Weather Bureau. There was a good share of the members of the Death Valley Expedition present. A warm and interesting discussion of the paper read was indulged in at the close. General Greeley, Gilbert Thompson, CHM and some other Geological Survey men criticized the statements of Prof. Harrington severely. Everyone with the exception of Mr. Harrington seemed to enjoy the remarks. The discussion was much better than the paper. General Greeley is one of the finest speakers I ever heard, speaks with perfect freedom and ease and quotes authors, dates, and figures as readily as if reading. He is a tall handsome man. Dr. M[erriam] is not a fluent speaker but hits hard and says nothing but what you want to hear.

In some of the remarks on weather it was stated as an established fact that in the interior of the continent winters of light snow fall were followed by dry summers and vice versa. I guess there is no doubt of its being the case.[11]

Work went on in Washington, and Bailey's self-confidence continued to grow, helped along by Merriam's constant support. Writing to his family on March 6, he reported:

Last night I read my paper at the Biological [Society]. The paper don't amount to anything but it is good practice. There were some other papers that were very good, especially Coville's. . . . I wasn't much scared. There were not over 30 in the audience and most of them I am well acquainted with. I told Dr. M[erriam] I hoped there wouldn't be more than 6 there. He said he hoped there would be a thousand. He is president of the society and Coville is secretary.

My group of Kangaroo Rats is finished and now I have to begin on other groups for the Worlds Fair. If any of you go to it you must look at the Dept. collection of mammals and remember that I planned them and had the mounting done. Probably I won't see the Fair but some of you may. . . .

Am examining gopher stomachs now in connection with the Gopher Bulletin. They are mostly stomachs that I collected in 1887 and 88. There is lots that I would like to do here, but still am glad to start out again before long. The field is where I do my best work.[12]

Merriam had other plans for him for the moment, knowing that young Bailey needed to develop his writing skills along with his outdoor expertise. Bailey wrote home in mid-March,

> *Have been at the same old work, writing about gophers and reading what others have written about them. M[erriam] is very good about helping me. After I write a lot about some animals he takes it and marks it up so I can't read it and then gives it to a typewriter and after it is typewritten marks it over again. He gives me all the help and advice possible. I never knew before how difficult it was to write smoothly and clearly.*[13]

The outdoors began to call to him more loudly as spring arrived. "This warm weather makes me restless and want to get out of doors more. I will not be sorry to start in the field soon."[14]

Meanwhile, Bailey received a letter from his colleague and friend E. W. Nelson updating him on his collecting work in Mexico. From near Colima, Mexico, Nelson wrote:

> *Dear Bailey, I remember that you asked me to drop you a line in your last letter—a long time since and I will give you a short account of progress to date, as I presume you are again in the field so news from here be of interest. The coast country is very unhealthy and filled with vermin to make one's life a torment. In the interior from 1500 ft up the country is a good one to work in. The immediate coast is not rich in mammals but from 500 to 2000 ft it is a fine region. I am just back from a week trip—was gone 9 days from this place—2 days taken up on road—and I brought back over 200 mammals. Had my assistant with me and we worked like windmills. I have been in the country a few days over 2 months and have over 550 mammals and about 100 birds on my catalogue with 48 species of mammals. This will give you an idea of the richness of the country. By the time I get to Mazatlan and take the steamer for home my collection should take in a fine lot of new things. I am only about 45 or 50 miles in a straight line from where I landed yet have taken 16 or 17 species of bats and all the others up to 48 kinds in this area. Tomorrow morning I go to the base of the Colima volcano for a brief stay to carry my work up to the pines on the west slope. Then I return here and start at once with a Mexican packer on a long overland trip to San Blas by way of Guadalajara. The road leads through some very rough mountain country*

> *but should yield excellent returns. . . . From here until I reach San Blas my chief danger will be the worthy bandit who is abroad in the country I must travel. However, I trust to luck and a good supply of fire arms to getting through all right. . . . Hope to meet you again in Cal. on my return. Let me hear from you and what you are doing. Sincerely yours, E.W.N.*[15]

The adventure and success of Nelson's trip had to make Bailey eager to return to the field and begin his own collecting and adventures.

25

Dixie and New Kinds of Wilderness (1892)

This season would be different, for Bailey had "pupils" to train. While nonchalant about the process of preparation, which was now completely familiar, his eagerness to leave Washington was hardly disguised in a letter written to his folks on April 3:

> *I feel cooped up here in town and am anxious to get out in the country. I look forward to the summer's collecting with some pleasure and feel quite confident of success. With good company it will not be a lonely trip. . . .*
>
> *I do not feel excited over starting out as I often do. It seems like an every day affair. My things are all packed except a few that I will pick up in a few minutes. . . . The overcoat and some other clothes that I can't take into the field may be of use to some of you at home. I have to abandon white shirts and starch. The large shirt was sent from the laundry by mistake. It is too big for me but may fit Charl or Henry. The fellow that got mine can get even by giving it to his little brother.*[1]

He was going to be traveling in new country—the South—where the Civil War had raged only three decades earlier. His travel instructions from Merriam were straightforward. He was to proceed to the Le Conte Plantation in Liberty County, Georgia, a few miles south of the town of Riceborough where he was to collect duplication types of mammals, reptiles, and batrachians collected there many years ago by Major LeConte, using a list provided to him by Dr. Stejneger.[2]

Heading west by going south was a new adventure in itself, and Bailey wrote home descriptively of the new country as he crossed it. In a week he was in Riceboro, Georgia, where he caught the family up with his travels:

Here we are away down in Dixie. It is Sunday and I have lots to write about but will begin back at the beginning of our journey.

We left Washington last Monday at 4 PM. Crossed the old Long Bridge and came south through Old Virginia, arriving at Richmond at dark. There was some very nice looking country along the RR and occasionally a good farm. Most of the farms were poor and in slovenly condition. The soil seems to be poor, a kind of faded out sand with very little surface soil. There were lots of Negro shanties surrounded by a few acres of cleared land. Timber and brush cover much of the ground and I would not clear it for the best farm I saw. Scrub pine and cedar cover the high ground and oaks, walnut and hickory, sycamore and lots of trees that I don't know grow along the streams. The country is hilly and somewhat picturesque and we often came out in sight of the broad Potomac.

The next morning we woke up down below Washington in the southern part of NC [North Carolina]. It was a beautiful warm morning and we found ourselves in thick woods of tall pines, oak, sweet-gum, sycamore and lots of new trees. There were small farms here and there along the RR, but the people and what are usually called improvements were the least interesting of our surroundings. The peach and cherry trees were loaded with flowers, great banks of pink and white. In the driest parts of the woods the Cornace bushes looked like white tents, and there were a host of flowers that I never saw before. The land is all flat and in many places flooded, especially as we came farther south through South Carolina.

We reached Charleston at noon, but did [not] go through the best part of town. What we saw of it was old and dilapidated and uninteresting. Some of the buildings seemed to have been quite good originally, but it must have been a long time ago, probably before the war. The streets were deep with sand and the vehicles that we saw were mostly two wheeled carts, clumsy things, drawn by one mule and a darkey for driver. We were glad to leave town after a 20 minute stop and be out in the swamp again.

We arrived at Savannah at 3 oclock and had to wait until after dark for the next train, so tramped about the town for several hours. It was another uninteresting place with a tired wornout appearance. All of the towns that we saw are thriftless and strikingly different from those farther north, but I did not come down here to study towns. Now we are out in the woods 10 miles south of McIntosh and about 40 miles south of Savannah. We are 3 miles from the old LeConte Plantations where a lot of new species of mammals were collected and described by Major LeConte many years ago. Our special object is to get specimens of those species.

Riceboro is the name of our post office and town, but there is not much to it but name, just a couple of grocery stores kept in the old tumbledown houses that were built "fo de wah." We are about 15 miles from the coast. The tide rises about 4 feet every day in our little creek. The highest land is not 15 feet above sea level. All of the country except small fields and some marshes along the stream is covered with thick timber of pine, live oak, sweet-gum, magnolia and cypress, and over it all a drooping load of long, gray Spanish moss. I cannot describe it so as to give you any idea of the effect, but hope to find some photographs of the woods. It shows to good advantage over the roads where the long branches meet overhead and the festoons of moss swing over your head like a curtain. The farms are small and not frequent now, but the whole country seems to have been cultivated once. The ridges of old cotton fields show all through the woods where pines 3 feet through are now growing and oaks and other trees as large.

Land is said to be worth $1.50 per acre here. It would cost $10 an acre to clear it and I doubt if it would hold out long. The soil is fine, white sand and seems to yield well but except the top thin layer of vegetable mould it is very pure sand.

The country is said to be very unhealthy. All the white people leave and go inland to higher land the summer. They leave here about May. The weather was pretty warm for a few days after we arrived. It was up to 87 degrees in Savannah Tuesday and we thought summer was here, but today it is so cool we sit in the sun to keep warm.

I wish "you all," to use a typical southern phrase, could see through my eyes for a few minutes as I sit here by the side of a big log in the sun and look across an old field at the woods, I see a solid background of tall, dark green pines and in sharp contrast against them the light-green blue-gums and rusty green live-oaks and over all the haze of gray moss. All of our enjoyment must come from the woods and natural surroundings. The people where we stay are poor trash. They can't cook and don't know how to live. Our food consists of rice, fried pork, corn bread and strong coffee, and not a thing decently cooked. I could live on rice if well cooked but find it hard to swallow dry, half cooked grains. This morning we had fried alligator's tail which would have been good if not cooked to a crisp. It was my first "gator," was 49 inches long and would have weighed about 20 pounds. They are common but we have not hunted for them. I went to a Negro church today. Would like to tell you about it but haven't time now.[3]

Happy to move on, Bailey's next stop was Chattahoochee. Florida may be the land of flowers, but the northern part was "hardly different" from the Georgia he just left as he noted in this letter to his folks written on April 17:

> *Is warm and clear, a hazy, lazy sort of weather. The same description would apply to people of the place. I have been on the train half of today which is why I have not written earlier and why this letter must be short. It was another case where I had to hold my expedition over two nights (which amounts to two days) in one place doing nothing or else travel on Sunday. Perhaps it is not right. I know that it is not good for me to lose a Sunday. Neither is it right to waste time for which I am paid.*
>
> *You will probably find Chattahoochee down on the map in large letters. We did and supposed it was a town. There are 3 white families here and a lot of Nigger shanties. The people are poor and lazy. Our quarters are not very scrumptious, but we can stand it a couple of days. The country is rather pretty, is not so flat and swampy as we have been in. Some of the hills are 20 feet high and most of the land is dry. Pine woods cover most of the country. In places there are good size pines, but much of it is too small for sawing. Cypress and Sweet Gum grow on the low ground and there are lots of oaks and other trees. There are lots of flowers in blossom and it seems like summer. We saw some good fruit farms along the RR but most of the country is a wilderness.*
>
> *It strikes me as very strange to find all of the cattle, as well as pigs, goats, dogs, and people through this country so poor. Our cattle winter on hay and come out in spring in better condition than the cattle here where grass is abundant all winter. The hogs, which are numerous and half wild are about as thick as a shingle. The people are as thin and slab-sided as the cattle and hogs, that is the whites. The darkies are plump enough. I wish you could see some Georgia and Florida darkies. Mulattos are scarce. They are mostly pure African and you can easily imagine yourself in Africa. I like to watch a crowd of them. Some faces are hideously ugly, others are fine looking in spite of color. One old and very black woman, "Aunt Margarita," where we staid at Riceboro seemed to be as earnest a Christian as I ever saw. I think that many of them are such.*[4]

On April 20, Merriam wrote Bailey chastising him for sending live snakes and other reptiles through the mail. Apparently, the box he had sent them in broke and a live snake escaped in the Washington post office that created quite a stir among the staff. Merriam was forceful and told him never again under any circumstances to send live snakes to the department by mail or by express unless he was specifically told to do so.[5]

Then, just two days later, Merriam had to send another letter to him, about the same problem. This time it proved to be a box turtle instead of a rattlesnake, although Merriam still regretted the incident.[6] The post office was important to the work of the division and Merriam disliked having sour relations with them.

Gloom set in briefly as Bailey and his traveling companion Coleman reached Bay St. Louis, Mississippi, on April 24:

> *They call it a town and say there are 2500 people here but it is all scattered through the woods and for 6 miles along the shore. You can never see more than a few houses at once and they are all one story cottages and in among trees so they do not show at a great distance. There are no streets, just roads and paths running around through town. The people are nearly all French (Creole). They are queer. Many of them are mixed with Negro or Indian. I have not seen any of those fabulously beautiful Creole girls yet. I think they keep them all shut up in convents.*
>
> *The greatest fault I find with the place is that they don't know how to cook. We are staying with a French family, Garibaldi, have very comfortable quarters and a good place for our work, but they give us tough meat fried like pieces of sole leather and no fruit or many fresh vegetables. The people don't seem to know what fruit is for. In the past week we have had just one mess of canned peaches, probably from Cal., and no other fruit. Orange, pear, and peach trees grow almost wild all through the place but just now there is no ripe fruit on them and the people seem to be too shiftless to save any fruit when it is plenty.*
>
> *Still, we don't find much fault with our grub or the people. The country itself is very interesting and in some respects pleasant. We cannot see ten rods from any side of our room for trees and bushes, hickory, live-oak, magnolia, orange, pear, and peach trees. There are half a dozen varieties of roses in blossom in the yard and lots of other flowers. The oaks and pines are loaded with Spanish Moss.*
>
> *I wish you could see some Magnolia flowers. Imagine water-lilies twice as large as you ever saw growing all over a beautiful, large tree and you get an idea of the Magnolia.*
>
> *We are right on the shores of the Gulf of Mexico. . . . We hired a boat the other day and rowed across the Bay St. Louis, about 4 miles. We did not find much on the other side of the bay and I am wearing several good sized*

blisters on my hands to pay for the row. The gulf is shallow for a long way out so no big waves come in. The highest part of the shore is about 15 feet above tide limit.

It rained for nearly 2 days last week and is now raining again. Water stood over most of the country, so we have not caught much in our traps, but we got a lot of lizards, frogs, and snakes. Cotton-mouths and Water moccasins are common. We got all we wanted in a short time. They were so plenty the first day that I have been wearing leggings since, though I doubt if they could bite through my pants.

Anna, you have got ahead of me. I never killed a Sand Hill Crane. We are driving the birds up that way. Have startled off a lot of warblers, and the Yellow-rumps all left when we were over in Georgia. Look out for a flock of Orchard Orioles that started yesterday but were taking it easy and may not reach you for a week or more.

It will not be possible for me to come to the wedding. I do not expect to get farther north this summer than eastern Kansas and not up there before July.[7]

News of his sister's marriage to John Mills of Elk River, when he could not be present to share in her joy, only added to his homesickness. A week later, on May 1, it was time to celebrate—at least for a day, at least in thoughts of home:

Wonder what you are all doing away up north this nice May Day. I expect the younger people have been out hanging May baskets last night and have some adventures to relate. Down here they don't know what a may basket is, and don't have any spring, or else it is spring all the year.

Coleman and I both feel the effects of the warm, damp climate in a dull, lazy, don't-care sort of feeling. We can overcome it now by an effort but a few years would make us as lazy as any of them.

I sent a box of Magnolia buds yesterday addressed to Flo and asked her to send one out home if they blossomed. The flowers are splendid. I measured one 10 inches across and they are very fragrant. If those buds open they can be pressed and will make good specimens.

You have not told me yet when the wedding is to be. Am sorry I can't send some orange flowers but the oranges are all out of blossom now. I might send some Spanish moss instead.[8]

A rare diversion for feminine company kept the young men occupied for several days at Houma, Louisiana, after visiting New Orleans where they saw:

> *the same old Miss. River that flows past you. It is Monday morning and I did not write a bit yesterday because am among very pleasant people and am trying to enjoy good company while there is a chance. There are three very lovely girls in the family where we stay and we have met about 15 others at a party. Am sorry we can't stay here all summer.*[9]

A week later on May 15 he smilingly noted that he was still at Houma, writing to his folks back at home:

> *Sunday finds us still at Houma which may cause a smile in view of what I wrote you last time. I am willing to acknowledge that we have staid as long as it seemed profitable to work the locality, but why not? We will not meet as pleasant people again for a long time. I must tell you about them.*
>
> *We are staying with a Mrs. Hall and her 3 sons and 3 daughters. They are one of the aristocratic families of the parish. Have been on a sugar plantation until this year, but are now part of them living near town. Two of the boys are on the plantation 9 miles from town, and Thompson and I have been staying there all of last week. It is a grand old place. One of the plantations that you read about with a big house and splendid grounds full of oaks, orange and other fruit trees and such splendid flowers. There is a large sugar mill on the place and a whole town of little houses, called the "quarters" where the slaves used to live and where the negro hands now live. Some of the old slaves are still on the place. One old negro, "Uncle George" remains with the family as much a slave as when owned before the war.*
>
> *We are in about as strong a rebel country as exists. The people who were not in the Confederate Army are proud of the fact that their fathers were, though they do not seem to hold hard feelings toward the north. The divisions in society are very rigid. There is the upper class of wealthy planters who look down on the French Creoles and small farmers and rule the country. This is one of the three parishes in the state in which the negro did not vote at the last election not because he did not want to vote nor because he would not vote the right way, but because the upper element said he should not vote and took their shotguns to the polls to inforce the command. They say the Nigger is all right in his place but that he must keep in it.*
>
> *To us the people are very pleasant but it is easy to see that if opposed they*

might make it unpleasant for outsiders. The old spirit is not dead nor is it quite asleep.

A week ago there was a very pleasant dance at the house where we stay and you may be surprised to hear that so sober an old man as I enjoyed dancing several sets. The girls very kindly showed me the changes in the set and forgave the blunders which I made at first. We danced the Lancers, which is quite easy to learn, somewhat like a Quadrill. Last night there was another dance at a place two miles from here and we had a very pleasant time. We met some of the people met before and some new ones. It was Saturday night so we danced till 12 and then came home.

You may think me rather fickle to be going to dances, but if you met nice people and pretty girls as rarely as I do you would enjoy good company. I am sorry not to be able to get better acquainted with some of them, but in this short time have made some friends that I will not forget soon. We will not stay much longer.[10]

Returning to New Orleans, he took time to describe it to the dear folks, in a letter written on May 17 from the St. Charles Hotel:

It is the best hotel in town and is a grand old castle. It's but 5 stories high but occupies a whole block. You might easily get lost in it. It has lots of winding galleries and large rooms for various purposes.

The Stock Exchange is down in the basement. I went in there today and found hundreds of men betting on horse races. One man was kept busy receiving deposits of bets and another in paying out money to winners. There was such a roar of noise from the crowd I could hardly hear a word said. It was not a Sunday school.

I have been out through town today to the lake and through some of the cemeteries. There are some pretty places out that way.

The St. Charles is not so nice a hotel as the California but in some ways is better. It is built of granite and would answer for a medieval castle. 'Tis almost as massive as the capital at Washington and is in such queer shapes.[11]

After leaving New Orleans, Bailey and his party traveled to Washington, Mississippi, six miles southeast of Natchez, where he wrote to his family on May 22 catching them up on the various places where he had been:

The town [Washington] consists of a little store, a PO, a school and two churches, though it used to be a good sized place and was the capital of Miss.

The country is pretty. Is hilly and all woods and fields. Like most of the south it seems to be worn out and the soil poor. The tops of the hills are not worth cultivating but the valley land raised good cotton and corn. The woods are pretty, large trees and mostly open beneath like the Michigan woods and some of our more northern trees reach down here. We left the cypress and wet swamps farther south. Here we are a hundred feet above sea level and nearly that above the Miss. R. Perhaps it is well for us too, as the levees were full and slopping over along the lower Miss. and one big break had flooded a lot of country and washed out a RR so that I had to go across the river and away around to get up here from New Orleans. I did not come up on a steamer as I intended because it took two days for a boat to make the trip.

I had to lay over half a day at Baton Rouge and looked over the town all I wanted to in that time. It is a dilapidated place and not interesting.

Natchez is a nice town, built on hills overlooking the Miss. R, and has nice residences and is full of trees and pretty yards.

I was very glad to see some ground higher than my head above sea level. It was very hard to leave the Louisiana sugar plantation but I should hardly want to live on one all of my life.

I staid overnight in New Orleans and went over a good deal of the queer old town and found that it had some quite pleasant parts. There are nice gardens and picnic ground and bathing places out by the lake (Ponchartrain) but the best parks are the cemeteries. They are open to the public and are laid out in nice walks and drives and full of tropical flowers and trees.[12]

Merriam wrote him again on May 31, with comments about his field assistants as well as providing further instructions. He complimented him on the shrews he had obtained and asked him to get even more so that they could settle the status of the various members of the genus *Blarina*. Then he questioned the ability of Thompson as a field man, suggesting he was careless in making up skins, labeling, and collecting. He suggested to Bailey that Thompson should not be kept on later than the end of June. He inquired about Bailey's other assistant, Coleman, wanting to know if he liked him and if he showed any promise.[13]

Enough of the South, as far as their boss was concerned. Merriam urged the young men to head for Missouri right away, to investigate reports of a special cave that had been discovered there to check out its mammalian contents. Addressing Bailey at Fort Gibson, Arkansas, on June 9, Merriam instructed him to locate and meet Mr. Truman S. Powell, editor of the local paper, when he arrived in Galena, Missouri. His instructions called for him to visit a cave on the Powell property. Merriam had previously visited the place and the Powell's had been kind enough to allow him to stay there and remove items from the cave. More specifically, Merriam explained:

> *About the cave as a whole, we care very little. Most of the bats that inhabit it by millions in winter have gone away in the summer. . . . But, in addition to bats, the cave is inhabited by coons and woodrats, both of which it is particularly desirable to secure, for the reason that remains of the ancestors of these species exist in the cave, as you will see when you go to explore the famous "ANIMAL PASSAGE." We do not care for many coons—two or three skins with half a dozen skulls will answer, but of the woodrats it is desirable to secure as many as possible. Besides the mammals, there are blind salamanders, white in color, and blind cray-fish, both of which we want, particularly the former. It would be well to send two or three dozen specimens of the blind salamander, if you can secure so many (and be sure to get adult specimens as well as immature).*[14]

Merriam added a postscript to the instructions for Bailey: "in addition to the cave plunder, get as many kinds of mammals as you can in the neighborhood. I told Mrs. Powell that you would teach her boys how to skin mammals and birds, so that they might indulge in this recreation hereafter to the profit of the Powell family."[15]

Before reaching the Ozarks in Missouri, Bailey crossed the eastern corner of Texas, his first foray into that region of the Lone Star state.

26

Ozark Country and Beyond (1892)

Texas was not new territory to Bailey, nor comfortable. It was here that he had become so ill that he left his job and returned home during his first season in the field. But he was getting more used to the work and the territory, as he wrote home from Paris, Texas, on June 12:

> *Am on the Texas Prairie once more where the wind can blow if it is hot. It is hotter than where we have been farther south but is high (500 feet) and dry and I don't mind the heat so much. . . . Am getting used to most everything good and bad. Don't think I could get used to Red-bugs [probably chiggers] though. They most eat me up, but I hope to leave them soon.*
>
> *The country here is not specially interesting, a sort of half prairie, half scrub oak, gently rolling land. The soil is hard clay so no mammals can live here and that spoils it for me. . . .*
>
> *S'pose you begin to think about 4th of July. I don't feel a bit of interest in holidays any more. Would celebrate anything though for the sake of company. It goes harder now to be alone than if I had not had company all along.*[1]

In addition to having company on the first part of this trip, part of Bailey's upbeat feeling related to the brevity of the Texas crossing. A week later he would be in Marionville, Missouri, territory much more to his liking, writing to his folks on June 19:

> *The country here has a homelike appearance. The crops are just such as we raise—wheat, oats, corn, barley, and potatoes. The trees are our own species, jack-oak and elms, though hickory, walnut, catalpa, mulberry, and various fruits grow as well. The grass and many of the flowers are our home*

species; so you can see I am with lots of friends. It would be very lonesome if I did not know any of these little creatures. . . .

It is a pretty country through the Ozarks though more like hills than mountains. For a farming country it is rather rough and as 'tis all covered with timber, a man would need a stiff backbone to clear up a farm there, then is mostly very stony and would not be pleasant land to work. I could not see that crops were better than we can raise. . . .

I have a new book to tell you about. It is Gray's botany—the new edition, but in coat-pocket-size. Has about 800 pages, is in small type on this paper with flexible leather cover. Will go in a coat pocket easily and is the neatest most perfect little volume I ever saw. . . .

Why don't somebody study up our trees?!! Am a good mind to pitch into Chet about it. John and Anna are off fishing I s[up]pose and out of reach. . . . Flo has her hands pretty full I presume in keeping track of Margarette and will not be likely to do much botanical work this summer. Now if someone among "you all" would identify the trees the rest could all learn their names at second hand. . . .

I am often up a stump by not knowing our home plants. Wish I knew the trees of Minn. as well as I do those of California and Louisiana. . . . I wish M.[erriam] would send me home to study botany for a few months. . . .

M.[erriam] says that cave is right among the "Bald-knobbers" so I am likely to have lots of trouble. May find a still in the cave, or may take to drinking moonshine whiskey.[2]

His goal, Marble Cave, came closer, as did the bald-knobbers,[3] when he reached Galena, Missouri, on the twenty-sixth,

a little town in Stone Co. which is in the SW corner of Mo., not far from the Ark. Line. It is a part of the Ozark Mts. though not much like mountains here, just long ridges 500 or 800 feet high, all covered with timber and brush. There are lots of rocky ledges and outcrops and caves.

The soil is made up of stones of all sizes and for miles along the ridges you can't see a bit of dirt—just a mass of stones. But grass and vegetation in general grow well in the stones. It looks odd to see corn growing in a mass of small stones without a particle of dirt in sight—still you often see good corn among them.

Some of the highest hilltops—or mountain peaks if you care to call them so—are bare of trees and have little other covering. These are called "Balds"—a name that you may recognize.

When M.[erriam] wrote that I would be among the "Bald Knobbers," I thought he was jesting, but find that he was quite in earnest. There is a gang of people here called "Bald Knobbers" but they are wild outlaws that we never see. I happen to be staying with a family of people of the best class found here. Mr. Powell is editor of the county paper, an Illinois man but he and his family have lived here long enough to acquire many peculiarities of the region. Still it is a pleasant place to stay and I enjoy the oddities of a new—to me—kind of environment. That's a long word but it means a whole lot. . . .

S[up]pose I ought to tell you something about Marble Cave. It is a wonderful place but I don't feel able to describe it. You go down through a hole on top of a hill, down a long ladder and into a room several hundred feet high and wide, a grand amphitheater that rings to the least sound, like the Rotunda of the Capitol at Wash. From this main room of the cave there are numerous tunnels and passages leading off in all directions, some going way down and through large rooms, sometimes so small you have to crawl on your knees. There are several good sized creeks of cold water and some waterfalls as high as 60 feet. The walls of the caves are of marble, lime and onyx. There are lots of stalactites and stalagmites and queer formations that interest curiosity hunters. The only part of the cave that is of special interest to us is a deposit of animal remains in one of the passages.

In the bottom of a long passage leading back from the main room we find the bones and dried carcasses of various animals, Coons, Skunks, Mink, Wood Rats, Mice, etc.

This passage is perhaps 100 feet long and from a size easy to walk in tapers back to where you cannot crawl through, though it is open to another room. Several inches of dust on the bottom is full of bones, then a hard clay floor 8 or 10 inches thick covers another layer of dirt and bones and these are very old, probably all of extinct species. M.[erriam] has hired the Powell boys to take out and ship him 10 sacks full of this bone dirt. It will be rich material for study and may yield many new species of old mammals. Am glad I do not have to get out the stuff myself as it is very hard and disagreeable work. M.[erriam] wanted me to be here while it is taken out to see that it was got from the right stratum. Meanwhile I am collecting the living species found here.[4]

After studying the cave and its contents, Bailey was off to Kansas, where he connected with Dutcher, just arriving in Belle Plaine from Washington, DC, with the good word that Merriam

> *intends to have me return to Washington early this fall. A long winter's work there will do me good if I improve this time. Am in hopes that another summer will take me to the Arctic Circle through Manitoba to the mouth of the Mackenzie. That will pretty near complete my tour of the continent. Perhaps I will be satisfied with traveling then.*[5]

It's small recompense to his family, who continue to miss their traveling son. Nor does it ring true for Bailey himself, more and more deeply involved in his pioneering work. It wasn't the travel that intrigued him so much as the discoveries. Even so, he continued to write home descriptions of new territory.

His next stop was the Oklahoma Territory, in Oklahoma City, where he and Dutcher found themselves on July 24

> *down among the "boomers" in a town a year old and with a population of 8500. We came in yesterday at 2 PM and are staying over Sunday. Came through Guthrie which is claimed to be larger than this place and is the capital of the territory but is not so nice a town. It is spread out on the prairie and looks bare like some mining camps. The houses are small but lots of them. That applies to this place as well. Little, one-story, two-room houses are the rule, though there are some fine, large business buildings of brick and stone here.*
>
> *Oklahoma has all the characteristics of a "boom" town and has not yet felt the full effects of a relapse. Perhaps it has life enough to carry it through, and if so is destined to become a good town. The town-site seems to me not well chosen. It is on the flats of the North Fork of the Canadian River, close to the river woods on one side, and below the hills on the other.*
>
> *Since writing the above I have been out for a long walk back through the town and over the hills, and think much better of the place from the other side. The best part of the town is built on higher ground and up in the cleaner air.*[6]

Texas has gained no charm in his mind in the meantime, returning to Gainesville, a month later, which he described as "a miserable town, or impresses me so, is dirty and dusty and stinks and has the lazy shiftlessness of a southern town. Have been feeling cross all the morning. First I got in a hotel where there were bedbugs and made . . ."[7] The rest of the letter is, happily, missing, perhaps eaten by the very bedbugs he suffered.

On August 14 he wrote from Gainesville to Anna, now addressing his letters to "Anna and John" since her marriage:

That Chiggre (as a school teacher told me to spell it) [chiggers] has caused great excitement and been a subject of wonder wherever I have showed it. At Pouca Agency, where we staid with very pleasant and intelligent people, I had to exhibit it several times a day until most of the people had seen it. The people are all very familiar with the animal itself. I can feel a number of them as I write, but none have ever seen them under a glass or knew anything about their structure. As I showed the drawing, I quoted some of your description and gave entertaining lectures on the Chiggre. If I had time I should experiment on them to see if anything would kill or keep them away. Perhaps I will take some to W.[ashington] with me to examine under the glass in our div.[ision].[8]

Bailey introduced Dutcher to many new experiences, including a camp meeting, which he'd never seen before. He answered his sister's curiosity about artichokes and her new husband's interest in pocket gophers. Writing from Wichita Falls, on August 18, he admitted that he didn't know the artichoke at all:

Have been very much mixed up on them this summer as I had supposed an artichoke to be a bulb, or tuber, but in Louisiana we had artichokes to eat as a common vegetable, and they were like little Agaves, or century plants and somewhat like a little cabbage head with rigid, sharp pointed leaves with soft pulp at the base. Inside the artichoke are a lot of sharp spines. They are very good, but I never could get one to examine and do not know what they are nor what related to.

Your question, John, as to whether Pocket Gophers ever live in clay soil comes right in my present line of work. I have been running all over southern Kansas, Ind. Ter. and northern Texas to see where they do range and to find why they do not inhabit certain regions and are common in others adjoining, and have found their range prescribed by the character of the soil almost wholly. Over a large part of SE Kansas they do not occur because the soil is a very sticky clay. Along the sandy valley of the Arkansas River they are common, but there are none on the clay prairie on either side. . . . Whether the clay bakes and becomes too hard for them to dig, or whether when wet it sticks to them, or whether, as you suggest, the water gets in their holes are questions not yet solved. . . .

Just at present I am experimenting on Prairie Dogs with carbon disulphide. So far the results are very gratifying and to me surprising. I had but little faith in the stuff but find that a few ounces of it in a P. D. hole will kill the P. D. in about 2 minutes. I catch them in traps, tie a string to them and let them run down their holes, then pour in the bisulphide, stop the hole and in a few minutes pull out a dead P. D. Am trying it on various mammals so as to be able to give a full report on it in our Gopher Bulletin. It is a cheap and easy means of exterminating all kinds of burrowing mammals.[9]

As the summer field season ended, Bailey was called back to Washington, heading there directly from Texas. As previously, he roomed with the Covilles, where he planned to stay all winter. His enthusiasm for his work was unabated. On September 6, he wrote to his family, "am just waiting for breakfast to get ready. I couldn't change my habits all at once and sleep till 8 o'clock, so got up at 6 and read the back copies of the Proceedings of the Biological Society. After this I shall have work to do evenings that will even up the day."[10]

He settled back into the work routine quickly, and learned a new skill that would keep him fit as well as outdoors, even in the city. After leaving the city previously before its summer lushness, he now finds, writing on September 11:

Washington is a much pleasanter and more beautiful place now that the trees are green, the streets shady, and the hundreds of little parks and circles full of flowers and fountains. Maybe I will get a wheel. I have learned to ride on Coville's. Have been on it twice and can ride all over town now without tipping over. Believe I shall get a wheel if I strike a good bargain in a second-hand one. Will wait till I learn to ride well and find out for sure whether I want one. Perhaps I will rent one for a month.[11]

The bicycle age was beginning, and the young adventurer welcomed its possibilities.

The upcoming World's Fair in Chicago began to take full attention of the Biological Survey staff, including Bailey. He relied on the folks at home to provide some of the materials he needed, as he created display cases for the small mammals in which he increasingly specialized. Such cases were not yet in use even in museums and were created from the imaginations of those who had been in the habitats of these fellow beings as a way to show their home territory.

One can almost sit with him at the worktable as he describes what he needs writing home to his family on October 10:

> *Now I want to write about some things that I need in fixing up cases for the Worlds Fair. We need about half a bundle each of good, clean wheat and oats in the straw. If you have not thrashed please save some for me. I will send official envelopes for it later. I also need some sticks that rabbits have gnawed to put in my case of rabbits. Should like a lot of little bushes that they have cut down, and some larger ones with the bark gnawed. Want to get up a case of 3 jack rabbits and 2 cottontails and have the gnawed and cut bushes in with them. I may want more things for fixing up cases after awhile. Preble is here now and will begin mounting mammals for our exhibit. I will have to plan all of the groups for about 70 specimens. Am going to have a coyote in one case killing a sheep.*[12]

Bailey constantly relied on his family to supplement his own growing knowledge. He had learned how to ask the questions in the field and to find answers that were intuitive for him as a boy on the farm, but not in the terms he now wanted them. Writing home on October 16, he asked:

> *Does anyone take notes on birds and animals? I wish that all of you would look out for any peculiar habits of mammals and write me any notes on them. Probably the only naturalist work that I will ever do that amounts to anything will be writing up the habits of our mammals and I should like to do that well and have every bit of information on the subject possible. I especially want to know when each species hibernates and comes out in spring and the number of young raised by different species. If it wasn't for just this kind of work that I now have a chance to do to the best possible advantage I should be with you on the farm. I feel that I am losing so much in not being with you while we all are strong and well and could enjoy being together so much.*[13]

Little did he realize—yet—the importance of his work, for no one had written the habits of so many mammals from such extensive fieldwork, nor had the opportunity to do so that he had. His family ties remained strong and gave him the balance for the aloneness in the field.

Anna meanwhile was creating her own niche in the world as a taxidermist, a balance to her new family ties. She continued to receive support from her brother, and from others in the field. As she wrote to him on November 1:

> *Geo. King brought me an owl to stuff yesterday, and I tried some of the improvements suggested by Hornaday. The wires fastened as he directs are*

> *very much better because so much firmer. I could twist and turn it as I liked and the wires held their place. It is a good specimen—for a poor taxidermist. . . . We have just received the sassafras and will send the wintergreen today. The wintergreen patch keeps about the same size, but the plants are rather small. I think they are a little out of their native soil and climate; though there are a good many berries on them this year.*[14]

Brother and sister both continued to risk using the courage that supported them so well throughout their lives. For Vernon, writing home a week later, it was speaking in public:

> *I must thank [Anna] for a fine bunch of wintergreen. I am chewing a leaf of it now and it is nice. I chewed a lot of it last night to keep up my courage till my turn came to read a paper at the Biological Society. My paper was on the Cross Timbers of Texas and their effects on distribution of animals. It was but a 10 minute paper and of no particular interest, but served to introduce an interesting subject for discussion. . . .*
>
> *Dr. M.[erriam] confided to me a piece of news the other day that did not surprise me at all; viz., that I would have to spend a month or so at Chicago next spring in preparing our exhibit. I hope some of you can manage to be there at the same time. My chief anticipation of the work is that some old friends may be there during part of my stay at least. Then I hope to come home and farm for a month. . . .*
>
> *We are having a much larger exhibit prepared then we had planned. The groups of mounted mammals will fill 10 large cases. We have a taxidermist working on them here and will send off a lot to be mounted. . . .*
>
> *Please write on both sides of the paper, Anna, as I want to keep your letters and don't want to carry blank paper around with me.*[15]

The Cross Timbers is a vegetation region in northeastern Texas that is made up of alternating belts of grassland and forest arranged in a north–south axis. It became a milepost for pioneers in their western march across North America.[16] Bailey's paper described its influence on the Texas fauna.

Bailey's lifelong interest in conserving mammals was also at work, though at first reading it may not seem such. He appreciated the role of wolves throughout his career, and he also understood the importance of acquainting the public with them. He asked family members, in a letter written on November 20, to collect—a euphemism for killing, even then—some wolves for the displays they were creating for the World's Fair:

I did not know that the bounty on wolves was so high but am glad that it is. I hope you will be able to get some, for we need them badly, though I doubt if M.[erriam] could pay more than the 8 dollars offered.

Charles, it seems strange to think of you as a man of 40 years when we have been boys together for so long, but 28 is not so young as I once was.

I thought it a good plan to have my life insured before I got any older, so have just taken out a policy of $5000. . . . It is a safe investment and if the grizzlies ever get me the insurance may be useful to someone. . . .

Since writing last week we have had a very good meeting of the AOU, where I met a lot of bird men that I wanted to see.

. . . As to the use of Aconite as an antidote for insect poison, Mother, I have not yet asked the Dr. about it, but as the statement of facts in that clipping are all a lie, I have not much faith in the remedy. I never heard of a scorpion sting being fatal. Have known lots of people being stung by them, and it is not considered serious. Such a remedy might be. . . .[17]

As the holidays approached and the work for the fair intensified, he wrote home to his mother prior to Christmas for help in gathering gifts for the family. This ploy was to work many times through his life, for it helped him stay close to the family, provide a little cash to supplement their meager supplies, and be a part of the celebration even though miles away. He addressed this letter, written on December 18, privately to "My Dear Mother":

I am going to write you a letter all by your self this time. Going to try to get out of work by taking you into partnership with me on the distribution of Christmas presents. I want to help make this a Merry Christmas but can not take time for doing anything myself. Now to get out of it easily I am going to send you $10 to get just what you want to for just who you want to. I know it is shirking work to shoulders that have always borne more than their share but you must be wise and plan to have others do for you, and help you all that you need. It is not going to give you much time between now and the 25th but do not bother to hunt up what can't be easily found.

Use the money just as you please, of course many of the presents will best be useful articles and you will know what things will do the most good in the places where presents will be scarce.

I will mention no names nor offer any suggestions but simply leave the money with you for carrying out the plans that you are always making for the happiness of others.

God's blessing be with it and with you—my Mother.

P.S. I make the checks payable to father's order so that he can make them payable to anyone who can conveniently get them cashed.[18]

Christmas Day passed in Elk River as it did in Washington. On December 27, Anna sensed his feelings and shared her own. Her husband's gift tells a lot about their relationship and her interests:

Christmas is passed again. How short the years seem, although there have been many changes in my plans and life in the past year. It seems strange and new to me yet to have a home of my own and a husband to love and make happy. I wonder if you are lonely this year spending your Christmas and New Year's away from home. You are among friends there though and you have spent them in much more lonely places sometimes. . . .

John's present to me was "Our Common Insects"—Packard. It is more simple and perhaps less scientific than his "Guide to the Study of Insects" and will make it easier for me to understand the latter, which I have found rather difficult to study at a time of the year when there were so few insects to study from.[19]

And so another year ended for the family in its many places, both internally and externally.

27

I Just Want to Remember (1893)

The prestigious National Geographic Society elected Bailey to membership,[1] and he proudly reported the fact to his family in a letter sent on January 17: "They have weekly meetings at which lectures are given by various explorers and scientific men. The lecture a week ago was by Lieut. Peary on his trip over the inland ice to north Greenland."[2] His stature, and his experience with the larger world, continued to grow.

New uses for plants also continued to intrigue him. Ginseng seemed to hold promise for the future. About the same time, silkworm culture held a similar intrigue on the West Coast, where people saw trainloads of cocoons pass through, shipped from the Orient and then taken to the textile mills on the East Coast. They tried unsuccessfully to grow mulberries and begin silkworm culture in California, where the labor-intensive process proved unprofitable to westerners. With time as valuable a commodity as labor in the West, would ginseng reach a similar fate? Writing to his family at home on January 27, he noted:

> *Some of the people here are getting excited over raising ginseng. Coville says it does not require over 4 or 5 years to develop roots of good size, though a seed requires a year and a half to germinate. Someone has tried it and has estimated the profit per acre as something enormous. The price is steadily increasing and the supply diminishing. Over a million dollars worth per year is shipped to China. The seed sells for a dollar an ounce.*
>
> *Coville won't accept my objection that it takes 14 years for a root to grow. He says it gets its growth and then remains nearly stationary and sends up a new stalk each year.*
>
> *It might pay to try a few plants of it or get Greenstreet excited and let him do the experimenting. Coville says the seeds must be planted when ripe*

and before drying, and says it can only be raised in woods, or where there is shade.[3]

Wet and muggy springs brought annual outbreaks of malaria to Washington. Bailey downplayed its presence in his own system as he described its cure in a letter written to his family on February 19:

It will take about 6 months in the Utah and Nevada deserts to clear my system of all traces of malaria, and that is the prescription I expect.

I am taking quinine and oranges for my malaria. All that worries me is that I don't dare eat everything that comes along. But I eat lots of oranges. Mrs. Coville just bought a box of 213 splendid oranges for $2.75. Most all fruits are cheap here and we use a great deal. Mrs. Coville does not keep a servant now, but she and Miss McMaster do all the work, and the fruits for dessert save work and are not at all bad.

It now seems as if I should be here over the 4th of March, and if so, I want to see as much of the Inauguration [of Grover Cleveland] as possible. All such opportunities seem like a last chance for me, for I never know what may happen next. The coming secretary of Agriculture, JS Morton of Nebraska, may not approve of our exploring the desert regions. . . .

Have been trapping a little lately out in the Zoo Park not far from here. Caught a Possum, a rabbit, a muskrat and a lot of mice and shrews. Just went out for an hour at a time once in awhile before breakfast and after office hours. Guess I will quit now. The boys stole a lot of my traps and the Zoo men got to watching me.[4]

John Mills sent a card in early March announcing the birth of his and Anna's first child, Laura. Bailey noted to the family, in a letter written on March 12:

She will probably be glad to see her uncle when I reach home. How strange it seems to think of our little girl as a mother. I read a paper at the Biological last night. Saw John Burroughs there. Maybe Anna will remember that he is one of our popular Ornithological writers. Has written some very interesting books on birds. He is a fine looking old man with white beard and hair. I had no idea he was so old.[5]

Just before leaving Washington in March, Bailey had a unique opportunity to go with a party of naturalists to the White House, where he *shook hands with Grover. About 75 of us went, mostly from the various museums and departments. Then in the evening we went to a social entertainment at the Arlington Hotel. It was given by the Geographic Society to its members and their friends. Was one of the pleasantest occasions of the kind I ever attended. The Arlington is more of a palace than the White House. Beautifully furnished parlors and halls. There were probably 200 people present, mostly from scientific circles, among them such men as Major Powell, Ward, McGee, Gilbert, Gannett, Cushing, several senators and representatives and 3 members of the cabinet. The princess of the Hawaiian Islands was there. She looks like a very pretty American girl.*[6]

A short time later, in April, he received a personal letter from his boss in Florida. Merriam's mother had died in Winter Park, and he was traveling back with his father to his brother's home at Lyons Fall, New York,

where the funeral was held—the snow being too deep to take the casket to our home on the hills. Mother died of dysentery and suffered much, but it was a comfort to her to have two of her children with her. My sister Florence is not at all well and is staying here with us, where she will remain until she goes west next month. My mother was a wonderfully good woman and her death is a sad blow not only to her family but to a multitude of friends, particularly among the poor and sick to whom her life was devoted.[7]

Merriam's concern for his family and grief for his mother did not deter him from overseeing the department's exhibits at the World's Fair in Chicago, the first major public display of his life zone theory. Bailey had been assigned to arrange the life zone exhibit, and Merriam wrote to him on April 17 in Chicago about repositioning the bighorn sheep in the exhibit so that it rested in the Arctic Alpine zone, just above timberline; apparently Bailey had arranged it as reaching through three zones, which Merriam didn't like.[8] Then, on April 26, Merriam wrote him again, this time regarding the forthcoming visit of President Benjamin Harrison, the twenty-third president of the United States, with more specific instructions about the exhibit:

Since writing you to-day the Assistant Secretary has requested me to telegraph you to put the mammals and birds on the mountain slope as far as possible before the arrival of the President and party on Saturday of this week. I explained that most of the specimens would have to be removed when the case was put on, if the case is not already finished; but he regards

> *the completion of the slope of so much importance, that he desires to have it in as good shape as possible, even if all the specimens have to be removed and re-placed. Some of the labels will be mailed to-morrow.*[9]

This had to be a tremendous hassle at the last minute but there is no indication that Bailey ever complained!

Summer began, and with it the field season, with instructions for his work. The letter was very detailed and included an ambitious agenda beginning in South Dakota and continuing to western Nevada followed by several stops in Utah and Wyoming. J. Alden Loring was assigned to act as his assistant for part of the summer.[10]

From Scotland, South Dakota, on June 4, Bailey wrote home:

> *It seems the most natural thing in the world to be alone again among strangers. I don't mind not having any company now, I have so much that is pleasant to remember and think over and over from my home visit. The visit seemed so short, but it will last a long time yet and keep fresh in my mind, and the dear old place will seem bright and green and the loving friends dearer than anywhere else in the world. I don't want to make friends now—don't want anyone to talk with but just want to remember. For a long time before it was looking forward—now it is looking backward.*
>
> *My work here in Dakota does not require much thought or study. I know just what to do and it depends on train connections as to how fast I can do it. I arrived here Saturday at 1:30, caught my gopher—a Geomys—and could have gone on to another locality last night, but no trains go west from here till Monday at 1:30. I have a fairly pleasant place to spend Sunday—might call it a "Sunday in Scotland."*
>
> *Scotland seems to have been so named because the people are all Germans and Swedes and because the country is the farthest from being like anything in Scotland—a boundless prairie.*[11]

In late June, the month of Bailey's birth, his mother remembered the occasion with a fruit cake for the family and reminiscences for her dear boy. She closed the letter with a special blessing, "I pray God that his light may shine brighter and brighter unto the perfect day, and that the same loving hand may lead guide and direct in the future as in the past, to keep you from all harm and to deliver from all evil."[12]

28

Fit for Scientific Work (1893)

In Ogden, Utah, Bailey received a complimentary letter, written on June 19, from T. S. Palmer, acting chief of the division in Merriam's absence, expressing pleasure with the exhibit at the World's Fair:

> *I have just returned from Chicago this morning and find your letter dated Pine Bluffs, Wyoming, June 15, together with a package of miscellaneous specimens sent in from that place. I was much pleased with the appearance of the exhibit at Chicago. The groups of course were all in place before I arrived, but many of the labels had not been put up. Considering the difficulties under which you worked, I think you and Preble did remarkably well.*[1]

Moving on into Utah, Bailey took time from work to visit a new friend. His boss's sister Florence was taking a trip west with her mentor, Harriet Mann Miller, known in ornithological circles by the pen name of Olive Thorne Miller.[2]

Ostensibly, Miss Merriam traveled for companionship and to recover from her mother's death, but she also was disposed toward lung difficulties. Though unstated, they remained an impetus for her physician brother to urge her to spend time in dryer climates. When Mrs. Miller informed her of her plans to visit Utah: Florence Merriam arranged to accompany her and her daughter, who was about the same age.

This set the stage for Bailey's brief mention in his letter home on July 8 from Ogden, Utah, "Spent the 5th of July with Miss Merriam and Miss Miller. Will run down there again tomorrow. I want to write to Mrs. Castle asking her about Phoenix. Miss Merriam thinks of spending next winter there."[3]

Soon Bailey's assistant, Loring, joined him, and they completed their outfits for the field season. Still at Ogden a week later, as he explained:

> *only waiting for my saddle to come. . . . My saddle horse cost me $13.00. He is 6 years old, sound as a dollar and a little beauty, will weigh about 850. He is perfectly gentle and tame. Can catch him anywhere from a drove and ride*

him without saddle or bridle. Horses are very cheap. Times are hard and a little money will buy a great deal. . . .

I did not get a chance to write last Sunday. Went down to Farmington and spent the day with Miss Merriam and Miss Miller. They had to give up the trip with us, though they hated to do so. We decided that they could not stand it.

You seem to have gotten the idea that it was Mrs. Miller that was going. Fortunately she never dreamed of such a thing. She is too fat and too cranky for such a trip. Miss Miller and Miss Merriam are both delightful girls. They came up here last Thursday and Loring and I took them up Ogden Canon with our buckboard and team. It was a splendid trip. We all enjoyed it so much that we did not mind the loss of half a day's work. Meeting them out here has been one of the pleasant incidents of the summer. But we have said goodbye to them and will soon be off.[4]

Off they were, for the Wind River Mountains of Wyoming. On August 13, writing to his folks at home, he described that they went through

South Pass and Atlantic cities—cities in name—there is a store in each, a P. O. and saloon and a dozen other houses, half vacant. . . .

For the past 100 miles our road has been over sagebrush plains. Mostly good roads but not very exciting country. We found plenty of water. 15 miles was the farthest between water places. We got lots of good specimens along the way and killed all the young sage grouse and ducks we wanted and saw plenty of antelope—40 or 50 some days—but did not get any. We live high. Have plenty of fresh meat and well cooked too. "Gus" cooks meat first rate. We have a broiler and he broils and fries and bakes game so it is delicious. We keep butter and canned milk and dried fruits and honey besides the staples of bean, potatoes, rice, and oatmeal. I don't think we ever lived better in camp and still our expenses are not high though we pay big prices for things out here. Potatoes are 4c, oats 3c, flour 4c, butter 35c and other things to correspond. $50 apiece will more than cover all our expenses per month including the cook's wages. We are dirty and ragged and hairy faced but we enjoy 3 good meals a day and most of the little incidents between: Such things as running a drove of antelope, rounding up a flock of young sage hens with the auxiliaries, crawling through sagebrush after prairie dogs or woodchucks, driving brush patches for bear (which we haven't succeeded in starting). Even getting rained on, or Loring's horse running away with him make a variety of life.[5]

These tales did little to ease the thoughts of his mother, at home in Elk River. She kept in touch with him more often, sensing the spoken and unspoken dangers he faced. "It is Wednesday afternoon yes almost suppertime but while I am watching the bread baking I shall have time to get a letter started at least, for I want to send it the first chance, for I am afraid you will not get many while you are in the wilderness and need them most."[6]

A week later, on August 20, his father sent a brief note bragging about the success Henry was having with trapping rats. The letter starts with a "ha! ha!" followed by a brief explanation of Henry holding a rat by the tail that he caught in one of Bailey's traps set in the woodshed.[7]

Bailey was well aware how little that numbers on a page can do to convey the altitude or scenery of Wyoming to those in Minnesota, but he continued to keep them abreast of his surroundings as best he could. Writing on August 23 from 9,600 feet elevation in the Wind River Mountains, fifty miles north of Lander, he painted this picture:

> *You would smile to see my position—sitting on the ground before a big fire writing on the back of my catalogue held flat against my stomach so the light can strike it.*
>
> *It is so cold I have to sit close to the fire and I have on a heavy flannel shirt and coat and vest and 2 pairs of pants and drawers and moccasins and leggings. We are camped only 400 feet below timberline at 9600 feet, and right in heavy timber of spruce and balsam and pine. We left our wagon down at Bull Lake (at 5800 feet) and packed up here. Farther up are the great snow capped peaks of the Wind Rivers. We have only been up to 11,800 feet as yet.*
>
> *We are right in the bed of an old glacier. It has scooped out an immense gorge in the side of the range, polished the granite bottom as smooth as glass, dammed up the outlet of the gorge with its terminal morain and left a deep lake (Bull Lake) 9 miles long. The old morains and debris and scratches are well preserved and plain. So you see we are on historic ground. (My fire is so low I can't follow the lines [on the paper]. Wait till I poke it.—Now it is better.)*
>
> *Perhaps you wonder what kind of game we get up here. We have had plenty of Blue Grouse and snowshoe rabbits and nothing else, though there are plenty of deer and elk tracks all around us. There are some bear tracks too, and I wasted 3 shots from my rifle at a Grizzly the other day. I was not very close and did not succeed in killing him and only had the three cartridges with me at the time. I have killed Coyotes with the rifle at longer range but maybe I was nervous. He was out on open ground and I lay behind a tree*

about 15 or 20 minutes waiting for him to come closer. But he has gone. It was a chance of a life-time and missed. Still have the satisfaction of knowing how a live Grizzly looks. It was not an extra big one. 600 or 800 I guess. . . .

Now I will hunt my blankets and write more another time.[8]

Keeping up his professional connections, a couple of days later Bailey received a response to a letter he had sent to Lewis Lindsay Dyche, superintendent of the World's Columbian Exposition, as the Chicago World's Fair was officially named, inviting him to join his collecting party at some time during the field season. What a different world it was in Chicago from life in Wyoming, as Dyche wrote back to Bailey on September 15:

Your favor of Sept. 3d which I was pleased to receive was rather a surprise to me, for I know how hard it is for a man to write when out on an animal expedition. Nothing would please me more that to be with you for a few weeks, but I cannot get away from this little show here. People are coming to the Fair now at the rate of about 175,000 paid admissions per day. There are crowds everywhere and the Fair is a grand success. . . . Theater "America" at the Auditorium is having an unparalleled run and people are buying seats two weeks ahead of time. Buffalo Bill is right in the push line with his show—making more money than anybody. He has a daily average attendance of 50,000 so we are told. . . .

The World's Congress on Zoology met Aug. 28th and lasted a week. Some excellent papers produced and one by J. A. Allen on geographical distribution of animals basing his argument on the distribution of mammals, provoked more discussion perhaps than any other paper read. Dr. Theodore Gill of Washington took a very lively interest in the discussion as Allen seemed to disagree with him in some respects. . . .

Am glad you are getting so many mammals. I would like to be along long enough to kill a two point buck and eat a quarter of venison. If there is any life I like it's a life in the woods.[9]

Soon it was time for Bailey to think about heading east again. Following Merriam, who visited him briefly in Wyoming, Bailey stopped for a day in Chicago and then returned to Washington. The difference in their itineraries was that Bailey would take time for two days at home in late August while en route. He told Anna, in a letter written on September 23:

You may think that a short visit. So do I, but I have yet the best thing to tell you. This winter I have decided (with Dr. M.[erriam]'s advice) to attend the Columbian University at Washington. I can take a special course in addition to my office work. Will tell you more about it when I come home. I hope to make this the first year of my college course. You will realize why I make so short a stop at home. I shall be late at best for beginning. The prospect is to me delightful. If I can take a course that will fit me for scientific work and place me on a footing with other naturalists, I may be able by hard work to sometime accomplish things that with my present knowledge would be impossible.[10]

His next letter is a quick catch up when he reaches Washington. Such small matters mean little to him, but he knows their importance to his family. Writing on October 10, he tells them:

I arrived here in good condition yesterday morning and have already settled down to work. Am at my old place with the Covilles. It is pleasant to meet again the people here that I have learned to like, and pleasant to find a welcome with them. . . . Have registered at the Columbian and begin class work tomorrow. Our train was late and did not reach Chicago till 1 PM so I had just a short half day at the Fair. . . . Found my wheel OK, and have not forgotten how to ride.[11]

Now it was Anna's turn for encouragement. When he sent her a copy of the draft of his first scientific publication, the "Gopher Bulletin," she read it and responded on October 17 that from it she was

learning many things which I am glad to know. I am not a competent critic but I can find no fault with it and I rejoice in your success. I am proud of "My Little Brother." You are going far beyond me in your work—work I still like to call "ours"—but I can still feel with you, for I love the work as well as ever, and I know, however great the success you win—you will not forget one who has worked with you through those happy years in the old home.[12]

Instead of the usual "Anna," she signed the letter "Anna Bailey Mills." In its own way, the letter and its signature quietly note the ending of an era, a signal that her priorities are now elsewhere.

Encouragement comes from other sources as well. His former assistant and continuing friend Basil Dutcher responded from New York on October 29:

The best thing that you told me in your letter was of the new opportunities that have been unfolded to you. Was I not something of a prophet when I said that a farm in Minnesota was not written down on your forehead as your ultimate destiny? Should any man, having a candle, hide it under a bushel, rather than let him put it on a candle-stick, that it light the house. And to apply the parable to things of today, is it right for one having talents to waste them in work not worthy of their greatness, or should he use them in such wise that the result of their application should redound to the glory and to the benefit of his common humanity. As I think of these things I count myself lucky that I have been brought into an atmosphere where work for the common cause whatever its nature is held up as the highest aim for manly effort, where it is thought that ability and intellect should not be direct[ed] solely toward personal advancement.[13]

Dutcher completed the letter a week later, writing:

The above burst of eloquence and moral settlement quite exhausted me a week ago, so that I had to go out and take a walk, and during the evening I was engaged in packing up my collection to ship the next day.

I suppose that if, as you say, you pursue some regular college course next Winter, devoting all your time to it, you will devote the time exclusively to special studies, without thought of continuing on an entire four years and taking a degree at the end thereof. It would hardly pay you I imagine to do the latter. Degrees are not worth anything among those familiar with them, and four years would be rather too long for you to spend in study alone.[14]

Eager to learn all he could, and with such encouragement from his friends and family, Bailey also took a course in German as noted in his weekly letter home written on November 5:

My studies grow more interesting as I get better control of them. Am taking German at the Berlitz School besides the college course. That gives me two lessons a week more, making 4 hours a week of German. At the Berlitz it is mostly practice in talking which I do not get much of in the college class. At the college there is a class of about 30, at the Berlitz there are but 2 in the class at present, so I have half the talking to do. At the college we study German in a more scientific manner. The two go well together.

I now have classes every evening, so I do not have much time to waste. Went to the Biological last night and staid through half the evening. There were some papers of special interest. It rained and I got damp but got home in time to study a couple of hours before bedtime. Guess I will have to take part of an evening for one of the Boston Symphony concerts this week.[15]

As the holidays approached again, Emily wrote to him on December 17 about her fondest dreams, and her memories,

It is almost Christmas and if our dear boy could only be with us it would be such a joy. The Holidays come and go and some of them leave their impressions more by what they are not than by what they are. For the last fifteen years the getting of our family together has been a very uncertain thing. But for 25 years before that we were always all at home at such times, and had each other to love and plan and care for if we did not have much to celebrate with, and in looking back we can remember a great deal of sunshine as well as some clouds, and all of our lives we have had so much to be thankful for that God in his love and mercy has spared the lives of our large family so long, and what is more than all temporal blessings combined drew the hearts of all to believe in and love and trust him. I cannot help but wonder at the love and mercy shown us as a family and at the care and love and quieting hand in your case through so many dangerous places.[16]

29

The School of Life (1894)

The year 1894 opened with a irritating request to Merriam from Congress wanting details about his special agents and field agents, including who they were, what they did, and why they were needed. This obviously raised the boss's hackles, and he responded on February 2 using Bailey as an example of the importance of these employees and their role in the agency:

Dear Sir:
Regarding to your communication of yesterday requesting a statement respecting the instructions, duties, reports, and so on of Special Agents *in this Division, I beg to say that in my judgment none of the employees of this Division can be classed under this heading.*

The work imposed upon the Division by Congress is the study of the geographic distribution and food habits of North American birds and mammals. The necessary investigations must be made in the field and the results elaborated in office. Persons engaged in this field work are in my judgment as clearly members of the Division force as are any of the office assistants. In fact it is customary for some of the field agents to spend part of the year in office in working up the results of their field investigations. For instance, Mr. Vernon Bailey, one of our so-called field agents, *has been employed in this capacity almost since the establishment of the Division. He spends the greater part of the year conducting biological exploration in the field and comes to Washington in winter to plot on base maps the results of his field work, and to perform other duties assigned him. Do you deem it possible to so construe the term Special Agent as to make it cover Mr. Bailey? In my opinion he is as much a member of the Division staff as I am.*

In my interpretation of the term, a Special Agent is a person appointed, usually for a brief period, to perform a specific task—not a person who is regularly engaged in the regular work of the Division. The last Special Agent employed in the Division was Col. Alexander Macbeth of Georgetown, South Carolina, who was charged with the special study of studying the depredations of the Ricebird in the rice fields of that neighborhood. His work was finished in October 1888, since which time he has not been on the roll of the Division.

If it is insisted that our Field Agents are Special Agents, I shall of course set about preparing the statement asked for. In this case I must ask to have an additional stenographer and two or three additional type-writers detailed as Special Agents to do this work, as it will involve several months of hard labor and the results will make a large volume of many thousand pages.

Respectfully,

C. Hart Merriam, Chief of Division[1]

In the meantime, Bailey headed off to South Dakota for some brief fieldwork between projects in Washington. His immersion in his work has affected his earlier strong discipline about how Sunday should be celebrated, as he laments to his sister Anna in a letter written on March 27:

My field Sundays get sadly mixed up with weekday work and very often it seems necessary to do much work on Sunday that I would rather not do. Still think you would do the same in the same place. Would you? But then, you do not know any more about it than I do until you have been there. What a quiet home-life you have! The very thought of it makes me homesick. Still I might get tired of a quiet life after awhile. Now it seems most desirable. Wish I could see baby Laura. Does she show signs of developing the taste of a naturalist?[2]

Foreseeing that the passenger pigeon was heading the way of the bison, Bailey urged his sister to keep "all records possible" on them: "They are probably doomed to extinction in a few years and you are in their last remaining region. It is a rare opportunity to observe the death of a species. Every note on them hereafter will be precious."[3]

On May 1, travel instructions came from Merriam directing him to proceed at once to Dakota and Wyoming and continue with the fieldwork he had started the last season. The letter included details about where to stop and what particular mammal species to collect. The trip was designed to conclude in Montana and included Basil Dutcher and John Loring as his assistants.[4]

Merriam sent Bailey a letter on June 20, outlining more problems with the post office and giving him very formal instructions for shipping specimens during the trip:

> *The frank privilege has been recently abused by Field Agents of the Botanical Division which has cause considerable excitement in the Post Office Department and in this Department, and has resulted in orders to the effect that no packages can be shipped by mail by any person in the field to himself or any other person in the field, but only to the Departments at Washington. Extreme care must be taken also in sending packages to the Department that they shall not be objectionable in weight or size, and shall be properly wrapped in paper. You are particularly cautioned against sending any large packages by mail during the coming season.*[5]

As Bailey reached the head of the Little Bighorn River in Montana for the summer's work, little did he envision the adventure that lay ahead when they followed the river to Ft. Custer, traveling across the Indian reservation. Writing his folks at home on July 1, he noted, "there are no ranches to bother. There is a good road and they are building a RR down the valley and have the end of the track half a mile below us. It is going to strike the NP at Billings and is under contract to be there by Oct. We will go through Custer's Battleground before reaching the fort."[6]

Before he has a chance to mail the letter, the Fourth of July comes and goes, and he adds a long postscript from the Crow Agency:

> *Today has been one of the red letter days in my western life. We have seen one of the greatest Indian dances and sham battles of the country and such a one as may never be seen again. Even now as I write late in the evening I hear the drum up at the camp. They are still dancing as they have been since morning. The whole thing was a complete surprise to us. As we came down the valley yesterday afternoon we saw the unmistakable sharp topped tepees of the Sioux and on coming nearer found ourselves in the midst of a swarming Indian camp. It is on the old Custer Battle Field and about 4000 Indians have gathered to dance and rehearse their old battles. There are about 3000 Crows, nearly a 1000 Cheyennes and a lot of Sioux. We counted about 400 tepees in a half mile circle and the place swarms with redskins and dogs while the hills are alive with horses.*
>
> *The great dance and battle was to be today and of course we staid over to see it. The scene was indescribable and so full of interest and novelty. Imagine a circle of 500 stalwart bucks dressed in every conceivable color and pattern of paint and ornamented with feathers and bells and queer skins and beads and shells and all the bright things they could ever get hold of. An orchestra consisting of big drums and rattles pounded by old men and a monotonous*

chant by thousands of old men, squaws, and all the gang, the decorated bucks dancing and hopping and running about in the circle as they sing or whoop and yell. Fights on foot and on horses with much shooting of blank cartridges and scalping of fallen victims and then the capture and distribution of spoils—blankets and horses. The whole show, though absurd in some respects, is "immense" and beats Buffalo Bill's Wild West out of sight.

The feature to me most interesting was the dresses and ornaments and saddles and hundreds of things I had never seen before.[7]

Alongside such adventures to write home about, Bailey's connection with Florence Merriam, sister to his boss, continued to grow, albeit subtly, with the good doctor's assistance. Merriam wrote to Bailey, then working out of Red Lodge, Montana, on July 27 informing him that Florence had gone from Twin Oaks to Flagstaff where she intended to go to a Mrs. Marshall's ranch to board. Reflecting on their time together in this region, Merriam commented, "Wish we could take a ride with her and point out a few hundred fine things to see."[8]

A month later, on August 23, he acknowledged Bailey's response to a copy of Miss Merriam's first published book,

Gratified to know you had so much pleasure from Florence's little book. It certainly is a good book—written with the proper spirit.

Now I have a disappointment for you as well as myself. You are not likely to see me in the field this year. I am pretty well, and doing a lot of work. So long as I can stand it and so much unfinished work remains ahead, I can hardly afford to leave. At all events I can't get away much if any before the middle of Sept. Then it will be too late to join you and I may take a hasty trip to Arizona and make the section we have so long wanted to make—from Phoenix to Prescott.

Winter will set in early in Montana and you will have to be thinking of a place to winter your outfit, as it will be clearly impossible to finish the Mary's Lake-Chief Mt. and Flathead country this fall. We will have to finish that job in the spring and then cross over to Oregon somehow.[9]

In his inimitable way, Merriam did manage to get away from Washington after all, heading immediately for Arizona. It was then October, and along the way he wrote to Bailey at Ann Arbor on October 4, where the latter had enrolled at the University of Michigan. Merriam informed Bailey that his gopher bulletin had not yet gone to press and likely would not before the end of the year.[10] He wrote to Bailey again three days later after his arrival in Flagstaff, informing him that Florence was doing pretty well and that the two of them were headed for fieldwork in the Flagstaff region. He talked about riding through the magnificent pines and reflected on the wildlife that he and Bailey had seen when they worked in the region five years earlier. He closed the letter with the comment that "Florence sends regards."[11]

About a week later, Bailey wrote his brother Charles who apparently was trying to decide between attending Michigan or the University of Minnesota. Bailey leaves little doubt about his recommendation on this matter as he described his course work and teachers at Michigan:

Dear Charles, I did not want to write to you until I had found out as much as possible about the courses & could judge of the advantages and disadvantages of the U. of M. Now I can begin to form opinions.

I am taking the following lines of work:

German, course 1, 4 hours a week, Prof. McLouth;
English, courses 1,5, & 10, 5 hours a week, Prof. Strauss, Heupel, Densmore;
Elocution, course 1, 2 hours a week, Prof. Trueblood;
Elements of Biology, course 1, 5 hours a week, Prof. Worcester & Johnson.

Am working at Latin a little by myself & will try & get some one to help me soon.

The course is not entirely satisfactory to me. McLouth is good in German, extra good I think, but there are 50 or more in the class & each student gets in a few words of recitation once in 2 or 3 days. In nothing else are recitations so important as in languages. The worst fault to be found is in my most important study, in English, course 1,—paragraph writing. Strauss is not master of the subject & is not a skillfull teacher. The class work does not amount to much. He has not returned any of the written work yet, so I do not know how he is as a critic, but I am much afraid he is NG. If he proves a failure I shall try to get into some other course. Trueblood is good in elocution. Densmore & Heupel are OK, but these are minor branches. My biological work is the most interesting of all and of the best practical importance. I enjoy it & like both the professors, especially Worcester. I am doing microscopic work on the lowest forms of animal life, began on the amoeba.

I begin to realize the disadvantage of a large institution. All of my classes are large—50 to 100. I do not believe there is any actual advantage here over the U. of Minn. The men with whom I am in contact with are not famous or great. The buildings & apparatus are apparently no better than at Minn. I believe that the only advantage I gain in coming here is in the name *& in the standing among the few with whom I work. My entrance fees were $60.00.*

As much as I should like to have you here this winter I would not urge you to come here instead of to Minneapolis. The law & medical schools are probably ahead of those of Minn.[12]

Continuing to encourage the friendship, Merriam noted in his next letter, written on October 21, that "Florence said she wanted to send you a note when I wrote next, but as she is not here I'll not wait. Very glad you like your work and have so good a start, but fear you are taking too much to handle it to advantage. You remember you used to tell me to be careful 'not to bite off more than I could chew'!"[13] Apparently, this was in reference to Bailey's decision to attend the university, and take a full course load, while at the same time continuing his professional work at the Survey.

Anna has now become his family reporter, and keeps Bailey in touch with their doings, as well as her own. Bicycles are all the rage, and she is among those who benefit, writing to him in October that:

now that I have a chance to leave baby. I am glad you have a wheel. I am sure the pleasure of riding it will tempt you out more than if you were to walk. The more enjoyable the exercise the more good it does, I think, when it is our mind that needs rest. . . . I wish you could have seen how happy father was over the wool business. He found it was going to make Chel and Charl join in the work, and do them all good and he is satisfied. It has done mother and all the rest so much good![14]

Trusting his judgment in evaluating traps, Palmer wrote him in Ann Arbor on February 12 requesting that he test some traps while taking his courses. "I sent you by mail today 10 traps of a new style called the 'sensible' mouse trap. We should like to have you try them, especially for shrews, to see whether you think they are equal to the cyclone trap. If they prove successful after a thorough trial we shall obtain a quantity for the use of our field agents."[15]

As another Thanksgiving approached, Bailey heard from his father who becomes a bit wistful. He didn't write often, but when he did, it was usually thought provoking and philosophical. He stirs his son to think more deeply about life, perhaps stirred himself by Vernon's own life. His limitation with words is less than he thinks, and the meaning more than makes up for it. Writing on November 18, he says:

> *Ma is writing and I want to write some too, but don't know how to express my thoughts in words. Do you think we ever think without words, I think we do. Now I think that study is a grand thing and the more the mind is expanded by learning the easier it will grasp new subjects. But the elements always seem the hardest, as learning the alphabet and spelling and the multiplication table, but they are necessary steps before we can see the light they lead us to. I think you are finding some of your studies elementary. But I suppose if a child could commence with the right studies and follow from one study to another that their minds are prepared for by their previous studies as first spelling than reading, arithmetic, and so on through the higher branches for 15 years they could accomplish more with the same labor that you can in the desultory way you have had to work for your education. And no doubt if you could have stayed in Minneapolis this winter and had Uncle John to have helped you, you would have accomplished more than you can there, but would not have the name of a great college. But what you do learn will not be lost if you should never go any farther, as it will help you to think clearer it seems to me.*[16]

The year ends, and another begins. The pattern sets new directions for Bailey. His letters to his family after about 1895 are distinctly different from those of his early travels. They are chatty and newsy, describing landscapes, wildlife, flowers, the experiences of the season, but they lack the deep imaginative engagement with home. There is no longer a sharing of knowledge—of farming from the one side and science from the other. They are the letters not of a farmer naturalist on an adventure, but of a loving son making his way in the cosmopolitan world of professional science.[17]

30

From Sermons in the Woods to Marital Bliss (1895–1899)

Always there to wave him on, Mother Bailey joined in the imagery so meaningful to her son as she shared his delight at college success. Writing to him on February 24, 1895, she exclaimed: "I am glad you passed . . . and if you need to be more perfect in any of your studies you can do it afterwards. You will soon be thinking of migrating now and I expect to see you in your flight."[1]

Bailey responded in kind, early the next month, sharing the loveliness of an early spring Sunday morning in Michigan, writing on March 3 to his folks:

> *Have been out tramping for an hour and down to the PO. Didn't get any mail but brought back a lot of sumack bobs and other dry brush to stick up in my room and a pocket full of Marchantia to study in the lab tomorrow. Most everybody has gone to church. I get the best sermons in the woods, and there was a little music thrown in this morning. The Tree Sparrows were singing. I am anxious to see the flowers come out. Shall enjoy renewing old acquaintances.*[2]

False spring is often soon over, and a week later on March 10 he wrote:

> *A regular blizzard was howling. About 6 inches of snow fell and it has not all gone yet. I went out in the woods this morning but could not find a genuine spring bird. I shall watch the migration as much as possible this year, but can not be very regular about it. Saw a Chipmunk this morning. I wish you would all notice the first chipmunks, gophers, woodchucks, skunks and all mammals that come out of hibernation and keep notes for me. Anna, you ought to work a bird corner into the Star News during migration. You could stir up a lot of interest in it. Ask others to send their notes to you and let you edit them. If other country papers would take it up it would be very interesting.*[3]

In May, toward the end of the spring semester at Michigan, Bailey received a personal letter from Florence Merriam imploring him to get Merriam out of the office and into the field. Although it is very formally addressed, the letter shows Florence's trust and confidence in Vernon:

Dear Mr. Bailey:
I am very anxious to get my brother into the field, and I want your help.

He has been used up all winter to do any work, and it is worse than folly for him to stay here through another summer in the vain hope of being able to pick up threads then. He would accomplish nothing by it and only unfit himself for next winter's work. He confesses that he can hardly endure the thought of even another month at his desk, he is so worn out.

Now will you help me by writing him—of course you will not answer this or "let on" that I have given you this hint—just write him a warm personal letter saying just what I know you feel about wanting him to be with you this summer, and putting in an earnest word or two of sound common sense about his work—the kind one man will take from another.

I shall be personally grateful. Sincerely yours,
Florence A. Merriam[4]

There is little in Bailey's family or professional correspondence about his experience at the University of Michigan or his intention to return. It seems likely that at his age the drudgery of basic courses required to complete an undergraduate degree, compared to what he was learning in the field and under Merriam's tutelage in Washington, convinced him that the cost and effort were not worth the reward. So, when the school term ended the next week, he quickly headed for the field, carrying official orders from the Department of Interior, issued on May 9, to visit the Blackfoot and Flathead Indian reservations, in the state of Montana, for the purpose of making a survey of the reservations. The agents and employees of the Indian service were instructed to facilitate his work.[5]

This was followed the next day by a letter from Merriam more fully outlining the work for that field season, which was to start at Blackfoot, Montana, where they had left off last fall. He was informed that Mr. Arthur H. Howell of Brooklyn, New York, was to serve as his assistant and would meet him at Blackfoot on May 16. The letter also reflected the growing confidence Merriam had developed in Bailey's work and judgment. Accordingly, he told Bailey, "it is not necessary for me to do more than outline where you left off last fall.

All details are left to you. . . . Take time enough to work the country pretty thoroughly so that we shall not have to go there again."[6]

With his papers and instructions in hand, Bailey immediately contacted the Indian Agent, George Steel, requesting permission to collect specimens of birds and mammals on the Blackfoot Reservation and to camp with his party, which included two assistants, four horses and himself. At the bottom of the request the reply was penned and duly signed on May 15, "the permission asked for is hereby granted."[7]

Less formal and more to the point was the note home soon afterward, written on June 9, "Our feet are sore. It is either gout or else chilblains from wading in the snow in thin shoes. Probably the latter."[8]

Merriam was pleased with the progress of the work. In uncharacteristic words of praise, he told Bailey how he felt, providing this accolade in his letter of June 27: "Your collection from St. Marys Lake is one of the most interesting ever received from a single locality. Your mammal report is unusually full and correspondingly interesting."[9]

At the end of July, sore feet notwithstanding, a hotel bed takes even more getting used to as he wrote to his family on July 23:

> *I am sitting in a chair and writing on a table. Am in a room in a hotel, feel strange and out of place. The change is so sudden I shall probably not be able to write much. Had to leave the outfit and come down here to catch a Perognathus, a little pocket-mouse that was caught somewhere around here and described and never seen again. My reputation depends on unearthing this mouse. It may take me a week or two and I may not get it then. Shall make a great effort. . . . This is not a trip that I enjoy. . . .*
>
> *Believe I promised to tell you something about the famous Flathead Valley. We have seen it about all and it contains better land than I supposed. There is a great deal of good farming country around Columbia Falls and Kalispell. They do not have to irrigate and crops look good but no better than we can raise all over Sherburne Co. They can't raise corn and fruit raising is still a doubtful experiment. But do not imagine that this is government land or cheap land. That part of the valley is settled as thickly and farmed as closely to the prairies between Anoka and Minneapolis. Farms are valuable and not for sale. There is vacant land back in the foothills and timber. We found lots of people starting to clear up farms that are covered with splendid looking but valueless pine and spruce and tamarack and saw them working in fields full of stumps from 5 to 8 feet across, stumps that will stand there for 20 years.*[10]

Merriam's determination was rarely in doubt, and certainly not this summer. He wrote to Bailey on August 14 that he would not be joining him in the field that season:

> *For 8 months I had no time for mammal work. Now I give more than half of each day to it. Can I afford to lose the chance to go on? I am reasonably well, so far as staying here is concerned, but cannot ride horseback until after I have another operation done—a slight one, but I want to put it off till cold weather. So I have concluded to stay & make hay while the sun shines, for I know from experience that it don't always shine.*[11]

Apparently, he was not going to listen to his sister, or Bailey, and take some time off.

Ever the critic, Merriam wrote to Bailey again nine days later criticizing the manner in which he had submitted his reports, noting that the same mistake had occurred before:

> *Your letter of the 17th instant from Spokane is just received, together with several reports and two boxes of specimens. The latter have not yet been unpacked. In looking over your reports I am deeply grieved to find that you have again combined two states in one report, namely, the report from Thompson to Coeur d'Alene. You made a solemn promise last year that you would never do this again, and I am at a loss to know what punishment to inflict.*[12]

When the field season ended, Bailey returned to Washington, writing to his folks on December 1, 1895, about spending Thanksgiving

> *as pleasant as usual here. I helped the Merriams eat their turkey and spent a very pleasant evening with them and the Gannets, playing caboush (if that is the way to spell it. It is like dominos with cards.) Mrs. M.[erriam] is already planning a lot of pleasant things for Christmas, so you see I am not entirely among strangers. If it was not for the Merriams and Covilles and a few other friends here I might find it easier to break away from my work and join you on the farm. As it is I employ my winters here full as well as the less civilized life in the field.*[13]

Shrews continued to fascinate Bailey, and he finally succeeded in taking the first specimen of *Sorex personatus* in the vicinity of Washington. He wrote up the account in an article, "List of Mammals of the District of Columbia," published in the *Proceedings of the Biological Society of Washington* in February 1896. His species account of *S. personatus* reads as follows:

> This tiny Long-tailed shrew is one of the rarest mammals of the region. It has not yet been taken within the District of Columbia, though no doubt it occurs in very limited numbers in some of the swamps. In the mammal collection of Dr. Merriam there is a much-damaged specimen, picked up in a path near Sandy Springs, Maryland, some years ago. During February of the present year (1896) I succeeded in catching three of these shrews in a sphagnum swamp near Hyattsville, 5 miles northeast of the Capital, but even in this semi-boreal swamp they seem to be scarce and are difficult to secure. Thorough and unsuccessful trapping for them in various localities about Washington proves to my own satisfaction that they do not inhabit the uplands.[14]

Soon the writing and the local mammals were left aside for another summer in the field, this time in Oregon. Merriam's instructions, written on May 5, 1896, included working the boundary between Idaho and Wyoming to ascertain what connection, if any, exists between the sage plains of the Green River basin and those of the Snake River basin of eastern Idaho. He specifically instructed Bailey to collect chipmunks (genus *Tamias*) in the Green River basin of Idaho and Wyoming, and then to head to Elgin, Oregon, to conduct a thorough series of experiments in killing pocket gophers and ground squirrels with bisulphide. After completing the experiments, he was to proceed westward with his outfit along the north base of the Blue Mountains as far as the Deschutes Valley, where he was to turn south and then east, toward Harney and Malheur Lakes, at which time Merriam would connect with him by mail at Prineville and other post offices from time to time. The instructions concluded with an explanation of the importance of the trip:

> *As you know, the special object of this trip is to ascertain the boundaries of the several life zones in Oregon, for the purpose of completing our biological map of the United States. You will therefore make this work your principal object throughout the season. Clark P. Streator, another Field Naturalist of this Department, has been sent north from Pyramid Lake into Oregon with an independent wagon outfit to assist in this work. He will be subject to your instructions. E. A. Preble of this Division will be detailed as your assistant, and will join you before you leave Elgin.*[15]

About a month later, on June 9, he received another letter from Merriam, sent to him in Oregon, about new federal regulations that just passed Congress regarding the mail that would affect their ability to ship specimens from the field to headquarters. The bill absolutely prohibited, without exception, the sending of mail in packages exceeding four pounds in weight. Because it meant a large increase in charges for express mail, Bailey was instructed to see that packages weighing more than four pounds were not to be mailed by him or anyone under his charge, and that smaller specimens had to be sent in small boxes. Large specimens were to be sent by express, and he was told to ship everything he possibly could before leaving Heppner.[16] This was just another of many bureaucratic hurdles that made fieldwork so difficult!

In the now familiar pattern, summer passed and winter found Bailey again in Washington. He had a chance to attend the American Ornithologists Union (AOU) meetings in Cambridge, Massachusetts, and enjoyed a look at Boston by bicycle. He described the experience in this letter to his family written on November 16, 1896:

> *Between [AOU] meetings I took bicycle rides about the old historic grounds around Cambridge and Boston and spent a good many hours in the museum, the public library and the art galleries. Cambridge is one of the most interesting and pleasant old towns I ever saw. The houses are built for comfort and are mostly rather unique in style. Wide yards full of trees and bushes give the town a pleasant country air. The grounds and buildings of Harvard College are the best of the kind I have seen. No wonder Harvard students are enthusiastic over their college. But the best of all was meeting lots of interesting people, among our naturalists.*[17]

In 1897 Bailey began an activity that would continue throughout the remainder of his life—working with young boys to teach them about the work of naturalists and the importance of natural history. On March 3, he received a brief note from William Derring, the director of the Boys Program at Pro-Cathedral church of St. Mark in Washington, DC, about his forthcoming talk, to be delivered the following Monday evening, about mammals and the study of nature. Derring exclaimed that "the boys were really very much interested and pleased with what you had to say at your last visit; and I believe that we will find that your little talks are really profitable to the boys."[18]

The following summer, Merriam planned an extensive field trip into the

North Cascades of Washington state. The outline he sent to Bailey on July 9, 1898, reads once again like an adventure tale:

> *Dear Bailey, Since writing you last my plans have become a little more defined. I am likely to leave here on the 16th and proceed direct to Spokane by the Great Northern. From Spokane I go to Lewiston, for which trip I suppose two days ought to be allowed, possibly 3. I then go direct to North Yakima, where I want you to meet me with a pack outfit about July 24. The only practicable way by which we can reach Paradise Park from the east, I am told, is to go from North Yakima west through Cowlitz Pass with a pack outfit, going by way of Longmire's Spring. . . .*
>
> *What to do with the buckboard outfit while we are gone on the Rainier and Olympic Mts. pack trip is difficult to decide. . . . Pack outfits are required for three trips—Mt. Ranier, the Olympics, and Mt. Baker. Pack outfits are extremely difficult to obtain on the west side of the Cascade, I am informed, so that it may not be possible to work two camps simultaneously as I had hoped.*
>
> *It may be necessary for us to take our pack outfit from Rainier through to the Olympics, and thence north through Skagit Valley to Mt. Baker, and thence east over Cascade pass to Lake Chelan. This would consume the whole summer, and would probably bring us into the Mount Baker country after the fall rains have set in. However, we can arrange details later.*[19]

Merriam's instructions illustrate the logistical difficulties of fieldwork prior to the availability of automobiles and good highways to facilitate rapid travel.

The Cascade trip was successful in producing large numbers of specimens and in resolving the life zone map for that region of the country. On returning to Washington time was productively spent working up the material and adjusting the maps. Bailey spent most of the following year, 1898, back in Washington where he stayed at the Merriam's home. His shyness about social occasions, especially when the Whist Club was in the house, comes across in this weekly letter to his family begun on December 11, 1898:

> *Things are going quietly and pleasantly here. My new quarters are delightful. I do not go out much. Haven't been to a theater or opera yet. Have been to church today and heard a pretty good sermon by Mr. Leavett, a Unitarian. I rather like the man. His views are broad and practical.*
>
> *Now it is Monday evening and the Whist Club is here—downstairs. There are 16 wimmen and now (at 11 PM) their husbands have come for them and the chatter and jabber coming up the stairway reminds me of a crows roost*

or the coots in Rice Lake. I refused to go down, even for the refreshments, though I know all of the people but a very few. I have been with them several times and always find myself very stupid among a lot of gossips, so prefer to stay in my den and write to you. . . .

Sunday, Dec. 17 . . . Christmas is almost here and I am not doing anything for anybody. The Merriams have invited a cousin from NY and Miss Florence will be here in a few days, so we will have a pleasant Christmas.[20]

The next spring on March 20, 1899, he received his long-awaited instructions from James Wilson, secretary of agriculture, to proceed with the biological survey of Texas. The orders called for him to proceed on April 1, under instructions from Merriam, from Washington to such points in the states of Texas and California as required to carry on the fieldwork of the Biological Survey. His railroad transportation, not to exceed two hundred dollars, was to be paid by the department from the appropriation for "Biological Investigations, 1899."[21]

And during that summer a long-kept secret comes out. Overjoyed at his good fortune, he let his family in on the news. Yet in the telling, nowhere does he mention the name of his intended! Perhaps they already knew, or could guess from the references dropped for so long. Writing from his summer headquarters in northern California, on October 3, after traveling over much of Texas, he coyly admits to his family:

I have been trying to keep a secret all summer. Have I succeeded? But I can't keep it any longer. I have a message to deliver. Other people are finding it out and I wouldn't have you hear it first from someone else. I wanted to wait till I came home so I could tell you what a noble, sweet souled woman has promised to be my wife. It is worth all the lonely years I've waited to know such a soul, such love at last.

So you see I will not be able to stay at home this winter, nor very long, because I want to go up to Locust Grove on my way back to stay a few days.

In spite of the weary letters I have written you when tired, for the summer's work has been hard, it has been the happiest summer I have known, and now I am getting well rested again. You can begin to look for me by Oct. 15 but I will write to let you know when I can tell closer to the date. I don't want to surprise you, so I am breaking the news gradually and don't want to waste any time, because I shall not have long to stay—scarcely a week perhaps and there will be much to talk of.

Can you see anything in this picture for a girl to admire? It reminds me of the "rough, ragged rascal that ran round the rocks."

I go to Sisson tomorrow and in a few days to San Francisco and then home. A letter might catch me at San Francisco but probably not. I shall probably hear from you again when I see you and that will be soon as possible.

A Merry Christmas to you all.[22]

Given the close relationship between Bailey and Merriam, it is not surprising that their friendship extended rather naturally to Merriam's sister, Florence. There is every indication that Merriam himself strongly encouraged their friendship and growing relationship that intensified in the 1890s as Bailey spent time out west where Florence was recovering from a serious bout with tuberculosis. In the summer of 1898, Florence served as a field assistant in Merriam's expedition to Mount Shasta, California. Bailey was also a member of that party, and they spent time together in the field and began to develop a deep fondness for each other.

On November 2, 1899, Bailey received a long letter from his close friend, Basil Hicks Dutcher, now a lieutenant and assistant surgeon in the US Army stationed in the Philippines. His purpose in writing is to congratulate Bailey on his forthcoming marriage scheduled for the following month. Dutcher's words express his strong satisfaction with their union:

I do not know of anyone more deserving of a fate more kind, nor do I on the other hand know of a kinder fate that Florence has to bestow. While I of course did not become as thoroughly or as completely acquainted with her beauty of character as you have, the little that I did see of her made us good friends, and infused me deeply with an appreciation of the kindness of her heart, the beauty of her spirit, and the depth of her mind. I trust that you will not regard these words as unthinkingly spoken, but as the true and mature expression of an event of so great importance in the life of the best friend that I have.[23]

On December 16, 1899, Florence Augusta Merriam and Vernon Orlando Bailey were married in Washington, DC, thirty-six and thirty-five years of age, respectively. The announcement the next day in the paper simply read:

Bailey—Merriam

The marriage of Miss Florence Augusta, daughter of Hon. C. L. Merriam of Locust Grove to Mr. Vernon Bailey occurred Saturday at Washington. Mrs. Bailey has gained renown in her writings on the birds and Mr. Bailey is a well known scientist. They have heartiest congratulations and best wishes for their future happiness.[24]

At first glance the marriage of Florence and Vernon seemed like an odd arrangement given their divergent backgrounds—Bailey being from a frontier setting, with limited education and worldly experiences, and Florence from a highly sophisticated and upper middle-class family. What could a government scientist like Vernon Bailey offer to Miss Merriam? His modest pay was little more than one hundred dollars a month at the time. But their union was to be a strong one that would last the remainder of their lives. According to Harriet Kofalk, Florence's biographer, they shared the most important priority—love of nature, and the enthusiasm and need to share that love with others. She loved the West with an enthusiasm equal to his own. And she was eager to discover more of it with him. Florence's grandniece put it simply, "Vernon was perfect for her, a very simple gentlemen. She fussed over details he wouldn't have. Vernon was outgoing and everyone adored him. Auntie Florence basked in his glory."[25]

31

Safe and Wild in Texas (1900–1905)

A few months after their marriage, the two newlyweds headed for the American Southwest on a field trip for their honeymoon. From April to September, they traveled, first by train to Texas where they studied the wildlife along the Mexican border and then into the territory of New Mexico.

Merriam considered Texas a keystone state for understanding the distribution of mammals and life zones. Eastern and western, as well as northern and southern, faunas intermingled there with many species reaching their distributional limits. Previously, several field agents of the Biological Survey, including Bailey, had worked in the state for brief periods. But Texas was not easy to work because of its extensive size, relatively poor infrastructure in its western regions, and harsh climate. But, after his marriage, beginning in 1900, Bailey was detailed to work in the state for the next four years. These trips, and others to New Mexico, with Florence his companion on occasion, produced some of Bailey's most memorable adventures and challenges.

Both of the newlyweds looked forward to the companionship of exploring the Southwest together. Bailey told his family in his weekly letter of March 11, 1900: "In about 3 weeks we will be in Texas if all goes smoothly. We are anticipating the trip with as much pleasure as if it was our first journey and without the feeling of starting off for a lonely summer. I hope Florence can stay with me till we both go on to Calif.[ornia]"[1] What would prevent that goes unsaid. Perhaps it was her health, always tenuous in spite of the rigor of outdoor life she so enjoyed.

From April to September they traveled, first by train to Texas where they studied mammals and birds along the Mexican border and then into the Territory of New Mexico. In writing to her brother, Florence recalled her earlier trips west:

How thankful I am not to be coming back to it alone! But all the years of loneliness and wandering, which have been brought back so vividly by the misery of the poor "lungers" alone on the train, seem now a part of another existence, for all the pain and weariness of my life have gone, and it is filled with peace and happiness. It seems now almost wicked to be so happy when the world is full of sorrow.[2]

After New Mexico they went on to California for more fieldwork as well as a visit to Twin Oaks, where she introduced her new husband to her Uncle Gustavus and his family. They stayed at La Mesita, the home that her father had built.

In her annual letter to her Smith College classmates, Florence described the summer of her honeymoon as follows: "My husband and I spent three months in Texas doing Biological Survey field work, and made an intensely interesting wagon trip across the prairies to the Mexican line. Then we crossed over to California and spent three months more with a pack outfit in the high Sierra."[3]

On his return to Washington, Bailey was among three scientists—L. O. Howard and T. S. Palmer were the other two—chosen to present public lectures, sponsored by the Trustees of the Public Schools of the District of Columbia, on the "Adaptations of Animals to Their Environment." Bailey's lecture was titled "Mammals in Relation to Environment."[4]

While in Washington, ensconced in various projects, the newly married couple made a big decision—to build a house in Washington where they would continue to spend at least most winters for the rest of their lives. The work got off to a slow start, with "rains and tardy materials" to blame, but by June 1901, Mrs. Bailey wrote to her sister-in-law Anna Mills that

a gang of men is to go to work tomorrow and we hope will get ahead well in the next few weeks.

I have been working night and day on my book trying to get it where I could leave it, and I have succeeded so well that I am actually hoping that I may be able to join Vernon next month.

Vernon is having such an interesting and enjoyable trip. Mr. Fuertes he finds an admirable camp companion with a deep appreciation of all the beautiful and grand things they see—a real enthusiasm for it all. He is a bright jolly fellow, full of a boy's nonsense and fun so that he will be a rest to Vernon.

> *The desert appeals to Vernon, you know, the wonderful desert ranges with their "atmosphere" and marvelous color effects—and all the bigness and mildness of it. He enjoys it intensely.*
>
> *I can hardly wait to go to him! You know what good fun it all is! We had such an ideal summer last year that it seems too good to be true that I am even hoping to go.*
>
> *He really needs someone to take care of him. He and Mr. Fuertes took a trip the other day where they were out 26 hours without food. They started with two biscuits apiece, and after eating them climbed so far they had to stay all night and 26 hours after 2 biscuits! Don't you think he needs a guardian? I scolded him properly.*
>
> *If I go it will be somewhere about the middle of July, as soon as the house is ready.*[5]

Their home was built at 1834 Kalorama Road, located between Eighteenth Street and Columbia Road. The meager but comfortable home would become a mecca for naturalists of all breeds and varieties. The dinner parties held there became legendary in the scientific community as well as with visitors. According to one account, "No one who ever visited that home in the old days will forget it; for it was the home of two devoted naturalists—devoted to nature and to each other—and every room, every nook and corner, was a testimonial to that devotion. It was a place where many kindred souls foregathered."[6]

Their home contained a unique showpiece on the panel of the library fireplace—a portrait of a fine Bengal tiger then living in the National Zoological Park, painted in repose by the famous wildlife muralist Charles R. Knight. In 1949, Mrs. Bailey bequeathed the picture to the Smithsonian Institution where it is now permanently deposited in the Smithsonian American Art Museum.

Bailey's 1901 spring trip into the Big Bend region would become legendary for its adventure and the risks that naturalists take while doing their work. Bailey was the expedition leader, Henry Church Oberholser was the ornithologist, and Louis Agassiz Fuertes went along to collect and paint birds. The adventure began on May 27 with Vernon Bailey in camp at the mouth of Tornillo Creek while Oberholser and Fuertes left for an early hunt along the Rio Grande. Apparently, Fuertes had sighted a rare zone-tailed hawk and was attempting to collect it, as recorded by natural historians Stanley Casto and Horace Burke in an unpublished manuscript:

The two men separated with Fuertes hunting along the canyon hoping to see the zone-tailed Hawk while Oberholser moved away from the river to hunt on the mesa. Fuertes soon found and shot the hawk, which lodged on the cliff face as it fell. Fuertes then descended by a side gulch onto the floor of the canyon and began to climb upward to retrieve his prize. At a point some 100 feet below the rim and several hundred feet from the bottom, he found that further ascent was impossible because of overhanging rocks and that it was equally impossible to descend because he could not see to secure footholds below. Realizing that he was trapped, Fuertes fired his gun and began to shout for help. Oberholser, who was already looking for him, heard his cries and soon arrived at the canyon where he peered over the edge to see his friend on a narrow ledge. Assuring Fuertes that we would return with help, Oberholser rushed back to camp greeting Bailey with the exclamation "Get all the ropes in camp. Fuertes is up on a cliff and can't get down or up." The two men gathered about 150 feet of picket ropes and hastened to the canyon, which was about a mile away. The ropes were quickly tied together and one end secured to a stout catsclaw bush while the other was thrown over the rim and swung back and forth until it could be reached by Fuertes and looped around his leg. Then, while Bailey and Oberholser pulled on the rope, Fuertes, with the prized hawk stuffed in his shirt, swung from ledge to ledge on the cliff face until he was finally hauled to the top.[7]

But the adventure was just beginning, as Castro and Burke described:

On June 8th, Bailey and Fuertes made their first excursion into the high country of the Chisos Mountains in what today is Big Bend National Park. Their destination was Plateau Mountain, one and a quarter miles southeast of Emory Peak and six miles distant from the base camp. At 1:30 in the afternoon they picketed their horses, ate their biscuits and bacon and began their climb onto the mountain. So intent were the two men on exploring the mountain that the sun had set before they got back to their horses, and they were forced to spend the night in a small cave. Their food was gone, and the cave was later referred to as "starvation camp." At daylight they arose and hunted for food but without success. Preoccupied by hunger they began their descent from the mountain and reached the horses just before noon. Arriving at the base camp in Pine Springs in the early afternoon, they eagerly gorged themselves on food.

Bailey was so intrigued by Plateau Mountain that two days later he departed for a second trip to that location, instructing Fuertes and Oberholser to meet him at "starvation camp" on the following day. Packing two days rations, the two naturalists left on June 12th to meet Bailey. However, upon arriving at the cave they found that Bailey was not there, but had left a note directing them to meet him at a location just across the ridge. They crossed the ridge and found Bailey at a cool spring where he had killed a buck. On the following morning (13th), Bailey packed the deer meat (about 50 pounds) off the mountain to the base camp. The meat was loaded on Bailey's horse, and Bailey rode Fuertes' mare "Fannie" back to Pine Canyon.[8]

As if that wasn't enough:

> The group left Pine Canyon on the morning of June 16th and arrived at Dugout Wells at about 5:00 that afternoon. It was soon discovered that a bag containing 60 pounds of deer meat had fallen off the wagon somewhere along the trail, and Bailey set out on "Fiddlesticks" to recover the meat. The meat was eventually found, and Bailey returned to camp about 10:30 that night. However, during his absence, Fuertes' mare "Fannie" and the mule, "Tobin," had strayed away from camp and could not be found. . . . Determined to find the missing animals, Bailey ordered Surber [the camp hand and cook] to saddle "Baylor," the pack mule. Upon being mounted the mule began to buck, and Bailey was thrown from the saddle and knocked senseless. Although bleeding from the head and neck, Bailey assured the men that he was okay. Bailey was then carried to his bed where he slowly regained senses with the aid of some of the "critter" [Old Crow? Wild Turkey?] provided by Fuertes. He was soon able to recall events up to the point where he was bucked off the mule but never remembered anything about what came later. It was nearly five days before the missing livestock was found.[9]

The next part of the trip was equally exciting, as chronicled by Bailey himself:

> Our next camp was at the lower end of the Grand Canyon of the Rio Grande [Santa Elena Canyon], where the river comes out between 2000 foot walls of black lava rock, a cut a little wider at the top than the bottom with many curves where the sun had never shown. The home of black phoebes and cliff swallows. The only way to get into the canyon

is at the upper or lower ends and we were camped as close to the lower end as we could get our camp wagon.

Early next morning Louis and I took our guns and traps and started up the river which was at low water that left shoves and shelves first on one side & then the other. Soon we had to cache our guns and traps and all of our clothes except shoes so we could swim from one side to the other when we came to sheer walls above and below the water but we kept going until long after noon. Toward night we were well up to the deepest and darkest part of the canyon but we knew we could make better time on the return.

On a high bank behind a sheer point we found old drift logs of cottonwood, worn to polished skeletons of trees from long days of beating the rocks in flood time. Some were 50 feet above the water and may have been there for many years. They were light and dry and it did not take us long to get a couple just right & float us in the swift current and each riding our "broncho" log in the swirling waters or lying flat and steering with both hands and feet like some prehistoric amphibians, we shot the rapids and dodged the rocks, paddled through the big swirls and in little over an hour covered the return trip to our clothes and guns and traps.

We guess we had been 12 miles up the canyon in about 8 hours and had come back at most of the way at racehorse speed.

There was still time to set traps and collect birds and get a few pictures and again we had good appetites for a hearty camp supper.

We left the Rio Grande with regrets as we had only skimmed the surface of the rare and interesting birds and mammals, reptiles, plants and insects of that blazing hot and fascinating valley.[10]

The trip continued into the Davis Mountains and New Mexico where more adventure awaited the naturalists, and Bailey was joined by Florence at Carlsbad where they talked with Fuertes about providing illustrations for her book on the birds of New Mexico. After Fuertes departed, the newlyweds headed to the Guadalupe Mountains, where Bailey wrote to his family from the head of Dog Canyon, in what today is Guadalupe Mountain National Park, on August 7, 1901:

This is Sunday morning and Florence says I can't do any work today—nothing harder than writing letters. But tomorrow we are going over the ridge into the head of a big canyon where there are lots of band tailed pigeons,

Microtus, and bears. It is a hard climb on foot and horseback, so I don't care if we rest today.

Wish you could see our little wickiup here under the nut pines and junipers. We are up at 6800 feet in the head of a wide canyon where we can look out over the whole world—at least over a whole valley and half a range of Mts. The valley is beautiful, with green grass and trees and the Mts. are just one everlasting great ridge.

We feel very safe and wild here, for this was the last stronghold of the Mescalero Apaches, where they came with stolen horses and cattle and what few scalps they could gather among distant ranches and ate beef and enjoyed a high old time up to 20 years ago. This valley was the farthest point from everywhere and the trails were rough and long and water was scarce and the good springs were covered up by the Indians so the poor soldiers on the trail usually got lost and often died of thirst and general stupidity long before they reached this valley. When they (the soldiers) did finally get in here, led by an old timer who told us about it around the camp fire the other night the Apaches fired a few shots among them and skipped out through a side canyon and scattered among the desert mountains.

Our tent stands almost over the old Apache trail leading out to west and we get water from a natural tank in the limestone gulch where the Indians have camped for ages. The ground is strewn with flint chips and broken (and a few good) arrow heads and pieces of broken pottery. There are little patches of corn and squashes growing now on rich bits of gulch bottom, planted by some prospectors on the ground where the Indians have raised corn and squashes long before white men saw the valley. But best of all the signs of savagery are hundreds of old mescal pits, where they roasted mescal—century plants—in pits just as you would burn charcoal, each pit 20 or 30 feet across and now appearing as a hollow topped mound with the rim of stones scraped back when the mound of delicious roasted mescal was uncovered. What a feast they must have had! We roasted some all night in the coals of our camp fire and in the morning found it like artichokes or sweet potatoes, but it should have been roasted 24 hours. . . .

The Indians are gone, all that remain of the tribe are on the Mescalero Reservation, 150 miles north of here, and they are tame. But the valley is very much as they left it. There is no water for ranches. One or two little seep springs supply the mining camp up above us and just now there is water enough in the tanks for us and our horses. Unless it rains soon we can't stay more than a week longer. There is splendid grass and many efforts have been made for water, but the mts. are tilted and the water drains back into them. . . .

But I have told you only about Injuns and nothing about ourselves and our little camp.

Two big junipers make a shady cover for the wagon and kitchen part of the camp and a few rods away our little tent stands under 3 nut pines and a juniper and gets shade all day and protection from wind and storm but gives a good outlook over the country. Just outside half under the branches of two of the pines our bough beds are well screened and sheltered but where we can see all the stars and constellations above us.[11]

The following year, 1902, began with a delay signing the appropriations bill, which in turn delayed their summer departure for Texas. No appropriations, no transportation. But springtime in Washington delighted them in their new home, an unexpected side benefit of the delay. Writing to his family in June, 1902, Bailey told them:

You probably think I am in Texas by this time but our appropriation bill is not yet signed so we can't get our transportation orders.

It has been so good to be here and see all the beautiful unfolding of a Washington spring, too, and enjoy our own little home together. The few minutes we can spend together in our garden among the weeds and grass and bushes, and the little plants that will someday be flowers, and admiring our beds of lettuce and spinach and radishes have been such a rest and happiness. We have our breakfasts out on the back piazza in the shade of the hickory tree and a meadowlark sings to us from the top of an old apple tree nearby, while the wood phoebe sits on the fence and calls to us.

The city is beautiful, such rows of trees and dense shade that you can ride for miles on a wheel and hardly get into the sunshine, and the parks are full of beautiful shrubs and flowers, some that I never saw before. I had no idea it was ever so nice. The weather has been pleasant so far and I hope it will not get hot for a month yet, until Florence can get away to a cooler region. We told you she was going up to Maine with the Dutchers, to Mt. Katahdin.[12]

Because the state of her health was unspoken, and in those days one didn't mention at all any childbearing difficulties, no record remains of what was at stake here. Speculation is either that her tuberculosis had flared up over the winter, or that she had a miscarriage. The Baileys were never able to have children, although the family knew that she had several miscarriages.[13]

Bailey headed to Texas shortly thereafter. Merriam's letter of instruction, sent on June 5, 1902, told him to proceed at once to Jefferson and begin fieldwork for the present season in continuation of the work previously conducted in Texas and the adjacent region. He was to be joined by Ned Hollister, and a little later by Merritt Cary and possibly one or two other assistants, to work under his supervision. Merriam's letter noted that the part of the state most in need of work at present is the eastern edge near the Louisiana boundary. After finishing there he was told to work along the edge of the mesquite area—along the boundary between the humid and semiarid parts of the state. He was told to de-emphasize work on birds as one of his assistants, H. C. Oberholser, would be giving special attention to them.[14]

Merriam reached him soon after his arrival in Jefferson to chide him about his writing. Bailey had recently submitted a rough draft of the "Fauna of Texas" to his boss, who responded, in a letter written on June 9:

> *It will stand a good deal of editing and elaboration. I have failed to find in it the description I hoped for of the boundaries of the zones and areas. It starts out on an unstated assumption. You know it isn't considered good form to begin a scientific treatise with an explanation of an unstated fact. For instance, you wouldn't begin an account of a wonderful dog by an explanation of why the dog had 1 red and 1 yellow eye, but would first tell the lie and then offer an explanation, wouldn't you?*[15]

That field season produced nothing particularly remarkable other than more specimens and documentation of wildlife in Texas, but Florence was able to complete her first notable book, *The Handbook of Birds of the Western United States*, which received considerable acclaim and later was to inspire Roger Tory Peterson to begin his own field guides, still renowned today.[16]

The next two summers, 1903 and 1904, found Bailey again in the field, covering Colorado, New Mexico, and Texas, reinforcing the workaholism and incredible stamina he maintained in his profession. In 1903, while A. K. Fisher served as acting chief in Merriam's absence, his orders called for him to give special attention to collecting data on the geographic distribution of birds, mammals, and plants, to working out the life areas of the country traversed, and whenever possible to take photographs of interesting plants and animals for use in illustrating reports.[17] The latter was a new opportunity that would open up a whole new dimension for his research work.

In his family, financial stress began to develop for Anna and her family back in Elk River, and he and Florence tried to help them out. A hint of the situation comes through in this postscript tucked in with a letter sent to Anna by Florence, written in 1903:

Anna, you are not to worry in the least about that money matter, for you are never to make any payment unless you can do it without the least inconvenience and should then feel that you would rather than not. The whole thing would not be a drop in the bucket on our debt and we could turn in other things and pay all we owe any day. As things stand now I would rather you would never think of paying anything on it. I am only too glad to have been able to help you get the start and you ought not to begrudge me that much pleasure.[18]

By the next season, in 1904, Merriam was back at the helm, sending his annual orders on July 2 instructing Bailey, as his chief naturalist, to continue his work mapping the life zones, this time in New Mexico where he was beginning a major faunal study. Merriam laid a very specific charge for him:

The chief object of your work will be to map the boundaries of the several life zones and minor faunal areas in New Mexico. In doing this you will keep careful records of the distribution of such trees, shrubs, mammals, birds and reptiles as you are able to make use of in the field, and will endeavor to secure such specimens as are likely to prove of value in working up the area. In addition to this work, you are expected to make observations concerning the availability for particular crops of the several life zones and areas of the region. You are expected also to ascertain as many facts as possible concerning the economic habits of mammals and birds in relation to agriculture, and whenever possible, to suggest means of dealing with noxious species. You are already so familiar with the details of the work allotted you that further instructions are unnecessary.[19]

In 1905 the first of the state faunal surveys prepared by Bailey appeared in print. The title page for the "Biological Survey of Texas" (*North America Fauna* No. 25) indicated it was authored by Vernon Bailey, Chief Field Naturalist, and prepared under the direction of C. Hart Merriam, Chief of the Biological Survey. The actual date of publication was October 24, 1905. In the annual report of the Survey to the Department of Agriculture, the publication was announced as follows:

A report on the life and crop zones, mammals, and reptiles of Texas, by Vernon Bailey, illustrated by a zone map of the State and numerous special maps, was published during the year. Full notes on the habits and relations of various mammals to agriculture in Texas, where such

> species as the coyote and prairie dog do enormous damage to farmers and stock raisers, are a feature of this report. Unfortunately the edition was so small that it was soon exhausted. It is hoped that it will be possible to issue a second edition of sufficient size to at least supply the demand from residents of the State.[20]

The quality of the Texas report received considerable praise, including from his colleague and friend, E. W. Nelson, who wrote, "Have looked over the Texas Fauna & consider it a fine piece of work & congratulate you on its completion. It is always good to get such a job on permanent record."[21] Given the many years that he had worked on the Texas fauna such a compliment had to make him feel good!

32

Wolves Dead and Alive (1906)

The year 1906 opened with a major budget crisis at the Survey. Because of a shortage in federal funding, they had run out of money to support fieldwork. Bailey wrote to Nelson in Mexico about the dilemma on January 15, offering to provide his own money, if necessary, so that the Mexico survey could be completed:

> *My dear Nelson:*
>
> *Henshaw has probably written you how we have come up against our picket rope. It is going to pinch all along the line & if I do any field work before July it will have to be entirely at my own expense. Some of the other fellows fare worse and will have to be furloughed. But one of the things we hate worse of all is to cut you & Goldman off when you are so near finishing your job. It seems a shame to have to give up & then go back such a distance when you are so near through. If there is any possibility of your scrimping along and finishing up without any more appropriation I will help stand the additional expense that it will throw on you and Goldman to the extent of $100 or if necessary $200. Of course I do not know just what work is ahead of you or whether you will think it worth while to try & finish it up in this way, but if you want to do it I shall be glad to help shoulder the load. I can send you $100 as soon as I hear from you and another $100 a month later. This is purely unofficial and without any red tape so do not hesitate to do as you please. I haven't any designs in keeping you down there (as Henderson might have) so don't get mad about it.*
>
> *You have been getting a fine lot of stuff but I shouldn't wonder if the camp dirt was getting pretty thick by this time. Wish I could trade places with you for awhile. We did not get into the field at all last summer & civilization is getting notorious.*
>
> *Guess you & Goldman will be glad to try a little civilization when you get a chance.*
>
> *Our best wishes and regards to you both. Sincerely yours,*
>
> *Vernon Bailey*[1]

In March 1906 Bailey was briefly transferred from the Survey to the Forest Service to assist with the wolf control program. The request came from Gifford Pinchot, head of the Forest Service, and was addressed to the secretary of agriculture:

> *I have the honor to request that Mr. Vernon Bailey, of the Biological Survey of the Department of Agriculture at a salary at the rate of Twenty-four Hundred Dollars ($2400) per annum, be transferred to the Forest Service, until further orders, at his present designation in the Biological Survey and salary . . . on March 15, 1906 to be paid from appropriation General Expense, Forest Service 1906. This transfer is requested in order that Mr. Bailey may undertake a study to determine methods for the extermination of wild animals which prey upon live stock in the forest reserves.*[2]

As a major landowner in the West, the federal government had come under pressure to help do its share to control noxious rodents and predators that farmers and ranchers felt were harming their operations and reducing their profits. In response, in 1905 the Forest Service began hiring trappers to kill wolves in the national forests.

A major part of Bailey's work for the Forest Service was to teach their trappers where the wolves lived and bred. Accordingly, he had spent the spring in Wyoming's upper Green River valley showing ranchers how to locate and dig out wolf dens. "Much interest in locating the dens was aroused among the ranchmen in the valley, first by personal intercourse and later by the distribution of publications," he explained.[3]

The Survey had taken an interest in this project in large part because Merriam saw in the issue a chance to reply to critics who claimed the agency was doing nothing practical. He spoke about the menace of coyotes and wolves, which "levy a heavy tax on stock . . . a loss generating several millions of dollars annually."[4]

The Survey hired David Lantz from Kansas to work on formulas and distribution equipment and to advise ranchers on the best way to get rid of "noxious animals." But Bailey was to be the man in the field working for the Forest Service.

In April came major news about career advancement, with Merriam informing him in Wyoming about the reorganization of the Survey and the role he would play in the new structure. Merriam's letter, written on April 3:

Dear Bailey:

With the approval of the Secretary, I have finally succeeded in reorganizing the Biological Survey along what I hope will prove to be rational lines. We have now established three divisions, or lines of investigation, on an equal footing, namely: Economic Investigations (comprising economic ornithology and mammalogy), under Doctor Fisher; Game Preservation under T. S. Palmer, as heretofore; Geographic Distribution under Vernon Bailey.

Owing to your present detail under the Forestry Service your appointment will not take effect until July 1, the others take effect on April 1. On the same date Henshaw was made Assistant Chief, and Nelson was put in your old place as Chief Field Naturalist.

Your appointment has been signed by the Secretary and is in the top drawer of my desk. You will have to go through the usual formalities of taking a new oath of office and filing a new record blank.

With best wishes, Very truly yours,

C. Hart Merriam[5]

The duties of the new office under Bailey were described as follows: "The office of Geographic Distribution has charge of field and office work relating to the collection, preparation, and elaboration of specimens and information illustrating the status and geographic distribution of North American animals and plants. It is engaged also in mapping the ranges of mammals, birds, reptiles, and plants, and preparation of reports thereon.[6]

After receiving his notification from Merriam, Bailey headed to Denver to continue his work with the Forest Service. Given his lifelong interest in the humane treatment of wildlife, he had never wanted animals to suffer—any animals—even under the demands of his job for the government. This led him to consider poison as the most humane way to "rid" farmers of animal "pests." Strychnine was the best-known poison at the time. From Big Piney, he wrote to Henshaw asking his opinion about the use of that product. Henshaw responded on March 31 with the facts:

According to German and French authorities on Toxicology, the smallest lethal (death producing) dose of strychnine for a dog is .75 milligram by subcutaneous injection, or 1.5 milligrams by the mouth, for each kilogram of weight of the animal.

According to the formula, if a coyote weights 25 pounds (12 Kilos), the least dose would be .27 of a grain (over 1/4 grain). If a wolf weighs 60 pounds (27 Kilos) the least dose would be over 1/2 of a grain.

Practically, 1/2 grain for a coyote and a grain for a gray wolf would produce the best results.

All the books agree that the effects of this poison appear more quickly in the case of dogs than of most other animals, but that there is much longer resistance to a fatal termination of the tetanic spasms. The only possible effect of giving the poison in a capsule would be to retard slightly its action. When the stomach is full of food the action of the poison is considerably retarded.[7]

Merriam followed up with his own encouragement to get on with the work:

Henshaw has already written you that Lantz looked up the literature on poisoning with strychnine, and found that the dose necessary for an animal weighing about 25 pounds is approximately a quarter of a grain; for animal weighing 60 pounds about three fourths of a grain; from which it is obviously safe to say half a grain for coyotes and one grain for big wolves. Lantz is this morning hunting up data as to the time required to kill by strychnine under various conditions. The literature on this subject is so voluminous and the experiments already made so numerous that it seems hardly necessary to make additional experiments now.[8]

Bailey, in effect, now had two jobs—one with the Forest Service to work on the wolf project and another with his new assignment in charge of Geographic Distribution to continue his collecting and distributional work as well as overseeing other field agents. In recognition of this dual role, he was awarded a salary increase from $2,400 per year to $2,500 per year, effective July 1 when his appointment with the Forest Service concluded.[9]

Before he left Wyoming in May, Bailey had shipped a box of young wolves to the National Zoological Park. One died before reaching Washington, but the letter of thanks from the park superintendent indicated that "the other two appear to be bright and lively. I am very glad to have these wolves, and hope that whenever you have a chance to secure anything of the sort you will bear us in mind."[10]

That same month, whether in jest, in a hurry, or for some unknown reason, Bailey also shipped a collection of skulls to the Survey headquarters in Washington. Henshaw, then acting chief, responded hastily, "The skulls forwarded by you have arrived and speak for themselves. They are what are usually termed loud, very loud, and I sincerely hope that if you have misfortune to collect any more you will take the trouble to partially clean, and above all things remove the brain."[11]

From Denver, on May 10, Bailey headed south, almost to the border with Mexico, to continue with his fieldwork. He stopped for supplies in Silver City, New Mexico, where he noted on the receipt from the Silver City Mercantile Company, "Last 15 days for 2 men and some left over. A good assortment." Here's what he bought:[12]

Flour	.75
2# b. powder	.40
salt	.10
sugar	.25
2# coffee grind	.80
5# sw[eet] choc	.65
1 box crax	.25
1 graham gum	.20
2 vanilla waf.	.20
cheese	.40
2 pc. bacon	2.75
5# prunes	.65
1 puffed rice	.10
1 sw.buiscuit	.50
15# of wheat (no price); subtotal $7.90	
spuds	.25
1 qt. m. syrup	.50
1 doz lemons	.30
4# b. beans	.40
2# b. beans	.35
2# corned beef	.35
2# chip beef	.35
2# veal scaf	.25
2# bat. salmon	.30
2# sardines	.35
1# walnuts	.25
1# pecans	.25
4# tomato	.40
2# peaches	.30
	$12.50 total

Still concerned about the use of strychnine as a humane way to kill wolves, he asked Henshaw how he could kill an adult wolf within three minutes. Henshaw saw the solution as

> *indeed a difficult one . . . you labor under a misconception if you think that an increase in the dose will accelerate the death of the animal, since after a lethal dose is reached increasing the quantity of poison has absolutely no effect except occasionally to cause the animal to eject the contents of the stomach and so to limit or altogether prevent the action of the poison.*[13]

Once again Merriam took up the issue about his writing more bluntly on May 19:

> *You had better go at once to the hospital in Albuquerque, or some other handy place, where you can find a good medical expert and have your head examined. I have just seen a letter from you in which you state unless a wolf can be killed inside of three minutes he might as well not be killed at all. Inasmuch as no sane man could possibly make such an absurd and utterly preposterous statement as this you are obviously in need of mental treatment. Trusting you will come out all right in the end.*[14]

In addition to ranchers and farmers, concerns about the impact of predators were expressed for national forests and parks like the Grand Canyon where they were thought to be decimating large game mammals. When the forest supervisor of Fredonia, Arizona, found the "stock interests" were "greatly suffered on account of wolves, cougars, coyotes and other wild beasts of the Forest," he wrote to the forester at the Forest Service in Washington, DC, "I have noticed in the past two years that there are but few fawns, and have frequently found carcasses of large deer that have been killed by these animals. Any steps taken by the Government for the destruction of these wild beasts of prey will be greatly appreciated by the stockmen of this country."[15]

The letter was forwarded to Bailey asking him to "take up the matter with Mr. Pratt and see what can be done with the view of ridding the section of the pests mentioned."[16] The story was the same in the Wichita Mountains of Oklahoma. By the end of July, Bailey received orders to go there to "carefully investigate the reported destruction of game there by wolves and coyotes with a view of devising protective methods. Incidentally gather as much data as possible on the kinds, abundance and habits of game animals and birds."[17]

Another part of the work involved testing various scents to better attract wolves to traps. One of his helpers, Merritt Cary, was working in Colorado that summer experimenting with "Siberian Musk" as an attractant.[18] Although at first unsuccessful in attracting coyotes, they had high hopes that a similar product could be found that would work even on the wily coyote. Meanwhile, Cary reported to Bailey that wolves were more scarce than previously, and in fact had done practically no damage that year. Even around the Laramie Divide, "a few are said to range that region, but in nowhere near their former numbers."[19] A man after Bailey's own heart, he agreed to continue trapping and experimenting with scents but expressed concern that the time spent on wolves was causing him to neglect his other work, including putting up representative specimens of small mammals.[20]

While conducting his mandated work to destroy predators, Bailey also continued to work toward increasing numbers of wildlife in ways the government could help. He suggested to his superiors in Washington that grain be planted to attract birds to a newly established game preserve. T. S. Palmer, in charge of game preservation for the Survey, replied in a letter written on August 21 that he already had that in mind, "perhaps as soon as we get the buffalo installed, or possibly before."[21] The preserve wasn't named, but Palmer commented that prospectors, not wildlife, were the biggest challenge to control.

The Baileys continued their extended honeymoon, camping, studying, and writing their way across the Southwest together. When they reached Silver City in southern New Mexico, near the end of September, a request came in from Palmer that encouraged Bailey because it involved work that would increase, rather than decrease, wildlife:

> *The Rhode Island Experiment Station has been trying for the past year to secure some wild turkeys from New Mexico and Arizona for crossing with domesticated birds. Their efforts have been thus far unsuccessful, largely because the laws make no provision for export of game for propagation. This defect can perhaps be remedied next winter. I should be greatly obliged, therefore, if you would bear this matter in mind during your trip and note where birds can be obtained to the best advantage and, if possible, ascertain the names of some reliable persons who would be willing to undertake the capture and ship them.*[22]

While Bailey had actively pursued finding effective methods to use poison and traps to kill predators as a means of local control, he was increasingly interested in finding humane ways to trap and remove them to areas where they could do no harm. However, local officials had little sympathy for working with humane—or even inhumane—traps. They wanted to kill the predators quickly and be done with it. The Wichita Game Preserve supervisor in Oklahoma noted that:

> *The setting of traps to catch wolves here has proved a complete failure, and I believe it would be better to invest the money in ammunition and have each officer carry a gun for the purpose of killing wolves or coyotes, to attend to four traps would take all of one man's time and the outlook is that we will have considerable work to attend to this fall and winter, however it would be a good idea to have the traps and if there should be time we could try and catch them especially if we should find a den.*[23]

Bailey's opinion was consulted, and he agreed that perhaps the best thing for the Service to do was to authorize the officers to purchase ammunition to shoot the wolves.[24]

In December, trappers in Utah rejected Bailey's suggestion of humane control methods for mountain lions. As they phrased it:

> *We believe the best and most practicable way in which to exterminate mountain lions, is to hunt them with hounds. The dogs will take the scent and soon tree the animal, in which case it is easily killed. At present there are no hounds in this part of the country. Mountain lions are very shy and it is very seldom that one is ever seen by men. It is also next to impossible to poison them from the fact that they prefer to kill their food.*[25]

Harriet Kofalk and Betty Hone, in their unpublished book about Bailey, portrayed him as "having different views" from his superiors with regard to the Survey's efforts in predator control[26] However, I have not found anything in the written record to suggest that he intentionally fought or was otherwise insubordinate to his instructions to proceed with the destruction of wolves and other predators. Later in his career, as we shall see, he became more resistant to the concept of broadscale destruction of predators in favor of nonlethal removal of problem animals. But, until his retirement in 1933, he publically supported the official position of the Survey regarding predator and rodent control.

33

Making Sense of Scents (1907)

The year 1907 opened with predators still front and center. His assignment with the Forest Service resulted in the January publication by the Forest Service of a booklet, "Wolves in Relation to Stock, Game, and the National Forest Reserves." The introduction to the publication makes its intent very clear:

> The enormous losses suffered by stockmen on the western cattle ranges and the destruction of game on forest reserves, game preserves, and in national parks through the depredations of wolves have led to special investigations by the Biological Survey in cooperation with the Forest Service, to ascertain the best methods for destroying these pests. The results appear in the present report, which includes also field notes on the distribution, abundance, and breeding habits of wolves.
>
> The chief object of the report is to put in the hands of every hunter, trapper, forest ranger, and ranchman directions for trapping, poisoning, and hunting wolves and finding the dens of young. If these directions are followed it is believed that the wolves can be so reduced in number that their depredations will cease to be a serious menace to stock raising. . . . Their complete extermination on the western range is not, however, to be expected in the near future, and it is only by constant and concerted effort that their numbers can be kept down sufficiently to prevent serious depredations.[1]

Beyond that, however, the thirty-one-page booklet served political aims for both agencies responsible for its creation. It intended to address anti-conservationist ranchers who might harbor continuing doubts about the Forest Service, and it also provided a rationale for the Biological Survey's detailed scientific queries. It reflected the congressional imperative to find practical—that is, economic—applications for the Survey's biological investigations.[2]

Bailey's pamphlet estimated that each wolf and mountain lion cost ranchers $1,000 a year, bears $500 apiece, and coyotes and bobcats $50 per animal. These numbers were used by the agency for more than a decade to justify the predator destruction program.

Meanwhile, information was accumulating in the field about the status and roll of predators, and the threat they also posed to game animals. Bailey received an update from the Forest Service in Utah, issued on March 5, that said:

> *I have secured what definite information I could about game, etc. killed by mountain lions on the Aquarius Forest Reserve. Men living in Escalante have seen sixteen deer that have been killed by lions, so soon after the combat as to leave no doubt that it was the work of lions. . . . From the tracks it would not seem that lions are very numerous. . . . Lions seem to have a preference for deer and horse flesh for we have never heard of them molesting cattle.*
>
> *We have not heard of wolves in the reserve but there are a few on the winter range adjoining the reserve that have killed a great many cattle. Cattlemen have offered a cow for every wolf scalp brought in, but not one has been killed, I think.*
>
> *Coyotes and wild cats are numerous on the reserve and their depredations are confined almost entirely among the sheep.*[3]

Now back on the full-time payroll of the Biological Survey, Bailey received new orders from Merriam on March 22, who addressed Bailey as "In Charge of Geographic Distribution." Soon afterward, Bailey headed for Michigan, Wisconsin, and Minnesota to investigate the extent of damage to stock and game by wolves, as well as ascertain the location of breeding dens of wolves in the timbered country, so it would become possible to devise a means of destroying them.[4]

Writing to his sister Anna three days later, Bailey described his new adventure from on a train near Marquette, Michigan:

> *In an hour or two I will be hustling to get out of town and 40 miles back into the woods, where I may not have a chance to send out mail for a week or more, even if I should have time to write letters. The country is rough and in places rocky, the woods are big and thick and the snow is over a foot deep here and deeper yet where I will soon be. Snowshoeing will be good and I shall not have to be back every night. I've plenty of matches and salt and there are rabbit trails in the swamps that I can see from the train. The*

tracking will be poor unless we get a little fresh snow, but I can follow a track even on the old, hard crust I guess. Wolves are heavy (100 lbs or more) and make a better track than coyotes. I followed one 8 miles on very hard crust last spring and got 8 pups out of the den.

I hope to get around home for 2 or 3 days after my work is done—about 3 weeks from now. Shall try to have wolf stories to tell you then. If a bear gets out and makes tracks I may have to investigate him too.[5]

In May, Merriam ordered Bailey to California to assist with the life zone and crop map of California. He also was instructed to make a record of the stomach contents of all carnivorous animals obtained, continue investigations of the habits of mammals and birds beneficial or detrimental to agriculture, and determine the most effective means of combatting mammal pests. If a disease among rodents became prevalent, he was told to secure material for a study of the disease in the laboratory and to secure all the field data possible on the nature and results of the disease. Finally, he was expected to obtain from ranchmen and horticulturists lists of the varieties of fruits, cereals, and other crops that have proved commercially successful in the various regions.[6]

The long train trip west in June, in the company of his wife, contained anything but the "idle hours" Bailey had envisioned. He wrote to Anna on June 7:

The first 2 days on the train I was too lazy and since reaching New Mexico and Arizona I have been running over the country so fast I couldn't write down the species of mammals and birds and plants and lizards and others as fast as they come along. I haven't written any reports and haven't even caught up with my journal. But I have colored in the zone map over a lot of new country.

Hay and grain have been harvested long ago and the country is dry except where irrigated. Around here there is very little irrigation or farming because no water except from windmills. Some day they will bring water out here from the Gila River and make a great country of this part of the valley.

If I had bought a patch of land near Phoenix 18 years ago, as I was tempted to do, at 15 dollars an acre I suppose it would be worth 300 dollars an acre now. This country has developed rapidly. Tucson is a city now, instead of the Mexican adobe that I knew in 1889. Lots that sold for 5 dollars then are now held at 5000, and business blocks are held at 1000 a front foot.

> *There are long streets of fine business buildings and beautiful residences and lots of trees and bushes and shade. It is really a very attractive city now. There are lots of street cars and a flourishing university.*[7]

The Bailey's visit to California was preserved not only in words but also in pictures. Albums of many of their destinations contain postcards and photos of Oceanside, Catalina, Idyllwild, and Palm Springs, as well as of San Juan Capistrano and other famous old missions.

While enjoying summer in Southern California, correspondence continued to focus on the predators farther north. One exception was a request from Survey Assistant Chief Henshaw to review a manuscript on field mice. The request itself shows the value they placed on Bailey's knowledge of small mammals:

> *Doctor Merriam requests that you give this the benefit of a careful examination with a view to detecting any errors in statement of facts concerning the several species of the group. He himself has not had time to look at it. Do not trouble yourself at all about the editing, but confine examination to subject matter, and indicate if in your judgment any portion of the manuscript can be omitted to advantage. I might say that [Prof.] Lantz's evident idea is not only to furnish practical hints to the farmer, but to a certain extent provide for use of the bulletin in an educational way.*[8]

The combination of helping the farmers specifically, and educating the public in general, was to become a major practice in agencies like the Biological Survey. At the time, so little was known about scientific matters by the public that such an aim was helpful indeed. As education became both broader and more specialized, the use of published bulletins took on meaning that today is questioned by many as advocacy rather than education. Even in the "predator control" realm then, the government position had a built-in audience through its outreach programs and bulletins.

Bailey's work with wolves was valuable to the administration as they prepared their part of the annual report of the Department of Agriculture for Congress. But, as Merriam pointed out to him in his August letter of instructions, money talked:

> *Are you taking means to collect and have ready in the early fall an* estimate of the value *of your wolf work to the Western ranges? We want the cattle*

> *man behind us and we want to know what has been actually accomplished in wolf killing (old and young) in each state and the value thereof in $s and cts in 1907. Sabe?*[9]

In October, Henshaw pushed harder for information to include in the year's report:

> *In the Annual Report for 1907, which I am now at work on, I mention your wolf work stating finally that as a result of investigations by one of the assistants of the Survey a preliminary bulletin was issued followed by a circular setting forth practical methods of reducing the number of wolves, and that these publications were widely distributed among ranchmen, hunters and trappers in the wolf infested regions. CH [Merriam] has seen this paragraph and suggests that I add to it what has been accomplished by these methods, meaning I suppose the number of dollars that have been saved to stockmen. Have you received any late information on the subject, and can you add a few lines giving the practical results in dollars and cents of the adoption of your methods? I have stated in the report which I am preparing for the Secretary to send to Congress that by the adoption of the method suggested as much as two millions of dollars may be saved annually. This, however, is really nothing more than a statement of our opinion of what may be made to follow by adoption of the method suggested in your bulletin. Do you think you can do any better than this?*[10]

Meanwhile, back in the field, in Minnesota a new hope was raised, at least by the sheepmen. Tapeworms were ravaging their herds, and they suspected that they might be transmitted by wolves. Henshaw brought Bailey up to date, noting:

> *An assistant of the Bureau of Animal Industry called to see me this morning to request the cooperation of the Survey in an attempt to secure specimens of tapeworms supposed to infest wolves, more particularly the wolves of Minnesota. It seems that the sheep of that State are seriously affected by one of the forms of a tapeworm which reaches the brain, and in nearly all cases proves fatal. The disease is causing great loss and consternation among the sheep owners of that State, and the B. A. are very anxious to know whether the parasite passes its final state of development in the intestines of the wolf. Should it prove that the wolf carries this parasite it will be an added and very important reason for efforts to exterminate them.*[11]

In November. Bailey was dispatched to Wadsworth, Nevada, to investigate a large outbreak of voles that were destroying crops. He penned this brief report back to Henshaw at headquarters detailing his thoughts and observations:

> *Am on the ground & find the Microtus even worse than reported. The loss has been enormous & is going on steadily. Fields are ruined. In ten minutes I caught 24 Microtus alive in my hands & put them in a tin pail. Great numbers of hawks, gulls, ravens, magpies, shrikes, etc. have gathered in the fields. Will work here for several days or a week & try all devices I can think of.*[12]

Although his primary scientific interest still remained with taxonomy and distribution, Merriam's agency, and consequently Bailey, were being forced more and more in the direction of animal damage control.

34
Movin' On (1908–1910)

Bailey followed up his publication on wolves of the previous year with a briefer circular with directions for the destruction of wolves and coyotes, this time published by the Biological Survey.[1] In this bulletin, for the first time, the killing of wolves (which received far more attention than coyotes) was inventoried on a national basis.[2] His report described the government campaigns to kill wolves and other livestock enemies, and for the first time he used the term "predatory animal." The Biological Survey apparently standardized this phrase with the creation of programs for control and destruction of predatory animals. This usage did not become commonplace in scientific literature until the 1920s, when it was shortened to "predator." Earlier references to wolves and other predators typically were made as "carnivorous animals" or "carnivores."[3]

Bailey enumerated the wolves and coyotes killed in or adjacent to national forests. He used Wyoming as his example because the Biological Survey had more systematic data from that state. His report concluded: "The Forest Service has made vigorous efforts to destroy wolves and other predatory animals on or near the national forests, and through its force of forest rangers has carried on the most systematic war on these pests ever undertaken."[4]

The federal government's mission to destroy wolves and other predatory animals throughout the western United States and its territories using the federally coordinated bounty system was taking shape. Bailey's report stated that government bounty hunters killed over 1,800 wolves (mostly in Wyoming) and 23,000 coyotes in 1907, resulting in an estimated savings to the livestock industry of $2 million.[5]

Despite these reports, western ranchers soon grew critical of the bounty method of destroying livestock killers. They saw it as too ineffective and subject to fraud. Livestock owners began calling for a federal program to take over the extermination efforts more directly and systematically. This would mean an increase in the Biological Survey's involvement, both in administration and as a source of scientific expertise. From 1908 until 1915, the Survey would gradually expand its control through the use of poison and trapping, and Bailey was periodically involved in addition to pursuing his scientific efforts to study the natural history of mammals.

By the autumn of 1908 the predator program was on the back burner and Bailey was back in New Mexico to work on his inventory and specimen collections. And, a major transition was underway within his family. His aging parents, as well as his young sister and her family, had decided to move away from the old homestead in Minnesota to seek "greener pastures" in Nevada. Things were changing and life was moving on!

His sister Anna had homesteaded with her new family in Nevada, where they were finding that life on the desert wasn't as easy as the early developers promised. She now had six children, with a final seventh to come the following spring. Apparently, Bailey had suggested the move after learning about a reclamation project that was under construction near Fallon, Nevada. This project, along with its promise of land, attracted the Mills family to relocate, and a homestead was settled in 1908 in Churchill County. Those that made the trek to Nevada included the immediate Mills children, their parents and grandparents, and several other relatives.[6]

Bailey's parents tried living in Nevada for a while, but soon moved to a tent city in Corvallis in western Montana to join some other family members already there, in what they hoped would be a more comfortable climate. Bailey began to take on more responsibility, though from afar, for the well-being of both their families, and he was to continue to do so throughout his life. His work—and his own simple lifestyle—gave him the means he needed. Bailey knew only too well what tent living was like! Although he loved to sleep on the bare ground until the day he died, he didn't expect others to live as he did.

His delight in his parents' move is evident, but he especially hoped for better housing for them than a tent. Meanwhile, he delighted in his own good fortune to be back in his favorite southwestern atmosphere and climate, writing to his parents on September 25, 1908:

> *Well it is good to think of you up there where things grow and big mountains loom up and there are trout and game. Only if you could all be together so none of you were lonesome or homesick for the rest. That is the only trouble now.*
>
> *I am caught up on my expenses and am sending you $30.00 for immediate use and can send more at intervals if you need it. Can you rent a comfortable house for the winter there or do you want to go to some warmer place for the winter? It is time to be getting out of a tent up in that country*

if I remember rightly. If you can't rent a house can you rent a couple of rooms where you can be perfectly comfortable? I can send you plenty for your rent and living expenses without missing it, so plan some way for as comfortable a winter as possible.

Our trip has gone on without any great events, all day in the saddle day after day gets monotonous, even among interesting canyons and painted desert and fossil forests and pueblo ruins that we have coming through.[7]

To Anna Bailey Mills, in a letter written the next day, he offered advice as well as money to help her struggling family:

[. . .] It is hard that you have had all this delay and uncertainty about your farm, and it keeps you back in building and making your improvements. . . .

In case you have to give it up I wish you could get the Black place but I would not run in debt for it. I wish I had the money to spare for it but couldn't raise the $450 now. . . . Have run pretty low but am gaining now and can spare a little now and then just as well as not.

I want you to let me pay the tuition for all the children you want to let go to school this winter. With all your other expenses it adds a good deal and to me it will be only a great pleasure. The enclosed $20 will start them, so let all go that can. I am glad Laura can take music lessons. What do they cost? I should like to help with that too.

Am sorry the place Father bought does not prove to be better, so you could use it in case you have to give up yours. I put all my spare cash in that and wish it could be of use to someone if Father doesn't want it. Why not build a temporary house on it this winter for the sake of the pasture if you can't keep the one you are in? Would it be as near to the schools?

So far we have had a good trip. I have young fellow with me from Amherst, Mass., pleasant and full of interest and energy. Then I have a good camp man, cook and packer with 7 horses, 3 saddle and 4 pack horses. This makes just a nice outfit, not too large for rapid traveling or getting into rough country.

We came up through the Gila National Forest and then over into Arizona to the highest peaks of the White Mountains, then north to Zuni, one of the best of the Indian Pueblos. Now we go north over the Navajo reservations and into country that has never been worked by any naturalists.[8]

Bailey's concerns for his aging parents and their state of being are voiced poignantly to his sister—but always with their mutual love of nature a part of their communication. Their mother had a bout of ill health while in Nevada that continued to be on their minds. Anna wrote to him on February 15, 1909, expressing her concerns:

> *Your letter came this morning and one from father saying mother is gaining and sitting up in bed. Still she is so frail that a very little would take her away from us. We can only hope that she will gain until the warm weather comes and then she will be safe until another winter. Every winter has frightened me for her for several years, but she has held out wonderfully. I shall probably get out there sometime in June and will see what can be done to ensure greater comfort and safety for another winter for her and father. The hard part of it all is that we are so scattered. I think mother has every care and comfort possible now, but it is hardest of all that she cannot have her children there. I am so glad Henry went out. He will be lots of comfort to her. We must all write to her often. I shall write a little every day, just to keep her cheered up.*[9]

The field season that year started a little later than usual, and Bailey returned to a familiar place in South Dakota, writing to his sister on July 29:

> *It seems strangely familiar to be out on these prairies where I worked 22 years ago, but I'm working them now in a different way. Then I was collecting the specimens and learning what they were. Now I seem to know most of the birds and mammals and reptiles and plants and can list the species at different places and trace out the boundaries of ranges very rapidly. At most of the places I stop but a day and in the past week I've covered the length and nearly the breadth of North Dakota and part of south. In a few days I'll be over in Montana and working westward toward Corvallis [Montana]. I have a young fellow, just graduated from Columbia College, with me part of the time but most of the time I leave him to collect specimens where needed. That relieves me most of the drudgery and makes my work all the more interesting.*[10]

After he visited his family in Corvallis, Montana, Bailey returned east for the winter season to write up his notes and work on reports for the Biological Survey. It was a hard winter out west, where his parents and his sister's family, each in their own place, lived out the season in tents. Springtime brought thoughts of shade, rather than warmth, both in Washington, DC, and in Nevada. Bailey urged his sister to look ahead to meet that need in a letter written on April 24, 1910:

I hope you can get shade for summer as rapidly as possible. Can't you set out pretty good sized cottonwood saplings along the ditches and close to the houses? They grow so fast they soon make good shade. Willows and cottonwoods make the best shade and windbreaks to deserts if you have plenty of water.

Wish you could see our shady yard. . . . For its size (25 by 75) there isn't a more satisfactory yard in town that I know of. . . .

We sleep out on the plaza and go birding before breakfast every pleasant morning. The migrants are coming thick and fast, and we see new ones most every day. Are you keeping notes and getting acquainted with all the birds. If the children will save scraps of plants and send me I will write the names on and send them back, same as I have to for our men in the field. I can't find any botany to cover that region. There isn't any.

How do Mr. and Mrs. Mills like the desert? I wish you all knew its most interesting side and loved it as I do. But you will soon change it—only not all. I am glad there will always be desert. Someday you will get over it more and into the Mts.[11]

That summer, for a change, Bailey stayed in Washington. His wife more often did that, working on books or caring for her tenuous health, which may have been an unwritten issue that summer. It might have been her lungs, or another miscarriage. Without children themselves, the Baileys happily parented any others within range. Vernon Bailey quickly found ways to do just that in the hot summer city, as he described to his sister in this letter written on the last day of July, while she was spending another summer on the Nevada desert:

Our summer here is pleasant and comfortable, mostly, and I am enjoying it. To Florence it is rather an old story, but not so bad as when she has to be here alone. We hope to get off for a week or so later, up to her old home. My chief amusement in odd times is showing the kids in the neighborhood how to do things. Yesterday we had a Wild West show, with my saddle and a barrel for a horse and plenty of kids to rope for steers. Then we built a camp on the vacant lot next to us. Wish I could be out there and have some real wild west with you all. Your children do not have to be taught to do the interesting things because they are doing them all the time. You don't half realize the advantages they really have over city children.[12]

Summer brought other challenges as well to the family in Nevada. Today we think of malaria as a tropical disease, but in 1910 it was still a part of life to be aware of in the north as well. Bailey had experienced it; now it was his niece's turn. His brotherly tone to her mother shows the level of understanding of the disease at the time, as expressed in this letter written toward the end of September:

> *I hope Laura's fever is nothing worse than malaria, tho that is bad enough. I remember how very "miserable" it makes one feel. But you must take every precaution to keep the rest from getting it. Of course you know all about its origin and habits, that it is conveyed by a certain species of nocturnal mosquito and in no other way. A mosquito that bites her will give the germs to the next person it bites. You must use very fine mesh mosquito net, or better yet tarlton [tarlton or tarlatan is a stiff, thin, transparent muslin or cheesecloth]. We have tarlton tents to sleep in on our piazza, tho malaria has been almost stamped out here. The malarial mosquito is a little thing and works only at night. . . .*
>
> *We had such a good vacation trip and have come back full of energy and pleasant memories. The hardest part of the trip was having to sleep in houses.*[13]

That last comment was to be Bailey's mark for all who remember him—that he loved to sleep on the bare ground until the day he died. For many years his wife joined in that joy, although later she too preferred houses to bare ground. That autumn, however, "We still sleep and eat out doors and maybe we will all winter."[14]

In noting their Aunt Sophrony's death that autumn, he shared his feelings with his sister in a letter written on October 23, 1910: "It is sad, but so much better for her to go. It has been a long weary waiting for her and I guess she was glad to go, tho we have to give up one of our loved ones here."[15]

The feeling extended to houses as well. Following his parents move to Montana, the old Minnesota homestead had been deeded to him. Now it had been sold, "but it is hard to have the old place go to strangers," he wrote to his sister. Closer to home, in closing the letter he wrote to her, "fine cold nights for sleeping out doors and no mosquitos."[16]

Bailey's sister Flo and her husband Chet Hill closed up the old house. Bailey wrote them the last day of October that he wanted nothing from it and suggested places for the old lantern and various journals. It was starting to get cold in Washington and he explained, "We have to pile on the quilts out doors these nights. The squirrels got up early and began to build warm nests this morning before we were up. Guess they slept cold. Old Bunnie and her 3 young were all on the piazza at once. They like to sit on the piazza rails to get warm in the sun."[17]

At holiday time, on December 1, Florence Bailey was the letter writer, admiring her sister-in-law's

> *brave home making and your happy outdoor life with the children met a deep response in our hearts; but when Vernon writes so often I am lazily content with thinking. I am sending you a few little things that may help piece out for Christmas, and as you know their tastes and needs better than I, will leave you to put on the names. The knives for the boys are not new but may whittle just as well! The one with the corkscrew was found on our steps and would not be given to every boy, but Vernon says Percy will find it handy opening pickle bottles! The other is one Vernon gave me, but I am such a poor whittler I think it had better be passed on! The pins for the girls have served me a good turn in younger days. The bird ones came from Chinatown in San Francisco, they may be interested to know. Vernon is sending you the American and Condor, and I have ordered a book—"Ethics for Children,"[18] that may be helpful.*[19]

Another year of adventure and satisfaction for "Mr. and Mrs. Dearie," as the Baileys referred to each other, ended by their fireside in Washington, DC.

The big development of 1910 had been the announcement that Merriam was leaving the Survey at the end of the fiscal year. This is something he had been considering since his friend and protector, Theodore Roosevelt, left the presidency in 1909. He was tired over his annual appropriation struggles with Congress and the need to justify his bureau's activities to that body, and he desired to free himself for full-time research. Railroad magnate E. H. Harriman had admired and respected Merriam's work ever since he asked him to organize an expedition to Alaska a decade before. After Harriman's death, his widow was approached to support Merriam's research in a tangible way, and the next year she set up a lifetime fund for that purpose. Merriam was then free to spend longer periods of time in the West, and he planned to move to the redwood country north of San Francisco where he could pursue his lifelong interest to study the vanishing California Indian tribes.[20]

Michael Robinson, in his 1905 book *Predatory Bureaucracy: The Extermination of Wolves and the Transformation of the West,* wrote about the ensuing struggle to determine who would replace Merriam as chief.[21] It was well known that A. K.

Fisher, who was in charge of the Division of Economic Investigations, desperately wanted the position, and Robinson speculated that Merriam was not inclined to support him because of his concern about overlooking Bailey, his brother-in-law and head of the Division of Biological Investigations—and the other obvious internal candidate for the position. In Robinson's view that led Merriam instead to throw his weight toward a third old friend and ornithologist, Henry H. Henshaw, a previous Survey employee whom Merriam had brought back to the agency in 1905 and installed as the number-two man.

I could not find any archival documentation to confirm Robinson's theory. Despite his contentious relations with some members of Congress, Merriam still retained enough clout to be able, in effect, to anoint his own successor, and he successfully lobbied for Henshaw. Henshaw, with less interest in pure science, was more fitted for the Washington political climate than Merriam. And, under his direction, the growing importance of predator and rodent control gave the Survey the means to thrive in the Washington political climate. Furthermore, Bailey's inclination for fieldwork, his disdain for Washington and administrative matters, and his lack of educational credentials would have made it very unlikely that he would have had any serious interest in the position. There is nothing in his correspondence or that of his wife that indicates he ever entertained the idea. But whatever may have happened in choosing his successor, with his mentor no longer in charge, Bailey's work at the Survey would now begin to move in different directions.

Before he left office, Merriam made a couple of moves that would benefit Bailey. In 1909, he changed the name of the Division of Geographic Distribution (under Bailey's direction) to the Division of Biological Investigations. Then, on May 30, 1910, he recommended a salary increase for Bailey that was approved. His justification statement to James Wilson, secretary of agriculture, read:

> *I respectfully recommend that the salary of Vernon Bailey, in Charge of Biological Investigations be increased from $2500 to $2850, to take effect July 1, 1910. . . . He was last promoted March 31, 1906. Mr. Bailey has been employed in the Survey for more than twenty years and has charge of the office of Biological Investigations, including biological surveys of the various States and Territories. He has published a number of reports of great value, including directions for the destruction of wolves and other noxious animals. Assistants in charge of corresponding lines of work in other bureaus receive from $3000 to $3500.*[22]

Florence Merriam Bailey, as a young woman, around the time she married Vernon Bailey. Courtesy of the Vernon Bailey Papers, Box 18, American Heritage Center, University of Wyoming.

Florence Merriam Bailey camped in the field in the Guadalupe Mountains, New Mexico, while on extended honeymoon with Vernon Bailey. Courtesy of the Vernon Bailey Papers, Box 18, American Heritage Center, University of Wyoming.

Photograph of Florence Merriam Bailey found in the field notebook of Vernon Bailey. Courtesy of SIA RG 7267, Box 2, Folder 4. SIA 2013-10188.

Pencil rendering of Florence Merriam Bailey, n.d. Courtesy of the Vernon Bailey Papers, Box 18, American Heritage Center, University of Wyoming.

Vernon Bailey and Florence Merriam Bailey feeding gulls along the Oregon coast, 1920. Courtesy of the Vernon Bailey Papers, Box 18, American Heritage Center, University of Wyoming.

Florence Merriam Bailey feeding young vole, 1924. Courtesy of the Vernon Bailey Papers, Box 18, American Heritage Center, University of Wyoming.

Anna Bailey Mills as a young woman, n.d. Courtesy of the Vernon Bailey Papers, Box 18, American Heritage Center, University of Wyoming.

Anna Bailey Mills as a young woman living near Fallon, Nevada. Courtesy of the Churchill County Museum, Fallon, Nevada.

John Mills, husband of Anna Bailey. Courtesy of the Vernon Bailey Papers, Box 18, American Heritage Center, University of Wyoming.

Anna Bailey Mills and Vernon Bailey on the trail up from Crater Lake, Oregon, July 17, 1927. Courtesy of the Vernon Bailey Papers, Box 18, American Heritage Center, University of Wyoming.

Laura Mills, daughter of Anna and John Mills, and Vernon's favorite niece, cooking outdoors. Courtesy of the Churchill County Museum, Fallon, Nevada.

IV

Work at the Survey After Merriam's Departure

The years 1901–1909, while Teddy Roosevelt served as president, were the heyday of the Biological Survey as a scientific agency, and the time when Merriam reached the apex of his career as a government official.[1] This also had been a period of great productivity and achievement for Vernon Bailey. But, with Merriam's retirement, the Survey continued to shift away from biogeographic and taxonomic work toward more strictly economic activities and ways to help farmers and ranchers. It gradually assumed the role of a regulatory agency, with its research functions much reduced in scope. As Congress passed wildlife laws, it charged the Survey with enforcing them as well as more practical problems associated with nuisance wildlife, predator control, wildlife management, and even the use of wild species of mammals for profits on farms and ranches.[2]

With this shift, Bailey's role within the agency also shifted. While he continued to do field survey work, particularly at some of the newly designated national parks (Grand Canyon, Carlsbad Caverns, and Glacier), he also received special assignments to investigate various wildlife-human conflicts and to promote the integration of wildlife into land management systems.

In 1915, the Survey was handed the full responsibility for predator and rodent control because of the pressure of livestock interests, particularly those in the western plains and Rocky Mountain states, whose senators or representatives held powerful positions on congressional committees. This would usher in an era of extreme scientific controversy about the pros and cons of predator control.[3] Bailey would not be immune from the controversy and criticism.

While still advancing in his career, Bailey decides to step away from administrative work and return to the field as chief naturalist. And, over the subsequent years, he begins to spend more time working on the development of humane traps and ways to use them to salvage wildlife. He invents several traps and receives six patents. He becomes widely recognized for his efforts on behalf of the humane treatment of animals, especially because of his inventions to capture animals alive and unhurt.

Bailey's personal life also begins to change and take on different meaning. His aging parents are increasingly unable to fend for themselves, and both he and Florence begin to struggle with their own health concerns. His beloved young sister, Anna, and her large family have homesteaded in Nevada and are experiencing difficult times with the relocation. Many of his other siblings have left the old homestead as well.

The chapters in this section chronicle the personal and professional changes in Bailey's life after the departure of Merriam from the Survey from 1910 until Bailey's retirement in 1933. He was forty-six years of age at Merriam's departure and would be sixty-nine when he retired. Over this period, he becomes more generous with his time outside of work, for example increasing his volunteer work for the Boy Scouts in the Washington, DC, area, and with his money by providing monetary and emotional support to his aging parents and siblings. Also, his fondness and devotion to Florence, his beloved wife, increasingly deepens. His self-respect increases as he grows as a professional and maintains his honesty and integrity in the face of pressures from both inside and outside of the Survey.

35

In Sickness and in Health (1911–1912)

While her husband reveled in the outdoors all his life, Florence Merriam Bailey continually had concerns for the air—within and without. She probably had tuberculosis as a young woman, but with the fear of it—both hers and that of society at the time—it was never mentioned by name. The new year started with another bout, and she apologized to his sister Flo for her unseemly delay in acknowledging holiday gifts. "If we could have enough fresh air all winter it would save *'being a great deal of trouble to ourselves'* as they say."[1]

Bailey continued to keep close tabs on the Mills family struggling in Nevada. In addition to another loan, he offered sage advice about natural predators for the latest agricultural scourge. In a letter written on February 10, 1911, he offered this advice,

> *In a very few years I am afraid the alfalfa weevil that is now all over Utah will reach you and then goodbye to alfalfa. But I should not hesitate to plant it now and get all you can started. We may find a bug or bird to eat em up by the time they reach you. . . . Florence is much better now and is up around the house most of the day, but hasn't been out doors yet. Guess she will get out by the time the birds come for spring.*[2]

That same spring brought out more of the philosophical side of his father's nature. The elder Bailey's increasingly deafness was a growing problem for Mother. His body responded by sleeping more, as he dozed in his chair much of the day.[3] Perhaps it was his own mortality that he watched or that of his wife—who was to pass on three years before him—as well as the changing seasons when he wrote on the last day of March, "no matter how nice the weather is nor how little or much there is to do night comes all the same and so it will go to the last.[4]

That aspect of humanity no medicine or physician can change. Not so with typhoid. The advent of inoculations made travel in the regions of its presence far more palatable, both to those traveling and to those waiting at home. Florence expressed her reassurance to her sister-in-law Flo, along with the joys of springtime that had enticed her out of her sickbed. Writing on April 8, she exclaimed:

> *Has Vernon told you that he is being inoculated for typhoid? My physician has been an army surgeon and so has been in close touch with all this movement. There is a special inoculation corps now, and all the 20,000 men in Texas are to be prevented! The doctor thinks it will be made mandatory in the army, and thinks that all young people should be inoculated. Vernon stayed home from office two days after the first hypodermic but had no headache or fever, just a little lassitude and local soreness. Last night he had the second hypodermic, and was out at seven this morning on his wheel for birds and flowers.*[5]

His father's philosophy was not lost on Vernon Bailey, and he passed it on to his sister Flo in reference to the loss of their uncle John. His letter, written on April 22, noted, "It is sad that we have to lose each other, but few of us will ever reach the age of 85. I have often wondered where he was and how his health held out. He always seemed so strong in mind and body. . . . Really he wasn't much older than we are now. Where will the next 24 years find us?"[6]

On June 1, 1911, he received notification that his title at the Survey had been changed to assistant in charge of biological investigations and that his salary had been raised to $3000 per year.[7] And then, a week later, his own mortality was put to the test. In the days before antibiotics, pneumonia was not a matter to trifle with. With her own concern for lungs, Mrs. Bailey was acutely aware of the effects. She hastened to assure his sister, however, that "the doctor's smile" was the best sign yet, and she put the responsibility squarely on her husband's shoulders for his own health, a perspective many have lost in the intervening years as we have come to rely on the physicians to do the healing. Her letter to Anna, written on June 9, commented on his pace of work, which she thinks contributed to his poor health:

> *It all comes from trying to act like 16 at 50! He has been crowding too hard, got run down, and a germ did the rest! A cold—acute bronchitis—and now bronchial pneumonia. . . . Tuesday I got the doctor to send in a trained nurse, so Vernon has the best of care and unremitting attention, with one of the best doctors in the country twos blocks away, and on the telephone. The*

> *doctor says he has no apprehension for him, but that he must go off with me for a real vacation.*[8]

In spite of her brave talk, her deep concern shows through as she advises his sister not to worry their mother with the details, but "I want you girls to know the exact conditions, as I should want to in regard to my brother." The cure was in his own nutrition, and a careful watch and loving care. "We are keeping his strength up with 6 raw eggs a day, buttermilk and strong beef and chicken broth."[9]

The prescribed vacation took the Bailey's to her brother's thousand-acre farm in upstate New York for a rest, although not for long. As soon as he was able, Bailey was eager to return to the outdoors, visiting his parents on a camping trip after the annual Merriam family picnic to celebrate the Fourth of July. As he gave them the anticipation of his visit, he outlined the summer vacation in this letter written on July 3, 1911:

> *I hope you will be well and strong by the time I get there so we can do lots of things, for I am getting so well I have to keep busy. . . . For a few days I am separating the cream from 35 cows, about 160 quarts of milk and 16 quarts of cream, separated by electricity. A very easy job at 5 o'clock these beautiful mornings. Florence's niece Augusta wanted to go down to New York a few days so I am taking her place in the dairy.*[10]

While Vernon traveled to Montana, his wife went north. As Emily wrote to other relatives on July 24, "She [Florence] is having a splendid time up in Maine living in her tent with nothing that she has to do yet very busy." As for Vernon, he "is getting stronger every day though he rushes around too fast for his softened muscle."[11]

Nothing could dissuade Bailey from his beloved outdoors. Well schooled in family picnics, he oversaw another one with the help of his protégé, Clarence Birdseye, who had met him for the field season. Time moves on, and Bailey looked back to describe the event to his relatives, in this letter written on July 28:

> *The time has gone fast since I came here but I couldn't stop it. Day before yesterday we went on a picnic—about 20 of us—down the river a couple of miles and the boys caught a fine lot of trout for dinner. Birdseye cooked the trout to perfection and I baked pancakes and broiled rabbit. We had a* big eat *and a very good time all round. . . . It is very pretty down by the river*

> *and we old folks sat in the shade of cottonwoods most of the afternoon while the young folks fished. Mother enjoyed it as much as anyone, but Father is so hard of hearing he misses all that is said unless it is shouted in his ear. He can see to read pretty well but hasn't much strength. I am feeling fine and will test my legs on some tall peaks soon.*[12]

Perception is everything, but rarely is the contrast so noticeable as in the following two versions of the same event. Bailey described his first "tall peak" outing with his nephew Bernard on August 6:

> *Bernard and I have just been off on a 4 days tramp in the mountains and had a glorious trip. We followed elk and bear trails were almost walked on by 4 white goats up among the big snow fields, caught trout and ate blueberries galore, found several species of mammals that had not been caught here before and settled several problems in distribution and corrected my zone map. It was a fine trip but pretty hard. I stood it well and proved that I am no invalid.*[13]

Mother Bailey, on the other hand, wrote this description two days later expressing what happened in slightly different terms:

> *Vernon and Bernard had an awful time in the Mts started Monday and did not get back till Thursday one night it rained all night and they built a fire and sat up against a big rock and slept a little and from the rain and wading in the snow were soaked and from Vernons condition it is wonderful that it did not use him up but they did not seem to mind it much only very foot sore but he coughs a good deal and it seems tight to me he thinks it is loose but now he is in a warmer and dryer climate I hope and think it will get better.*[14]

Summer passed in some "very interesting" work in Southern California, including one long trip with Dr. Merriam: "but the best of all was getting home . . . We sleep out on the piazza and enjoy it very much. . . . There is a family of young squirrels in the tree house, just big enough to poke their noses out. The two old squirrels are tame as ever."[15]

In November, with the approach of cold weather, Bailey expressed his concern for his parents' financial ability to get their house "comfortable" in time and forwarded another sum. In Washington, the first freeze killed all the geraniums and sent the Baileys indoors to sleep for the first time. "Awfully stuffy. Glad you all keep so well and are in such a healthy country."[16]

He took time to encourage his sister's decision to live in healthy country, sending her his old saddle to use. Winter in the city was not his cup of tea, and he longed for the desert while the snow began to fall in Washington: "Your life there should grow more and more interesting and full and some day your farm will be a beautiful oasis, or one of a great oasis in the big clean desert. Wish I could come out there oftener and stay longer and be with you in that kind of life. I love it."[17]

Anna's son Perry turned sixteen that year, and for Christmas "Uncle Vernon" sent her a book for him to read, *From Youth into Manhood*,[18] "and for him to lend to all the boys he knows. It is the best of its kind and is used in the YMCA and recommended by them for all boys. It can do no harm and can do great good. I wish every boy in the country could read it and know all it teaches."[19]

Sitting by the fire together in Montana that winter, on February 4, 1912, Father Hiram Bailey and his wife reminisced over their sixty years of working together, recognizing how few:

> *are so well able to recall so many years that their interests have been the same. Still focused on the welfare of our children, though we can do no more for them but are a charge on them, yet I believe the love we have for one another makes our relations pleasant duties. I am afraid my infirmities will prevent me doing much work but if my eyesight is as good as at present I can do much to help yet. I can't do much at getting wood or any hard work but can do all the chores, take care of the cow and horses and chickens and saw and hammer some and help Mother and hope to be able to work in the garden this spring. I don't go to church because I can't hear or can't understand the preacher, yet I can understand common talk very well when directed to me. My left ear is entirely deaf and my right eye blind but I am so thankful for what is left of me and would get along very well only for a dizziness that the jar of motion gives me. [. . . .]*[20]

Getting old is not for sissies, as it is often said!!

Bailey's sister Flo kept their mother posted on other family members, and the letters were kept and passed along to be savored by those away. Their brother Henry passed in and out of poor health, and his wife Helen likewise. Then, on May 3, 1912, the family was informed that their beloved mother, Emily, had succumbed that day at the age of eighty-one. The cause of death was not indicated.[21]

After coping with the loss of his mother, Bailey headed for the field for the summer, accompanied once again by his wife. They stopped at his sister's home in Nevada in June, and in a letter written on June 6, 1912, he noted the old place

> *never looked better than it does now with grass headed out and all vegetation dense and green and birds and flowers all around. The prairie chickens were crowing loudly this morning at 4:30. Florence never saw or heard them crowing before and she was wild over their antics. Watched them with a glass at close quarters as long as we wanted to.*[22]

Always alert to times and ways to quietly help his family, just before Christmas Bailey inserted ten dollars in a letter to Anna written on December 6, 1912, "for a turkey and fixing" just to help with a good time, for I know you are all working and saving with all your might and this will make it a bit easier."[23]

36

So Long to Administration, Back to the Field (1913–1914)

As the new year began, Bailey's work with the Boy Scouts increased. Writing to Anna on January 26, 1913, he apologized that "I rarely get time for a letter. Hope you are having as mild a winter as we are. Grass is green and dandelions and pansies are in blossom."[1] Bailey loved his work with the Scouts and, in his absence, Florence was always ready to stand in.

Increasingly chafed at being held to Washington supervising the Division of Biological Investigations, in May Bailey requested and received a change in title back to chief field naturalist, retaining the same salary of $3,000 a year. The written reason for the change was recorded in an official memo as, "Mr. Bailey desires to be relieved from administrative work in order that he may be free for more field work and for the completion of investigations he has in hand."[2]

E. W. Nelson was appointed as assistant chief and placed in charge of the Biological Investigations Division. As chief field naturalist, Bailey reported to Nelson.

Bailey's official instructions for that summer, which came from Henshaw on July 1, 1913, had a familiar ring to them, as the Survey chief specified that he would be traveling to Minnesota, North Dakota, Wyoming, Montana, and Idaho to gather data on the geographic distribution of animals and plants.[3] Tall order, even for the head field naturalist and even using local men to supplement, as was suggested. No longer does he long for companionship. He is given assistance and has the loving company of his wife during many seasons. The times have changed, if not the purpose.

In his new role, Bailey continued to be the envy of the men in Washington, for his summers in the field. Nelson stated his feeling, along with his request, written at the end of July:

> *I envy you your motor trip through the [North Dakota] country where waterfowl are breeding in large numbers. . . . In connection with waterfowl I wish to remind you that the collection is very short of specimens of blue herons from their breeding localities, and consequently please make every effort to get several specimens this season, if possible.*[4]

This is the first reference of Bailey using an automobile in his fieldwork, which had to have been a welcome change given all the years he had had to use the railroad and horses and wagons!!

From North Dakota, Bailey moved to Wyoming where he received a letter from Nelson, written on August 8, 1913, about exterminating prairie dogs,

> *I wish throughout the work you are doing this summer you would try and map as accurately as possible the extent of all the colonies of prairie dogs that you notice. It will soon be up to us to definitely map the distribution of the prairie dogs in connection with plans for their extermination, and this mapping must be done more definitely and on a much larger scale than anything we have attempted before.*[5]

On October 11, he received notification that his original travel plans for the season were being extended to go to Arizona "to cooperate with the Bureau of Plant Industry in studying the distribution of the Arizona cotton boll weevil in their relation to life and crop zones."[6] This came after the chief clerk notified him that he was suspending $2.05 of his monthly expense account, "July 4th, the item of admission to fair grounds, 50c, is suspended because this expense is not covered by your letter of authorization."[7] He was also overcharged for a railroad fare and requested a refund. Notary fees were not allowed, and if that wasn't enough, "an error of 80 cents is noted and deducted." The total "passed," incomprehensible in today's terms for a month's expense, was thus perfunctorily noted by the clerk: "$113.95."

When one considers his itinerary, the business with the clerk appears ludicrous. Even Nelson recognized this, commenting on his itinerary, "The number of places mentioned in your itinerary to wind up the season appears rather formidable, but probably looks larger than it really is."[8] I guess it's all in one's perspective, but Bailey never complained because he was doing what he loved.

Yet throughout all the travel and travails was the ongoing devotion of the Baileys for each other. Now married fourteen years, they continued the romance that was to last throughout their life together. While he was away from Washington, she continued to carry on his work as scout master, writing him on October 15, 1913, with an update on his scouts and teasing him about how she had heard he was not properly taking care of himself,

> *I don't like the combination of your weather, your colds and your self-forgetfulness. Better take care of yourself or the Head Nurse will go and see to it! Sterling say's you've been going around bare-headed in the rain. A nice example! . . . Love to you Mister & tell your boys that I'm hoping it will clear up so they can have a glorious time the rest of the work. Your humble, obedient (on occasion) Acting Assistant, FMB*[9]

This letter was followed by another written the next day while she was sitting on the piazza that autumn, telling him to "have a beautiful time darling, & take some time to love your Old Wife."[10] On occasion Mrs. Bailey also would sign her letters to her husband as "Wifikin."[11]

Continuing the correspondence two days later, on October 18, she reported on the meeting she had attended in his absence, commenting:

> *It was good to see the boys & they seemed glad to come. When a noise was heard downstairs three valiant Protectors of the Weal (Edward C, Edward W[ingate] & Orville) rushed downstairs & dealt summarily with the Indian baskets that had gone on the floor! The tall one with all its arrows had gone down for some inexplicable reason.*[12]

Florence also helped with his family responsibilities while he was away in the field. Writing to Anna on October 16, she urged her "to take up the offer of the Red Cross and get an Instructor Visiting Nurse. It seems to me a great opportunity. Zenaida [C. Hart Merriam's daughter] and I took the Red Cross nursing course last winter, and though I thought I had reason to know a good deal about nursing, I found that it was quite possible to learn more!"[13] Florence also mentioned one of her own special interests, stargazing. "Your children know the constellations, don't they? Vernon and I always feel at home at night in camp, which we are, for we have old friends in the sky. The Boy Scouts have to know a few constellations and I take the opportunity to teach them as many as I can!"[14]

Not much of Bailey's personal writings have survived, including his poetry. One suspects he did more; perhaps he saw no need to sign them and so they cannot be identified by today's readers. Part of Florence Bailey's adoration of her husband were these poems, and she confided to Anna Mills, "Has Vernon ever given you copies of his poems? I know you would love them, as I do."[15]

Very few of Bailey's poems have survived, although I did find this one about a pocket mouse that he had captured and kept as a pet on one of his field trips:

BOBBITY
Dear little mouse with shiny coat
Bright black eyes and dainty hands
Watching us with a wistful look
And a far away gaze that understands
More than we think of our intent
And more than we know of distant lands.
Deserts and wastes of sandy soil
Where treasures of seeds in a cool deep cell,
The rich rewards of nights of toil
Are the dainty foods that pleased him well.
But when he came to share our life
And freely his valued trust to give
To accept from our hands problems and care
And teach us how his people live
It was only for us to understand
And write his life with a friendly knowing hand.[16]

Bailey's work authorization for 1914 arrived in May, and it was signed by Nelson who was now in charge of biological investigations. Although the appropriation bill was once again late in being approved, he was told to work in Oregon and other states west of the Mississippi River to continue investigations concerning the distribution and habits of native bird and mammals of that region.[17]

The concluding paragraph of the official letter was clearly intended to reflect Nelson's confidence in Bailey's judgment about matters of fieldwork:

> *As you are already entirely familiar with the requirements of the field work you have in charge there is no necessity for detailed specifications. The matter of securing the best results will be left entirely to your discretion as with the order in which you will take up the work in the different states.*[18]

The next month he received notification from Nelson that the appropriation bill had been approved and that he would be allocated $500 to support his work but that more could be available if needed.[19] This was a far cry from the old days when he often had to pay his own expenses while doing fieldwork!

In August, Bailey was notified by Nelson about some changes in the administration of the Biological Survey:

> *Dear Bailey:*
> *It will interest you to learn that today I received my appointment as Assistant Chief of the Biol. Surv. in place of Dr. Palmer who is placed in charge of Game Preservation. I plan to continue in charge of Biol. Investigations as heretofore!*
> *Sincerely yours,*
> *E. W. Nelson*
> *PS. The change was considered to be for the good interest of the Survey.*[20]

Nelson still remained Bailey's immediate supervisor. But, as we shall see in the next chapter, changes in leadership and direction were just beginning in the agency.

37

Changes in Leadership and Direction (1915–1919)

Although the Survey was developing its own expertise for predator control, before 1915 predator work was usually done in conjunction with the Forest Service. Congress soon provided formal responsibility. On June 30, 1914, the US Congress authorized the Predatory Animal and Rodent Control (PARC) branch of the Biological Survey and made it responsible for experiments and demonstrations in destroying wolves, prairie dogs, and other animals injurious to agriculture and animal husbandry. The sum of $125,000 was appropriated for 1914–15 to employ three hundred hunters. By the close of fiscal 1916 the PARC had been organized into control districts and staffed.[1] By killing animals—wolves, coyotes, and cougars—that stockmen claimed were killing their valuable assets, the Survey built an alliance, albeit strained at times, with a powerful constituency with growing influence over management of the public domain.

In addition to the arguments of the livestock industry, two subsequent developments facilitated the Survey's predator control programs. In 1916, an outbreak of rabies, primarily from coyotes, hit southeastern Oregon, northern California, southern Idaho, and northern Nevada. Congress responded with an appropriation of $75,000 to the Survey to tackle the problem. When the United States entered World War I the following year, increasing the food supply became a national goal. As a result, Congress allocated $250,000 to the Survey to curb livestock losses from predators and to prevent rodents from destroying crops. By 1917, the Survey employed up to three hundred hunters and trappers and killed 30,512 predators, chiefly coyotes, a destruction of wildlife that generated little criticism, even from wildlife advocates.[2]

Then, in 1916, Henshaw retired as chief of the Survey because of health problems, and he was replaced by Bailey's colleague and friend E. W. Nelson. Nelson would serve as chief from 1916 to 1927—a period characterized by major controversies over hunting and predator control. Also in 1916, the

National Park Service (NPS) was formed and Stephen Mather was designated to head that agency; he immediately began to actively promote the parks, emphasizing their ability to generate profits. Nelson supported his efforts, and the Survey cooperated with the NPS on many projects that often involved Vernon and Florence.

Against this backdrop, Bailey continued to hold the title of chief field naturalist and to pursue his fieldwork and studies throughout the West, but he seemed to enjoy more support under his good friend Nelson than he had under Henshaw. Nelson trusted and had great confidence in Bailey, and he expanded his role even further to include projects all over the United States. Also he began to assign Vernon and Florence to work on selected wildlife projects within the national parks, including the task of preparing bulletins describing wildlife in the parks. But the main emphasis at the Survey continued to be on animal damage control that was primarily under the direction of A. K. Fisher with Bailey tangentially involved.

The year 1915 started off as a difficult year for Bailey. In May he received word of the passing of his father Hiram, at the age of eighty-four, and as requested he was buried next to his beloved Emily in Montana. The grave marker was a simple stone rock with both of their names etched along with the year of their deaths. Both of his parents were now gone and only his siblings remained.

On July 4, Nelson sent Bailey a lengthy, personal letter, marked confidential, in which he confided plans for adding personnel as well as promotions and salary adjustments that had been approved by the secretary. He also reported to Bailey that he had received several manuscripts from Florence and that she was writing his mother numerous cheerful letters, which she greatly appreciated. Nelson deeply respected both Vernon and Florence for their kindness to him and his mother.[3]

Bailey's work assignments in the years leading up to the involvement of the United States in World War I (1915–1917) involved varied field activities, including a mixture of new projects and continuing with projects already underway. In 1915 he spent time in North Dakota completing his mapping of life zones and distributions of mammals as well as taking charge of field operations in Oregon. In addition, he was asked to determine the status of gophers (genus *Thomomys*) in Saskatchewan, Canada. The superintendent of Yellowstone National Park gave him free range to study mammals in the park, including permission to secure specimens by trapping and shooting.[4] It was rare for national parks to grant such broad permission.

In 1916 he worked on life zones and mammal reports in North Dakota,

Oregon, and northern California, and he was charged to investigate the winter conditions of the elk herds in Yellowstone Park and to census the elk and other large game populations in the park.[5] The status of elk in the western states was a hot-button issue for the Survey, and one in which Nelson had a personal interest.

Travel orders for 1917 were not much different. They called for work in Montana and Wyoming to continue investigations of bird and mammal life of both Yellowstone and Glacier National Parks for the purpose of securing data to be used in connection with the biological survey of Montana and Wyoming as well as provide reports on the wildlife of the national parks.[6]

Earlier that year, Nelson issued a memorandum to all of the fieldworkers, including Bailey, which represented a major departure from previous Biological Survey policy concerning the collection and preparation of specimens. The letter, issued on June 12, 1917, instructed them to pay less attention to collecting and specimens and more to observing life histories and behaviors of the animals. Nelson noted that while collecting rare or very young specimens to supplement existing collections was okay, the Survey's collection of most species is "well-supplied" and that time "will be more profitably spent in obtaining more detailed information on the life habits of these species than in largely increasing the number of specimens." His final piece of advice was revealing: "These suggestions are made to bring to the notice of field men the need of close attention to a phase of field investigations which is often neglected in favor of the interesting pursuit of specimens."[7] There is nothing in the record that indicates Bailey's response or attitude about this change in direction, although he continued to collect and prepare specimens throughout his career at the Survey.

Although the war years had resulted in reduced appropriations for the agency, Bailey continued to receive adequate resources for his field surveys and work, and he continued to receive his travel and work instructions directly from Nelson. In 1918 he worked in Texas and New Mexico to oversee demonstration work in the destruction of prairie dogs and to ascertain the effectiveness of the various methods required to keep down the abundance of rodent pests in the region. After completing this work, he was dispatched to Belton, Montana, for a brief trip into Glacier National Park to inspect the wintering grounds of moose, elk, and deer to learn more about their winter habits and the extent to which predatory animals preyed on them during the time of deep snow. Then he proceeded to the Olympic Mountains in western Washington to determine as nearly as possible the numbers of elk inhabiting the different valleys, their condition and whether or not they were suffering from lack of winter feed, and the extent of loss to predatory animals.[8]

Although she had assisted Bailey on many of his field trips since their marriage, Florence had never been given an official title or a salary. That changed in September 1918 when the secretary of agriculture received a memorandum with a recommendation for the appointment of Mrs. Florence Bailey as special assistant at 75 cents per hour, total compensation not to exceed $300. Her work involved studying the birds at Glacier National Park while Vernon worked on the mammals.[9]

Vernon's work with the Boy Scouts also began to take on two new directions. One involved building a troop museum that he helped the boys construct. It included the construction of museum cases for housing specimens and teaching the boys how to collect and prepare specimens as well as how to identify and study local wildlife species. According to Bailey, the boys were taught to "trap for field mice, shrews, moles, and such small game as they can catch in woods and wildlife places. They measure, skin, and stuff the specimens, clean and number the skulls to agree with the numbers on the skin labels, and later will clean and prepare some skeletons."[10]

These are the very same things that Merriam taught him how to do more than thirty years earlier. The other project with the scouts had to do with assisting in the war effort by establishing, maintaining, and harvesting a "boy scout cornfield" on part of the Potomac Park in Washington to help feed the soldiers.[11]

Following the 1918 armistice to end the US involvement in the war, work began to return to normal at the Biological Survey. Bailey's orders for 1919 were to continue his many years of work in the Dakota region, investigating the distribution, abundance and habits of birds, animals, and plants, and to study the life zones in North Dakota and adjoining states.[12] However, midway through the field season he was suddenly dispatched to Deadwood, South Dakota, for the purpose of consulting with congressmen and local citizens on the establishment of a bird refuge on Mt. Theodore Roosevelt. His full instructions, sent on September 22, 1919, were issued by the acting chief of the bureau:

> *Dear Mr. Bailey:*
> *In response to the request contained in your telegram from Grandforks, North Dakota, under date of September 20, just received, I am sending you under separate cover by this mail copies of the Geological Survey sheets of the Spearfish and Sturgis Quadrangles, which show the location of Sheep Mountain now*

known as Mt. Theodore Roosevelt. This is the location for which the Society of the Black Hill Pioneers has suggested for the establishment of a bird refuge.

Upon arrival at Deadwood you should consult Ex-Congressman Eben W. Martin, Captain Seth Bullock, or some member of the Deadwood Club or Pioneer Society and ascertain from them how large a reservation is contemplated in the proposed plan. Having secured this information the next step will be to ascertain the ownership of the lands on the mountain. Either Mr. Martin or Captain Bullock can perhaps obtain this information for you. If the lands are in private hands it will be necessary to obtain a list of owners and a detailed map of their holdings. We should know what plan, if any, the Pioneer Society has for the acquisition of private lands which may be necessary to include in the reservation. If the greater part of the land is in private hands it will hardly be worthwhile for you to attempt to collect all the detailed data. These can be supplied possibly by the Pioneer Society. You will need to know the general facts, however, in making your recommendation as to whether it is possible to acquire a large or a small tract.

Your principal work will be to ascertain the birds now on the mountain and to make a list of the species which come under your observation; to ascertain which species are likely to be attracted to or benefited by the proposed refuge, and what natural advantages the location offers in the way of supplying food. Your report should also show clearly how far Mt. Roosevelt is from the outskirts of Deadwood, and what provision, if any, has been suggested for protecting it; also whether the birds are likely to suffer to any extent from the depredations of cats, dogs, or any native predatory animal.

As you probably remember, Congressman H. L. Gandy brought this matter to the attention of the Biological Survey sometime ago, and the data indicated above are necessary for us to act intelligently on his request for the establishment of a bird reservation on this area.

Very truly yours,
W. C. Henderson, Acting Chief of Bureau[13]

The letter clearly reveals the extent to which the Survey was now willing to go to appease members of Congress.

His trip also produced some scientific successes as he wrote to his partner-naturalist sister Anna on November 26, 1919:

I was 2 months in North Dakota and got a lot of good material for my report on the mammals, caught a lot of mice and some gophers alive to study and brought home and still have a pocket gopher, and meadow mouse which stores beans in the fall that are greatly prized by the Indians as food. I've been trying for years to find out what mouse it was and this time found the mice and brought one home alive with its cache of wild peanuts and artichokes. . . .

I hurried back so Florence could go to the hospital for an operation for gallstones. That was nearly 2 weeks ago and now she is able to sit up and will be home in a few days. They found 22 gallstones as big as hazelnuts. No wonder she has been miserable for the several years back. Now she will be perfectly well and already she is eating all sorts of things she hasn't been able to touch for years.[14]

As the year ended, interest and discussion were percolating among a group of Survey workers who felt there was a need for a scientific society devoted to the study of mammals similar to those already in place for ornithology. A key organizational meeting had been held at the Bailey's home on December 5, 1918, with Bailey presiding over the topic of forming a society for the study of mammals. It seemed appropriate for the now prominent government bureau to help nurture its own scientific roots. Further, despite the increasing number of scientists specializing in the study of mammals, no mammal organization similar to the ornithological union existed. At this meeting it was agreed that a committee would be appointed to assist with the establishment of the new society.

Bailey was present at a meeting of the "Committee on the Organization of the Mammal Society" held in Washington, DC, on January 23, 1919, and both he and Florence were elected charter members and present at the organizational meeting of the American Society of Mammalogists (ASM) at the United States National Museum in Washington on April 3–4, 1919. His former mentor and now brother-in-law, C. Hart Merriam, was elected as the society's first president. In 1919, the ASM began publishing the *Journal of Mammalogy* and holding an annual meeting. Bailey was an active member and supporter of the ASM throughout his career and held several organizational leadership positions within it, including the presidency.

C. Hart Merriam toward the end of his tenure as chief of the Biological Survey. Courtesy of US Geological Survey, Patuxent Wildlife Research Center. Courtesy of USGS-PWRC, Biological Survey files.

Henry Henshaw, second chief of the Biological Survey. Courtesy of USGS-PWRC, Biological Survey files.

Edward D. Nelson, third chief of the Biological Survey. Courtesy of USGS-PWRC, Biological Survey files.

Paul G. Redington, fourth chief of the Biological Survey. Courtesy of USGS-PWRC, Biological Survey files.

38

Rats, Bats, and Beaver (1920–1924)

In 1920 the bureau began publishing a formal newsletter as a medium for furnishing information regarding its work.[1] The first issue included information about Bailey, noting that he brought a number of live rodents (*Geomys, Microtus, Perognathus,* and *Peromyscus*), captured in North Dakota, to the meeting of the Biological Society of Washington on November 29, where information concerning their habits and relations was discussed. The report also noted that despite a typical North Dakota blizzard, with the accompanying uncomfortable weather conditions, Mr. Bailey was successful in definitely locating the bean mouse of North Dakota, the activities of which were mentioned by Lewis and Clark, Maximilian, and others. This proved to be a new subspecies of the meadow vole, *Microtus pennsylvanicus wahemia,* described by Bailey.[2]

His travel itinerary for 1920 called for him to head west to North Dakota again, then on to Idaho, Montana, and Oregon, and for the ensuing winter farther south to Nevada, Arizona, and New Mexico. His instructions called for a field study of the life habits of rodents and other animals with special reference to their control and eradication.[3] He was allocated $1,100 for expenses. On June 22, he received official notification that his salary was being increased from $3,000 to $3,250 per annum with his title remaining chief field naturalist.[4]

On June 25, a nice personal note arrived from the survey chief, E. W. Nelson, that he had handwritten while traveling on a train in Ohio. The letter expresses Nelson's gratitude to both Bailey and his wife for their friendship and support:

Dear Bailey:
In the rush of getting away from the office, I omitted to have a last word with you. I am now strengthening my own back to a favorable hope & to express

all my best wishes for your health and success on your western trip. I hope you will come back to Washington next spring with renewed vigor and good for real strong field work for many years to come. I scarcely need tell you & Florence how much I prize you both among my few really & truly good friends. The field work should be fine for both of you . . .

With love & good wishes, as ever yours,

E.W.N.[5]

Bailey was now given considerably more flexibility in his travel and work schedule, as revealed in a letter from acting bureau chief, W. C. Henderson, written on June 29, granting him permission to stop off at Minneapolis, Minnesota, while en route to southern Idaho and eastern Oregon, for the purpose of taking two or three days annual leave. Amazingly, the letter stated:

Inasmuch as you will be employed during the next year or longer on independent field work, should you desire to take a few days leave from time to time, not exceeding five days at a time, you are authorized to do so provided you do not exceed in the aggregate the amount of leave to which you are entitled during the calendar year and leave blanks are promptly submitted to this office for any leave taken, which should be completed to show date of return to duty.[6]

This was a far cry from the strict, dictatorial days of working with Merriam!

Fieldwork was beginning to change because of modern technology developments, such as the automobile. Apparently he had requested the use of a car for his work in Arizona where roads and travel were still very skimpy. In late November 1920, he received word from E. A. Goldman, now in charge of Biological Investigations, that his request had been denied but they hoped to accommodate automobile travel in the future:

In regard to the possibility of securing a Ford Truck, I have discussed the matter with Mr. Thompson and learn that efforts are being made to secure several trucks formerly used by the War Department, and there seems to be a chance that one may be available, but considerable delay may be involved. It seems very doubtful, therefore, whether you can plan at all on securing any such transportation during the period you will be in Arizona. I hope, however, that we shall be able to secure one for the rest of the Arizona work.[7]

Having seen the limitations of train travel and experienced the hassles involved with the old pack mule and wagon days in the early years of his fieldwork, no one could have appreciated the value of automobiles for field survey work more than Bailey. With an auto, a collector could reach areas that previous collectors could not reach in a day's walk from any town or railhead. Also, because they were not confined to rails, autos were good for overland travel in open and empty terrain. As early as 1913, the Baileys had begun using a car to travel to some of their field sites, but now Bailey wanted the Survey to acquire cars to aid in field survey work. As soon as it became practical, the Baileys adopted the auto as their main means of travel in the West.

He and Florence spent the winter of 1921 in southern Arizona, near Continental on the slopes of the Santa Rita Mountains, taking a rare opportunity to watch wildlife through the colder weather. By the end of March he could count forty-four mammals (fifteen species) in the tent, telling his sister in a letter penned on the March 29 that "some are lovely pets. Have 3 of the smallest species of Perognathus not so big as some of the grasshoppers here. Probably the smallest of our rodents."[8]

Florence was watching his health carefully. It's possible that he had had a heart attack and his wife was solicitous of his well-being throughout the season, keeping him close to home in the tent. They had planned to drive to Albuquerque, but she dissuaded him, and they traveled by train instead. Nelson was concerned enough to have included a handwritten inscription on the bottom of his travel orders that read, "In going into the mountains you should not in any case try to work above 5000 feet and be very careful about hill climbing. Better go easily so to be able to build up and keep going instead of overdoing and getting out of commission. I know how it is from personal experience."[9]

Nelson asked Florence to keep him informed about the situation, and she provided this update in a letter written in December 1920:

Dear Dr. Nelson:
You said you wanted to be kept informed as to Vernon's condition and I have something definite to gauge it by now, that I know he won't tell you himself.

A couple of weeks ago he found a gopher working up the canyon and, wanting to get it, went up for two days twice a day. It was about a mile and a half and as I found to my horror afterwards by the contour map 4000–5000 feet by gradual slope and Clint [C. Hart Merriam, Florence's brother and a former doctor, who was advising Bailey about his medical condition] had said he must not ever go up hills! The result is that he did not get over it for a week.

He gets along well if he does not overdo and takes a long rest at noon—he works at night—in place of it—but any over exertion taxes his heart too much.

Clint says I should not return home until the hot weather is over and I know that is so, as it used him up in North Dakota last summer. He also says that he should keep the same altitude—nothing above 4000–5000 feet. And of course in going back he must take up no high passes.

He will probably write you part of this himself but I wanted you to know before making any plans for the summer.

He is in no condition to have the responsibility of a car, but there is a man here with a Ford who will take us where we need to go.

Don't "let on" that I told you all this. Just keep it in the back of your head.

Your letters do him good. Sincerely,

F.M.B.[10]

The new year, 1921, brought good news on the financial front. Nelson and Fisher wrote to him in Arizona in March that henceforth his travel would be on a per diem basis, $1.50 a day in camp and $3 a day at other times, thereby relieving him of the considerable drudgery and work involved in itemizing his expenses. This would free up even more time for fieldwork.[11,12]

In June, 1921, he and Florence were in Duluth, Minnesota, investigating the life habits of muskrats and beavers in the region to acquire information for the possible establishment of fur farms stocked with these animals.[13] At the end of the month, Goldman wrote that one of the live kangaroo rats he had sent to Washington had escaped in his (Goldman's) cellar but that, "one of the boys placed a baited cage trap, which this morning contained the little fellow, and it is now safely back again in its regular place."[14] One has to wonder how many residences in Washington had wild kangaroo rats running around inside!

His calendar diary for 1922 opens with documentation of a visit on January 1 to his old friend and colleague, Basil Dutcher, "who is far gone with pneumonia, poor fellow." He visited Dutcher a week later on January 8 and simply noted that he "is slowly losing ground."[15] Dutcher died at Walter Reed Hospital on January 16 at the age of fifty-one.

In writing to his family on March 9, Bailey notified them of his election to the presidency of the Biological Society of Washington, "the highest scientific honor I ever expect to attain," and then he wrote about other things that were taking up his time:

My boy scouts are mostly running themselves, with two good assistant scoutmasters and some voluntary assistants from the old members of the troop. I have become mainly a figure head, a sort of ornamental heirloom. I have just finished a bulletin on Beaver Farming which I hope will be published soon. There seems a chance to get some other reports published that have been waiting since before the war and I've had to bring them up to date. . . . Had a rather discouraging letter from Henry not long ago. The chicken business down at San Marcos [California] is not a great success it seems. . . . It is only a passing wave of disadjustment and surely will come out all right before long.[16]

In September, he was invited to be a regular contributor to the recently established *Nature Magazine* published by the American Nature Association, which he happily accepted. He immediately sent in an article on baby beavers for which he was paid ten dollars, and shortly thereafter he became a consulting editor to the magazine, using it as a means to supplement his income and to inform the general public about interesting species of mammals.[17,18]

By autumn Bailey was expanding both his dreams and his practical life, learning new things about the small mammals by watching them at home. As he proudly announced to his sister, in a letter written on September 4, "I've a mouse house under the back piazza, full of wild animals of various kinds, kangaroo rats, pocket mice, grasshopper mouse, Zapus, and lots of meadow mice. Wish I could get a female grasshopper mouse to go with my male from Oregon. Should like to raise some."[19]

The next spring (April 1923) a controversy erupted over the actual date of his birth. Apparently he had provided different dates when he submitted his personal statements sheets required by the new Civil Service act. The chief personnel officer wrote to Nelson, on April 25:

In three personal statement sheets received from Vernon Bailey, Chief Field Naturalist, he gives as date of birth June 21, 1864. In two other statement sheets submitted by him, he says that he was born June 21, 1863. As the correct date of birth is very essential information, especially in view of the Retirement Act, it is requested that Mr. Bailey be directed to submit a statement, under oath, showing the exact date he was born.[20]

It would take more than a year to fully resolve this given the poor records that were available at the time Bailey was born.

His interest in beaver brought a new assignment a few months later that would prove to keep him close to home but still in the field. His travel instructions, issued on June 6, sent him from Washington, DC, to Oakland and other localities in Maryland and adjoining states for the purpose of determining the source of food supply for beavers and other furbearers in that section of the country, and to note any areas suitable for rearing fur-bearing animals in captivity.[21]

A more detailed letter from Nelson, written the next day, left no doubt about the hoped-for outcome of his beaver work:

> *If you can demonstrate that beaver farming is a practical proposition, it will be an admirable thing. The only question that I have concerning the experiments, is the possibility of raising large enough numbers of beaver on limited areas to make the business profitable. If owners or large tracts of land could guard them from poachers, then I believe they could succeed excellently in beaver farming, by protecting the animals and giving them an opportunity to increase in a natural way, taking each year the surplus. . . . However, you now have the opportunity to demonstrate the matter and I merely wish to urge the necessity of using good judgment in handling the proposition*[22]

Later in the summer, on August 4, Nelson wrote Bailey in Michigan about the sudden death of President Warren G. Harding and its impact on the work of the Survey:

> *The death of the President has been a great shock and has carried a universal sense of loss throughout the country. President Harding was a man who appears to have won the deep personal regard of everyone, regardless of political affiliations. From his speech at Seattle on his return from Alaska, he made it plain that he had seen through the misrepresentation which had been put out regarding Alaska by certain interested people during the last few years. His expression of opinion concerning the situation in the Territory as a result of his visit agreed exactly with the contention that I have maintained from the first as to the situation there and naturally filled me with great pleasure. As Secretary Wallace, Hoover and Work were with him, no doubt the results of the trip will put an end to the campaign of misrepresentation and efforts to change things radically will slow down. I am hoping very much that the result will be beneficial in stabilizing our work and giving us a better opportunity to assist in the building up of the wild life resources of the Territory.*[23]

That autumn, beaver took him to Michigan to place some beaver for farming at Boyne City. Once again he and his wife teamed up, as she continued to observe the habits of the birds—from camp—while he livetrapped the beaver. He described the process to his sister in this letter written on September 7:

> *Have been away from camp a week and have a night's run yet to get back. Hope to find more beavers in the corral, as I left several traps set with a boy to watch them and Florence to keep camp. Have had some trouble in getting my live traps to work but finally got them to catching beavers and caught four. Have permits for 20 and want to get 3 places stocked with them as experimental farms to test out the practical side of beaver culture.*
>
> *We have had four fine boys—17 to 19—helping us all summer with the work but only one with us now. The rest have gone back to school.*
>
> *Have a beautiful camp place by a lake with two beaver houses in it and lots of other lakes and beaver houses not far away and have had a most interesting summer. . . .*
>
> *Wish you could see the beavers we have had in camp, 3 fine big young of the year and their mother, all tame enough to be handled and petted and all beauties.*[24]

Back in their comfortable home in Washington, Mrs. Bailey continued to encourage his helping young people. After telephoning a response that he was still in the field, she forwarded a letter to him, of October 10, 1923, from the DC Council of Boy Scouts, penning at the top a comment that "this looks good—a not too hard chance to help." The letter called for the establishment of a "Corps of Experts," with a request that he be a part of it:

> *During the past few years, there have been a large number of men who have served the Boy Scout Movement in Washington, as Scoutmasters. Of this group, there are a few men like yourself, whom we feel have rendered distinguished service, and the severance of whose connection with the Movement, we feel has been a distinct loss to Scouting. For some time I have been endeavoring to work out some means of recognizing such service, and retaining in the Movement in some capacity such men. After careful thought we have decided to create a special Corps of Experts, who will have the rank of Assistant Deputy Commissioner, and in which Corps we would like to offer you a Commission.*[25]

The recognition for his scouting work continued. Columbia University had been offering a home study course for scoutmastership for about a year, when they decided to organize an "Advisory Board" to assure that "future changes in the Course are genuine improvements." They would simply refer questions to the board and were most eager to include Bailey as a member. Atwood Townsend, the Columbian instructor, assured him "there will be no arduous duties attached to this position. All we want is your occasional advice upon problems that confront us."[26,27] Bailey accepted.

Meanwhile, his sister Anna continued her busy life, raising seven children in the homestead town of Fallon, Nevada. The youngest was named Vernon, after his uncle. Two days before Christmas, 1923, she wrote to her brother about her latest adventure with wildlife, their mutual passion,

> *We have had a tame Ring neck Pheasant, which we raised from a setting of eggs broken up in the mowing last summer. He is a beauty now, and I like him so much I would like to raise pheasants. Do you know if I could get a permit to raise them in captivity and sell the mounted birds? Vernon is much interested in them.*[28]

The Southwest was once again on Bailey's itinerary the next field season in 1924. He joined the first large expedition into Carlsbad Caverns with instructions to explore it and other caves in that vicinity in southeastern New Mexico.[29] The expedition was sponsored by the National Geographic Society, and Bailey's special assignment from the Biological Survey was to report on the bats. Not only was their presence of interest, but also their potential for helping the farmers by providing fertilizer. How little was known at that time is evident by the detail given by Bailey in his letter of official travel directions prepared on March 1, 1924:

> *These caves are reported to be inhabited by enormous numbers of bats of which careful and intensive studies are to be made. The species that occur should be determined and their relative numbers, mode of occurrence, food and breeding habits should be studied and also as definite information as possible should be secured concerning the rate that guano is deposited in the caves. . . . A stop should be made en route at San Antonio, Texas, to examine the bat roost of Dr. C. A. R. Campbell with a view to determining its value in the production of commercial fertilizer. Visits should also be made to some of the larger caves in Texas, which have been alleged to produce many tons annually of guano, and a thorough study made both there and*

in New Mexico of the economic value of these bats as producers of fertilizer. Samples of a pound or more each of the guano deposited by the various species should be taken for examination in connection with the study of food habits and to determine chemical contents. Specimens should be taken of other mammals, reptiles, and batrachians that inhabit the caves or their neighborhood. Your familiarity with the work is such that further detailed instructions are unnecessary.[30]

While Bailey was in New Mexico, an old friend was working in Washington to begin manufacture of his design for an effective live trap. To keep the trap project going in his absence, he had arranged with Charles Knight to build prototypes of the traps.[31,32] Bailey's passion for livetrapping wildlife was to keep him going throughout the rest of his life, bringing him several patents and the opportunity to continue to travel after he left the Survey a decade later.

In response to Bailey's initial report that the bats "were still sleeping quietly in the highest parts of the caves," he received a suggestion from headquarters as to reasons, among them the weather and the altitude. He also received a veiled sigh of relief that he had obtained a permit and was not violating the game laws by collecting the bats: "We were a little afraid that you might have forgotten that bats have state-wide protection and might undertake to collect some without a permit and bring us into conflict with the State officials. As it is one of the functions of this bureau to enforce the game laws, we have to be especially careful."[33] In the same letter, he was encouraged to check on the antelope reported nearby, another mammal about whom little was yet known.

Meanwhile, back on the plains of southern New Mexico, Bailey received directions from headquarters in Washington on April 23, 1924, to learn more about antelope in order to verify whether they were increasing or decreasing. The letter noted that owing to the dry seasons of 1917 and 1918 settlers had left the country and, together with protection extended by stockmen, this was protecting the antelope so that it was now increasing in numbers, following a decade of considerable reduction in their numbers.[34] Apparently, they wanted him to verify the situation.

Bailey's former boss and still close ally Merriam, who was deeply involved with Indian history in his "retirement" aerie in northern California, on learning of Bailey's work at Carlsbad, wrote to him on May 12 to keep the Indians in mind, *lest your mind is too deeply imbedded in Bats to think of the Indian lore that may be connected with the caves. I am writing to call your attention to the importance of that part of the investigation. Don't fail to get from the Indians their old tales in regard to the caves: how they were formed, who lived in them, whether or not they were the abodes of giants or hob-globins. If you get solid with them and don't hurry them (put on brakes for once) you are sure to learn a lot of most interesting things.*[35]

From Carlsbad Caverns, Bailey continued the field season with official directions issued in July to investigate the food habits of injurious animals.[36] At the same time, he was designated officially as a "Biologist" with a $750 salary raise to $3,800 annually and still retained the title of chief field naturalist.

Beaver were seen more as a problem to farmers in timbered country than as a valuable part of the wildlife. While studying the "problem," after being sent to northern New York, Bailey received a state license to trap a pair to send to the National Zoo in Washington, which he did in September 1924.[37]

Beaver weren't the only wildlife "problem" that year. While Bailey was still trapping in New York, his colleague, E. A. Goldman, wrote him from Arizona about the deer problem there along with some information about a possible bait for beaver:

I am forwarding you under separate cover a small bottle of what is claimed to be a successful bait for trapping beaver in Alaska, which has been submitted by Ernest P. Walker for any use that we may wish to make of it. Mr. Walker remarks that it looks like a fake to him, but he would be glad to be advised as to what we think of it. You may have an opportunity to try it out, and if it seems to be worth while possibly a sample might be retained for analysis.

I had an interesting and also very profitable trip to the Kaibab Plateau with the committee appointed to investigate conditions affecting the deer. I was very much surprised to find a forage condition that I had anticipated two years ago has arrived much sooner than I expected. The reduction in carrying capacity of the area has been very markedly advanced by the drought of this year, but it would have come in any case. Conditions are approaching or may be said to have reached a very critical state, and unless some very drastic measures are taken to reduce the number of deer very soon I do not see how the starvation of thousands can be long prevented.[38]

These turned out to be prophetic words as the Kaibab deer explosion turned out to be one of the classic examples of overpopulation and habitat destruction, with extensive die-offs of animals, resulting from excessive predator removal.[39]

Bailey's reputation as a naturalist with a gift for interpreting natural history to the public was spreading. In a letter written in September 1924, he received high praise from Joseph Grinnell at the Museum of Vertebrate Biology at the University of California:

> *I have met up with at least a half-a-dozen Sierra Club people, back from their Glacier Park trip, who are clear in their praises of one Vernon Bailey! You certainly did arouse lots of real interest in the animal life; and they all are enthusiastic about you! Incidentally, let me express admiration of your Microtus contribution. That is a most significant record—bearing on all sorts of questions, both biologic and economic.*[40]

As a "popularizer of natural science," Bailey was asked to address the American Nature Study Society in August at its annual meeting with the American Association for the Advancement of Science.[41] Bailey offered a choice of subjects for his hour-long presentation, and the society chose "Our Friends and Foes in the Mouse World."[42]

Having just published *Wild Animals of Glacier National Park* with his wife, he discussed their work on the animal life in a brief talk to the Biological Society that fall as well. This talk included pictures in the form of glass slides showing the major life zones in the park and photos of the game species in the park along with population estimates of their abundance. He also noted that the hoary marmots, Franklin's grouse, and ptarmigan were so tame that they could be photographed at four feet from the camera and sometimes could be picked up, fed, and their backs stroked![43]

But, as they like to say, "trouble was brewing in paradise," as controversy was coming to a head over the predator control program at the Survey. During the early years of the 1920s the problem of predator control began to boil up with many people, and in particular academics and conservationists began to attack the program. Personnel at the Survey, including Bailey, quickly became embroiled in the issue. Discontent became open opposition at the 1924 meeting of the American Society of Mammalogists held at Harvard in May.[44,45] In the sanctuary of the venerable buildings of America's oldest institution of higher learning, several academics gently took issue with the Survey's extermination policy and, in turn, listened courteously as the agency's senior biologists responded.

Critics maintained that the Survey was not controlling predators but exterminating them. Valuable material, they claimed, was being lost to science. Local populations were being wiped out and some subspecies might already be extinct, making it impossible to reconstruct their place in the area of their relation to other populations of the same species.

Goldman, who bore the burden of defending the Survey, told the scientists not to be alarmed. Predator control might cause "local extermination," he explained, but the Survey did not intend to kill off whole species, and was not doing so. He maintained that the smaller predators, particularly the coyote, were in no danger at all.[46]

Goldman's rhetoric did not satisfy everyone, and the ASM membership took a vote to direct its president to appoint a committee to report on the Survey's predator control work. An attempt was made to insure the committee was balanced—Bailey and Goldman were selected to represent the Survey, and three academics (Joseph Dixon of the Museum of Vertebrate Zoology; C. S. Adams of the New York State College of Forestry; and Edmund Heller, chairman of the committee, from the Milwaukee Museum) were chosen to represent the general ASM membership. Adams was the only committee member with a professional academic education (PhD degree). Bailey and Goldman had no college degrees; Heller had a BA degree from Stanford and built his reputation on the Roosevelt African expedition of 1909–1910; and Dixon had done some graduate work and was employed as a collector and naturalist at the Museum of Vertebrate Zoology of the University of California at Berkeley.

The committee would not make a report until years later, and when it did, controversy erupted again (see below). The predator control problem would haunt the Survey throughout its existence, and Bailey would be in the center of the debate until he departed the agency. He sought his way out by developing live traps that would allow the capture of predators, without harm, so they could be relocated to areas where they could be protected. This opportunity was becoming one of his greatest passions.

39

Family Time and Professional Success (1925–1927)

The new year of 1925 produced a photo of Lake Tahoe from the Nevada relatives, giving the Baileys pause to reminisce about their time there when they had packed to the area around the west shore of the lake and then met up with Dr. Merriam and John Muir, of the Sierra Club, for a trip in the mountains south of the lake. As a result of his work on a Sierra Club outing there, Bailey was elected a life member, "an honor I had never expected but greatly appreciate."[1]

In April Bailey was dispatched to Pennsylvania by the Survey to assist that state with removing beavers from localities where they had become pests, to demonstrate the best methods of carrying out this kind of work, and at the same time to test the effectiveness of an improved type of trap.[2]

The trap in question was a live trap recently developed by Bailey himself. Although Bailey had collected many beavers on his early collecting days for Merriam, he began to study them in detail in 1920 for the purpose of restocking areas where they had been depleted as well as "farming" them as a source of breeding stock and fur. Most of his work had been in Pennsylvania, Wisconsin, Minnesota, New York, and the Upper Peninsula of Michigan which he felt showed great promise for the development of fur farming businesses because of the excellent quality of beaver pelts from that region. He was quoted in a newspaper article in a Michigan newspaper about the potential of beaver farming in the Upper Peninsula:

> I believe there are possibilities for establishing beaver farms on the upper peninsula which will bring rich returns within a comparatively short time. . . . My prediction is based on the plain facts that there are large areas of ideal beaver ground along the south shore of Lake Superior, as well as in other parts of the peninsula, and that beaver raised in this district are in great demand and will bring top prices as

> breeders. The value of beaver as breeding stock is several times greater than their fur value and beaver-raisers in other parts of the country are eager to get Lake Superior stock.
>
> Pennsylvania beaver farmers have tried to get breeders from this territory, but have not been able to. The Pennsylvania men turned to Ontario for their stock. Ontario beaver rank next to the Lake Superior animals, but do not compare with them. Yellowstone park beaver, far inferior to those in the upper peninsula, are being used as stock in the Adirondack mountains. Even with this inferior stock beaver farmers in Pennsylvania and the Adirondacks are making money, so there is no reason why the industry could not be built up here.
>
> I have found several places that are especially ideal for starting beaver farms. . . . and I have interested several persons to go into the business. They will apply to the state commission for permits to carry on the industry and the state department stands ready to co-operate to the fullest extent.[3]

The key to success in these endeavors was the ability to capture live beaver in sufficient numbers to house and raise them, and Bailey's ingenious trap potential could address that problem. The trap had been patented by the Survey but was available free of charge to manufacturers. For the next several years, Bailey would be extensively involved with people in an effort to make beaver farming successful and profitable in the Upper Peninsula.

His efforts to develop live traps were beginning to draw public attention. Edward Break, president of the Anti-Steel Trap League, wrote him several letters in May and June urging him to continue with his efforts,[4,5] and he started corresponding with W. E. Sanderson, field representative of the American Humane Association, who urged him to enter his traps in their annual live trap design competition.[6]

Anna's reputation as a taxidermist was spreading, and she wrote her brother in July about a major opportunity that had come her way:

> *There is to be a big exposition at Reno in 1926. Prof. Fransen and his assistants have asked me to mount a collection of the smaller birds of the state for the exhibit. The price is good, and I think I am to have most of the arranging of the large case which is to be classed as song birds, and some other groups besides. It is work I have always wanted to do and I will have a year to do it in.*[7]

Bailey responded the next month from the field where he had been studying muskrats in Louisiana:

> *Am delighted to hear of your new job—mounting birds for the state exhibit. You will enjoy it greatly I know and do it well. Do you know the new method of mounting is to cut out bodies from a soft wood lighter and easier to cut than cork that makes perfect mounts, very light and strong. It is called Balsa Wood and kept in stock by dealers. Bernard told me about it first and I will get the address of some dealer who keeps it for you. It cuts like cheese but lasts like time in things like these.*[8]

Bailey's experience for the Chicago Columbian Exposition a quarter century earlier was still coming in handy. By now museums had begun to display animals and birds in similar fashion, with attention to their natural environment, as Merriam's life zone theory became the norm. Bailey sent his sister pictures to show how such displays could be arranged professionally. He also offered his own invaluable suggestions, in a letter sent to her on November 22, 1925, to show the development of this art form that continued to be so important in his own work:

> *Glad to get your letter and we are sending some papers with pictures of bird groups, not all mounted but full of suggestions for grouping and sitting. The National Museum groups would not help you at all, as they are not well done or well grouped.*
>
> *Wish I knew more about the plans for the collection you are making but for a general collection showing the common birds of the region you should have group cases, with each group, as a case of sparrows on the ground and in the bushes with the back of the case painted to blend in the distance, a case of warblers in branches of trees with tree trunks and branches painted on the back, all the chickadees and nuthatches and creepers in another case with bark and branches and the background to correspond. Then gamebird groups, water birds, shore birds, gulls and terns, a pelican group and so on.*
>
> *Wish I could be there to help you with it. Why don't you run over to San Francisco and see the groups in the California Academy of Sciences and in the public museum in Oakland. You would get lots of ideas and see some of the best work of modern taxidermists. Go to Dr. B. W. Evermann, Director of the Calif. Academy at the Golden Gate Park and tell him who you are and what you want and he will do all he can to help you. At Oakland the Public Museum is one of the best of its kind in the whole country and its system*

of labeling specimens and groups to make them interesting is ahead of anything I have seen.

Have you any good book on taxidermy with instructions for making earth and logs and groundwork generally out of paper mache? You make it out of wet newspapers, plaster and glue over wire screen and cover with sand and grass and leaves. Put in glass for water and use bark for tree trunks and real branches and bushes. Laura could paint the backgrounds and these colored pictures in the papers we are sending will help.

Are they paying you enough to make it worth while? Don't do cheap work and make them furnish good cases and pay someone for painting the backgrounds. Put in lots of birds, males, females, old and young and all the different plumages you can get. Don't worry about bothering anybody and ask for all the help you want.

Give me your plan for groups or cases and I can help you more.[9]

His correspondence with his sister continued, this time focused on passenger pigeons. These birds had been extinct for many years, and their value as specimens—including their eggs—continued to rise. Bailey and his sister had been among the collectors as young people on the northern plains but the passage of time, like the passage of the pigeons, dims in memory. He tried to awaken his sister's memory in order to pinpoint their history with scientific precision. Writing to her after Christmas, on December 27, he inquired:

I've been trying to remember to ask you about pigeon eggs. There are seven sets in our old collection, one egg in a set, and a number of people are wanting to buy them. I tell them they can have them for $100 apiece but they want to give about $25. I laugh at them and tell them I am in no hurry. They are getting more valuable all the time. The only trouble is I've lost the old egg catalogue and do not remember the dates. Do you remember collecting any of them or when they were collected or anything about them? Or do you have any idea what became of the egg catalogue? Think hard.[10]

A subtle shift seemed to be taking place in his routine. Never one to complain, especially about outdoor activities, he let down his reserve briefly in this letter to his sister written at the end of December:

At last I am out of the woods and home and it is very pleasant to be comfortable again. I've had a most interesting summer and much of it very

> *delightful but at the last from Oct. 18 to 21 it was real winter with 3 inches of snow and cold. I was snowed in for 3 days in camp before I could get a team to move my outfit to the railroad and then I caught the first train for home. Was alone for the last two weeks and had a fine time as long as the pleasant weather lasted. Got some good big beavers at last, the largest weighing 49 lbs., but got only 14 in all, not so many as I wanted but enough to stock two ranches pretty well. That will give me a chance to continue the study of them in captivity next year and for a series of years.*
>
> *My traps did not work very well at first but now I can make a trap that will hold any beaver. . . . But the best of the trip is getting home for the winter. . . .*
>
> *I brought back some little chipmunks and some red-backed mice for pets and find some of the animals I left with others still alive, so my mouse room is fairly well started again. . . .*
>
> *I haven't heard from Matie all summer but will write her now. I simply couldn't write letters during the summer. It was strenuous work for all of the daylight and some of the night, but I stood it surprisingly well, though getting pretty tired and worn out and running down from 140 to 123 lbs. in weight. It hasn't hurt me any though and I am catching up as fast as possible.*[11]

His words suggest the arduous nature of field work, particularly at his age, is catching up to him, and he hints at wanting to spend more time with the development of his humane traps and ways to use them to encourage wildlife.

Bailey had an interesting experience at the annual meeting of the American Society of Mammalogists, held in May at the American Museum of Natural History in New York, where he presented a paper about some of his experiments on the hibernation habits of mammals. At the conclusion of his talk, Bailey casually speculated that, "It is quite within the range of possibility that hibernation may be applied to human beings—when we understand it—especially in nervous troubles where absolute rest and quiet are essential." This was picked up by the media and sensationalized far beyond the merits of possibility! One article had a byline that read, "Hibernation Might Cure Us of a Lot of Human Ills, Especially NERVOUS DISORDERS, Says Dr. Vernon Bailey, of the United States Biological Survey, if We Just Curled up and TOOK IT EASY UNTIL SPRING." Another article appeared with the title, "HIBERNATION IS URGED AS CURE FOR HUMAN NERVES."[12]

The year 1926 was a time of government austerity (Calvin Coolidge was president) and there was not much funding for fieldwork, but it did prove to be a good year for other accomplishments, including publications and patents. Bailey's long awaited biological survey of North Dakota appeared in the *North American Fauna* series,[13] and he authored a paper about mammals in the vicinity of Washington, DC.[14] The patent for his live beaver trap was granted, and the pamphlet describing its construction and operation appeared in print.[15]

Toward the end of the year, he once again used the holidays to catch up on family correspondence. Writing on Christmas night, 1926, Bailey described the Christmas fare to his sister as well as reminiscing about their visit earlier in the year:

> *It has been one busy time since we got home but Christmas is almost over, the guests are gone, and now we are free for a quiet evening at home and a letter to you. Dr. and Mrs. Merriam and Zenaida were with us for dinner, our second Christmas dinner, with turkey but no muskrat this time. I couldn't find a muskrat in the market, tho there were plenty of rabbits and possums and one black bear. . . .*
>
> *We had a lovely trip home through raging blizzards across Nevada, Utah and Wyoming and snow to Omaha and zero weather at Chicago but we enjoyed it all from a comfortable train. . . . [It was] a wonderful trip all the way around and it was good to see you all there again. We were telling Dr. Merriam about it today and that he ought to go over there and study those Indians and get you or Laura and Vernon to go around with him. I only wish it were possible for me to spend a summer there on caves and bats and domesticating sage grouse and mountain sheep and antelope.*
>
> *Or better yet if there was any way to start a survey of Nevada as Laura suggests. After next presidential election there may be funds again for field work but not unless we have someone at the head interested enough to get them and to use them where needed.*
>
> *Perhaps I was too discouraging about naturalist work but it makes me so mad that we can't do the things that ought to be done, we never have been able to since Dr. Merriam left the Survey.*
>
> *But I needn't kick. If I had done administrative work instead of fieldwork I would have been in a position to control such matters now. There will be a change of chiefs in the spring for Nelson is dropping out and we will have a new one but probably not so able a man as Nelson has been. Still things keep changing, up and down. Don't discourage Laura and Vernon from being naturalists. Someday it will be appreciated and anyway they will get more out of life from their knowledge of what is in the world. . . .*
>
> *It would probably pay Vernon [Mills] to make up all the muskrats he can*

> *get for specimens as topotypes generally sell well and they ought to bring at least three dollars apiece at any of the museums.*
>
> *It would be possible to make a collecting trip pay by getting specimens from type localities and advertising them in the Mammal journal for museums and private collections. I can send you a list of Nevada type localities if you want and help find a market for specimens. . . .*
>
> *You and Laura and Vernon could have a lot of fun collecting all over the state and make something if not as big wages as at some less interesting work. You have lots of rare species out there that would sell well in this and other countries. It could be worked up into a big business eventually with a worldwide market and would be worth doing. The collecting could be done in fall and winter when other work was not so urgent. I would be glad to help all I could and if a good business could be started there would be plenty of chance to write up and publish reports without waiting for government aid which comes slowly. Think and talk it over. There are still new species to be collected in Nevada and you would not be limited by any state lines. The whole desert country is rich in interesting animal life.*[16]

He was encouraging his sister and her young son to do what he had successfully done as a young boy forty years earlier, but the Mills family had its own agendas. Laura continued to teach and work at taxidermy. Young Vernon would later get interested in natural history as a possible career, and mother Anna continued to hold the family together on their homestead. The following summer all three of them joined Bailey for an outing to Oregon, which would prove to be a highlight in the memories of each of them.

Bailey spent the first part of the spring field season in 1927 in northern Michigan helping the State Conservation Department with beaver farming by teaching the game wardens and state trappers how to catch alive and handle their beavers. As Bailey noted, "It's a big problem and I am glad to help with it."[17]

In July the family clan had gathered for the Oregon trip, with Vernon Bailey footing the bill for hiring an automobile and all the other trip expenses, "for the sake of having you all with me for as long as possible"—rather than get involved in the red tape and restrictions on hiring relatives to be his assistants. He had hoped Merriam could join them and still anticipated that they might meet up with him in the Klamath country of southern Oregon on his own drive across country. Bailey's directions for his relatives' equipment were specific and enlightening to those of us now dependent on modern synthetics to meet such needs:

> *You will each need a light waterproof sleeping bag, made of 2 1/2 yards of double width (2 yards wide) unbleached, close woven sheeting. This should be first dyed seal brown or dark green or any dark color, then waterproofed and sewed across the bottom and halfway up one side for a bag. To waterproof it melt a pound (2 lbs. will do for 3 bags) of parowax and pour into two quarts of gasoline and dip the cloth in and soak up the bottom. (A gallon of gasoline will do for the three bags.) Do this a long way from any fire as the air gets full of explosive gas.*
>
> *Then hang up the cloth and let the gasoline evaporate, which will take a day or more if the weather is not hot and dry. Then iron each piece of cloth thoroughly with a hot iron to melt and force the wax well into the fiber of the cloth. It is better to do the waterproofing before the bags are sewed up.*
>
> *One good soft quilt sewed into a bag, across the bottom and halfway up the side and slipped into the waterproof bag makes a good summer camp bed. The bag is long enough to hold all your clothing in the fold above your head and keep the rain off at night and I can show you how to make the ground pretty soft and comfortable. You and Laura can sleep in the tent when you want to and Vernon and I can be perfectly comfortable on the ground outside, rain or shine.*
>
> *I will get the cooking outfit and grub when we are ready to start and we will keep everything as light as possible. Will have a few traps along but not count on doing very much collecting. I want to check up my life zone maps and get certain specimens to complete ranges and get all I can on crop adaptation.*[18]

The trip created many special memories, but by the end of July, the Mills participants had returned home, while Bailey continued to work in Oregon.

The predator control problem that had started to surface at the 1924 ASM meetings surfaced again in 1927 when C. C. Adams, chair of the society committee to look into the Survey's programs, called on its members, including Bailey, to make recommendations for the report. For a number of reasons, the committee made no report because many of its members were in the field and away from the office. Also, Nelson's retirement as chief of the Survey brought a further delay because the group wanted to give Paul Redington, his successor, a chance to get settled in office.

These circumstances, as well as professional differences among the members, made it hard for them to reach agreement on the predator control program. So, they presented two reports.[19] One, signed by all, was a noncommittal recital of common ground. Predators, it said, had values—educational, scientific, and economic—and should be preserved. It suggested either the national parks or isolated parts of the public domain but did not recommend any specific areas. The second report, signed by Dixon, Adams, and Heller, but not by Bailey and Goldman, charged that the Survey and the western livestock industry were conducting an extermination campaign against western wildlife that could not be defended on scientific or economic grounds. It went on to conclude that the estimates of stock lost to predators coming from ranchers and state officials had exaggerated the extent of the danger and that Survey analyses of the stomach contents of dead predators was inaccurate and biased. This second report was a direct attack on the scientific integrity of the Survey and caused much consternation and a defensive reaction on the part of Survey leadership.

The following statement, presumably approved by the Chief Nelson, was released on February 23, 1927, to explain the Survey's position.[20] Interestingly, it couched predator control as a form of wildlife conservation.

> WILD LIFE CONSERVATION ENGAGES
> ATTENTION OF BIOLOGICAL SURVEY
>
> The Biological Survey, one of the scientific bureaus of the Department of Agriculture, has as one of its chief functions the conservation of wild life. Its research work deals with the habits, relationships, geographic distribution, migration, and requirements of birds, mammals, reptiles, and amphibians. The information developed is important in determining the forms that may be broadly termed useful and those that are to be relegated to the category of the harmful, and in prescribing what man's attitude should be with regard to the protection of deserving species or the suppression of forms that are found to be economically or biologically injurious. Regulatory activities over the administration of several acts of Congress for the conservation of our heritage of wild life, including the preparation and enforcement of regulations for making effective a treaty for the protection of the birds that migrate between the United States and Canada.
>
> Although concerned chiefly with the conservation of wild life, the functions of the Biological Survey properly extend also to the control and in some cases the local suppression of such wild mammals and birds as menace success in agriculture, horticulture, forestry, or livestock production, or that threaten the continued existence of useful game birds or other harmless forms of wild life. When the suppression of wild-animal pests becomes necessary, this bureau does not hesitate

> on sentimental grounds to take drastic action, and it enjoys the cooperation of State agencies and other organizations and individuals interested.
>
> The actual control or destruction of injurious rodents and predatory wild animals becomes in the end a conservation measure, however, of great economic importance. The eradication of rodents from an industrial area and of predatory animals from livestock and game ranges makes room for production enterprises and for living creatures that are by comparison more useful and pleasing to man, and consequently more deserving of conservation and perpetuation. The attitude of the Biological Survey toward wild life is therefore three-fold. It stands for a wise and well-coordinated conservation and along with it, utilization and control.

The multiple faces of the Survey made the bureau function sometimes with a conservation perspective, sometimes with a preservationist perspective, and sometimes with a combination of both. The added responsibilities of protecting, managing, and killing wildlife—unlike the Survey's early work in mapping flora and fauna—lacked a strong scientific foundation, a deficiency that caused Survey scientists to question their assumptions about nature and their methods of investigation.[21] The predator control controversy seemed to stir a deeply rooted humanitarian ethic in Bailey, and although he continued to defend the Survey publicly, it would eventually bring him into conflict with its views and policies.

40

Beaver, Deer, and Cross-Country Trips (1928–1929)

Hopeful that the new year would prove to be less controversial, 1928 began with Bailey creating some unanticipated excitement at the meeting of the Biological Society of Washington. He brought a live, wild beaver to the event that, as he described it, "sat on a little table before 200 people and ate a big sweet potato and some crusty rolls and let everybody come around and feel of his fur and his tail and see his big teeth without making a bit of fuss. It was big medicine."[1]

In February, Bailey began a series of serious interactions with some men in Michigan about the possibility of establishing a commercial fur farming business in that state. In particular, he developed close ties with John A. Doelle, from Lansing, Michigan, the executive director of the Michigan Real Estate Association. Doelle contacted Bailey about an opportunity to put together a group of wealthy investors—including Dr. Clarence Cook Little, president of the University of Michigan—that would purchase significant acreage to establish a beaver farm. Many of the interested men were associated with the Hiawatha Sportmen's Club, and they had been discussing the possibility of establishing the proposed farm as a Michigan corporation, known as the Lake Superior Fur Corporation. Later the plan was modified to include a partnership with an already existing entity, the North American Fur Farm.[2]

Doelle suggested the proposed farm could be used as an experiment station for the federal government with Bailey as an employee. Bailey responded favorably, writing on March 5, 1928,

> *If you want to develop this property and will take me in to handle the beaver work for you at a small salary to start with and on a profit sharing basis that would be fair and reasonable, I would be strongly tempted to resign my present position and join you. There are great possibilities in it. The first thing*

would be to make a careful survey to locate the beavers and the best land to be enclosed for them, then to get the right kind of fencing and see that it is properly constructed at a reasonable cost.[3]

Apparently, Bailey took up the matter with the higher-ups at the Survey and in the Department of Agriculture who quickly nixed the idea because of the potential for a conflict of interest. Accordingly, Bailey responded with this somewhat apologetic handwritten letter to Doelle:

Only today have I discovered that it had been answered by Mr. Ashbrook, in charge of fur resources of the bureau and violently jealous because I have made a study of beavers and beaver management and published on them without taking him into joint authorship. He knows nothing of beavers or any wild animals and is not in any way a naturalist. From the first he has tried to interfere with my study of the beavers and in this letter which he wrote for the chief's signature he is merely trying to prevent my having any more to do with them.

I am sorry because I should like very much to come and could do a lot to advance beaver industries in that region, but time will do much of it anyway. I am tempted to throw up my job and come out there and start a beaver farm and make a demonstration that would show whether it would pay. But for two or three reports I am trying to finish I would do it this year.

For the present however I will have to stay here and drop all my work with the beavers which has seemed to me well worth doing.[4]

In thinking this through, Bailey must have realized that by resigning he would have placed his career at the Survey (and his retirement pension) at risk for something that was less than certain. There is no indication in the record that the beaver farming operation ever took off at the proposed scale, probably because of the financial difficulties imposed by the Great Depression that started about a year later.

Bailey's attention then shifted to deer management. In May 1928, at the request of the Game Commission of Pennsylvania, he was detailed to visit the areas in that state where deer were dying in large numbers to determine the causes and to make suggestions for remedial measures. Over several decades, Pennsylvania had realized almost unbelievable success in restoring its white-tailed deer population through protection, restocking, and a system of state deer refuges. A key part of their plan was to only allow the hunting of bucks with one or more forked antlers. Does and other antlerless deer (spikehorn bucks) were rigorously protected. A strong education program was then initiated to inform the public, especially sportsmen, about the need for protecting does, and this quickly became the "dogma" for deer management. But the deer population steadily increased and deer soon began to be a nuisance and damaged farmland crops.[5]

The Game Commission took action in 1923 by setting up a limited open season on antlerless deer. Public outcry was strong, and both sportsmen and landowners opposed the action. By 1925, the deer bubble was beginning to show signs of collapse. The animals killed by hunters showed lower average body weight, poor antler development, and increased parasite loads. Well defined "browse lines" began to appear across the landscapes, and that winter deer began to die by the thousands.

Bailey was appalled by what he found when he visited the area in 1928. In four townships, he counted more than a thousand deer carcasses as well as the depletion of nearly all vegetation within reach of the deer. With the backing of Bailey's report, the Game Commission took further action, announcing a complete closure on the hunting of bucks and an open season on does. Despite the public uproar, the commission held firm and the state deer population returned to sustainable levels. Bailey's recommendations were soon adopted in other states with large deer die-off situations.[6,7]

His report on Oregon mammals and life zones continued to progress and occupied him well into the next summer. His wife was even more preoccupied with her own writing, as her monumental life's work, *Birds of New Mexico*, neared completion. He was already looking forward to her completion of proofing the galleys because in just a few weeks he was scheduled to travel to the Grand Canyon for the purpose of participating in a study, under the auspices of the National Research Council, to advise the National Park Service about scientific and educational needs in Grand Canyon National Park.[8]

Bailey was excited about this opportunity not only because he had collected and studied animals in the park for many years, but also because he was working on some papers about the mammals and life zones in the park that were scheduled to be published in 1929, and his old friend and mentor, Dr. Merriam, with whom he had first visited the region four decades earlier, was also a member of the committee. Although he gave several talks and participated in meeting discussion, he refused to let these formalities interfere with opportunities to get in some fieldwork! In his trip report, issued on July 23, 1928, he declared, "Have started the boys here collecting mammals, birds and reptiles and building up a local collection. A glorious place to be and every minute more than full."[9]

Bailey also visited the Kaibab Plateau, part of the North Rim of the Grand Canyon, accompanied by Park Service officials, to check on the status of the deer population there, which had become a national controversy.[10] The deer population had undergone dramatic fluctuations since the government had assumed management over most of the region decades earlier. A common interpretation was that decades of predator control had reduced the natural predators of the deer to the point the deer increased exponentially in numbers and subsequently damaged the range so severely that thousands of deer began to starve. There were strong disagreements between the National Park Service, the Forest Service, and the Biological Survey about how to address the problem. The Forest Service had opened a hunting season on the deer that was adamantly opposed by the Park Service.

In his report on the mammals of the Grand Canyon (which included the Kaibab), Bailey noted that, while there could be as many as twenty thousand deer on the plateau, they were for the most part in prime condition, suggesting that the range was not currently overstocked. But, he cautioned that conditions were ripe for the deer to once again begin increasing rapidly, thus starting another starvation cycle. One of his major recommendations focused on the importance of minimizing domestic grazing of livestock. "If the accursed range cattle can be eliminated from the National Park there will be abundance of feed for antelope and deer all along the south side of the Grand Canyon."[11] But he also wrote that it was important to keep predators down, and no one challenged him. Although he didn't realize it at the time, Bailey was becoming drawn into the larger controversy about predators and deer management, the burden of which had heretofore been born primarily by E. A. Goldman in the Biological Survey.

Just before the year ended, a letter arrived from the Civil Service Commission wanting immediate clarification about the exact date of his birth and the inconsistency about the date in their records. After the new year, he wrote his older brother Charles in California who provided the necessary verification from the family bible. On January 28, 1929, the secretary of the Civil Service Commission notified the secretary of agriculture that the matter was finally resolved by a statement signed by Charles Bailey, and witnessed by Helen Bailey, that according to the family Bible record he was born June 21, 1864, and not 1863, which had been provided in some official records.[12]

Never one to sit idly by or have only one project at a time, Bailey wrote his sister on March 1, 1929, that "now I have to hustle to finish another book before I go west in the spring, probably to the Grand Canyon." This was the book on the mammals of Yellowstone Park, to which his wife contributed, but he hastened to disclaim to his niece Laura, "it will not be any such book as [Auntie Florence's] 'Birds of New Mexico.'" He concluded the letter with a brief note about a few of the new pets in his home, "mouse room, but not very many, just enough to keep me busy and learning a little all the time." He also made time to keep at bay his old nemesis—house cats—using his live trap, "and now the young squirrels and a family of young cardinals have a fine time in the yard, living largely on rolled oats."[13]

On March 20, before leaving for their annual trek out west, Bailey composed and sent to Paul Redington, the new incoming chief of the Survey, a lengthy philosophical letter about the "Balance of Nature." Why he did this is unknown because there is no indication that it had been requested by Redington. As the Survey was under attack over its controversial predator control program, perhaps Bailey thought it would be of use to Redington since his previous background was with the Forest Service.

THE BALANCE OF NATURE

The balance of nature is a much overworked slogan with little foundation in fact. There may have been such a thing before the discovery of America, but if so, it has not been satisfactorily recorded or described and it rapidly vanished before the advance of civilization.

With a sparse and scattered human population there may be a somewhat stable adjustment of animal and plant life, but with a dense human population such as we have now, or the far more dense population in European and Oriental countries, every form of wild life is dominated by the needs and activities of man. Many of us within the past 50 years have seen the middle west and western States change from abundance of wild game and other native animal and plant life to pastures of domestic stock, fields of cultivated crops, and exotic weeds. The game and fur animals went first, the carnivores had to be killed to protect the stock, and the rodents had to be killed to protect the crops. We who grew up among them know.

Some game and carnivores were crowded into National Forests and National Parks and unoccupied lands, and if we let them alone, as some advocate, to maintain a *balance of nature*, there will be in a few years a large number of carnivores and a rapidly diminishing number of game and livestock until these are all or nearly all gone; then the carnivores will starve or scatter out and a few [will] live on the small animal life.

Man has destroyed any balanced nature that ever existed and unless he controls present conditions intelligently animal life and even man will disappear.

These statements are truisms, so patent to us that they may sound foolish, but to most people the real facts of relationships among animals are little known that any pretty theory is accepted as fact and the false claims that if all animals are let alone all will be happy and harmless appeals to them so.

Tirades against the killing of carnivores have been widely circulated within the past few years and most of these can be traced directly to two sources, Dr. C. C. Adams and Dr. Joseph Grinnell, both able naturalists but with very restricted vision. Articles by M. P. Skinner, Edmond Heller, Edmond J. Sawyer, and others, associated with or dominated by Adams are along the same line, attacking the policy of the Biological Survey, the Forest Service, and the Park Service. . . .

It worries me when such intellectual men advocate policies so absolutely fatal and destructive to our best interests and highest good but how can we help it unless we can get the facts before the public.

The Biological Survey has never advocated the extermination of any animal much less accomplished it. Some species must be vigorously controlled or they will do great harm and we can get along with very few mountain lions and big wolves. Coyotes and bobcats will be with us for a long time in too great abundance for our needs, but they must be controlled or we will lose not only much valuable stock but the best of our game animals. The incidental or accidental killing of some badgers and skunks and valuable fur animals has brought criticism but has not been very serious and can be mostly avoided with proper care.

In no place is the control of animal life especially mammals and birds more important than in our National Parks. No species should be allowed to increase beyond a reasonable abundance for our use now and in the future, or beyond its ample food supply, and every native species should be maintained up to the abundance desired and to the best advantage of itself and others. In other words every species should be regulated as to numbers and distribution according to our knowledge of the habits and requirements of each and all. This is not difficult. It is being done to a great extent now and rapidly progressing to greater perfection, but such propaganda as Adams is putting out is hampering the Park Service. . . .

The same principles apply to National Forests and should apply to the Public Domain.

The Biological Survey has always stood for intelligent control and regulation of animal life, based on as full knowledge of habits and requirements as possible. If more of this fundamental knowledge

> could be made public the opposing propaganda would be largely overcome. Our position is sound and unassailable and if better understood would be more popular. We should guard against enthusiastic individuals discrediting the Survey by ruthless killing methods and especially wholesale poison distribution. Control and education of our field men are as important as are they important in education of the public.[14]

The statement clearly represents an effort by Bailey to justify, in philosophical terms, the Survey's position on predator control.

The Baileys didn't relish a drive west to Arizona and the Grand Canyon alone, so they had arranged for a family friend, Barbara Hastings, to take her car and drive them. The planned itinerary included a stop at the Mammoth Cave in Kentucky and at Carlsbad Caverns in New Mexico.[15] The purpose of the trip was for Bailey to work out some of the life zone inconsistencies in the Grand Canyon by collecting specimens in the bottom and on both sides, taking the whole summer to complete the task. Florence worked on birds and helped with his reports as well as a book they were both authoring. That book, *Among the Birds in the Grand Canyon Country*, was their last collaboration and major work of writing, as their professional lives quieted down with the passage of time.[16] He was then sixty-five, his wife sixty-six.

Bailey encouraged his niece Laura to join them at the canyon, then recanted and offered her the choice of that or a summer's outing with the Sierra Club to Mono Pass in the Sierras of northern California. Pushing a bit for her to join them, he described the possibilities in this letter sent to her at the end of March:

> *You can easily drive in to the north rim of the Canyon with a car and there is good camping there or all along the way. The north side is most interesting and you can go down the trail to the river and stay all night at a nice place there and up the south side next day, or go around by Lees Ferry by auto in a day.*
>
> *We couldn't be together all the time but could part of the time and it would be lovely to have you out there with or near us.*
>
> *I will have to be on many trips with the Park Rangers but will have to leave the rest somewhere. Will have lots of collecting and work to be done at many places in and out of the Canyon.*
>
> *I wish your mother and Vernon [Mills] could come with you but you would have to plan your party as would be best for all. Am afraid your mother would not enjoy the Canyon trails, but she wouldn't need to go on them.*[17]

Anna Mills had not been well, but she was getting stronger and they hoped for continued improvement as the summer weather warmed. The choice for Laura Mills was easy, and she began to pack for an outing to the canyon with her favorite uncle. He kept in close touch, writing her on stationery from Bright Angel Camp, about his work first in the bottom of the canyon before the weather got too hot.[18] The biggest thrill of the summer was his first opportunity to fly, with a young Ranger, across from the South to the North Rim. His enthusiasm was unbounded, so much so that his wife "feared he would discard all other methods of transportation for ever after!"[19]

On the return trip to Washington, the Baileys and their young driver stopped at Mammoth Cave in Kentucky. While Bailey worked on what he had found, his wife wrote to his niece Laura, on August 14, bringing her family up to date on their activities,

> *Uncle and I took a six mile trip in the cave the other day and he is just back from one to the River Styx and the lowest one, Echo Rim, where he saw white blind fish, crayfish, and worms white and blind after how many generations of adaptation to darkness? He says that the saltpeter made there before the war of 1812 and during the Civil War was made from bat guano, which supplied the niter, so perhaps we'd all be using bows and arrow but for the bats!*[20]

The ranger from the Grand Canyon, Edwin McKee, drove east with them. One of the Baileys' favorite roles was that of matchmaker, and once again they succeeded with their young traveling companions, who married on the very last day of the year.

As the Baileys looked toward a time of retirement not too far off, they headed west again to further plans for a new home in Southern California. It would be on land owned by Florence Bailey's cousin Helen, near that of her uncle Gustavus Merriam, who had been one of the first homesteaders in northern San Diego County. Vernon Bailey's brother Henry, a widower without means, would manage things for them meanwhile. Bailey wrote to his sister on September 13, 1929, about their plans:

> *I staked out my farm in a corner of Helen's place, 3 acres up on a bench where we can look over the whole Merriam Valley and enjoy all its beauty without much work or taxes. Henry will look after it and later explore for water and reservoir sites and set our trees and start building. No hurry for it will be several years before we can go there to stay and Henry is helping*

> *Helen with her chickens and has a comfortable place to live and not too much hard work. It's a beautiful valley and I want you to see it someday. There are lots of birds and kangaroo rats and wood rats on my farm. I'd rather have them than crops but I want plenty of fruit for them and us too. About half of it is irrigated now but the other half is most interesting.*[21]

The California experience was to be short-lived. The excuse for returning to Washington was that their house hadn't sold. The real reasons only they knew. After many trips west and enthusiastic reports about their new house, they closed it up, returned east, and did not return to Twin Oaks again. The house was later sold and is no longer part of the old homestead.

41

Predator and Prey and Patents (1930–1931)

In the nation's capital and in small towns across the country, "predator control" had become one of the big wildlife issues of the day at the beginning of the decade of the Great Depression. Bailey did not favor extermination of any animal but had certainly "done his duty" as he saw it in helping the farmers and ranchers through the work of the Biological Survey, and he often defended the Survey in public venues. But the dispute was beginning to affect the entire wildlife professional community and nowhere was it more volatile than in the American Society of Mammalogists where it pitted friends against one another both inside and outside of the Biological Survey.

In 1930, A. Brazier Howell, a former worker at the Survey and onetime friend of Bailey's and now on the faculty of the Department of Anatomy at Johns Hopkins University, entered the dispute in a highly vocal manner.[1] Complaining that the mammalogists had been handling the Survey with "kid gloves," he drafted a petition calling for an end to the predator control program as currently constituted. He circulated it among scientific institutions and societies and sent it to Chief Redington in April 1930.

Then at the annual meeting of the American Society of Mammalogists in New York in May, with Bailey on the board of directors, the ASM membership once again took up the predator control issue, this time appointing yet another special committee on the problems of predatory mammal control, instructing this committee to attempt a critical investigation of actual conditions in the field, in which the committee personnel would cooperate as far as possible with special investigators from the Survey.[2] Official members of the committee, which did not include any members of the staff of the Biological Survey, were H. E. Anthony (chairman), Lee R. Dice, M. P. Skinner, Charles T. Vorhies, and E. Raymond Hall.

Apparently, in an effort to defend the agency during the debate, Bailey and other Survey people made some harsh comments to A. Brazier Howell (although there is no written record of what exactly was said), causing Howell after the meetings to pen a letter to Bailey on May 7 in an attempt to make amends. Both Bailey and Howell were members of the board of directors of the ASM:

> *My dear Mr. Bailey:*
> *I am suspicious of these men who never get mad, but you did hand me a jolt for the time being. I feel like you do, that life is not worth living if we can't keep our friends, and I have forgotten already what you said. In fact, I feel that we are on better terms for it, and besides, I meant it when I said you can cuss me up one side and down the other, and altho I might flare back, I would still have the same affection for you.*
>
> *Just be patient and have a little confidence at least in my motives and sincerity for a while longer. I was under forced draft the other day and could not qualify statement as I should have liked, but you will hear the whole story before long. I know whom you have in mind when you mention soreheads. I think I have all such spotted and their statements have not an ounce of weight with me. Naturally I have gathered some chaff with the wheat. I have some misinformation, and other facts I don't know, but I also get some things that you don't. For instance I was told yesterday by a senator that Redington had told him that the destruction of other fur bearers incidental to coyote poisoning was of no moment anyway for the future of the fur industry lay in fur farming. That may have been twisted, but I get too many straws of that kind from the same direction for it not to indicate the trend of the wind.*
>
> *There are some who say that I enjoy this sort of ruckus, but it is most distasteful to me and I realize that personally it will likely do me more harm than good. And you may be sure I would never have tackled it without making sure that I am voicing the opinion of the great majority—at least, I am convinced, 95% of the non-BS [Biological Survey] members of the Society. It makes no difference whether the majority of them know coyotes or not, they can judge of what is sound biological practice. . . .*
>
> *And in regard to my methods, they may not be the best, but you know that kid glove efforts would never be successful, for we have been trying that for five years. Only vigorous action can succeed, and no considerable job of construction can be accomplished without some degree of destruction as a byproduct.*
>
> *But anyway, we are good friends and will stay so. Sincerely yours,*
> *A. B. Howell*[3]

There is no record of a response to this letter by Bailey, but it seems unlikely that he would have maintained a grudge as this was not in his nature.

A month earlier, in April 1930, Goldman and Bailey publicly defended the Biological Survey's poison program over the protests of mammalogists and before a US Senate committee considering the bureau's ten-year funding plan. Bailey took a complicated stance on the poison issue, noting that it was important to deal with predatory animals on a case-by-case basis, with the Kaibab situation representing a special case. His emerging concern was for management that placed humans in control of habitat, deer, and predatory animals,[4] along the lines of his philosophy about the "Balance of Nature" (see chapter 40).

With predator control so much at the forefront, the Survey dispatched Bailey to conduct field inspections of Survey predator control programs in Montana, Washington, and Oregon from October 17 to December 16, 1930. His trip report continued to laud Survey efforts and protocols, and his recommendations did not depart from previous Survey viewpoints.[5]

But what he saw at Kalispell, Montana, in November caused him to alter his previous views about the use of poisons as he described in his official report:

> Before coming on this trip I was in favor of giving up the use of poison by the Biological Survey on account of its possible injury to other forms of wild life and because the moral effect of its use seems not to be good. After seeing the careful way in which our men are handling it I am not prepared to condemn its use until we have something better and more human than the brutal old steel traps in general use. With a type of trap that would not injure the animal caught so that any useful, harmful, or unprized animal can be released, trapping could be made to answer every purpose of predatory animal control by being more effective than at present and less revolting to most right thinking people. It could be made a science and followed by more intelligent people. Until then I consider poison preferable to traps in controlling predatory animals.[6]

It also seems evident that his statement was intended to promote his work in developing live traps to be used in the manner described.

With all of this going on, and "as the new year rang in," Bailey was at last at a point to patent his humane trap. His patent attorney, Bayard H. Christy, a partner in Christy, Christy & Wharton "patents and patent litigation," in Pittsburgh, entered the fray, at least philosophically, in a series of letters to his client written in 1931 that intermingled their business with the larger context.

Christy entered into a discussion with Bailey on the subject. It is one sided in this telling, but Bailey's responses may be inferred from Christy's ongoing remarks: "In spite of what you say about the brutality of the steel trap, which is perfectly true, I think you should condemn the use of poison, if only because of the unintended victims. To my mind nothing can justify that."[7]

Two weeks later, on February 11, Christy continued with a much more extensive statement:

I understand the functions of the Survey to be essentially two-fold: one, to collect data; and, two, to cooperate in the accommodation of wild life to the needs of society. The criticisms focus on the second activity.

I understand it to be an avowed principle of the Survey that no species is to be exterminated. I may be mistaken in this, but that is my understanding. I cannot reconcile with this principle either the statements or the activities of the Survey, so far as concerns the Timber Wolf. It seems to me quite plain that the end desired, and certainly the end which is being accomplished by the Survey, is the extermination of the Timber Wolf.

My second point of criticism is the use by the Survey and its agents of steel traps and poison, because of the incidental and unintended victims. I am not prepared to say that these measures should never be taken, but I am satisfied that they have been taken and are being taken under circumstances beyond justification. Furthermore, I think the example of the government resorting to these measures is a very bad example, and encourages the use of such measures with respect to outlawed animals by ruthless persons with deplorable results.

My third criticism of the Survey is that, pressing forward keenly and eagerly for the destruction of certain species, it is supine as to protection. If it ever has done anything to rescue the Condor, for example, from extinction, or the Bald Eagle, or any other predator, I personally do not know what it is. There is now sufficient land over which the Survey has authority to make demonstrations to the public for the preservation of a considerable number of splendid and interesting species threatened with extinction. I cannot understand why the Survey is all on the side of destruction, and in these respects is inactive for preservation.

I have no sufficient knowledge to say whether the Survey's activity with respect to wild fowl is or is not all that it should be. I have read the gist of what has been published on both sides. The Survey may be entirely right, but in view of the nature and the weight of the criticisms I have felt that the Survey's position has at times been equivocal when it should have been clear and emphatic. It should be in a position to lead, not follow, when it comes to increasing the stringency of the game laws.

I say these things because I have been given to understand that you are one of the committee to review and report on the activities of the Survey. The vindication of the Survey is unimportant; the conservation of wild life is greatly important.[8]

Undaunted after reading the Biological Survey chief's report, Christy continued two weeks later:

A difficulty in the situation is this: a contention, a struggle has constantly to be carried on and carried on gratuitously against the overreaching and the subtlety of individuals and elements in society that are definitely and selfishly interested. It is but natural that the gratuitous contestant should at times yield ground! It needs exceptional wisdom, understanding, and moral fiber never to yield.

All of your letter is good, excepting only the sentence, "We have enough of both [wolves and mountain lions] and in some places too many, but I doubt if you want either back in Pennsylvania." That sentence has implications that I'm sure you did not intend.

Spring is upon us. I have seen the early morning robins and crows. Have you any plans for the field?[9]

Despite spending so much travel time and working with his live traps, Bailey continued to produce important publications for which he was recognized. The book he wrote on *Animal Life of the Yellowstone National Park* drew high praise from US Senator Frederic C. Walcott of Connecticut.[10] Also, he submitted for publication his manuscript on the "Mammals of New Mexico" and published two articles in *Nature Magazine*—"The Mammals of Texas" and "The Mammals of the Arid Southwest."[11]

That summer held in store a trip west, partly to accompany the Sierra Club on an outing north of Yosemite. They drove west with two young nieces, stopping to visit relatives north of Santa Fe, New Mexico, where he took Betty Hone to Seton Village to meet his friend, Ernest Thompson Seton. When they reached the gate to Seton's ranch, Bailey looked at the ground—a usual practice for the naturalist wherever he went—and quietly commented, "Oh, he's not home." His young niece couldn't figure out how he knew, until he explained. A wolf always leaves his sign and then scratches three times as he passes through his territory. Seton had left three scratches by the gate post so that those who knew him would know he had passed through and was gone.[12]

From New Mexico they traveled on to Nevada in March to visit the Mills family and gather more participants for the summer outing. If it wasn't so hot there, he wanted his wife to stay with Anna Mills at Fallon, but decided that the cooler climate at Lake Tahoe would suit her better, while the more agile members hiked for a month. Bailey wrote of his plan to his sister, on March 23, 1931:

> *Am very glad that Laura will be able to go and I want to bring Florence and if possible have her and you go with us to the first camp at Soda Springs in Tuolumne Meadows where we gather and stay over one day before starting out. That would give you and Florence one or two campfires and an idea of the way we travel and the kind of people in the party.*[13]

Laura Mills was excited at the prospect of the Sierra Club outing and offered various suggestions for her aunt's comfort in their absence while they continued with their fieldwork.

His official travel instructions, issued on June 27, were to visit various places in California, Nevada, and Arizona to study animal life and life zones in the Sierra Nevada Mountains of California and the Grand Canyon country of Arizona. In California he was told to join a Sierra Club party covering the high part of the mountains east of Yosemite Park and cooperate with them as far as possible in a detailed study of the fauna and flora of that region. The Sierra Club agreed to pay all expenses for this part of the trip. After leaving the Sierra Club party in California, he was instructed to proceed to the Grand Canyon country to continue the fieldwork he previously started there in 1929.[14]

Back in Washington after the summer, Bailey again heard from his attorney Christy, who continued corresponding on his philosophy of predators:

> *You will not, I am sure, think it merely contentious of me to discuss a point which came up casually last night and which under the circumstances could not be discussed then. Mention had been made of a biological principle, that the predator is valuable to the species preyed upon. You remarked (or so I understood) that if this were so, war was valuable to the human species. Since you spoke with conviction and since I feel deeply the importance of the whole subject I venture here to set down some comment on the matter.*
>
> *The principle that the predator is valuable to the species preyed upon is I*

believe well recognized: it is no mere fancy, conceived by those sentimentally interested in predators. Its operation has been particularly observed on the grouse moors of Scotland, where the relentless activity of gamekeepers in shooting hawks has resulted in disastrous increase of grouse diseases. This observation is current in the writing of men of first reputation; it can hardly be rejected by the open mind.

But does the observation follow that, the principle being accepted, warfare must be recognized to be valuable to humankind? No, for two reasons. First, *the principle has to do with* two *species: that of the predator and that of the prey; warfare is a phenomenon wholly within one species. Man at war is* both *the "predator: and the "prey."*

Second, *the principle operates beneficially in that it removes the physically unfit. Warfare in its operation removes the physically fit; and of all those who go to war it is the bravest that are exposed to the greatest danger. The biological effect of war, then, is to remove the fit, not the unfit.*

If application is to be made of the biological principle in question to human life, the best illustration must be found (the parallel is an imperfect one) in infantile diseases. They eliminate children of little stamina. It is children of relatively great power of resistance (of "high opsomic index") which overcome and outlive.

You will pardon my insistence. Too much is at stake to assent by silence to what one understands to be misunderstanding.[15]

The special committee, as the ASM was in the process of completing its report on the predator control practices of the Survey, and Harold Anthony (committee chair) distributed reports he received from Bailey and Goldman defending the Survey. The committee paid little attention to what the Survey people thought. The committee report was presented at the annual ASM meeting in Philadelphia on May 14, 1931. After summarizing the conclusions and opinions of its members and the feedback of others, the committee recommended to the society the following resolutions, which were passed:[16]

1. That the society strongly urges the Biological Survey that the use of poison as a control measure against predatory mammals be drastically curtailed, with the view of complete suspension of poisoning as soon as it is reasonably possible.
2. That the society deplores the propaganda of the Survey which is designed to unduly blacken the character of certain species of predatory mammals, giving only part of the facts and

withholding the rest, and which propaganda is educating the public to advocate destruction of wild life.

3. That the society asserts the claim of the great nature-loving public to a voice in the administration of our wild life resources, and challenges the right of a federal organization, such as the Biological Survey, to consider only the interests of a very small community, the live stock interests.

Clearly, the Survey was losing its argument in favor of predator control at least in scientific circles. Bailey looked at this and undoubtedly saw an urgent need to keep working on his development of live traps to help resolve the dilemma.

Christy was getting down to business on the Verbail trap, as it has been named, when the patent office responded to their initial application. He informed Bailey in a letter written at the end of April that they have asked for "revision in details of form, but, manifestly, the case is allowable. I am making response, and expect favorable consideration."[17]

The traps were already in use, and success stories added fuel to Bailey's desire to see the trap accessible on a larger scale. Then, on July 16, he received a letter from another live-trap inventor, E. D. Foster of the Folding Trap Company, the manufacturer of Live Catch Animal Traps for muskrat, mink, marten, beaver, otter, raccoon, rabbits, and cats in Tomahawk, Wisconsin. His admiration of Bailey is evident, as well as his interest in a joint endeavor. He wrote:

During the past few years of live trap manufacturing we have crossed your trail in a great many different sections of the country, until now we feel that we have almost had the pleasure of meeting you.

Our most recent contact was at the National Trap Contest in Albany, in which your beaver live trap received a place. It is about this trap that we wish to write you and am afraid you will find the length of the letter rather tiresome.

. . . From different sources we understand you make no pretense of building or selling your trap, and that anyone is permitted to use the idea in building and selling them. We feel this way about it, that you are really entitled to some royalty or percentage of profit on such traps sold to the public, and want to say we are willing to do just that. While our traps contain your original idea it varies considerably in size and general proportions, with improvements important enough to warrant this request of patents covering

those improvements. It occurs to me that any particular trap you might recommend for use in National Parks and Forests would certainly be given preference when such traps were needed, and if we can convince you that our models will give more efficiency and longer service than other makes, so that you could recommend them, we certainly would want you to get the financial benefits you are entitled to through your patent rights.

. . . In writing you we feel that if you find our trap to be the very best on the market to-day, you could recommend them for Government use, conscientiously, and at the same time get some return to which you are entitled.

If you wish we can send you some of the very finest of testimonials regarding them, but they would perhaps mean nothing to you, as your own judgment would be worth a great deal more than all the testimonials.[18]

Christy continued to correspond on details of the trap, involved not only professionally, but ethically and philosophically as well. Writing on September 2, he inquired:

I wish you would consider whether there be, in the simplification of material and manifest cheapening of cost of manufacture, anything which seems to you to be the expression of creative thought, and therefore patentable, as distinguished from good workshop sense, which is supposed to be possessed for the benefit of the world, and therefore not to be restrained by adverse patents.[19]

Correspondence with Foster also continued later in the month, as they worked together on the practicalities of the use of live traps. The trust and collaboration are evident. One is much less likely to find such interchanges today, further evidence of the change in attitudes in the intervening years:

Relative to the other live traps that you are perfecting, it occurs to us that perhaps we can help some in perfecting and field testing them, if they come within the possibility of our doing so. We have access to adjoining fur farms for making the tests in the wilds as the trap operation may be seen in actual process.

We are somewhat familiar with one or two of your experimental models for taking muskrat, with sets under water, and believe something along this line is going a long way toward the ultimate live trap for fur bearers. . . .

In line with your contention, that in the future most all fur bearers will have to be taken alive, we are in constant touch with all State Conservation

Departments, stressing the use of live traps, getting them to use and try them, so they may be more favorably inclined toward legislation along this line. The common steel trap is so well established that it's going to require a lot of pioneering to turn their thoughts to some other more humane and efficient method, but if live trap manufacturers can stick it out the effort may be justified.[20]

A break from the ethics of trapping mammals came for Bailey in attending the annual meeting of the American Ornithologists Union in October in Detroit when he received word that Florence's older brother, Charles, had just died at the age of eighty.[21] Mrs. Bailey returned to her hometown for the funeral directly from Detroit, where she had received the Brewster Medal—the first woman to do so—which was the highest honor possible in ornithology. As Bailey reported to his niece, it was awarded every two years for the most meritorious work in ornithology and was given for her New Mexico book. She received a medal and several hundred dollars with it.[22]

By the time Bailey returned home in November, he received the first very, very crude sample of his foot-snare trap from Foster, who found the lock on the chain not at all satisfactory and questioned the sales appeal of this kind of trap. In the same breath he lauded its humaneness and noted that if it works properly the animal would have little chance to escape or hurt himself very much. But would it sell? In a letter written on November 9, 1931, he asked Bailey to consider what advantage it had over steel traps:

You are considered a genius in figuring out traps and believe you can figure a lock that will meet all requirements. It occurs to me that perhaps the chain type of hand-cuffs used by police must have a perfect lock. I did not try them anywhere except on my dog and it seemed to work well, much to his discomfiture."[23]

In response, Bailey urged Foster to cut the costs so the traps could be sold more cheaply and thus be more accessible—another kind of ploy that fit more closely with Bailey's philosophy. Foster wasn't used to that kind of thinking and sputtered his response in a follow-up letter written on November 21:

I do not see how it is going to be possible to make them any cheaper as it seems these frames with springs can be built for not more that 10 or 15c, and if the trap is better than steel traps your competition there should not

> *be considered. For small animals they would cost more than steel traps but for larger animals they should be cheaper. If we can get something good the competition will not trouble us.*[24]

The year ended on a good note. In December, his lifelong work, "Mammals of New Mexico" (*North American Fauna* No. 53), came off the press and copies were distributed across the country.[25] Then it was announced that he had received a prize for his humane beaver trap. The official announcement, as stated in the Official Record, United States Department of Agriculture, read:

> For the Biological Survey beaver trap, designed to trap beavers alive and uninjured, chiefly for propagation and restocking, Vernon Bailey, the inventor, of the Bureau of Biological Survey, recently received second prize in the alive and unhurt class of the 1931 annual trap contest of the American Humane Association. The trap was developed by Mr. Bailey during his extended beaver studies made for the bureau.
>
> Patented in 1926 by the department, the Biological Survey beaver trap has proved efficient and practical and has been used by conservation officials in Arizona, Maine, Michigan, Minnesota, Montana, New York, North Dakota, Pennsylvania, and Wyoming, and by many individuals in this country, in Canada, and abroad.
>
> The main feature of the trap is the humane manner in which it catches the animal. It is a much enlarged steel trap with a bed of wire netting attached to the jaws, which are operated by coiled springs rather than by the familiar U spring. When sprung by the beaver, the jaws close above the animal and the side mesh confines it. The trap may also serve for carrying the beaver. Technical Bulletin 21 furnishes descriptions and specifications showing how a machinist or practical mechanic can manufacture the trap.[26]

Whether unsolicited or not, the testimonial that arrived in December from W. E. Sanderson, a field representative of the American Humane Society, certainly boosted enthusiasm for both Bailey and Foster on the importance of their collaboration on creating a humane trap:

> *I hardly know how to express my appreciation for the wonderful work that you have done and are doing for taking the cruelty out of trapping. You can imagine that I was especially pleased to see the statements you made with*

> *reference to humane trapping in your report of the game refuge trip that you made here in New York State.*
>
> *. . . I consider that you have made to date the greatest contribution for humane traps. I am speaking especially of your type of beaver trap. Your trap which was produced by the Folding Trap Company of Tomahawk, Wisconsin was found to be a success both in Pennsylvania and Michigan. This past fall they sent me one of these traps which I used in the exhibit in New York and at Grand Rapids. After the Grand Rapids show I took this beaver trap with me to northern Wisconsin where I caught two beavers on two separate nights before 8 p.m. I liberated them again as soon as I had taken some movies of them. This same trap I loaned to the New York State Conservation Department along with the other two that we have. One of these is the new one that you sent after the contest and the other is the one that I traded for with Mr. Slautterback of Pennsylvania. Along with the three traps belonging to The American Humane Association there were two other traps made after your specifications. Throughout the test the two that were made for the Conservation Department went out of commission. Four beavers were caught, three in the same trap that I had used in Wisconsin and one in the new trap which we received from you this past summer.*
>
> *I do not pretend to be an expert trapper, neither am I a gambler. However, I would like to see any other trapper with one steel trap or any other trap make a better showing that I was able to make with the Bailey trap catching beaver in Wisconsin.*
>
> *The American Humane Association feels greatly indebted to you for what you have done to help us with our work of giving to the wild life of the field and forest the same protection now afforded domestic animals.*[27]

Likewise, Foster received affirmation from the state of South Dakota, which had been experimenting with both the Bailey trap and another one. They chose to order from Foster, and he reported his pleasure to his collaborator on December 22, with a proviso, "Despite these occasional bright spots business is pretty bad, so will probably have plenty of time to work out your ideas."[28]

Perhaps because he wanted his views recorded for posterity, earlier in the year Bailey sat down and composed a handwritten document, that he called "Wild Life Policies," expressing his views about the underlying principles of wildlife management in relation to public and private lands. Though never officially published, it is presented here exactly as he wrote it.[29]

WILD LIFE POLICIES

Abraham Lincoln said *with public sentiment nothing can fail, without it nothing can succeed.*

Not only the sportsmen but all classes must be back of conservation if it is to be a success. Wild life covers all kinds, the farmers, the scientists, the foresters, the recreationists. Let them all contribute and feel the same ownership and interest that is so often limited to sportsmen. This will demand a policy.

Practically all wild life has some value in some way to some of us, but too much of any kind is not desirable anywhere. There must be control, protection, regulation, segregation or much of the most valuable wild life is wasted. But let us think in broad terms and give each form of wild life its full value, to others as well as to ourselves.

To the farmers and land owners, why not give a fair share of the value of the game this land supports and their crops help to feed and so have the advantage of their good will and cooperation in practical conservation rather than their opposition. At best the farm yields but a meager return and the game could in many cases be made a valuable crop that should be encouraged.

The problem of devoting public land to its highest use for all of the people is often complex but on certain types of land, not well adapted to agriculture, game and fur bearing animals will often yield valuable returns and at the same time allow the slower process of reforestation to take place over a long term of years. Not all such lands are adapted to all of many kinds of wild life however and a definite policy of management must be developed for each type.

Game and wildlife management becomes a serious problem requiring the application of much scientific as well as practical knowledge on a wide range of subjects, but especially on the habits and requirements of both mammals and birds. It also must include a full knowledge of plants and food cover for wild life and of the endemic and contagious diseases to which game animals and birds are subject.

There must be safe and simple methods of control of all forms of animal life so that none shall unduly injure or destroy others. A wholesome relative abundance should be established for such species as can successfully occupy the same ground and this relative abundance should be maintained. With other species which can not live together without the serious destruction of one or more defenseless forms either the destroyed or destroyers must be removed to other areas or utilized in some way to avoid conflict.

Any mammals or birds may be taken in live traps that will not injure them and they can be then moved to such areas as are suitable to them or confined in inclosures [*sic*] or handled as seems most advantageous in any general plan of management. Complete or partial segregation of species will in many cases be found necessary and it should not prove difficult.

Domestication or semidomestication of many of our native mammals and birds is bound to take place in the not distant future and certain species would be of great value as additions to our present list of Old World stock. This however has only a secondary bearing on the present plan of wild life management.

Private ownership of game and fur bearing animals on fenced and owned or controlled land will demand recognition in the future more than in the past and definite plans for control, regulation, and disposal of privately owned game could well be involved in a general system of wild life management.

Protection of rare or depleted species of game mammals or birds often requires great care and skill to bring back or build up a satisfactory abundance but in most cases it can be done and the national disgrace of extermination of a species be avoided. Usually the species in danger have some peculiar value for game or food or fur and their restoration is a national asset.

Valuable native species of game or fur bearing animals should be maintained in such abundance as desired on their natural ranges and in some cases their ranges may be slightly extended within their natural life zones where they will not conflict with other forms of native life. In most cases there is less danger in extending the range of ones own species than in introducing others from foreign countries.

Introduction of exotic species of game or other mammals and birds is always attended by risk and real danger to some of our native species and should be very carefully considered and in most cases avoided. In many cases they will only supplant and crowd out more valuable native forms or they may bring in new diseases that are fatal to some of our most valuable native life. Still it is not necessary to bar all importation and the ringneck pheasants and Hungarian partridges have proved valuable additions to our game list in extensive agricultural areas from which all native game has been crowded out. Much careful study should be given to importation of any exotic species.

Control of forest and grass fires is one of the essentials of conservation and game management. More efficient methods must be devised for both prevention of fires and quick control.

Regulations for hunting and other methods of taking game and fur should be in the hands of a commission that can act promptly in determining when other seasons can be allowed and when closed seasons are necessary. At least the commission should have authority to close the hunting season promptly when there is danger of too much game being removed.

Local and limited licenses would often afford the best means of regulating the number of animals to be taken on any limited area, limiting the number to the known surplus for a county or group of counties or for smaller areas.

Bag limits for game, fur and fish are of course an important check on the take and in some cases could be restricted instead of closing the season prematurely.

With deer an occasional open season on does for the whole or part of the regular season or on both does and bucks without restriction of sex may be necessary to keep a well balanced herd and afford the greatest amount of hunting and best grade of game. A large number of deer does not necessarily mean a large number of full grown bucks for hunting or for breeding purposes. So far as we know about five does to one buck is a good proportion.

Regulation of fire arms, traps and all means of taking game should be part of the duty of the game commission, not only for protection of game but protection of the public. Any carelessness or dangerous methods should be penalized.

Publicity, or education of the public to a full understanding of the necessity of control and management of wild life is absolutely necessary for successful operation. Education of the public takes time and in many cases should be started several years ahead of any new move, such as an open season on does. All game officials should be primarily educators.

This remarkable statement is consistent with the modern conservation philosophy of wise use, as opposed to complete preservation; it outlines a rationale for endangered species management; it points out the potential problems with exotic species; and it supports the role of state and local management of game animals and other forms of wildlife. Bailey's practical experience and his many years of fieldwork gave him an enormously practical perspective about wildlife management and conservation.

42

Rewards and Sudden Announcement (1932–1933)

The South Dakota order for beaver traps and other orders had pressed Foster to the limit, and he apologized for the delay in proceeding on the foot-snare trap while adding his own reservations about it. Writing on January 24, 1932, he noted:

> *One thing about this type of trap, if it can be made to operate 100%, is that it will be rather hard to set on account of the chain which is so hard to keep in the proper position. This may be a serious handicap in marketing them. The average trapper is now so accustomed to the convenient steel trap that he may object to using another type unless it has decided advantage, in ease of setting and results. I will continue to give it thought and would be glad to receive any suggestions you make.*[1]

At Bailey's suggestion, Foster tried some sample traps on cats, but without results. His next target was muskrats. Meanwhile, business was picking up with a new order for fifteen aluminum beaver traps in March that greatly satisfied Foster.[2]

After sixteen months of waiting, the patent office allowed the proposed patent improvements, and Christy advised Bailey to forgo paying the fees to register it in other countries, based on Bailey's indication of its ultimate value elsewhere.[3] Now, it was on to the next, an application for a new pole trap. Christy requested a sample or drawing, or both, so he could understand it in order to advise Bailey about the next steps to take. Writing on April 1, he noted:

> *Surely it would be a humanitarian thing to have a pole trap whose use would not involve mutilation and suffering. As a conservationist, I have doubt whether, in the present state of mind, people who use pole traps would pay much regard to distinctions between good and bad birds of prey. That,*

however, has nothing to do with the humanitarian considerations, nor has it anything to do with the question of patentability.[4]

Bailey responded ten days later with a description of the new trap and a justification for its patentability:

The object of the trap is to do away with the cruelty of catching birds in steel traps on poles and to allow the destruction of injurious species and the release of useful species of hawks and owls without injury. The peculiar features in this trap that differ from all others are the motion of the spring which jumps upward and throws the chain high around the legs of the bird, and the soft flexible chain which will hold the captive without injury or discomfort. I have looked at a great many designs of somewhat similar traps in the Patent Office but I did not find one that has these features, or that could possibly be a success for such purposes. I believe that this trap is not only patentable but that it will be a thorough success.[5]

Negotiations to manufacture his traps continued with Foster offering a royalty of two dollars per beaver trap. Their honesty with each other is quickly appreciated as Bailey responded on January 10, 1932, "In regard to the beaver trap your offer of a royalty is perfectly satisfactory and a similar arrangement for the other traps would be equally so. In fact I think that two dollars on a beaver trap is rather high, but if the business will stand it, so much the better."[6]

Bailey returned to the field once again in the summer. His letter of authorization, issued on May 26, 1932, directed him to proceed to St. Paul, Minnesota, and other points in Minnesota, Michigan, and Wisconsin for the purpose of field investigations on beaver to mark them for age and sex and condition of fur.[7] Then he and his wife trekked west to his home area of northern Minnesota, lamenting as he went its development into a "great summer resort for the farm country and cities." The effect on wildlife was startling. He reported to Anna that he didn't even see a spruce grouse. "They are so tame anybody can kill them with sticks so they are most all gone."[8]

In July he was notified that he had won first prize of $100 in the annual trap building contest—in the category of traps taking animals alive and unhurt—supported by the National Humane Society. The prize was awarded for "a trap made in different sizes that catches either mammals or birds by a looped chain that is thrown upward and around the leg as the trap is sprung and holding the creature securely but without injury."[9]

As the year rolled into winter, Bailey's nephew, Bernard, the son of

Bailey's older brother Charles, who had been collecting small mammals in California, received an invitation, apparently on the recommendation of Bailey, to do some collecting in Mexico for the Museum of Comparative Zoology at Harvard. Bailey agreed to accompany him to assist with the work, and the two of them spent most of the months of November and December collecting in the Mexican states of Sonora and Chihuahua, apparently with considerable success. Bailey had not worked in Mexico since 1889, and he hoped this would provide his nephew an opportunity for additional employment.[10]

On his return east after the new year, Bailey worked on a longtime project to list all the deer specimens in the museums across the country. During his stay in Chicago, while he listed those housed in the Field Museum, he wrote his niece Laura, acknowledging her Christmas gift of a book of her own production, "On the Heights." Writing on January 30, 1933, he complimented her that "you do such exquisite work in your pictures, type and text that your books are treasures."[11]

Trapping continued to be the focal point of his professional life. In March 1933, he published a leaflet for Cornell University's Rural Education Department titled "Trapping Animals Alive." They printed 90,000 copies.[12] Laura Mills provided the photographs of coyotes and the traps for this and other articles, and her brothers helped experiment with the traps. Anna welcomed the boys' involvement. Bailey had tried to get his brother Henry in California to experiment with the traps, but he replied that all the coyotes had been caught down there, since "so many people had nothing else to do."[13] So he was counting on the Nevada contingent of the family to help with his ongoing experiments to perfect the traps.

In May 1933, at the fifteenth annual meeting of the American Society of Mammalogists (ASM) in Cambridge, Massachusetts, Bailey was elected to a two-year term as president of the society of which he was a charter member. His election came after T. S. Palmer, his colleague at the Survey, had declined to serve. The minutes of the recording secretary of the ASM recorded the election episode as follows:

> On the first ballot for President Dr. T S Palmer received the greatest number of ballots, and on motion he was formally and unanimously elected but Dr. Palmer promptly resigned, even after those present refused to accept his resignation. Persisting, however, a new ballot was taken, undecisively, and the third ballot showing a preponderance of ballots for Vernon Bailey, and as this was a formal ballot,

Bailey was declared elected, and he took the chair and thanked the members for their approval.[14]

On hearing the good news, his old friend and protégé Olaus Murie wrote from his home in Jackson, Wyoming, on June 9, congratulating him on his election and offering "any help I have a chance for."[15]

The ASM meetings that year also witnessed the first positive agreement between that society and the Survey in many years, namely, the passage of a resolution by the society in support of the Survey's research budget that was under threat of serious reduction. Survey Chief Paul Redington responded with a brief note of genuine appreciation for the action regarding the research activities of the Biological Survey.[16]

The end of Bailey's official career at the Survey came quickly. On June 27, 1933, he received a form letter that his classified appointment as senior biologist was being terminated on July 31 "without prejudice because of reduction of force."[17] This was followed a week later on July 3, 1933, by an official memorandum from Redington advising him that his separation was "due to the necessity of reducing bureau forces because of greatly reduced appropriations for the fiscal year 1934."[18] Redington expressed his regret that the action was necessary because of the Depression and the need to cut back on the staff. The official announcement was followed on July 5 by a personal letter from Redington to Bailey expressing appreciation for his forty-six years of service to the agency and for standing up in defense of the bureau's predator control program. An excerpt from that letter stated:

> *Your reputation as a painstaking investigator, as a lover of all forms of wild life, as an explorer, and as a very friendly soul has already been written in the records. I cannot add much to this statement except to hope that you and Mrs. Bailey may keep on in the splendid nature work which has appealed to both of you, and that in your years of retirement you may continue to have the peace of mind that is one of your characteristics.*[19]

On July 7, Bailey responded with this personal letter to Redington noting his appreciation for his kind expressions:

> *Dear Mr. Redington:*
>
> *My notice of retirement is received and also your very kind letter of the same date.*
>
> *For over forty-six years my whole life and work and interest has been centered in the Biological Survey of which my field reports and specimens and*

publications are a permanent part, and it is needless to say that the best interest and development of the Survey along scientific and practical lines has been and always will be my highest interest and ambition. My separation from the official service at this time, a little earlier than I had expected, is no great hardship, and Mrs. Bailey and I both feel that it is better for us to go than for some of the younger employees, to whom it would have been far more serious. We appreciate the spirit of fairness in which you have acted and also your expression of confidence and friendship. This change will in no way lessen our loyalty to the Survey, nor our high regard for you and your most estimable family.

I shall have much to finish up, including proof reading on our Kentucky Cave Life book, now in press, and I hope on proof of the Oregon Mammals and Life Zones, as my last contribution to the series of North American Faunas. At all times I shall count it a pleasure to be called upon for any help that I can give in any of the future work or plans of the Biological Survey. As president of the American Society of Mammalogists I also hope to be able to establish a better spirit of cooperation among the working naturalists of the country of which the Biological Survey should and generally has taken a leading part.

With sincere regards, I am, faithfully yours,

Vernon Bailey, Chief Field Naturalist, Division of Biological Investigations[20]

Accolades poured in from colleagues and friends across the country expressing congratulations on his many achievements. William J. Hornaday, the first director of the New York Zoological Park (known today as the Bronx Zoo) and a pioneer in the early wildlife conservation movement in the country, penned this letter on July 21, 1933:

The American public is to be sincerely congratulated on the fact that your life and health has been spared for 46 years of expert and valuable service in expounding the wild life of North America. Your record of work and successful achievement is one of which you and your family and friends can forever be immeasurably proud. If there is anyone in the field of zoology who appreciates your work any more than I do, I have yet to discover him. Sincerely and permanently . . . your friend, W. J. Hornaday[21]

Horace Albright, director of the National Park Service, wrote this on August 7, 1933:

You have had a wonderful career in the service of the United States Government. As a scientist and as a naturalist everybody knows and can understand that you have made valuable and lasting contributions to the Government, on the one hand, and to public welfare, on the other, through your labors for the conservation of the Nation's wild life. I feel sure that your record in the field of biological research and in the conservation of wild life is so notable, so widely known, and so much appreciated that it must surely be a cause for supreme satisfaction as long as you live.[22]

His lifelong friend, colleague, and boss at the Survey, E. W. Nelson, who would be dead less than a year later, wrote this on August 2:

You are to be congratulated on the splendid usefulness of your services to the Bureau and to the development of mammalogy especially in this country. You have started many beginners in the study of mammals, including myself, and I hope you will have many years ahead during which you may put your store of information in permanent form and at the same time continue your field studies in life history. You will be free to choose your subjects and can please yourself in your programs. . . . You and Mrs. Bailey are among the few long time good friends that are left on my list and become more and more prized as time goes on. . . . Always, sincerely your friend, E. W. Nelson[23]

Then on September 1, a brief note was received from Henry Wallace, secretary of agriculture under President Franklin Roosevelt, that read:

Dear Mr. Bailey,
I learned some days ago of your retirement, and it has been on my mind ever since that I should say to you how much we appreciate the record of your forty-six years of fine service. It reflects credit upon us all, and it should be a source of great satisfaction to you.
Sincerely yours,
H. A. Wallace, Secretary[24]

Bailey penned a handwritten response back to Wallace and mailed it from Ranchos de Taos, New Mexico, on September 14. It read:

In Santa Fe yesterday I was much pleased to receive your good letter of Sept. 1, in regard to my forty six years of service in the Biological Survey. It is a great satisfaction to feel that my work has seemed worthwhile and that I still have many warm friends there. Most of my interests are still with the Department and I have great hopes for its future under your administration.[25]

A retirement ceremony was held in Washington on July 21, and Bailey was presented with a book of photographs and autographs from the event as well as a retirement gift. The following encomium accompanied the photographs and gift:[26]

TO
Vernon Orlando Bailey
Pioneer explorer and leader
in the
Bureau of Biological Survey
United States Department of Agriculture
Life-long student and lover of wild life
Eminent naturalist and writer
Devoted champion of birds and mammals
Friend and Inspirer of humankind
Loyal and helpful citizen
His fellow-worker in the Survey
Extend whole-hearted wishes
For health, contentment, and
Long-continued service

On August 30, he penned this handwritten letter of thanks to Walter Henderson who had organized the event:

Dear Mr. Henderson:
I can never get over the pleasure and deep satisfaction of the many expressions of friendship given Dr. Palmer and me on our retirement from the long service in the Biological Survey. The book of photographs and autographs will always be one of my most prized possessions and I am sure that the beautiful all leather traveling bag will be useful as long as I shall need it.

But most prized is the true friendship and good will back of it all. At the time I could not express half of my appreciation of all you did and said and again I want to extend my thanks and best wishes to each and every one of my friends in the Biological Survey.

I hope to work with you still for many years to come, Sincerely yours,
Vernon Bailey[27]

It was officially finished after forty-six years of devoted service, and on August 18 he received a form indicating that he had been granted an annuity of $1,200.00 per annum, under section 1 of the act of May 29, 1930, commencing Aug. 1, 1933. His record of service and compensation follows:[28]

May 10, 1887–Nov. 18, 1887	$ 40/month
May 15, 1888–July 1, 1890	$125/month
July 1, 1890–April 30, 1895	$150/month
May 1, 1895–June 30, 1896	$1,800 per annum
July 1, 1896–June 30, 1902	$2,000 per annum
July 1, 1902–June 30, 1903	$2,250 per annum
July 1, 1903–June 30, 1906	$2,400 per annum
July 1, 1906–June 30, 1910	$2,500 per annum
July 1, 1910–June 30, 1911	$2,850 per annum
July 1, 1911–June 30, 1920	$3,000 per annum
July 1, 1920–June 30, 1924	$3,250 per annum
July 1, 1924–June 30, 1927	$3,800 per annum
July 1, 1927–June 30, 1928	$4,000 per annum
July 1, 1928–July 31, 1933	$4,600 per annum

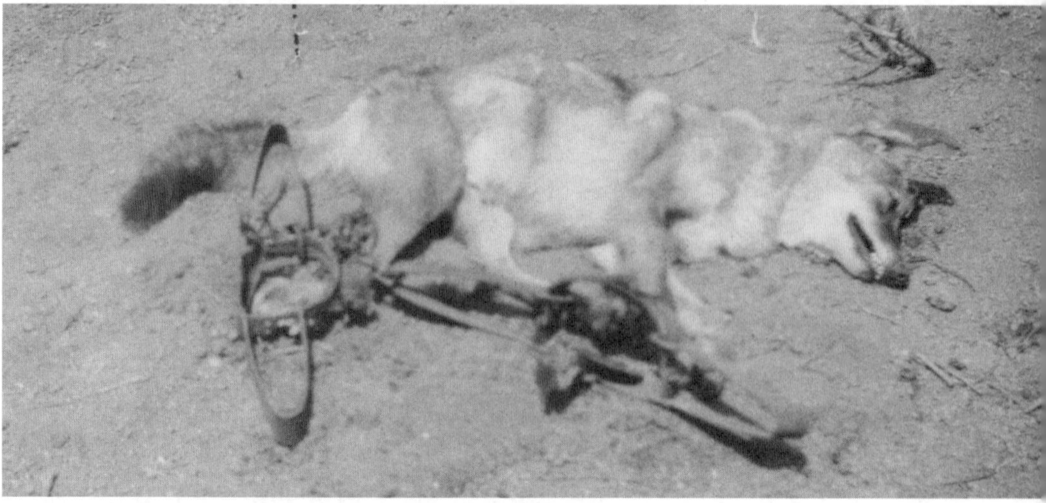

Coyotes in two No-3 steel traps, leg broken and left to die. Courtesy of the Vernon Bailey Papers, Box 18, American Heritage Center, University of Wyoming.

Coyote in Verbail Trap. Courtesy of the Vernon Bailey Papers, Box 18, American Heritage Center, University of Wyoming.

Female gray wolf in a steel trap about to be killed by the Biological Survey on the east fork of the Gila River in New Mexico. Courtesy of the Denver Public Library, Western History and Geneology Department. Stokley Ligon Collection.

Biological Survey hunter and his catch of coyotes. Courtesy of USGS-PWRC, Biological Survey files.

Biological Survey hunter Cleve Miller in Arizona, with mountain lions, 1922. Courtesy of USGS-PWRC, Biological Survey files.

V

Retirement and the End

There has been speculation that Bailey may have been "forced out" of the Survey because he had changed his position on the predator control problem, favoring humane treatment instead of extermination, and because of rumors that Mrs. Bailey had contacted Eleanor Roosevelt asking her to intervene with her husband and end the program.[1] The major reference to support this comes from Stanley Young's manuscript on the history of predator control, a work completed in the 1960s toward the end of his life, but never published. Young neglected to note the all-important date or the name of the First Lady's informant, making it impossible to confirm the speculation.

As we shall see in the chapters in this section, Bailey's retirement years were as notable as those that went before—in writing, in motion picture photography, in humane work, in lecturing and counseling and continuing fieldwork as a consultant for the Biological Survey. Although retired as a full-time employee, he was soon added back on a part-time basis to continue his fieldwork and special projects that had not been completed, including continued field trials and improvements of his recently patented Verbail traps. Compensation was not included with his appointment, which only allowed for reimbursement of travel expenses.

Practically every season of his involvement with the Survey after retirement was marked by fieldwork in some part of the United States, including work in Texas, Oklahoma, New Mexico, North Dakota, and Oregon, as well as publishing papers for scientific journals and popular articles for *Nature Magazine* and other outlets.

43

Trapping a New Life (1933–1939)

In retirement, Bailey shifted full steam into his trap projects, while his wife recovered from an auto accident in which her knee was damaged. He wrote to his sister Anna on July 23, 1933:

> *Maybe we will get out there occasionally now that I am out of office and our time is all our own. I've got to test my traps on coyotes and make them work the first thing. Then I will have to start a company to manufacture them and put them in the market.*
>
> *Just now we have to wait for another week for Florence to have the plaster cast sawed off her leg and then some time for the knee to get limbered up so she can get around. She has been very patient and her recovery will be perfect but it takes time.*
>
> *I hope we can go to Calif. this winter to get things all fixed up there. Henry has the walls of the house up to the windows but it goes slowly. . . .*
>
> *Here is a copy of my obituary from the Department of Agriculture, highly colored for public news consumption.*
>
> *I feel greatly relieved to be free and hope to be able to live on my annuity of $1200 per year and what else I can make in various ways. Anyway Henry and I think we can raise enough to eat on our place in California and we will not be so far from you there and I hope we will see you oftener.*[1]

Professional recognition for his career achievements continued to pour in. On May 22, 1934, he received a letter from Gilbert Grosvenor, president of the National Geographic Society, that he had been elected a life member to the organization for his contributions "for the increase and diffusion of geographic knowledge."[2] He was the forty-third recipient of the honor; other life members included Charles Lindbergh and Bailey's friend and former boss, E. W. Nelson.

Just a few days earlier, as recorded in his field diary on May 19, he went to see Nelson at Garfield Hospital where he was taken a few days earlier following a serious heart attack. Bailey found him "very feeble but still keeping his courage and saying he would get up again," but the next day the diary entry simply stated, "Nelson died early this morning, a brave old scout and very useful man."[3] Both he and Palmer had retired and now Nelson was dead. The old guard, with the exception of Goldman, was no longer in place.

As is often the case, "retirement" was not all leisure with both Vernon and Florence remaining active in their Washington social circles. They were invited as special guests to a banquet in the capital city on February 27, 1935, at the Roosevelt Hotel to celebrate the fiftieth anniversary of the Biological Survey.[4] They attended along with Merriam who gave a speech honoring the early contributors to the organization, including Bailey.

Then, in August 1935, Bailey was reappointed back to the Survey as a "collaborator," without compensation but with authorization to incur expenses and per diem, for the purpose of assisting with investigations of wildlife conditions and wildlife management.[5] One of his first assignments was to investigate the economic relations and develop management plans for game and fur species at the Wichita Mountains Wildlife Refuge in Oklahoma and to test the efficacy of his new Verbail live traps. In his trip report, submitted on December 19, he noted that his traps for coyotes had not worked as he had hoped they would but that overall the trip was a success. Ever the specimen collector, he reported that he was sending in one salted elk skin and skull, a coyote skeleton, and a few other specimens by express and one box of smaller specimens by mail.[6] Old habits die hard! Over the next several years he would work on special assignment under this collaborator arrangement, further testimony to his valuable experience and capability as a field naturalist.

His new book, *Mammals of the Grand Canyon*, appeared in 1935 and prompted a nice congratulatory letter from his old mentor Merriam, even though it came with some constructive criticism:

Dear Vernon:
A copy of your "Mammals of the Grand Canyon Region" has just reached me. I have read it with acute interest and congratulate you on being father to such a useful publication.

If I were called upon to criticise [sic] *I would say that you have been mighty lenient in accepting the alleged new sub-species that have been described during the past few years, many of which impress me as based on imaginary differences.*

The number of these will prove rather distressing to those who want to know what mammals inhabit the glorious region which you have been so fortunate as to familiarize yourself with more intimately since our joint work there 36 years ago.

Your present contribution is one to be proud of and one that I am sure will prove helpful to many visitors to the Canyon as well as to professional naturalists.

With congratulations, As ever yours,

CHM[7]

When Bailey did not respond right away, Merriam followed up with another letter on August 30 about the book, this time specifically questioning the status of the bobcat:

No word from you since you and Florence started north for the Adirondack country. Hope you had good luck and that you will soon return to your old stand.

In again looking over your recent "Mammals of the Grand Canyon" I have had a thought in connection with the Giant Wildcat that Elizabeth spotted and I killed on San Francisco Mountain, September 28, 1889, and to which I applied the name Lynx baileyi.

On page 31 of your Grand Canyon Mammals I notice your remark that the type of baileyi from Moccasin Spring, Arizona, north *of the Grand Canyon, is only "about the size of the eastern Bobcat."*

Referring to my San Francisco Mountain Fauna *(p. 80) I find that the measurements of the type specimen, an adult female, are: length 780, tail 130, hind foot 170. You saw this animal before it was skinned—in fact if I remember clearly—while it was across the back of my horse. If so you will remember that as it hung over the horse its feet nearly touched the ground on both sides. I admit that this is a slight exaggeration for the distance from the feet to the ground was probably a full foot. Nevertheless, there seems to be no doubt whatever that this beast was* very much larger *than your Moccasin Spring specimen which you say was about the size of the eastern Bobcat. My San Francisco Mountain animal, although a female, was about double the size of the biggest Bobcat I ever saw.*

In view of the above circumstances it strikes me that the San Francisco Mountain cat must have been about double the size of your Moccasin Spring animal and therefore is likely to be undescribed. You can easily determine this by going to the Museum and comparing your Moccasin Spring specimen with my San Francisco Mountain one.

> *It's so long since we last heard from you or Florence that we begin to be worried.*
>
> *As ever yours, Hart*[8]

Merriam was ever both the critic and the mentor! There is no record that Bailey ever responded to these letters.

But Merriam refused to drop the matter, penning yet another letter to Bailey the following spring on May 1, 1936:

> *For some time past I have been forgetting to speak to you about the Big Lynx I shot on San Francisco Mountain many years ago—part of which you broiled and ate, along with the rest of us!*
>
> *Now, this cat doesn't seem to fit in which type of* Lynx baileyi, *having in spite of its short tail a length of 780 mm (30.75 inches); tail 130 mm (5.1 inches). The hind foot measured 170 mm (6.7 inches). The type of L. baileyi measured 745 mm, 132 mm, 16 mm.*
>
> *In comparing these measurements with others, this particular cat seems to have been a giant, which sets me wondering whether or not it may be a species, or at least a subspecies, different from baileyi from Moccasin Spg, North of the Grand Canyon. It might be worth while to compare the skulls.*
>
> *If you chance to have time to do this and also compare the skin with the type of baileyi I should be glad to know the results. As ever, Hart*[9]

Again, there is no record of a response from Bailey. However, Donald F. Hoffmeister in his 1986 opus on Arizona mammals, published fifty years later, referred all of the specimens in the state, including Merriam's specimen from the San Francisco Mountains, to the subspecies *Lynx rufus baileyi*, thus vindicating Bailey's taxonomic assignment.[10]

Testing his live traps also kept Bailey well occupied during his first post-"retirement" years. In 1936, he, along with a partner, Douglas Hays, formed a company to market and find a manufacturer for his Verbail traps. The Verbail Trap Company, headquartered at 807 District National Building, Washington, DC, listed Bailey as director and Hays as business manager. That same year he entered some of his traps in a national competition sponsored by the American Humane Association (AHA), which had taken up the cause of banishing steel traps along with several other organizations concerned with animal welfare. On June 8, 1936, Bailey was notified by W. E. Sanderson, director of the Wild Life Department of the AHA, that he was awarded an "Appreciation Award" of $50.00 for noteworthy improvements in the construction of his leg-hold type of trap and for helping to solve this humane trapping problem.[11]

Then, Lucy Furman of the Anti-Steel Trap League took up the cause of banning steel-trapping focused initially on the state of Kentucky.[12] Miss Furman, a retired schoolteacher and novelist, had written an eloquent article on the cruelty of trapping in 1928. It attracted the league's attention, and it had made her a vice president. She returned from her retirement home in Florida and set out to convert Kentucky to the cause. But she needed an alternative to the other trap, and Bailey's device gave it to her. Instead of rigid steel jaws, Bailey's had a chain circle. When the trap was sprung, the chain contracted to make a tight but flexible loop around the animals's foreleg that would hold the animal without breaking its leg.

Bailey and Furman corresponded often, and she made Bailey's trap the centerpiece of her campaign. In 1936 she enlisted the Kentucky Federation of Women's Clubs to her cause. Two years later she convinced the country's largest trap manufacture, the Animal Trap Company of America, to manufacture Bailey's device. The Kentucky legislature passed her bill in 1940.

Bailey was eager to experiment with and improve his trap design across the country, to see what it would do under varying conditions. And he used this as an opportunity to reconnect with his Nevada family and once again involve them in his work. He and Florence decided to make one more trip to California by car instead of by train, giving them more opportunity for side trips, including visiting the Nevada portion of the family.

As the summer auto trek to California began to take more definite shape, he reported to his niece Laura they would be traveling in a 1935 Ford driven by Betty Hone and her college friend,[13] Nancy, who furnished the car. Furthermore, he noted, as "Betty and Nance are both good drivers so we, Auntie and I, will have an easy time in the back seat where we can nap as much as we like." It was his intention also to "do all the trapping I can along the way and more out there, trying new traps, tho I think our fox and Coyote trap is about perfect, and we plan to have them in the market by August."[14]

A major milestone happened when his book on the mammals of Oregon was published in 1936 (*North American Fauna* No. 55).[15] This would be the last of his major works on the mammal fauna of western states, and it received accolades from mammalogists across the country for the thoroughness and quality of the work and for setting a new standard for faunal survey.

Bailey kept busy with his usual list of activities, including writing and other projects. In January 1937, he was elected director of conservation for the American Trappers Association, the major organization in the country that supported trapping and trappers.[16] He encouraged them as an organization to get more involved with increasing furbearer populations and thus making them more profitable on both private and public lands.[17]

His Verbail trap was declared lawful for use in Pennsylvania,[18] and other trappers began to correspond with him about the deficiencies and difficulties of using his traps. He would make use of this information in the improvement of his product. The Biological Survey issued a revised version of his 1934 pamphlet on the proper way for capturing animals uninjured. The newly issued version included a photograph of the latest model of his foothold trap.[19]

Bailey received praise from many private citizens opposed to steel traps and in praise of his leg-hold live trap. A feature article about his traps appeared in the *Sunday Star,* a Washington newspaper, based on a talk he had given before the Biological Society at the Cosmos Club. The article noted that Bailey's long experience with wildlife had impressed him with the cruelty of steel traps and that he was now devoting his new leisure in retirement to perfecting live traps that are humane and testing them in nearby Maryland and Virginia. The article described one incident as truly amazing. It showed Bailey capturing a live skunk, then approaching the trap and mollifying the captive skunk, and then bringing it home, quite contented in a sack! Someone in the audience exclaimed that he might be the only man in the world to succeed in such an undertaking, whereupon Bailey smiled and said,

> Oh, no, I'm quite sure that many others have caught live skunks without regretting it. It's all in the approach. This particular little animal, you see, has not been hurt. I drew near very slowly, made no sudden motion or sound, and presently the little fellow let me release him without protest.[20]

Bailey was thought by his contemporaries to have a magic touch with animals. For example, it had been noted the foxes he caught and presented to the National Zoo would fight each other for a chance to lick his fingers and nibble at tidbits when he visited them in their new home.

In October 1937, his good friend and former mentor, Leonard Stejneger, retired from the US National Museum, and as requested Bailey provided a congratulatory statement for his retirement celebration, commenting on the time when they first met out back of the San Francisco Mountains in Arizona forty-eight years ago. He also expressed his personal gratitude about having personally helped in the broad field of biological investigations.[21]

In November he published an article, "Humane Trapping," in *National Nature News* magazine that was previewed with the following announcement:

> For many years Vernon Bailey has been striving to perfect humane traps and now holds patents to six different types that have proved more or less successful. He is also constantly urging upon the trappers the importance of visiting their traps often and using every care to prevent suffering or even fright when the animals are caught. He has given a lifetime to studying animals and knows and understands them as few do.[22]

The following is a list of the traps he produced and patented: Verbail Leghold Trap, Muskrat Killer Trap, Beaver Cage Trap, Cat Cage Trap, Pole Trap (leghold for large birds) and Kingfisher Pole Trap (cage trap for small birds).[23]

After more experimentation with his traps, Bailey closed out the year on December 22 with this letter to his business partner Douglas Hays after he had sent him some new traps with improvements to the chain loop and pans.

> *Dear Douglas:*
> *I wrote you yesterday but have some good news today. In the six new traps you sent me I caught a fine big coyote, a bobcat, and a cottontail the first night. Got 100 feet of fine movie film and 4 rolls of stills including monoxide execution of [the animals]. Left them in 5 minutes but they were dead in 3. Am saving the coyote and cat for mounting when I get home. Hope to get more in the morning.*
>
> *Had 6 of the old traps set but got nothing in them, tho two were sprung. These new traps have better springs, limber chains and good pans. I am greatly pleased with them and will have good proof of their efficiency. Will have a few good lectures and plenty of magazine articles to write with good illustrations.*
>
> *Next year I hope you can come out with me and we will show the trappers a few tricks worth knowing.*
>
> *I just had to tell you the news right off, but am hoping for more game in the morning. Tell the trap co. the traps are all right.*
>
> *Love to you all,*
> *Vernon Bailey*[24]

The next year, 1938, began with Bailey providing an explanation about how to remove live animals from his traps. In a letter to Ford E. Spigelmyre, chief ranger at Sequoia National Park in California, written on January 11, he commented:

I wish I could show you how to take skunks and foxes out of traps gracefully, but it's a difficult thing to tell so you can do it every time. In the first place, catch your fox, and it's not always so easy, but once in the trap, approach any animal very quietly and slowly and talk softly to them in a low tone until they get over their panic of fear and become quiet. Carry a gunny sack and two sharp sticks three or four feet long, but keep low down and work up very slowly and quietly on your knees until close enough to the animal to push the gunny sack in front of it, suspended from one edge on the points of two sharp sticks, letting two thirds of it hand down with the mouth open in front of the animal. Keep it between you and the fox or skunk as much as possible and move it up very slowly, no matter if you waste five or ten minutes doing it. You will save time in the long run and once you get the open sack over the animal's face and eyes the battle is won. Even a bobcat will welcome a sack to crawl into and by pushing it over any animal you can gradually get the whole animal, trap and all, into the sack without any trouble. Once in the sack they are in the dark and not afraid and can be held and controlled with your hands. Getting the left hand round the mouth of the sack, with the right draw the trap chain or trap out, if it has gone into the sack, to you very slowly, and clasp the sides together with the hook. Then you can shake the chain loose from the foot and let the animal draw the foot into the sack. Tie it up and carry it on your back anywhere. This may sound difficult, but it is not if you take plenty of time to it and I have plenty of moving pictures to show with skunks, foxes, bobcats, and coyotes being put in sacks and carried away. A little practice will give you all the technique and skill necessary for the whole operation and it's lots of fun to feel that you can handle animals in a way that doesn't injure or frighten them.[25]

Some of the difficulties with using his traps are reflected in this letter he sent to Lucy Furman, one of his biggest advocates, on February 16:

Dear Miss Furman:
Your air mail letter of February fourteen and postal card of the following day have just arrived. I am sorry you are having so much trouble with the traps, but hope the young fellow from the mountains will be able to handle them for you. It is largely a matter of practice and mechanical skill, but seems to be difficult for many people to catch on to. The adjustment on the No. 2 trap is just right for coyotes and bobcats, but possibly a little too strong for foxes. We have no trouble in making the changes to suit the animal we are trapping for, but none of these traps are intended for continued practice on a naked finger.

I think your present arrangement of the bill to go into effect in November, 1939, is perfectly all right. That is only a month earlier than we talked of, January 1, 1940, and the traps will surely be available by that time. Your senator is perfectly right about not dating it beyond the next season and you can leave such matters safely to the men who are getting it through. Also I think you can leave the matter of proper strength and tension of these traps to us and the trap makers with perfect assurance that we will make them just as humane and comfortable for the animal as possible.

We could probably arrange for Mr. Hayes to come down and demonstrate the traps for you if his expenses were paid, but it would be very much better if you can get an intelligent local trapper to do this as he cannot be accused of partiality. I am enclosing a copy of THE NATIONAL NATURE NEWS with illustrations of these traps. Also in the last number of NATURE MAGAZINE for March 1938 you will find a considerable article on management of predatory and fur-bearing mammals, with illustrations of dogs, foxes, and bobcats in these traps on page 159. You can probably get it on news stands or from some subscriber there. I have no duplicate copy of this to send, but will have in a few days if you need it. Don't be discouraged. The traps are coming along all right.

With best wishes, Sincerely yours,
Vernon Bailey[26]

He continued his extensive correspondence with Mr. W. E. Sanderson of the Animal Humane Association who informed him on February 24 that Mrs. Edward Breck, president of The Anti-Steel Trap League in Washington, DC, had announced the manufacture of the humane Verbail leg-hold trap by the Animal Trap Compamy of America, Lititz, Pennsylvania. As part of the announcement, Mrs. Beck urged her members to write their daily paper about this and send a card of congratulations to the trap company.[27]

Then on March 5, 1938, Doug Hayes provided information to the Animal Trap Company about the number of each size trap sold to date so that they could plan their production schedules:[28]

Trap No.	1935	1936	1937
#1	46	200	254
#2	87	237	497
#3	12	57	192
#4	16		
Totals	161	494	943

Bailey continued his family correspondence especially as the holiday season approached. He wrote to Anna on December 10 concerning a recent medical problem he had experienced:

> *I thought I told you all about my trouble last summer and since but now that it is all over I can look at it more cheerfully. In New Mexico in the hottest part of summer, I rode all day in a cold rain and wind and got chilled and my prostate gland, which has been slightly enlarged for several years, swelled up and closed the neck of the bladder. I was in considerable pain and misery until I got to a doctor and got fixed up so I could come home in a hurry. The worst of it was I had out a fine line of mountain lion traps and Wendell had to pull them up and take me 200 miles to a railroad.*
>
> *I got home pretty comfortably but the doctors here said an operation was the only safe solution, so I went to the hospital and had the glands burned out with electric wires. There was no cutting nor any great pain. The spinal anesthetic hurt the worst, paralyzing my whole body by hyperdermic injections in my spinal cord.*
>
> *They kept a rubber tube in my bladder for 2 weeks while I drank 20 glasses of water and other liquids a day to wash out all the refuse, a kind of irrigation not enjoyable but very effective.*
>
> *Now I am all right again and back to normal or better. Am getting fat from drinking so much milk but not to worry about.*[29]

Nonetheless, it seems as if old age is beginning to catch up with him—slowing down, savoring memories, collecting and saving letters and memorabilia.

The year 1939 proved to be a banner year for publications with ten titles appearing in that single year, including four papers in the *Journal of Mammalogy*, three in the *National Nature News*, and one each in *Nature Magazine*, *North Dakota Outdoors*, and *Pennsylvania Game News*. His papers continued to reflect his scientific professional work as well as efforts to educate the general public about mammals.

He also wrote down his thoughts about the humane treatment of animals and trapping without cruelty, something he had become very vocal about the past few years. This handwritten document is presented here exactly as he wrote it:

TRAPPING WITHOUT CRUELTY

Trapping and hunting are the oldest industries in the World and our cave dwelling ancestors depended on them for both food and clothing. While early hunting was largely with clubs and spears the trapping was just as crude. Pitfalls, deadfalls and snares were probably among the earliest forms of trapping and they were still in common use among primitive tribes. It was only four or five hundred years ago that the diabolical steel trap came into use and untold millions of wild animals have suffered the torture of its crushing jaws of iron. About 60,000,000 fur bearers a year is the estimate of animals taken in this country at the present time, mostly in steel traps.

In my lifelong study of animals I have of necessity collected a large number for specimens. My catalogue number is 11300 mammals now in the U.S. Nat. Museum and many of these were taken in traps. Comparatively few of these were taken in steel traps however and as far as possible they were taken in traps that killed instantly or caught them alive and uninjured. A few of the larger kind had to be taken in steel traps because there was no other way to get them but for years I have studied on methods of getting any animals without injury. Now I can see my way clear to capturing any of the animals that we need to take without harming them and with very little discomfort. The fright of being caught and held causes most of the suffering but this can be partly avoided by approaching the animals quietly and by talking softly to them to allay their fear.

I hate to show pictures of animals in traps but must make my point clear. Some of these larger kinds are now scarce and will not suffer much more, but just think of the sixty million a year of fur bearing animals, back for 300 years since the fur industry began in this country and you will see why some women refuse to wear furs.

There is much money in the fur business and no possibility of stopping it. In fact there is no need of stopping it if we can give the trappers a better trap that will obviate the cruelty of it.

Fur is the warmest, most beautiful clothing in the world and in very cold countries is almost a necessity to life and comfort. Some day we will of course make fur synthetically and then the fur bearing animals can have a holiday, if they are not all gone.

> At present we are raising a vast amount of rabbit fur and with it making beautiful imitations of many more valuable furs. We are raising great numbers of silver and black foxes, and using the coats of numerous kinds of domestic animals. All of these can be and generally are produced without any more cruelty or hardship than in the utilization of other domestic animals.
>
> Now if we can cut out all cruelty from trapping and develop wise and humane methods of dealing with our wild life generally we can certainly feel more respect for our animals and our civilization.[30]

Clearly this had become his professional creed at the end of his career.

44

The Early War Years and Prairie Trek (1940–1942)

Bailey spent much of 1940 getting caught up on his publications by expanding his portfolio of popular articles. He placed stories about mammals in two new outlets, *Natural History Magazine* (published by the American Museum of Natural History) and *Frontiers—A Magazine of Natural History* (published by the Academy of Natural Sciences, Philadelphia). He received a nice check from each magazine but more importantly, his popular writing was expanding his notoriety. In February, he was invited to speak before the Association for the Protection of Furbearing Animals in Toronto, Canada, on the topic "Making Friends With Our Wild Animals."[1] And, his professional colleagues in the American Society of Mammalogists invited him to address their annual meeting in Denver on the subject "Handling Animals Without Fright or Injury."[2] Clearly, his work with live mammals and how to handle them was gaining recognition.

In April the trapping regulations under the new anti-steel trap law in Kentucky, which Bailey had assisted Lucy Furman with, were issued. The law directed that "only those devices were to be used which either took the animal alive unhurt or killed it at once. Land animals . . . were to be taken with the non-injuring Verbail chain-loop leghold, in proper sizes, or with the old-fashioned deadfall, or the home-made box or cage trap, or with instant killers set in furrows or holes."[3]

But soon thereafter problems began to develop in the trapping business. Disappointed with their slow progress in manufacturing his Verbail traps and with the prices they were planning to charge, he abruptly cancelled his contract with the Animal Trap Company (ATC). On hearing this, and fearing that her efforts to ban steel trapping would fail without an alternative means of trapping animals unharmed, Lucy Furman wrote to him in April 1940, begging that he reconsider his decision, which he reluctantly agreed to do.[4] With Furman acting as mediator, Bailey and the ATC attempted to find cost-effective ways of overcoming the problem that the trap did not properly work in the hands of ordinary people.

To try and get some relief, Bailey wrote the Rockefeller Foundation to gauge their interest in funding the project. His letter of May 3 documents how much of his own money had gone into the development of the traps:

Dear Dr. TenBroeck:
The fur industry is world wide and millions of animals are taken every year in steel traps that break and mangle the legs of animals in unnecessary torture.

For many years I have been trying to devise traps that would take animals without injury and now have traps that will take any animal with reasonable comfort or kill them quickly if not desired alive. I hold patents on six different types of traps and have perfected others that are not patented, but it is a slow and expensive process to get them manufactured and into the hands of the trappers and teach the trappers to use them.

I have spent about $7,000 in patents, manufacture, and advertising which is about all I can afford to put into it. It will still require about $4,000 a year for three years to get the traps well made and into the market at prices to compete with steel traps, to teach the trappers how to use them and to make necessary improvements. That would be without any profits to anyone beyond wages of makers and cost of materials and introduction.

The business ought to carry itself after three years and possibly before.

Is there any possibility of aid from the Rockefeller Foundation?

Enclosed are a few circulars and notices of the traps.

Sincerely yours,
Vernon Bailey[5]

He received a reply a few days later that while the project was deemed worthy it was beyond the scope of the foundation to fund.

Then in the next month came an announcement, as a form letter, explaining a change in the status of the Biological Survey,

Dear Sir:
The Bureau of Biological Survey and the Bureau of Fisheries have been consolidated into the Fish and Wildlife Service, in accordance with the provisions of the Reorganization Act of 1939 . . . and the President's Reorganization Plan No. III, and you have been transferred, without change in position, grade or salary, to that Service effective June 30, 1940.[6]

The agency he had devoted his entire life to was now history!

In November, Bailey received a nice letter from Walter P. Taylor, leader of the Texas Cooperative Wildlife Research Unit at Texas A&M, imploring him to write his life story:

> *It seems to me that you owe something to the science of mammalogy and to the naturalists, namely, an autobiography or some rather comprehensive work of that sort. Your life and experiences have been absolutely unique, and as one of the leading figures in world mammalogy, it seems to me that you have a real responsibility to write up your life story and, of course, in that connection would be able to put in an immense amount of information and interesting detail regarding the natural history studies you have made. I do wish you would consider this if you have not already, and see if you cannot arrange to write the proposed autobiography or its equivalent.*[7]

Other than his 1928 autobiographical account about his family and early years as a young man,[8] which was never published, he never attempted an autobiography.

Always eager to spend time in the field with his relatives and true to his commitment to the education of young boys, Bailey spent time with his niece, Betty Hone, assisting with one of her favorite projects in New Mexico. Betty had just finished college—thanks to room and board from her uncle and aunt—and was teaching at a private school in New York. Rossiter Olmstead, the science teacher there, was associated with the Cottonwood Gulch Foundation, a New Mexico-based organization that provided "wilderness treks" for teenagers. Separate outings were arranged for boys and for girls. Miss Hone had participated as a science advisor for the girls for two years. Bailey, at her suggestion, signed on as a science advisor for the boys for the summer of 1940.

The young men on the Prairie Trek that summer vowed, as young groups more often say than do, to keep in touch with one another. This group did so. In 1993, fifty-three years later, the mailing list was still current; the communications still active. In contacting the list for their reminiscences of Bailey, more than half responded to the inquiry. Each added a piece to the puzzle of what the summer was like for young easterners, most in the West for the first time, many coming face to face with an old-timer like Bailey for the first time. He awed them; he inspired them. Some went on to become naturalists in their own right, or at least to accept and appreciate their role within the context of the natural realm. Here are some of their comments as recorded for posterity by Harriet Kofalk, the biographer of Florence Merriam Bailey:[9]

> What I remember most is how very spry, nimble and gentle he was. I couldn't get over how an old, old man (remember, I was about 15) could do all the things he did! I remember his foisting rattlesnake meat and pac rat meat on me after telling me they were something else! I've never knowingly had either since—but at the time they were good.
>
> The half century hasn't erased from my mind a clear picture of the 76-year-old naturalist's craggy face, wiry body, hat, and as I remember, leggings. I seem to remember that he wore the same sort of garb up in the mountains and down in the desert.
>
> Growing up, I had almost no exposure to older people. I had no grandfathers and my only grandmother lived far away and I saw her only four or five times for a few days before she died when I was 13. As I think back on it now, I believe that summer 1940 was the first time I got to know on a sustained basis anyone of Mr. Bailey's age group. Perhaps that's why I say I was "intimidated" by him. I didn't know what to expect. What I found (to my surprise, I guess) was someone absolutely at the top of his form physically and mentally, who had great knowledge and energy, and who still was a productive and purposeful life in the middle of his eighth decade. That was an important revelation to me. (Especially now, as I approach my 70th birthday.)
>
> He wore khaki pants. He proclaimed that the khaki pants should never be washed. Well hardly ever. If they were they must be washed with coffee grounds. I guess that was to maintain the color. I think it's just as well that I never did but I always have felt guilty when I don't.
>
> As did the whole Prairie Trek experience, he certainly heightened and gave depth to my love of nature. I remember him as a very intense and driven man but also very gentle and considerate. He was a nice guy.
>
> I went out on a number of rides with him on his daily trapping trips, as I recollect just the two of us. My major recollection was the sheer impact of his basic philosophy. He was "all business," friendly

> but interested in his mammals, and I was not a boy at that time to be close to anybody so no real intimacy developed: we related through his trapping. I recollect we caught a coyote—on his peg leg!—with the Bailey trap and numerous mice, rodents, etc. Once we caught a skunk in the Bailey trap. I was incredibly impressed when we got down off our horses, he used two sticks to push a burlap bag over the skunk, until it was in the bag trap and all. Then he reached in and undid the trap spring. And then, he put the bag over his shoulder and rode back into camp without any unfortunate episodes! Incredible. When we let it go at camp, it just ambled away as if nothing had happened.
>
> I remember that we were all kind of shocked to see Vernon Bailey. He was a little, thin, kind of dried up man—the sort of person you might want to help across a busy street. And we wondered at first how much he would slow the group down as he tottered around. No way. My god, he had more energy and zip than any of us, young or old. He was the first up and the last to bed. He was out with his traps before anyone even opened an eye. He could out-hike anyone in the group. And he was so full of stories about his life in out-of-doors, and his love of it was so obvious that we were fascinated by the rare experience of being with a man like that.
>
> Mr. Bailey would sometimes take over the cooking. We always cooked over an open fire. And, of course, having spent so many years chasing after mammals, he was a camp cook without peer. Without being specific, I remember some odd combinations, however, that he dreamed up that were not on our standard menu.

Seldom do we have such a clear picture of one person's influence in one short span of time. Of course the influence was the result of a much longer span of time as he shared with the boys his lifelong love of nature, which subsequently became theirs.

Bailey continued to draw accolades and recognition as one of the country's foremost naturalists known for his deep interest in humane trapping. In March 1940, he was invited by the Association for the Protection of Fur-Bearing Animals to give the keynote address at their annual meeting at the Royal Ontario Museum in Canada. His lecture, "Our Fur-Bearing Animals," was presented along with motion picture illustrations, including some in color. Bailey was ahead of his time in using motion pictures to illustrate his work. In his lecture he solicited the help of women to be more aware that animals captured by steel traps had suffered great pain that could be avoided with the use of live traps. If we could only educate the public in this manner a great good will be done, he told the audience, fur dealers would realize that buyers were interested in the method in which the animals were caught, and they would in turn make trappers more conscious of the fact that animals can be caught without injuring them or causing them to suffer.[10]

A few months later the Honorable Sam G. Bratton, of the US Circuit Court of Appeals in Albuquerque, New Mexico, proposed that the University of New Mexico confer an honorary degree on Bailey as they had done for Florence in 1931. On June 6, President J. F. Zimmerman responded to Judge Bratton that the Graduate Committee had met and had decided to confer the award on someone else.[11] Unfortunately, the university never got around to awarding an honorary degree to Bailey, and there is no record that it was ever proposed or discussed again.

The early war years, 1941 and 1942, proved for the most part uneventful although Bailey remained active pushing forward with his publications and advocating the use of his traps. He continued to publish popular articles, with several appearing in *Nature Magazine*, and in a scientific article published in the *Journal of Mammalogy*, he and a colleague (J. Kenneth Doutt) described two new beavers from Labrador and New Brunswick. This would prove to be his last scientific publication.

There was to be no resolution to his problem with the American Trap Company, but in June 1941 he received a letter from the US Predatory Animal Control office in Washington, DC, offering to distribute information and marketing materials to aid the sale and distribution of his traps.[12] Unfortunately, the Allcock Manufacturing Company, manufacturers of the Havahart Trap, declined to manufacture any of his traps after they were approached.

But this didn't keep Bailey from trying! On June 9, 1941, he penned a handwritten letter to Kermit Roosevelt, son of President Theodore Roosevelt and president of the American Association of Audubon Societies, summarizing all that he had accomplished and requesting support to continue with the development of the traps. The letter also provided an excellent summary of progress and what Bailey had hoped to accomplish with his trapping work.[13] Unfortunately, the Audubon Society did not agree to be involved with the project, and by 1942, given the urgency of the war effort, antitrapping efforts had nearly ceased in the United States.

For the first time since the organization was formed, Bailey had missed the annual meeting in Chicago of the American Society of Mammalogists the previous spring, prompting a letter from Walter P. Taylor, dated November 19, 1941, one of the leaders of the society:

> *Dear Mr. Bailey:*
> *There is nobody in the country who was missed at the Chicago meeting of the American Society of Mammalogists anything like as much as you were. We all regretted very much that you were not present at the annual convention; it did not seem like the same old place without you present.*
> *We trust that next year you will be sure to attend. We missed you so much this time that we cannot properly hold another convention without having you right in the middle of it.*
> *Here is hoping that you are feeling fine, and Mrs. Bailey, too, and wishing you every success and happiness in your work.*
> *Very sincerely yours,*
> *Walter P. Taylor*[14]

On December 23, Taylor wrote Dr. W. B. Bell at the Fish and Wildlife Service asking to secure the services of Bailey to assist with certain research projects in Texas. The letters explained that Bailey was wanted to experiment with his chain-loop traps on gray fox, the reestablishment of beaver colonies in central and eastern Texas, and the relationship of the coyote to game animals in south Texas. Compensation offered was $100 per month, an amount similar to his retirement annuity.[15] Bailey received permission to do the work in April, May, and June of 1942, one of the few commitments that he was not able to keep.

Throughout the year he had continued his correspondence with his extended family in Nevada, including a letter from Anna describing her trip to San Francisco to visit the California Academy of Science, a trip that her brother had helped to arrange, and her upcoming exhibit of birds to be presented at the grand opening of the Nevada State Museum in Carson City later that year.[16] She had worked on the taxidermy for the exhibit for several years with the assistance and advice of her brother.

The mounted Nevada birds from the collection of Mrs. Anna Bailey Mills of Fallon proved to be the outstanding display at the Nevada State Museum when it was opened to the public in October 1941. In recognition of her gift to the museum and of her ability, Anna was officially named honorary curator of ornithology at the museum and was presented a certificate during the ceremonies.[17]

Bailey had to be proud of his "little sister" and lifelong lover of nature!

The year 1942 opened with a series of very lengthy letters in January, February, and March from his nephew and namesake, Vernon Mills, in Fallon, Nevada, keeping him informed about his various wildlife projects and observations around the home of his parents.[18] His older brother Charles sent him a long letter from Redlands, California, where he was living and in poor health. The letter is very nostalgic and laments the fact they have lost touch the last few years. It harkens back to their days of growing up and their happy days on the Meadow Vale farm and their mutual interest in natural history. The letter closes with a note that he has been confined to his room for three weeks and with best wishes to his brother and to Florence. This would be the last letter between the two brothers.[19]

45

Gathering (1942)

The Prairie Trek was to be Vernon Bailey's last summer in the field. On April 20, 1942, he succumbed to pneumonia, quite suddenly after a short illness, and approximately one month after the death of C. Hart Merriam. At the time of his death, he was still planning the expedition to Texas as a collaborator for the Fish and Wildlife Service.

His widow wrote to his sister the next day:

> *Dear Sister Anna,*
> *How can I tell you? It is heartbreaking news. After a short illness, with pneumonia, Vernon passed away yesterday. The service is to be in the house tomorrow afternoon.*
>
> *Of course we should think of all his long life has stood for, of the wonderful influence for good that it has been. But the heartache is here just the same.*
>
> *Your sorrowing*
> *Sister Florence*[1]

The unexpected letter came as a "sad blow" to the Nevada relatives. Laura Mills passed the word to her sister May, including news about the country they had traveled together on their trip to Oregon:

> *Mama is being very brave about it. Even so I was glad that Vernon [Mills] got in late last night or early this morning. Just having him to talk to, and to listen to as he tells what he has been seeing and doing, helps her a great deal. He spent most of the week up in Humboldt Co., and traveled back and forth across the places where we went with Uncle Vernon on that Oregon trip, and reports a decidedly improved range condition since the live stock men cut down on the size of their flocks and herds. They saw antelope, and marveled at their keenness and speed; and lots and lots of sage hens.*[2]

Back in Washington, his funeral was a gathering of the faithful. A relative, Harry Mills, described the service, which was held at the Bailey home on Kalorama Street in Washington, in a letter written to the family on April 22, as "a notable gathering of scientists most all were greyheaded. The minister was a friend of Vernon's from Boston. The casket was loaded with the nicest of flowers. The house was packed with the friends. Even the policeman on the sidewalk was a friend of Vernon's. What a lot of friends he had."[3]

At his services, the Reverend Dr. John Van Schiak eulogized him by quoting from the Eighty-Fifth Psalm—"Mercy and truth have met together." The text of the eulogy follows:

> Mr. Bailey, who had lived for almost 78 years, had devoted his most strenuous efforts to the advancement of knowledge about natural history and to the development of kindliness toward wild animals. Truth he honored and discovered in field investigations in every State of the Union and in Mexico and Canada, in studies that formed the basis for writings that are listed in more than 200 publications. Mercy, in its most practical forms, he practiced through many years of work for conservation and gentle, patient, but persistent agitation, years that included his own accomplishments in designing and promoting the use of traps that make their captures alive and unhurt.
>
> The influences of such a character for good are, of course, inevitable, yet they were all the more effectively exerted by Mr. Bailey because by inclination he was a guide to other men and to women and boys and girls. Whether these influences, aside from those perpetuated within his writings, are considered as they were felt by other members of his profession, by the Boy Scouts of America, for which he was a great leader, by his numerous audiences or only by casual acquaintances and the general public, they must be valued most highly.
>
> To many who knew him personally, and surely to some others also to whom he was known only at a distance, he will be remembered all the more preciously because of the companionship which, with the help of Florence Merriam Bailey, he created and perpetuated for 40 years. The reassuring and enriching influences of this companionship have a precious reality for many who must now only remember it.
>
> His rich personality was one of the greatest inducements that one could feel toward a life devoted to science and conservation. Those who have known him well can surely hope that others in the future who

will benefit by his contributions to science and the literature of the outdoors may also feel the personality of the man behind them.[4]

Two days following his death, Florence received a touching letter from Ira N. Gabrielson, director of the recently formed Fish and Wildlife Service and formerly chief of the Biological Survey:

> *My dear Mrs. Bailey:*
> *I want you to know how deeply and sincerely the members of the staff sympathize with you in the loss of your husband. Words are futile things with which to express in any adequate measure the love and esteem with which he has been regarded during the long years of his devoted and productive service in the Biological Survey.*
>
> *The fine spirit of friendliness and cooperation that he invariably displayed since his retirement will also live as a continuing memorial and inspiration in the minds and hearts of all of us who had occasion to draw upon his vast store of knowledge of the ways of the wild creatures that he so dearly loved and understood or were in other ways associated with him. His far-reaching influence upon the public mind, including the hosts of young people who have been reached through his personal contacts and writings, will long continue to serve well the cause of wildlife conservation and management. This will make for enriched lives and a better country in which to live and enjoy the beauties and benefits of the things of nature in which he found inspiration and such deep delight.*
>
> *I can only wish for you the comfort that can come from reflecting on the helpfulness of the influence that he has left at work in the world in which he has lived and extend to you my personal sympathy and that of his associates in the Service. Please let us know of anything any of us can do to be of service to you.*[5]

In the next issue of *Nature Magazine* his friend and colleague Edward Preble eulogized him with the following written remarks:

> It is particularly fitting that our Association should mourn his passing, for he was co-author, with his wife, of the leading article in [our] first number. . . . This joint authorship was symbolic of the Bailey household, for their married life of more than forty years has been an object lesson worthy of a pair whose entire lives have been governed by the principle of "working together," and working for others,

> whether in natural-history studies, or in any field—social, educational, or humane—that called for cooperative effort.
>
> Vernon Bailey was, perhaps, best known as a mammalogist, but he was also a practical ornithologist of the outdoor type, and had a field knowledge of the plants of the country that many a botanist might well envy. His knowledge of the geography of the West was, I believe, unsurpassed. There have been few years, during the past five decades, that did not find him traveling, by some method, through desert, forest, mountain trail, or river valley. His memory of places visited was the most exact that I have ever known. He added to a genius akin to that of the Indian for memory of topographic details the broad geographic viewpoint of the cultivated scholar. With all these various fields of interest, advanced by a tireless energy, Vernon Bailey has accomplished much. He had no need for the time-consuming amusements that so many crave, for with his interest and enthusiasm in all Nature's products, including his fellow-man, he was always busy, and all his work was play.[6]

Other accounts of his death and accomplishments appeared in *Science*[7] and *The Auk*.[8] Surprisingly, the *Journal of Mammalogy* (volume 23, page 244, 1942) mentioned his passing in a brief unsigned paragraph, but the promised longer piece on this former president of the American Society of Mammalogists was never published.

Bailey was cremated and interred at the Merriam family cemetery in Locust Grove, New York, along with Florence, who died six years later in 1948, and C. Hart Merriam, who also died in 1942 two months earlier than Bailey. His beloved sister, Anna Bailey Mills, lived until 1951, passing away on Tuesday, August 14. Laura, his favorite niece, continued to reside in Fallon, Churchill County, Nevada, where she led scout outings, worked with the 4-H program, and was a local expert on natural history. She died on Christmas Day, 1973, at the age of eighty. Today, there is a park in Fallon, Laura Mills Park (dedicated in 1976), that bears her name and is testimony to the respect she earned for her work in education and the natural sciences. She was a "chip off the old block," and her uncle Vernon would have been most proud of her achievements.[9]

Biological Survey staff, front row center (*L to R*) A. K. Fisher, Walter Henderson, Vernon Bailey, Paul Redington, and T. S. Palmer on the occasion of Bailey's and Palmer's retirement, July 21, 1933. Courtesy of American Heritage Center, University of Wyoming.

Vernon Bailey demonstrating foothold bear trap. Courtesy of the Vernon Bailey Papers, Box 18, American Heritage Center, University of Wyoming.

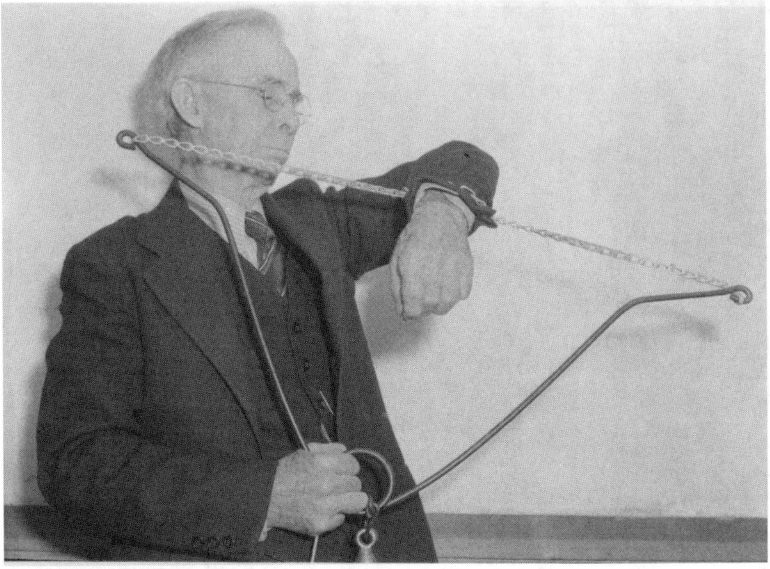

Vernon Bailey, 1935. Courtesy of the Vernon Bailey Papers, Box 18, American Heritage Center, University of Wyoming.

Vernon Bailey toward the end of his career. Courtesy American Heritage Center, University of Wyoming.

Vernon and Florence Bailey at their home on 1834 Kalorama Road, Washington, DC. Courtesy of the Vernon Bailey Papers, Box 18, American Heritage Center, University of Wyoming.

Coyote, caught in Verbail trap, being released from gunnysack by Vernon Bailey on September 3, 1936, at San Marcus, California. Courtesy of the Vernon Bailey Papers, Box 18, American Heritage Center, University of Wyoming.

Vernon Bailey, January 27, 1936, bringing home a live bobcat in a gunnysack on his back. Courtesy of the Vernon Bailey Papers, Box 18, American Heritage Center, University of Wyoming.

Vernon Bailey holding two wild foxes just caught at Lyon Fall, New York, in September 1940. According to Bailey, "These two gray foxes were caught in No. 1 chain loop (Verbail) traps and kept overnight in the house, then taken out and let go for moving pictures. They were not hurt and were very gentle and quiet but made good time when released." Courtesy of the Vernon Bailey Papers, Box 18, American Heritage Center, University of Wyoming.

Vernon Bailey with his movie camera in 1942 just a few months before his death. Courtesy of the Vernon Bailey Papers, Box 18, American Heritage Center, University of Wyoming.

Bailey in Perspective

Vernon Bailey had a fascinating life and career. Growing up on a farm on the edge of the American frontier, and without much formal education, he distinguished himself as one of the leading field collectors and naturalists to ever live, earning recognition not only for his scientific achievements but also for the quality of his personal character and demeanor and for his devotion to American wildlife.

Bailey was among the last generation of naturalists to be made entirely in the field. He entered his scientific apprenticeship at a time when natural history was for some already a career, and thanks to Merriam's preference for men trained in the field, Bailey's career did not suffer because he lacked education, although he felt the lack of it.[1]

With the rise of academic science, and the accompanying demand for academic credentials and the rise of research programs oriented around natural history, a career path like Bailey's became impossible. He retired in an era of ecologically based science that was driven by research programs developed within professional communities and carried out in academic institutions, and he left an agency transformed by changing science and new missions. The replacement of self-taught naturalists doing descriptive work by people with academic credentials pursuing theory-based research problems marked a major shift in the institutional and intellectual structure of science that took place during Bailey's lifetime.

Three major developments affected Bailey's life and career. One was growing up on a farm on the western frontier in Elk River, Minnesota, where his parents moved when he was about six years old and where, as a young lad, he developed a strong interest in natural history through his work on the farm. It was family farming—bringing in the hay and finding the cows—that connected Bailey's love of skilled outdoor work with a desire to know nature scientifically.[2]

The second development was meeting and coming under the tutelage of C. Hart Merriam at the US Biological Survey at a time when a career in natural history was fully possible without a formal education. Although he possessed little formal education, Bailey served a grueling apprenticeship under Merriam and became a mainstay at the Biological Survey responsible for its fieldwork and surveys. As he progressed through his apprenticeship with Merriam, it became obvious that Vernon Bailey had the knack for fieldwork and that he enjoyed and took pleasure in it. To him, collecting seemed almost like an addiction, recollected with pleasure and keenly anticipated.

The careers of these two men became intertwined during the years that Merriam served as chief of the Survey, and the mentoring and teaching that Bailey received affected his entire life and career. Merriam came to appreciate Bailey's dogged determination, willingness to accept instruction and criticism, and consistent improvement. He quickly came to realize how vital Bailey could be to his idea of a systematic western survey of mammals. He could see that his discovery of young Bailey potentially could bring those dreams into the realm of the possible.[3]

Bailey adopted Merriam's scientific method for fieldwork and mapping life zones and followed it throughout his career. Merriam grew to have great confidence in Bailey. In 1896 he was given the title of chief field naturalist, and when Merriam reorganized the Biological Survey into a bureau in 1906, he placed Bailey in charge of investigations in geographic distribution, one of three major responsibilities of the Survey, the only one Merriam had created, and the one that sustained most of Merriam's interest during his years as survey chief.

The third great development in Bailey's life was his marriage to Merriam's sister, Florence Merriam Bailey, an accomplished naturalist in her own right and one of the leading female ornithologists of her age. By all accounts their marriage was a happy and productive one, although in many ways it represented an alliance across a social chasm. Bailey was an unsophisticated country boy raised on the frontier with virtually no education. Florence came from a wealthy sophisticated family, and she combined the qualities of a real Victorian lady with an adventuresome spirit. Throughout their forty-two years together, "Mr. and Mrs. Dearie," as they called each other, shared a deep, abiding love of nature and the outdoors. The Baileys were listed among the forty-nine "notable couples" in science before the 1940s. Clearly, their marriage and relationship sustained each other, both personally and professionally.

Florence also influenced his approach to his work in subtle ways. She was an ardent believer in studying live birds as opposed to collecting specimens.[4] Although Bailey excelled in specimen collection, he became equally fascinated with observing living animals, and he often studied animal behavior in his home using mammals that he and Florence had obtained on field trips. He also developed a deep humanitarian ethic about how animals should be treated.

Vernon and Florence married late compared to the custom of their time and were never to have children, although Florence is known to have suffered several miscarriages. Despite this disappointment, both Vernon and Florence were devoted to young people. Working with the Boy Scouts was of particular interest to the Baileys, and Vernon served as a scoutmaster for many years. They also devoted time and resources to support the education and lives of many of their nieces and nephews.

Bailey's work did not produce any major theoretical contributions to natural history. For the most part, his work produced records about where animals lived and how they lived. His knowledge about the geography and physiography of the West was greater than nearly anyone else who had ever lived. His collections of specimens and written descriptions and documentation of habitats and life zones in the "inner frontiers" of the western United States constitute the baseline information for modern taxonomy and biogeography, and they provide an essential information base for addressing critical conservation issues such as habitat deterioration and climate change.

What really stood out about Bailey was his remarkable endurance and capacity for fieldwork. At one time, he stayed in the field almost continuously for four consecutive years. Anyone who has ever undertaken fieldwork, and has experienced the daily grind and difficulty of such work, would know that was nothing less than remarkable, especially given the infrastructure available during the times that Bailey worked, mostly before automobiles and good road systems were available. Survey work required physical qualities of fortitude and courage as well as cerebral qualities, in other words skills of both head and hand. One had to have knowledge about camping and woodcraft skills as well as organizational and managerial skills. Collectors had to be skilled marksmen and trappers, and they had to know animals and where to find them.[5] Bailey excelled in all of these capabilities.

In most of his scientific works, Bailey adhered to the Survey's older traditions. He was obsessive about obtaining specimens to document his work. This was not surprising, considering the critical place they occupied in the Survey under Merriam, and the fact that preparing them was easy for him since he had learned that art as a young boy. The focus on collection and analysis of specimens was in accord with the early mission of the Survey since this was an effective way to illustrate Merriam's life zone theory, and it provided the basis for describing new species and subspecies of mammals for publication in the newly established *North American Fauna* series. Although the desire for specimens resulted in the gathering of essential factual information, scientists would later argue that it was done at the expense of discovering larger patterns in nature.[6]

Because he lacked a broad education in biology, especially in evolutionary and ecological theory, some of Bailey's work was overly simplistic. For example, he focused on individual species, studying their behavior, physical characteristics, breeding habits, and the animal's "economic status." Unlike some of the more educated members of the Survey, he was not inclined to devote much attention to the relations between species, nor was he inclined to think of animals as components of a community and ecological system.[7]

Growing up on a farm close to nature, Bailey personalized his interactions with wildlife, and this was something he never gave up. He described animals in anthropomorphic terms, often gave them names, and occasionally kept them for close observation. And he often used anthropomorphic language in referring to their behavior, as for example, the chestnut mantled ground squirrels are "pot-bellied, lazy little philosophers of the woods" that spend much time lounging around, "as if thinking about a long comfortable sleep."[8]

He rationalized a clear beneficial/injurious dichotomy about animals with regard to their impact on agriculture and ranching. In one of his books, for example, he described the Texas jackrabbit as an "asset" because it is preyed on by coyotes, eagles, hawks, and owls, thus reducing the "more serious depredations" caused by these predators. Conversely, the mountain lion was portrayed as "troublesome" to the stockman, and black-tailed prairie dogs were treated as a "serious handicap to stock raisers as well as any form of agriculture and are generally destroyed in every way possible."[9]

Bailey also never lost confidence in Merriam's life zone theory, since it formed the theoretical underpinning of many of his works, even after it was discredited. Bailey was unable to fathom why there might be a problem with the theory.[10] To him, it had been developed and approved by his mentor Merriam and he saw no reason to question it.

Bailey prepared three philosophical position papers toward the end of his career that were never formally published but expressed his philosophy and views about wildlife management. These papers reflected his deep personal feelings about important principles that he had learned over many years observing and collecting animals. The first, titled "The Balance of Nature," was written shortly after Redington took over for Nelson as chief of the Survey in 1929 (see chapter 40). In this statement, Bailey articulated his views on the predator problem with a defensible rationale for the Survey's position and its programs, even though in later years he greatly modified his position. The second document, "Wild Life Policies," was written two years later and two years before he retired; in it he laid out his understanding and thoughts about the underlying principles of wildlife management (see chapter 41). He wrote his third philosophical statement in 1939 addressing the importance of humane treatment of animals and trapping without cruelty (see chapter 43).

Following his retirement, Bailey spent less time in the field trapping and collecting and began to devote more of his efforts toward improving his humane traps and ways to use them to salvage wildlife. He became legendary for his ability to humanely trap mammals alive as well as handle and tame them without harm. He successfully developed live traps for small mammals (mice and rats), beaver, and large carnivores and constantly experimented to improve them. He held six patents on various traps that were manufactured and used to some extent.

Bailey was ahead of his time on the issue of reducing cruelty to animals. He invented both a beaver trap for the Biological Survey, that was used in restocking operations, and the so-called foot-hold trap, which instead of rigid steel jaws had a chain circle, released by a spring, that would catch and hold without breaking the leg of the animal caught in it. The foot-hold trap was developed for use in capturing a variety of mammals and birds. He received prizes from the American Humane Association for both inventions that were patented as Verbail traps.

Bailey was deeply involved in the predator control controversy that rocked the Biological Survey over much of its history. Early on, he was a strong advocate of the Survey's control program, even authoring its first instructional materials for killing wolves. But later, the controversy seemed to have stirred a deeply rooted humanitarian ethic in him, and by the 1930s he had developed misgivings about the bureau's policy.[11] In a 1936 departmental memorandum, he expressed reservations about the future of predator and rodent control, claiming "no species or group can be wholly condemned."[12] In 1937 he provided a glowing review in the *Journal of Mammalogy* to *Wilderness Wanderers* by Lucy and Wendell Chapman. The authors, noted Bailey, advocated studying animals by getting to know them in their natural habitat, "instead of carrying guns and traps and shooting or collecting the animals on sight."[13]

Bailey's legacy includes publishing more than two hundred articles, although the exact number has been difficult to determine. Howard Zahniser listed 244 articles published by Bailey,[14] and a file of his papers at the University of Wyoming, American Heritage Center, contained a "cut and paste" version with 202 titles.[15] Through an exhaustive search for more than four years, I was able to document 234 published works.[16] Among his most significant publications were accounts of the life zones and mammals in the states of Texas, New Mexico, North Dakota, and Oregon , and in four national parks. In addition to his scientific publications, he contributed numerous articles to popular weekly and monthly magazines as well as to outdoor and trade journals, thus effectively disseminating information about wildlife to the public. A complete list of his publications is available at http://www.nsrl.ttu.edu/publications/specpubs/sps/SP64.pdf.

Among other significant accomplishments, he contributed over thirteen thousand specimens to the US National Museum and Biological Survey mammal collection, and he described seventy-eight taxa of mammals with another thirteen named after him. A list of these are available at the same website listed above; they include a bat, a shrew, an armadillo, two rabbits, sixty-nine rodents, two carnivores, and three ungulates.[17] He clearly played a major role in describing the mammal habitats and fauna of the western United States. During his career, he worked in every state of the Union, in Canada and in Mexico. Probably no one in North America ever knew more about its native mammals.

As he became famous for his work with mammals, he won various nicknames indicative of his pursuits.[18] Theodore Roosevelt called him "Wolf" Bailey because of his efforts to protect farmers and cattlemen of the West against this predator. "Gopher Jim" Bailey was applied to him after his first bulletin on pocket gophers. "Beaver" Bailey was earned during his research on their natural history and potential to be raised profitably on farms.

Bailey was highly respected among his scientific peers and became affiliated with many professional organizations and associations, but he was especially devoted to the American Society of Mammalogists (ASM), of which he was a founder and charter member. He attended the first twenty-two meetings of the society and presented papers at all but six of those meetings. At these meetings he was always a focus of enthusiasm. His papers and comments never failed to rally attention, and his consideration for the younger members was for them an outstanding benefit of the meetings. He published in the first issue of the *Journal of Mammalogy* and in half of the first twenty-two volumes of the journal. He served on the "Life Histories of Mammals" (later the "Life Histories and Ecology Committee") for a decade. He was elected to the board of directors for the class of 1927–1929 and again for 1929–1931. He was elected as the ASM's eighth president in 1933 and served a two-year term.

Other scientific society affiliations included: membership in the American Ornithologists' Union, president of the Biological Society of Washington, president of the Audubon Society of the District of Columbia, fellow of the

American Association for the Advancement of Science, life member of the National Geographic Society, and member of the Cooper Ornithological Club, Washington Academy of Sciences, the American Forestry Association and other societies interested in wildlife and conservation.

On a personal level, Bailey was known to be scrupulously honest and fair, and a model of integrity. He was quietly generous and admired by most all who knew him. He was especially generous to his immediate family, supporting them emotionally and monetarily throughout his adult life. His correspondence with his immediate family (parents, sisters, brothers) is indicative of a loving, trusting nuclear family. His family unit was a major source of strength as Bailey often endured weeks and months alone in the field.

A few of his colleagues had mixed impressions about him and some even downright contempt. Howard McAtee, a career scientist with the Biological Survey, was quite harsh in talking about Bailey, as reflected in these comments:

> He had only desultory schooling, which can not be held against a man, but he did not make use of contacts with better informed men and books in improving his education to anything like the extent that others in the organization did, e.g. E. A. Preble. He was essentially a field collector who trained others in the art but never rose above that status in ability. Dr. Merriam made him, and Dr. M[erriam]'s sister, Florence, (much superior to Bailey in every way) married him. He was a perfect toady to Merriam, disgustingly so, some of us thought.
>
> He was really illiterate and his writings were put in shape by others, the official editors, especially E. A. Preble and his wife. He was too ignorant to know his own ignorance. . . . Like other ignoramuses, he could not appreciate good work when he saw it.
>
> V. B. was spare in frame and ascetic in habits; he never swore, "O pshaw," being his strongest but a very characteristic expression. He was not a bad, but a weak man, and being elevated to places and associations where he did not fit, made more or less of a mess of things.[19]

There is much evidence to suggest this characterization was overly harsh and perhaps driven by professional jealousy. Bailey's official "fitness" reports reveal relatively high scores regardless of who was serving as chief.[20] Also, he made several attempts to return to college to improve his education. Other naturalists (Stejneger, for example), recognizing the desire to improve his education, provided him lists of books to read to strengthen his biological knowledge. And, his wife Florence, who had a degree from Smith College, is known to have assisted him with his zoological interpretations.

McAtee's petty attitude toward Bailey comes across in these comments from his notes, "Preble told me that Bailey once commented (and it would be considered as prophetic from his close association with the Chief) 'It's too bad, they'll have to let McAtee go, as he can't write.' Coming from one who couldn't even spell, this was a 'corker.'"[21] It should be noted that Preble eulogized Bailey's work in glowing terms.

Albert. K. Fisher, who was a colleague of Bailey's throughout his career at the Biological Survey, and who was known to be considerably more gregarious and outspoken, described Bailey as a very pious person who would not do any official work on Sunday, instead spending considerable time in reading the Bible. According to Fisher, Bailey seldom cursed and usually under stress would utter nothing more stringent than, "oh, Pshaw." But he went on to say that even with his shortcomings and being handicapped by insufficient foundation, he thought Bailey deserved a great deal of credit for an advancing forward the study of mammals of the United States, even though in that he was aided by his wife in working out his zoological problems.[22]

Regarding Bailey's pious tendencies, Fisher and Hartley H. T. Jackson recounted this story as told to them by Ned Hollister, another Survey naturalist, regarding Bailey's aversion to alcohol. As Hollister told the story, he met up with Bailey at Jefferson, Texas, in 1902 on his first field trip for the Biological Survey. Merriam had assigned him to work with Bailey and "learn the ropes" of fieldwork. At their initial meeting Hollister innocently suggested that they go into a saloon that they were passing where they could talk over a glass of beer. This apparently "horrified" Bailey who ended up taking Hollister to the village cemetery in Jefferson for his first instructions in field methods! Hollister, who had never met Bailey previously, pictured him in his mind's eye as a huge heavy man, rather slow and deliberate in action, and mentioned how surprised he was to find him small, quick, and of rather nervous temperament. Another incident on this trip that struck Hollister's sense of humor occurred at the first camp. In unloading the supplies from the wagon Bailey gave his suitcase a quick jerk from the wagon, causing its cover to open; pins, needles, thread, nails, screws, pencils, ink bottles flew everywhere, and Hollister noted there was not a single item in the suitcase larger than the bottle of ink or a hand mirror.[23]

Fisher recounted his own story about an experience he had with Bailey in the field in Death Valley:

> When we left the mining camp of Coso we borrowed without permission a number of tools so that we could get our outfit over a sandy stretch. When we returned to the general region, I told Jim Wilson the owner of the tools what we had done and was it his pleasure for us to take them back to Coso or leave them with him at Darwin. Bailey seemed relieved that we got out of the trouble so nicely but was somewhat perturbed when Wilson suggested that we drink with him. Wilson wanted to show me his outfit so I went to the cellar where he drew out considerable brandy from a barrel and when we started to drink, Bailey asked for soda water and I gave him a gentle kick in the shins and suggested that he meant cider, which the bar-keep furnished him.[24]

As a general rule, many field naturalists of Bailey's era had a reputation for being rather boisterous, "rough around the edges," not overly religious, and more comfortable in khakis and jeans than in suits. Clearly, Bailey did not fit this description as he was for the most part decidedly understated, generally quiet, although with a subtle sense of humor, a complete teetotaler, and seriously religious. These characteristics may not have endeared him to some of the "coarser" gentlemen in the naturalist crowd.

Rollin Baker, a senior mammalogist whom I knew for several decades, met and talked with Bailey at the US National Museum in Washington in 1940, prior to Baker's assignment as a naval officer. Baker provided this recollection of the seventy-six-year-old field man,

> Vernon Bailey was a talkative gentleman when we visited in March 1940. This was in the Biological Survey quarters. . . . Bailey was a slightly built, wiry fellow probably weighing 140 pounds at most. He had an unruly mop of hair and almost owl-like eyes enhanced by a rather small face and "weak" chin. At least at the time that I saw him, he appeared to be not what one might call a classy dresser, and if you will please pardon my saying so, he looked a mite slouchy.[25]

At the 1940 ASM meeting in Denver, Baker asked Bailey if he had any regrets about his work at the Survey. After giving the matter some thought, Bailey readily admitted to young Baker what he considered to be one of his greatest mammalogical blunders, indicating that he was indeed an error-making human after all. He told Baker that when he was engaged in Survey work in North Dakota in the latter years of the nineteenth century, he observed by a railroad siding a huge pile of bison bones, gleaned from killing sites for shipment east to rendering plants. His tragic mistake, he admitted, was to neglect to salvage skulls and other significant skeletal parts from this pile for preservation in the Smithsonian in Washington. The sad fact is that neither he nor any other collectors saved significant samplings from northern and southern bison herds in the Great Plains.[26]

Science changed during the times that Bailey lived, moving from a focus on fieldwork, collecting, and taxonomy to a concentration on theory supported by laboratory experiments and ecological work. While Bailey earned a position of prominence despite lacking a college degree, newer members of the Survey had college and graduate degrees and were more specialized than "the naturalist of the past."

Although Bailey was of the "old school" of naturalists, he deserves to be recognized as one of the greatest field naturalists to ever live. He was a well-respected scientist throughout his life, despite not having a college degree. Scientists respected his skill in observing nature and trapping animals, although his methods of investigation exemplified the nineteenth-century naturalist tradition, an approach that had largely lost its ground to ecology.

Bailey's experiences with the hardships of fieldwork and living in nature for much of his life imparted in him a philosophy of life guided by self-reliance and optimism. Overcoming his frontier background, Bailey developed renaissance tendencies and greatly enjoyed cultural activities. He attended plays, lectures and readings, the opera, musical performances, and he loved poetry, occasionally writing some himself. He also collected poems that he admired, and in perusing his files, I found this one written in 1903 by Edmund Vance Cooke that seems to capture the essence of his philosophy about life and provides a fitting way to conclude this opus about an unusual man the likes of which we are never likely to witness again.[27]

HOW DID YOU DIE?
Did you tackle that trouble that came your way
  With a resolute heart and cheerful?
Or hide your face from the light of day
  With a craven soul and fearful?
Oh, a trouble's a ton, or a trouble's an ounce,
  Or a trouble is what you make it.
And it isn't the fact that your're hurt that counts
  But only how did you take it?

You are beaten to earth? Well, well, what's that?
  Come up with a smiling face,
It's nothing against you to fall down flat,
  But to lie there—that's disgrace.
The harder you're thrown, why the higher you bounce;
  Be proud of your blackened eye!
It isn't the fact that your're licked that counts;
  It's how did you fight—and why?

And though you be done to the death, what then?
  If you battled the best you could;
If you played your part in the world of men,
  Why, the Critic will call it good.
Death comes with a crawl, or comes with a pounce,
  And whether he's slow or spry,
It isn't the fact that you're dead that counts
  But only how did you die?

Appendix

Biographic Profiles of Naturalists Associated with Vernon Bailey

Naturalists, other than Bailey, Merriam, and the leaders of the Biological Survey, are mentioned at various places throughout the text. A brief biography for each of these figures, listed alphabetically, is presented below. They include some well-known figures in American natural history as well as lesser-known individuals who only had brief tenures with the Survey. For a few of the individuals no biographic materials were available.

Charles C. Adams (1873–1955) was an ecologist who spent most of his career as the Forest Ecologist at the New York State College of Forestry at Syracuse University. As a member of the American Society of Mammalogists, he chaired the 1924 committee appointed by the society, which included Vernon Bailey and E. A. Goldman, to study the government policies on predatory animals. He challenged the argument of Nelson and Goldman of the Biological Survey about the "balance of nature" and became a vocal opponent against the predator-control programs of the Survey.

Joel Asaph (J. A.) Allen (1838–1921) was an American zoologist, mammalogist, and ornithologist. He became the first president of the American Ornithologists' Union, the first curator of birds and mammals at the American Museum of Natural History, and the first head of that museum's Department of Ornithology.

John Burroughs (1837–1921) was an American naturalist and nature essayist who became active in early US conservation in the early decades of the twentieth century. He was friends with many personalities of his time, including President Teddy Roosevelt and John Muir, and often accompanied them on field excursions. He became involved in the infamous "nature faker controversy" and attacked, along with President Roosevelt, some popular writers, such as Ernest Thompson Seton, for their fantastical representations of the wildlife. Bailey met and accompanied him on a few field excursions.

Merritt Cary (1880–1918) was one of the lesser-known naturalists who worked for the Survey during Merriam's tenure, although he was listed by Merriam (1935) as a key member of the agency during this time. He was born in Nebraska and studied at the University of Nebraska in Lincoln. His government personnel records (National Personnel Records Center, St. Louis, Missouri) show that he joined the Survey in 1902 and worked off and on in various capacities until his final termination in June 1917. He resigned in 1917 because of ill health and died not long afterward in 1918 from a very serious case of bone tuberculosis. He participated in fieldwork in many western states and Canada and also worked on food habits research (National Archives Record Center). His most important published works were his mammals of Colorado (1911) and life zone investigations of Wyoming (1917).

George A. Coleman received an appointment to do fieldwork in 1892, and after a few weeks training (along with Loring) under Vernon Bailey was assigned to work in Georgia, Mississippi, Louisiana, and Tennessee during that summer and fall. Coleman began work in Mississippi, and later collected with Bailey in Louisiana, Kentucky, and Nebraska. He departed the Survey in 1893.

Elliot Coues (1842–1899) joined the Army Medical Corp in 1864 and spent the next twenty years doing fieldwork, collecting specimens, and publishing extensively on mammals, birds, and other vertebrates. He served as the first curator of mammals after Baird had organized the United States National Museum within the Smithsonian Institution, in 1879.

Frederick Coville (1867–1937) was a botanist who befriended Bailey and was one of his companions on the Death Valley expedition. Coville became chief botanist of the US Department of Agriculture and was the first director of the US National Arboretum. He made numerous contributions to economic botany and became especially well known for his research on blueberries. While on assignment from the field at Survey headquarters in Washington, DC, Bailey often stayed with Coville and his wife.

Basil Hicks Dutcher (1871–1921) was the son of William Dutcher, the longtime president of the National Audubon Society. At the age of nineteen he was appointed a field assistant in the Division of Ornithology and took part in the biological reconnaissance of Idaho under the direction of Bailey in 1890. In the following summer he became a member of the Death

Valley Expedition and would go on to work in several other states including California, Montana, and Wyoming. Shortly after receiving his medical degree he secured an appointment in the army as an assistant surgeon with the rank of First Lieutenant. During his twenty-five years of service he was stationed at several posts in the Southwest, in the Philippines, Puerto Rico, and Panama, and during World War I he was in charge of a hospital in Brest, France. While working for the Survey, he did considerable fieldwork with Vernon Bailey, and the two became close lifelong friends. He died in 1922 at the relatively young age of fifty-one.

Albert K. Fisher (1856–1948) was born and raised in New York and graduated from the College of Physicians and Surgeons of New York in 1879, where he was a classmate of Merriam. Merriam convinced him to give up further thought of practicing medicine and join him in the new Section of Economic Ornithology when it opened in 1885. He remained with the agency until he retired in 1931, following forty-six years of continuous service. For nearly a quarter of a century, Fisher was in charge of economic investigations and the agency's programs for controlling predatory animals and noxious rodents. His ability in dealing with members of Congress, as well as with his fellow workers, played an important part in successfully administering the continually broadening scope of the Survey. Fisher was also the peace keeper among the conflicts that often developed between Merriam and the other staff. An inveterate practical joker, Fisher was popular in scientific circles and cultivated most anyone who could be useful to the Survey.

Louis Agassiz Fuertes (1874–1927), the great wildlife artist, was lifelong friend and correspondent of Vernon Bailey. In 1901, Fuertes joined Vernon Bailey and H. C. Oberholser for a four-month survey of the Trans-Pecos region of Texas. Fuertes found the experience exhilarating and produced hundreds of bird portraits, as well as paintings and sketches of a number of mammals, a whip scorpion, and several lizards. Most of his works from that trip were purchased by the government for $20–30 each. Bailey and Fuertes remained friends throughout life and Fuertes contributed many drawings and illustrations for both Bailey and his wife's publications. Fuertes was killed at age fifty-three when his car was struck by a train in Unadilla, New York, on August 22, 1927.

Ira N. Gabrielson (1889–1977) was a career employee of the Survey, having joined the organization in 1915 after having worked for several years as a school teacher. He started out in the Survey's food habits laboratory, but by the time Darling became chief, Gabrielson was in charge of predator and rodent control in the Northwest. He proved to be an able administrator and continued as director of the Fish and Wildlife Service until he retired in 1946 to take on new wildlife-related responsibilities in the private sector.

James Gaut (1879–1914) worked as a field agent for the Survey from 1899 to 1906 collecting in many areas of North America including Virginia, Maryland, California, New Mexico, Texas, Coahuila (Mexico), Chihuahua (Mexico), Oklahoma, and Colorado. He too was trained by Bailey and while working for the Survey collected almost four thousand mammals. He was known as a "go-getter" and was sent hither and yon for topotypes or other much-wanted material, usually "delivering the goods." He was also known for his reckless disposition and in the horse-and-buggy days managed to have an accident that cost him an arm. He resigned from the Survey in 1906 and died in an automobile accident in 1914 at the age of thirty-five.

E. A. Goldman (1873–1946) joined the Survey at the age of eighteen after meeting Nelson and subsequently working with him on a biological survey of Mexico. Their work in Mexico, which would prove to be monumental, became a significant part of Merriam's scientific agenda to define life zones and document the vertebrate fauna of North America. Nelson and young Goldman traveled to all parts of the Republic of Mexico and much of Guatemala over fourteen years collecting birds, mammals, and reptiles. In 1910 Goldman was dispatched farther south to survey the region around the canal zone of Panama, while the canal was under construction, on assignment to the Smithsonian Institution and supported by the War Department. In 1918, he served as a major in the US Army Sanitary Corps in France during World War I, trying to prevent the food and other supplies from damage by rats. On returning to Washington, DC, Goldman resumed employment with the Biological Survey, serving as head of the Section of Biological Investigations from 1919 to 1925. He became chief of the Division of Game Reservations from 1925 to 1928, and in the 1930s Goldman was assigned to assist in negotiations between the United States and Mexico to add Mexico as a signatory to the Migratory Bird Treaty Act. Goldman was often referred to as the real "Noah" of the Biological Survey because of the large number of mammals, birds, plants, reptiles, and mollusks named for him, totaling something more than fifty. Most of his early studies focused on small mammals, particularly small rodents such as pocket mice and pocket gophers.

During his lifetime, Goldman described well over three hundred forms of mammals, most of them subspecies, including a substantial number of pocket gophers. Goldman died on September 2, 1946, in Washington, DC, and was buried with full military honors in Arlington National Cemetery. Educationally, he was very much self-made. He completed grammar and high school, but he never received a post secondary degree. His command of Spanish was almost perfect. He also took up photography and became one of the best outdoor photographers in the Biological Survey.

Joseph Grinnell (1877–1939) became director of the Museum of Vertebrate Zoology at the University of California at Berkeley in 1908. This was the first major center for academic mammalogy in the United States, and Grinnell is widely acclaimed as the father of academic mammalogy. An outstanding scientist, who published 554 papers, Grinnell strongly opposed the predator-control program of the Biological Survey and spent years fighting it along with his students.

Henry Wetherbee Henshaw (1850–1930) spent his early career in the western United States, and he was a member of the famous "Geographical Explorations and Surveys West of the 100th Meridian" led by George M. Wheeler. Because he was in poor health, he moved to California in 1892 and then to Hawaii in 1894. Having recovered, he returned to Washington, DC, in 1905 to work at the Biological Survey and was named chief of the Biological Survey when C. Hart Merriam resigned in 1910. He held that position until 1916, when he retired because of health problems. Henshaw's finest moment as chief came on October 1, 1913, when, appropriately enough, it was he who handed President Woodrow Wilson the quill pen with which the chief executive signed into law the Weeks-McLean act, better known to history as the Migratory Bird Law, to protect migratory birds. During his service as chief of the Survey, Henshaw also interested the secretary of agriculture, James Wilson, in the publication of a bulletin on common birds to be profusely illustrated with colored plates by Louis Fuertes. As a result, in March 1913, the US Department of Agriculture Farmers' Bulletin 513, "Fifty Common Birds of Farm and Orchard," was issued. This proved to be one of the most popular publications ever issued by the department. The first edition of two hundred thousand copies was quickly exhausted and several others followed a few years later.

Ned Hollister (1876–1924), from Wisconsin, joined the Survey in 1902 when he was invited to accompany a Biological Survey party in Texas as assistant to Vernon Bailey. He worked with Bailey for a time and soon proved competent for independent assignments and made important collections of mammals and birds at many places in Texas and New Mexico. In 1903, he served as a field assistant on a Survey trip to Alaska. In 1904, he served as a representative for the Survey on a hunting trip to Louisiana, and in that same year he was appointed full time to the field staff of the Survey where he remained continuously employed until 1910. During his time with the Survey, he traveled and collected in Utah, Nevada, Oregon, California, Arizona, and New Mexico in 1905. Hollister's genius in the museum was immediately recognized and he was placed in charge of the care and arrangement of the huge mammal collection brought together by the Survey. In 1909, he accepted the position of assistant curator of mammals at the US National Museum and found himself with the entire responsibility for moving, installing, and rearranging the great reference collection. In 1916 he was appointed superintendent of the National Zoological Park, a position he held until his death in 1924.

William T. Hornaday (1854–1937) was an American zoologist, conservationist, taxidermist, and author. He served as the first director of the New York Zoological Park, known today as the Bronx Zoo, and he was a pioneer in the early wildlife conservation movement in the United States.

A. Brazier Howell (1886–1961) was affiliated with the Survey in the early 1920s and deserves mention because of his role in the predator-control controversy that rocked the agency in the early years of the Depression. Known as a "dollar-a-year man" because that yearly salary was necessary to justify him occupying an office, he became the most vocal critic inside the agency about the predator extermination program. He also was a critic of the life zone concept that the agency continued to use to explain plant and animal distributions. Howell was independently wealthy and had the financial means to pursue his own agenda. In 1928 he moved to Baltimore to accept a faculty position in the Department of Anatomy at Johns Hopkins Medical School.

Arthur Holmes Howell (1872–1940) came to the Survey in 1895 serving his apprenticeship in northern Montana with Vernon Bailey. For four months the two men camped together in Montana, Idaho, Washington, and

Oregon. Later Howell traveled in Colorado, Idaho, and Utah. In May 1896, Howell received a second appointment of six months, and at the end of this period he received a permanent appointment, at first as a special assistant. During his first few years his work consisted of the preparation of scientific study skins and curating the collection of mammals. As time passed Howell's activities became more varied, and he eventually became one of America's leading ornithologists and mammalogists.

Howell continuously worked for the Survey for forty-four years until his voluntary retirement in 1940. During his career, he conducted extensive fieldwork in Alabama, Arkansas, Florida, Georgia, Illinois, Kentucky, Louisiana, Missouri, Montana, New Mexico, and Texas. In addition to his reputation as a keen naturalist, he was also known for his acumen with a shotgun.

Hartley H. T. (Harrod Thompson) Jackson (1881–1976), from Wisconsin, was one of the last of the professional staff employed just as Merriam was leaving the Survey, and he went on to have a long and illustrious career with the agency. He received his BS in zoology and chemistry from Milton College in 1904. After graduation, he was offered the first Rhodes Scholarship at Oxford University, but he turned it down because he wanted to do his post-graduate work at an American university. He obtained his PhD in zoology at George Washington University in Washington, DC, in 1914. Jackson joined the research staff of the Survey on February 16, 1910. He worked under the supervision of Bailey, who at that time was chief of the Division of Geographic Distribution, on the immense Biological Survey research mammal collection housed in the new National Museum. During his early years with the Survey, Jackson conducted fieldwork in Arizona and Wisconsin. In 1917, E. W. Nelson, while chief of the Biological Survey, arranged for him to study the mammal fauna of Wisconsin that resulted in the major publication of his career, *Mammals of Wisconsin* (1961). In July 1925 he was promoted to the position of chief of the Division of Biological Investigations and from 1917 to 1935 was in charge of taxonomic mammalogy. Jackson was made chief of a new unit in the Division of Wildlife Research that in 1936 became known as the Section of Wildlife Surveys, and he remained in that position until his retirement. During World War II, Dr. Jackson served on two War Production Board committees and supplied them with a volume of important information. He also assisted the Office of Strategic Services in obtaining important information on Alaska. Jackson played a prominent role in the formation of the American Society of Mammalogist and became a devoted member of the society throughout his life. He retired on May 31, 1951, after forty-one years of government service. He was the last of the Merriam men to die, succumbing on September 20, 1976.

J. Alden Loring (1871–1947) of New York joined the Survey's field force in April 1892. He was an enthusiastic collector and during the next few years was involved with field surveys in many regions of the western United States, where he was trained by Bailey, and in Canada and Mexico. He left the service in 1897 and served as curator of animals of the New York Zoological Park from that year until 1901, and then he spent 1903 in Alaska studying mountain sheep and bears. In 1909 he accompanied President Theodore Roosevelt on his scientific expedition and hunting trip to East Africa, representing the Smithsonian Institution as a field naturalist. After his return from Africa, he established a lecture series, "Through Africa with Roosevelt," which had a foreword by President Roosevelt. In 1916, Loring was commissioned to go to South Africa to purchase wild animals for the zoological parks in New York, Philadelphia, and Washington, DC. He was reemployed for special duties by the Survey on several occasions, most notably in 1920 when he spent the summer on the great waterfowl breeding grounds in central Canada.

Herb Keys, according to R. E. Kohler, was a neighbor of Vernon Bailey and accompanied him on his overland trip to Arizona in 1888. I could not locate any additional information about him. He left Bailey in the middle of their trip to work in Arizona and never made any sort of reputation in collecting or science.

Frank W. Knowlton (1860–1926) was an American botanist, ornithologist, and paleontologist who worked for the US Geological Survey. He collected fossil and living plants in the American West from Montana to Arizona. He accompanied Merriam and Bailey as a member of the field party to survey the San Francisco Mountains and Grand Canyon region in Arizona.

Waldo L. McAtee (1883–1962) joined the Biological Survey in 1903, following his education at the University of Indiana, as chief assistant in economic ornithology and later was placed in charge of the Division of Food Habits Research. More importantly to the purpose of this book, he recorded anecdotes and remembrances of staff associated with the Survey and in 1951 sent these to the Library of Congress with provisions they would be restricted for use until any individual treated was dead. From these notes, we have at least some idea about the personalities and idiosyncrasies of the various people employed by the Survey.

Edward William Nelson (1855–1934), some months senior to Merriam in age, was the eldest of the leading figures in the Biological Survey's early days and came to the Survey with about as much experience in field research as Merriam. He was another of the Survey people who had no formal college education. In the summer of 1872, he worked briefly in the West with Edward Drinker Cope, the distinguished paleontologist. In 1877, Spencer Fullerton Baird offered him an appointment as an enlisted man to the US Army Signal Service to study the mammals and birds of Alaska. Nelson hired on as a special field agent for the Survey in November 1890 where he worked with Bailey, Fisher, and Palmer. Nelson remained with the Survey for the next forty years, eleven of which (1916–1927) he served as the third chief of the agency. During his role as chief, he instituted the development of programs bearing on the conservation and general administration of wildlife from a national standpoint. He was instrumental in the negotiations for the Migratory Bird Conservation Act, Migratory Bird Hunting Stamp Act, and the Alaska Game Law, all of which gave better protection for migratory birds, especially waterfowl. Also, during his tenure as chief, many of the controversies associated with the predator-control program and policies of the Survey would come to public light bringing much attention to the role of the agency. Nelson retired from administrative work in 1927, and two years later at the age of seventy-four he retired from active work with the bureau.

Harry Church Oberholser (1870–1963), of Ohio, joined the Survey in the same year as Howell, receiving an appointment as an ornithological clerk in the Division of Economic Ornithology. Among Survey personnel, he had one of the best formal educations, having received BA, MS, and PhD degrees from George Washington University. For the first fifteen years of his career, he worked under Merriam with principal duties including the identification of thousands of birds sent to the Survey. He was appointed assistant biologist in 1914, biologist in 1924, and senior biologist in 1928. Most of his fieldwork was done between 1895 and 1903, principally in the West. His lifelong interest in Texas bird life began with a biological reconnaissance of the state that he made in 1900 with Vernon Bailey. He produced a monograph on the birds of Texas that remained unpublished at his death. A condensed version of this work, *The Bird Life of Texas*, edited by Kincaid and others, appeared in 1974. *Bird Life of Louisiana* (1938) was the other important work Oberholser published during his lifetime. He worked for the Survey forty-six years until retiring in 1941.

Wilfred Hudson Osgood (1875–1947) came to the Survey in 1897 from California. He had entered Stanford University shortly after its founding, coming under the influence of the eminent zoologist David Starr Jordan, then president of the university. He left Stanford before completing his BA degree to take a position in 1897 with Merriam at the Biological Survey and eventually received his degree in 1899. Osgood was greatly influenced by his association with Merriam, not only working for him but also living in his house in Washington where he met and interacted with many of Merriam's influential friends and other workers at the Survey (such as Vernon Bailey). He spent over a decade with the Survey, publishing a number of papers in the *North American Fauna* series, including his classic revision of the deer mice of the genus *Peromyscus* in 1909. He left the Survey and went to the Field Museum in 1909 where he served as assistant curator of mammals and birds (1909–1920) and chief curator of zoology (1921–1941).

Theodore Sherman Palmer (1868–1955) came to work for the Survey in 1889 after having graduated from the University of California at Berkeley in 1888 with a BA degree. He later earned an MD from Georgetown, possibly in emulation of Merriam and Fisher, although he never practiced medicine. He did some notable fieldwork (especially with the Death Valley Expedition) and authored several important publications about mammals and birds before turning to the field of conservation and game protection. Palmer was known for his ability to handle administrative matters and spent much of his time in Washington, DC, working on wildlife laws, game management, and conservation. He administered the branch of the Biological Survey that dealt with regulations concerning the hunting and protection of wildlife and headed it for decades. Palmer influenced much of the wildlife legislation passed from 1900 to 1924 and in some instances was the principal factor. He helped to write the legislation that resulted in the landmark Lacey Act of 1900 giving the Survey new regulatory and managerial responsibilities. He also drafted the preliminary version of the treaty governing the protection of Canadian and American migratory birds and helped prepare the first federal regulations under the Migratory Bird Treaty Act of 1918. He was also involved in the creation of what became the National Wildlife Refuge Program, counseled innumerable state legislatures as they formulated their game laws, and was a director and vice president of the National Audubon

Society for thirty years. After forty-four years of service Dr. Palmer retired from the Survey in 1933, the same year as Vernon Bailey. His great avocation had to do with compiling the necrology of members of the AOU, of which he was secretary for several decades. This very useful activity earned him the somewhat dubious sobriquet of "Tombstone Palmer."

Edward Alexander "E.A." Preble (1871–1957) of Massachusetts joined the Survey in the same year as Loring, receiving an appointment as a field naturalist and remaining employed there continuously until 1935. He began his fieldwork in 1892 with Vernon Bailey in Texas, and worked in Georgia, Maryland, Oregon, Washington, and Utah, conducting life zone samplings. In 1900 he began a major field exploration to the Hudson Bay region of Canada where he worked extensively with his brother and Merritt Cary for several years. In 1907, he and Ernest Thompson Seton made a canoe trip to the Barren Grounds about Aylmer Lake, a region to the northeast of Great Slave Lake along the Athabasca peninsula. As a senior biologist, in his later years with the Biological Survey, Preble became very interested in wildlife management and conservation, and for some years he was one of the judges in a contest for humane trap designs held by the American Humane Association. One of his greatest services was the editing of papers written by other members of the Division of Biological Investigations of the Biological Survey. One of the chief beneficiaries of this editing—Vernon Bailey—publicly acknowledged the aid in 1939: "We . . . felt safer when Preble went over our manuscripts . . . and I welcomed this opportunity to express my own obligations for such help,—always cheerfully given even if his work suffered by delay." In 1925 Preble was appointed consulting naturalist for *Nature Magazine,* and in 1935 he retired from government service to become associate editor of that magazine. Until his death in 1957, he edited, reviewed, and wrote articles for *Nature Magazine,* the publication of the American Nature Association.

Paul G. Redington (1878–1942) was the first outsider to serve as chief of the Biological Survey, taking over in 1927 from E. W. Nelson. He came from the Forest Service and returned to the Forest Service in 1934. He based his administration of the national wildlife resources on three needs, which he labeled the three Rs: (1) Research to establish a factual basis for public policies that had long been too much determined by political rather than scientific factors; (2) Regulations to reduce the overshooting that had depleted the country's wildlife; and (3) Refuges to provide areas where wildlife could find sanctuary.

Ernest Thompson Seton, a British-born naturalist and artist, long resident in Canada, collected specimens for Merriam from the 1880s to about 1908. In 1907, he made a two-thousand-mile canoe trip in northern Canada with Preble as his traveling companion. He learned how to describe animals properly from Merriam, and he completed a number of illustrations for publications put out by the Biological Survey.

Leonard Stejneger (1851–1943) was a Norwegian-born American ornithologist, herpetologist, and zoologist who specialized in vertebrate natural history studies. He gained his greatest reputation with reptiles and amphibians while working for the Smithsonian Institution and was elected to the National Academy of Sciences in 1921. Bailey spent time in the field with Stejneger and came to have a very high regard; the two men were friends throughout their lives.

Clark P. Streator (1866–1952) already well known for his fieldwork in the West Indies and in British Columbia, joined the Survey as a participant in a field expedition to south-central Idaho in 1890 where he trained under Bailey. He remained with the Survey for several years and did important work in various parts of the United States, mainly on the West Coast, including British Columbia and southern Alaska, but also in Colorado, California, Nevada, and Texas. His service terminated in 1896. His specimens, judiciously selected and well prepared, were always known to be as representative as possible of the local fauna.

Russell J. Thompson received an appointment to do fieldwork in 1892, and after a few weeks training (along with Loring) under Vernon Bailey was assigned to work in Georgia, Mississippi, Louisiana, and Tennessee during that summer and fall. Coleman began work in Mississippi and later collected in Louisiana, Kentucky, and Nebraska with Bailey. He left the Survey in 1893.

In addition to these men, a few other individuals, who were only employed briefly with the Survey, went on to distinguished careers outside of the agency. Notable individuals included:

Frank H. Hitchcock, who became postmaster general in the administration of President Howard Taft; **Frederick Funston**, a congressman's son who later became an army officer, won the Congressional Medal of Honor in the Philippine insurrection, and became a major general; **Clarence Birdseye,** who would later invent the first products of the frozen-food industry; and **Alexander Wetmore** who rose to become secretary of the Smithsonian Institution.

Notes

CHM—Clinton Hart Merriam Papers, Bancroft Library, University of California, Berkeley

FMB—Florence Merriam Bailey Papers, Bancroft Library, University of California, Berkeley

LOC—Library of Congress

LOC-TSP—LOC, T. S. Palmer Papers

LOC-WM—LOC, William McAtee Papers

OPM—Office of Personnel Management, St. Louis, Missouri

OPM-AKF—OPM, A. K. Fisher Files

OPM-TSP—OPM, T. S. Palmer Files

OPM-VB—OPM, Vernon Bailey Files

SIA—Smithsonian Institution Archives

SIA-N&G—SIA, Nelson & Goldman Papers

SIA-ASM—SIA, American Society of Mammalogists Papers

SIA-VB/FMB—SIA, Vernon Bailey and Florence Merriam Bailey Papers

SIA-HHTJ—SIA, Hartley H. H. T. Jackson Papers

VOB—Vernon Orlando Bailey Papers, American Heritage Center, University of Wyoming, Laramie

Preface

1. V. Bailey, "Biological Survey of Texas," *North American Fauna 25* (1905): 1–222.

2. D. J. Schmidly, *Texas Natural History: A Century of Change* (Lubbock: Texas Tech University Press, 2002).

3. D. J. Schmidly, W. E. Tydeman, and A. L. Gardner, eds., *United States Biological Survey: A Compendium of Its History, Personalities, Impacts, and Conflicts* (Lubbock: Texas Tech University, The Museum, Special Publication Number 64, 2016).

4. D. J. Schmidly, "Vernon Bailey (1864–1942): Chief Field Naturalist of the Biological Survey," in *United States Biological Survey: A Compendium of Its History, Personalities, Impacts, and Conflicts*, ed. D. J. Schmidly, W. E. Tydeman, and A. L. Gardner (Lubbock: Texas Tech University, The Museum, Special Publication Number 64, 2016), 25–53.

5. K. B. Sterling, *Last of the Naturalists: The Career of C. Hart Merriam* (New York: Arno Press, 1977).

6. H. Kofalk, *No Woman Tenderfoot: Florence Merriam Bailey, Pioneer Naturalist* (College Station: Texas A&M University Press, 1989).

7. H. Kofalk and B. Hone, "My Game Is Mice: A Life in the Field" (unpublished and unfinished biography of Vernon Bailey, no date), copy of manuscript deposited at the Southwest Archives, Texas Tech University, Lubbock, Texas.

8. R. E. Kohler, "From Farm and Family to Career Naturalist: The Apprenticeship of Vernon Bailey," *Isis* 99 (2008): 28–56.

9. The Biological Survey was known by several titles in its historical evolution. In the beginning it was known as the Division of Economic Ornithology (in the Department of Agriculture). The next year (1886) saw the phrase "and Mammalogy" added to the title, and in 1896 it was named the Division of Biological Survey. The Division became the Bureau of Biological Survey in 1905, and it remained under that designation until it was merged into the United States Fish and Wildlife Service in 1940. Throughout this text, it is interchangeably referred to as "the Biological Survey," the "USBS," "the Survey," or simply as "the bureau."

10. R. E. Kohler, *All Creatures, Naturalists, Collectors, and Biodiversity, 1850–1950* (Princeton, NJ: Princeton University Press, 2006).

11. Hiram Bailey autobiography, VOB, Box 11.

Introduction and Background

1. R. E. Kohler, *All Creatures, Naturalists, Collectors, and Biodiversity, 1850–1950* (Princeton, NJ: Princeton University Press, 2006).

2. D. Lunde, *The Naturalist Theodore Roosevelt* (New York: Crown Publishers, 2016).

3. Kohler, *All Creatures.*

4. Ibid.

5. T. R. Dunlap, *Saving America's Wildlife* (Princeton, NJ: Princeton University Press, 1988).

6. The Cyclone Mouse Trap was patented by John Morris in 1883.

7. K. B. Sterling, *Last of the Naturalists: The Career of C. Hart Merriam* (New York: Arno Press, 1977).

8. C. H. Merriam, "Biology in Our Colleges: A Plea for Broader and More Liberal Biology," *Science* 21 (1893): 352–355.

9. Bailey was the second person hired by Merriam and the first to work strictly in the field. The first employee, Albert K. Fisher, had been a classmate of Merriam's in medical school, and he worked primarily alongside Merriam in Washington, although he did occasionally go into the field. Shortly after Bailey hired on, Theodore S. Palmer, who had just received his BA degree from the University of California at Berkeley, joined the team. Palmer also worked out of Washington and only occasionally went into the field. All three of these men would serve the agency for more than four decades, far beyond the twenty-five years that Merriam served as chief. They were joined in 1890 and 1891, by E. W. Nelson and E. A. Goldman, who worked for the agency forty and fifty years, respectively. These five senior scientific staff became colleagues and giant figures inside the agency, and each played a prominent role in its mission and accomplishments.

10. R. E. Kohler, "From Farm and Family to Career Naturalist: The Apprenticeship of Vernon Bailey," *Isis* 99 (2008): 28–56.

11. Sterling, *Last of the Naturalists.*

12. A. L. Gardner, "The United States Biological Survey: A Brief History, 1885–1940," in *United States Biological Survey: A Compendium of Its History, Personalities, Impacts, and Conflicts*, ed. D. J. Schmidly, W. E. Tydeman, and A. L. Gardner (Lubbock: Texas Tech University, The Museum, Special Publication Number 64, 2016), 1–14.

Section I

1. Hiram Bailey autobiography, VOB, Box 11.

2. 1928 Bailey Family History, VOB, Box 11.

3. VB letter to Houghton Mifflin Company, VOB, Box 8, Folder 6.

4. 1928 Bailey Family History, VOB, Box 11.

Chapter 1

1. This chapter is adapted from Hiram Bailey handwritten account of the early history of the Bailey family, VOB, Box 11.

Chapter 2

1. This chapter is adapted from Vernon Bailey's 1928 "Bailey Family History," VOB, Box 11.

Chapter 3

1. This chapter is adapted from Hiram Bailey's account of the early history of the Bailey family as told to his son, Vernon Bailey, VOB, Box 11.

Chapter 4

1. This description of hunting and fishing around the Bailey homestead is taken from Vernon Bailey's 1928 autobiographic account of his life, VOB, Box 11.

2. 1928 Bailey Family History, VOB, Box 11.

Chapter 5

1. Once he had set the stage for his own development halfway through the 1928 autobiography, Bailey subtitled it "The Making of a Naturalist—Field Work of a Biologist," in which he described how school work began to kindle his interest in natural history, 1928 Bailey Family History, VOB, Box 11.

2. Oliver Davie, *Methods in the Art of Taxidermy*, (Philadelphia: David McKay, 1900).

3. Wilk Schneider to Bailey, 12/30/1885, VOB, Box 1.

4. D. J. Schmidly, "Vernon Bailey (1864–1942): Chief Field Naturalist of the Biological Survey," in *United States Biological Survey: A Compendium of Its History, Personalities, Impacts, and Conflicts*, ed. D. J. Schmidly, W. E. Tydeman, and A. L.

Gardner (Lubbock: Texas Tech University, The Museum, Special Publication Number 64, 2016), 25–53.

5. C. H. Merriam, *The Mammals of the Adirondack Region* (self-published, 1884), Press of L. S. Foster.

6. J. M Wheaton, "Report on the Birds of Ohio," *Report of the Geological Survey of Ohio* (Vol. 4, 1883).

7. R. E. Kohler, "From Farm and Family to Career Naturalist: The Apprenticeship of Vernon Bailey," *Isis* 99 (2008): 28–56.

8. Ibid.

Chapter 6

1. CHM to VB, 1/13/1886; VOB, Box 1, Folder 1.
2. CHM to VB, 3/28/1886; VOB, Box 1, Folder 1.
3. CHM to VB, 6/15/1886; VOB, Box 1, Folder 1.
4. CHM to VB, 7/16/1886; VOB, Box 1, Folder 1.
5. CHM to VB, 8/16/1886; VOB, Box 1, Folder 1.
6. CHM to VB, 10/8/1886; VOB, Box 1, Folder 1.
7. H. Widman to VB, 1/31/1887; VOB, Box 1, Folder 2.
8. ? to VOB, 2/20/1887; VOB, Box 1, Folder 2.
9. CHM to VB, 3/18/1887; VOB, Box 1, Folder 2.

Section II

1. VB to CHM, 7/20/1886; CHM Reel 35, UC-Berkeley.
2. R. E. Kohler, "From Farm and Family to Career Naturalist: The Apprenticeship of Vernon Bailey," *Isis* 99 (2008): 28–56.
3. Ibid.
4. R. E. Kohler, *All Creatures, Naturalists, Collectors, and Biodiversity, 1850–1950* (Princeton, NJ: Princeton University Press, 2006).
5. Ibid.

Chapter 7

1. Comm. USDA to VB, 5/4/1887; VOB, Box 1, Folder 2.
2. 1928 Bailey Family History, VOB, Box 11.
3. CHM to VB, 5/5/1887; VOB, Box 1, Folder 2.
4. VB to CHM, 5/10/1887; VOB, Box 15, Folder 11.

Chapter 8

1. CHM to VB, 5/18/1887; VOB, Box 1, Folder 2.
2. VB to Dear Family at Home [DFAH], 5/15/1887; VOB, Box 8, Folder 8.
3. CHM to VB; May/nd/ 1887; VOB, Box 1, Folder 2.
4. VB to DFAH [Postcard], 5/23/1887; VOB, Box 8, Folder 8.
5. VB to DFAH, 5/29/1887; VOB, Box 8, Folder 8.

6. VB to DFAH, 6/nd/1887; VOB, Box 8, Folder 8.

7. CHM to VB, 6/4/1887; VOB, Box 1, Folder 2.

8. VB to CHM, 6/5/1887; VOB, Box 8, Folder 8.

9. VB to DFAH, 6/10/1887; VOB, Box 8, Folder 8.

10. CHM to VB, 6/7/1887; VOB, Box 1, Folder 2.

11. King to VB, 6/8/1887; VOB, Box 8, Folder 8.

12. VB to DFAH, 6/10/1887; VOB, Box 8, Folder 8.

Chapter 9

1. CHM to VB, 6/15/1887; VOB, Box 1, Folder 2.

2. VB to DFAH, 6/20/1887; VOB, Box 8, Folder 8.

3. Ibid.

4. VB to DFAH, 6/26/1887; VOB, Box 8, Folder 8.

Chapter 10

1. R. E. Kohler, "From Farm and Family to Career Naturalist: The Apprenticeship of Vernon Bailey," *Isis* 99 (2008): 28–56.

2. VB to CHM, 7/1/1887; VOB, Box 8, Folder 8.

3. R. E. Kohler, *All Creatures, Naturalists, Collectors, and Biodiversity, 1850–1950* (Princeton, NJ: Princeton University Press, 2006).

4. Emily Bailey (EB) to VB, 6/28/1887; VOB, Box 8, Folder 8.

5. VB to DFAH, 7/10/1887; VOB, Box 8, Folder 8

6. H. Kofalk and B. Hone, "My Game Is Mice: A Life in the Field" (unpublished and unfinished biography of Vernon Bailey, no date), copy of manuscript deposited at the Southwest Archives, Texas Tech University, Lubbock, Texas.

7. Ibid.

8. CHM to VB, 7/11/1887; VOB, Box 1, Folder 3.

9. VB to DFAH, 7/17/1887; VOB, Box 8, Folder 8.

10. CHM to VB, 7/20/1887; VOB, Box 1, Folder 3.

11. CHM to VB, 7/23/1887; VOB, Box 1, Folder 3.

12. VB to DFAH, 7/24/1887; VOB, Box 8, Folder 8.

13. VB to DFAH, 8/7/1887; VOB, Box 8, Folder 8.

14. VB to DFAH, 8/14/1887; VOB, Box 8, Folder 8.

15. VB to DFAH, 8/21/1887; VOB, Box 8, Folder 8.

Chapter 11

1. CHM to VB, 8/26/1887; VOB, Box 1, Folder 3.

2. VB to DFAH, 8/28/1887; VOB, Box 8, Folder 8.

3. VB to Anna, 8/30/1887; VOB, Box 8, Folder 8.

4. VB to DFAH, 9/18/1887; VOB, Box 8, Folder 8.

5. VB to DFAH, 10/9/1887; VOB, Box 8, Folder 8.

6. VB to Anna, 10/9/1887; VOB, Box 8, Folder 8.

7. VB to Anna, 10/10/1887; VOB, Box 8, Folder 8.

8. VB to DFAH, 10/10/1887; VOB, Box 8, Folder 8.

9. VB to DFAH, 10/30/1887; VOB, Box 8, Folder 8.

10. H. Kofalk and B. Hone, "My Game Is Mice: A Life in the Field" (unpublished and unfinished biography of Vernon Bailey, no date), copy of manuscript deposited at the Southwest Archives, Texas Tech University, Lubbock, Texas.

11. Ibid.

12. Ibid.

13. CHM to VB, 11/1/1887; VOB, Box 1, Folder 3.

14. VB to DFAH, 11/6/1887; VOB, Box 8, Folder 8.

15. VB to CHM, 11/19/1887; VOB, Box 15, Folder 12.

16. CHM to VB, 11/21/1887; VOB, Box 1, Folder 3.

17. CHM to VB, 11/29/1887; VOB, Box 1, Folder 3.

18. CHM to VB, 12/15/1887; Box 1, Folder 3.

19. Barrows to VB, 12/30/1887; VOB, Box 1, Folder 3.

20. CHM to VB, 12/31/1887; VOB, Box 1, Folder 3.

21. R. E. Kohler, "From Farm and Family to Career Naturalist: The Apprenticeship of Vernon Bailey," *Isis* 99 (2008): 28–56.

22. Ibid.

Chapter 12

1. CHM to VB, 3/10/1888; VOB, Box 1, Folder 4.

2. VB to DFAH, 5/20/1888; VOB, Box 1, Folder 9.

3. CHM to VB, 6/5/1888; VOB, Box 1, Folder 4.

4. VB to DFAH, 6/10/1888; VOB, Box 8, Folder 9.

5. VB to DFAH, 6/17/1888; VOB, Box 8, Folder 9.

6. CHM to VB, 6/19/1888; VOB, Box 1, Folder 4.

7. VB to DFAH, 7/1/1888; VOB, Box 8, Folder 9.

8. CHM to VB, 7/16/1888; VOB, Box 1, Folder 4.

9. VB to Anna, 7/8/1888; VOB, Box 8, Folder 9.

10. VB to DFAH, 7/8/1888; VOB, Box 8, Folder 9.

11. VB to EM, 9/16/1888; VOB, Box 1.

12. R. E. Kohler, "From Farm and Family to Career Naturalist: The Apprenticeship of Vernon Bailey," *Isis* 99 (2008): 28–56.

Chapter 13

1. VB to DFAH, 10/7/1888; VOB, Box 8, Folder 10.

2. VB to Anna, 10/7/1888; VOB, Box 8, Folder 10.

3. VB to DFAH, 10/14/1888; VOB, Box 8, Folder 10.

4. CHM to VB, 10/21/1888; VOB, Box 1, Folder 4.

5. VB to DFAH, 10/28/1888; VOB, Box 8, Folder 10.

6. CHM to VB, 11/1/1888; VOB, Box 8, Folder 10.

7. VB to DFAH, 11/11/1888; VOB, Box 8, Folder 10.

8. VB to DFAH, 11/25/1888; VOB, Box 8, Folder 10.

9. Hiram Bailey (HB) to VB, 12/1/1888; VOB, Box 8, Folder 10.

10. Ibid.

11. VB to DFAH, 12/2/1888; VOB, Box 8, Folder 10.

12. Herb Keys was a neighbor of Baileys (according to Kohler, "From Farm and Family, 2008"), and apparently Merriam had agreed that he could join Bailey for the overland trip to Arizona in 1889.

13. VB to DFAH, 12/11/1888; VOB, Box 8, Folder 10.

Chapter 14

1. CHM to VB, 12/7/1888; VOB, Box 1, Folder 4.

2. CHM to VB, 12/18/1888; VOB, Box 1, Folder 4.

3. VB to DFAH, 12/30/1888; VOB, Box 8, Folder 10.

4. CHM to VB, 1/3/1889; VOB, Box 1, Folder 5.

5. CHM to VB, 1/10/1889; VOB, Box 1, Folder 5.

6. VB to Anna, 1/20/1889; VOB, Box 8, Folder 11.

7. VB to DFAH, 2/10/1889; VOB, Box 8, Folder 11.

8. CHM to VB, 2/12/1889; VOB, Box 1, Folder 5.

9. CHM to VB, 2/12/1889; VOB, Box 1, Folder 5.

10. VB to DFAH, 2/17/1889; VOB, Box 8, Folder 11.

11. VB to Anna, 2/17/1889; VOB, Box 8, Folder 11.

12. VB to DFAH, 2/24/1889; VOB, Box 8, Folder 11.

13. VB to Anna, 3/3/1889; VOB, Box 8, Folder 11.

14. VB to DFAH, 3/3/1889; VOB, Box 8, Folder 11.

15. VB to DFAH, 3/17/1889; VOB, Box 8, Folder 11.

16. VB to DFAH, 3/21/1889; VOB, Box 8, Folder 11.

Chapter 15

1. CHM to VB; 3/12/1889; VOB, Box 1, Folder 5.

2. "Down the Colorado, March 1889"; VB's handwritten account; SIA RU 7176; VOB, Box 8, Folder 11.

3. CHM to VB, 5/7/1889; VOB, Box 8, Folder 12.

4. R. E. Kohler, "From Farm and Family to Career Naturalist: The Apprenticeship of Vernon Bailey," *Isis* 99 (2008): 28–56.

Chapter 16

1. VB to DFAH, 4/3/1889; VOB, Box 8, Folder 11.

2. VB to DFAH, 4/7/1889; VOB, Box 8, Folder 11.

3. CHM to VB, 5/1/1889; VOB, Box 1, Folder 5.

4. VB to DFAH, 4/28/1889; VOB, Box 8, Folder 11.
5. VB to DFAH, 5/5/1889; VOB, Box 8, Folder 12.
6. VB to Anna, 5/5/1889; VOB, Box 8, Folder 12.
7. VB to DFAH, 5/27/1889; VOB, Box 8, Folder 12.
8. CHM to VB, 5/31/1889; VOB, Box 1, Folder 5.

Chapter 17

1. CHM to VB, 5/25/1889; VOB, Box 1, Folder 5.
2. VB to DFAH, 6/21/1889; VOB, Box 8, Folder 12.
3. VB to DFAH, 6/26/1889; VOB, Box 8, Folder 12.
4. VB to DFAH, 6/30/1889; VOB, Box 8, Folder 12.
5. VB to Anna, 7/7/1889; VOB, Box 8, Folder 12.
6. VB to Anna, 7/13/1889; VOB, Box 8, Folder 12.
7. VB to DFAH, 7/21/1889; VOB, Box 8, Folder 12.

Chapter 18

1. VB to DFAH, 7/28/1889; VOB, Box 8, Folder 12.
2. VB to DFAH, 8/4/1889; VOB, Box 8, Folder 12.
3. VB to DFAH, 8/30/1889; VOB, Box 1, Folder 5.
4. K. B. Sterling, *Last of the Naturalists: The Career of C. Hart Merriam* (New York: Arno Press, 1977).
5. VB to DFAH, 10/9/1889; VOB, Box 8, Folder 13.
6. VB to DFAH, 10/27/1889; VOB, Box 8, Folder 13.
7. VB to DFAH, 10/13/1889; VOB, Box 8, Folder 13.
8. Ibid.
9. Ibid.
10. VB to Anna, 10/13/1889; VOB, Box 8, Folder 13.

Chapter 19

1. VB to DFAH, 10/20/1889; VOB, Box 8, Folder 13.
2. CHM to VB, 10/23/1889; VOB, Box 8, Folder 13.
3. VB to DFAH, 10/30/1889; VOB, Box 8, Folder 13.
4. VB to DFAH, 11/3/1889; VOB, Box 8, Folder 13.
5. Ibid.
6. VB to DFAH, 12/1/1889; VOB, Box 8, Folder 13.
7. Ibid.
8. CHM to VB, 12/5/1889; VOB, Box 1, Folder 5.
9. VB to Anna, 12/22/1889; VOB, Box 8, Folder 13.
10. VB to DFAH, 12/22/1889; VOB, Box 8, Folder 13.
11. VB to DFAH, 12/27/1889; VOB, Box 8, Folder 13.
12. Ibid.
13. Memorabilia, VB's deerskin notebook, 1889; VOB, Box 20.

14. CHM to VB, 12/30/1889; VOB, Box 1, Folder 5.

15. R. E. Kohler, *All Creatures, Naturalists, Collectors, and Biodiversity, 1850–1950* (Princeton, NJ: Princeton University Press, 2006).

16. VB to DFAH, 1/17/1890; VOB, Box 9, Folder 1.

17. CHM to VB, 2/8/1890; VOB, Box 1, Folder 6.

18. CHM to VB, 2/15/1890; VOB, Box 1, Folder 6.

Chapter 20

1. R. E. Kohler, "From Farm and Family to Career Naturalist: The Apprenticeship of Vernon Bailey," *Isis* 99 (2008): 28–56.

2. CHM to VB, 3/8/1890; VOB, Box 1, Folder 6.

3. CHM to VB, 3/10/1890; VOB, Box 1, Folder 6.

4. CHM to VB, 4/7/1890; VOB, Box 1, Folder 6.

5. VB to DFAH, 4/13/1890; VOB, Box 9, Folder 1.

6. CHM to VB, 4/15/1890; VOB, Box 1, Folder 6.

7. VB to DFAH, 4/20/1890; VOB, Box 9, Folder 1.

8. Ibid.

9. VB to DFAH, 4/27/1890; VOB, Box 9, Folder 1.

10. VB to DFAH, 5/1/1890; VOB, Box 9, Folder 1.

11. VB to DFAH, 5/17/1890; VOB, Box 9, Folder 1.

12. VB to DFAH, 5/25/1890; VOB, Box 9, Folder 1.

13. VB to DFAH, 6/1/1890; VOB, Box 9, Folder 1.

14. VB to DFAH, 6/8/1890; VOB, Box 9, Folder 1.

15. VB to DFAH, 6/15/1890; VOB, Box 9, Folder 1.

16. CHM to VB, 6/6/1890; VOB, Box 1, Folder 6.

Chapter 21

1. VB to DFAH, 6/22/1890; VOB, Box 9, Folder 1.

2. VB to DFAH, 6/29/1890; VOB, Box 9, Folder 1.

3. CHM to VB, 7/2/1890; VOB, Box 1, Folder 7.

4. Dept. Ag. To VB, 7/1/1890; Box 1, Folder 7.

5. VB to DFAH, 7/6/1890; VOB, Box 9, Folder 2.

6. VB to DFAH, 7/13/1890; VOB, Box 9, Folder 2.

7. CHM to VB, 10/27/1890; VOB, Box 1, Folder 7.

8. CHM to VB, 11/5/1890; VOB, Box 1, Folder 7.

9. CHM to VB, 12/3/1890; VOB, Box 1, Folder 7.

10. VB to DFAH, 12/31/1890; VOB, Box 9, Folder 2.

11. W. Jenkins to VB, 1/2/1891; VOB, Box 9, Folder 3.

Chapter 22

1. V. O. Bailey, "Into Death Valley 50 Years Ago," *Westways December 1940* (1940): 8–11.

2. Ibid.
3. VB to DFAH, 1/25/1891; VOB, Box 9, Folder 3.
4. VB to DFAH, 4/5/1891; VOB, Box 9, Folder 3.
5. VB to DFAH, 5/13/1891; VOB, Box 9, Folder 3.
6. VB to DFAH, 6/14/1891; VOB, Box 9, Folder 3.
7. VB to DFAH, 6/20/1891; VOB, Box 9, Folder 3.
8. VB to DFAH, 6/26/1891; VOB, Box 9, Folder 3.
9. VB to DFAH, 7/5/1891; VOB, Box 9, Folder 4.
10. VB to DFAH, 7/26/1891; VOB, Box 9, Folder 4.
11. VB to Anna, 8/2/1891; VOB, Box 9, Folder 4.
12. VB to DFAH, 8/9/1891; VOB, Box 9, Folder 4.
13. VB to DFAH, 8/16/1891; VOB, Box 9, Folder 4.
14. VB to DFAH, 8/29/1891; VOB, Box 9, Folder 4.

Chapter 23

1. R. E. Kohler, "From Farm and Family to Career Naturalist: The Apprenticeship of Vernon Bailey," *Isis* 99 (2008): 28–56.
2. VB to DFAH, 6/10/1888; VOB, Box 8, Folder 9.
3. VB to DFAH, 9/28/1888; VOB, Box 8, Folder 9.
4. VB to DFAH, 9/28/1890; VOB, Box 9, Folder 2.
5. VB to DFAH, 12/29/1889; VOB, Box 8, Folder 13.
6. VB to DFAH, 7/14/1889; VOB, Box 8, Folder 12.
7. VB to DFAH, 2/21/1891; VOB, Box 9, Folder 3.
8. Bailey does not say who he thought was stepping over him, but it may have been T. S. Palmer. Recently appointed, in 1889, Palmer was four years younger than Bailey and had a BA degree.
9. VB to DFAH, 8/24/1890; VOB, Box 9, Folder 2.
10. Kohler, "From Farm and Family."
11. Ibid.
12. Ibid.
13. Ibid.

Section III

1. R. E. Kohler, *All Creatures, Naturalists, Collectors, and Biodiversity, 1850–1950* (Princeton, NJ: Princeton University Press, 2006).
2. Ibid.

Chapter 24

1. VB to DFAH, 1/3/1892; VOB, Box 9, Folder 5.
2. Ibid.
3. VB to DFAH, 1/10/1892; VOB, Box 9, Folder 5.
4. VB to DFAH, 1/17/1892; VOB, Box 9, Folder 5.

5. VB to DFAH, 1/22/1892; VOB, Box 9, Folder 5.
6. VB to DFAH, 1/31/1892; VOB, Box 9, Folder 5.
7. VB to Anna, 2/18/1892; VOB, Box 9, Folder 5.
8. Ibid.
9. VB to Anna, 2/28/1892; VOB, Box 9, Folder 5.
10. Anna to VB, 2/28/1892; VOB, Box 9, Folder 5.
11. VB to DFAH, 2/28/1892; VOB, Box 9, Folder 5.
12. VB to DFAH, 3/6/1892; VOB, Box 9, Folder 6.
13. VB to DFAH, 3/13/1892; VOB, Box 9, Folder 6.
14. VB to DFAH, 3/25/1892; VOB, Box 9, Folder 6.
15. EWN to VB, 3/27/1892; VOB, Box 1, Folder 9.

Chapter 25

1. VB to DFAH, 4/3/1892; VOB, Box 9, Folder 6.
2. CHM to VB, 4/10/1892; VOB, Box 1, Folder 9.
3. VB to DFAH, 4/10/1892; VOB, Box 9, Folder 6.
4. VB to DFAH, 4/17/1892; VOB, Box 9, Folder 6.
5. CHM to VB, 4/20/1892; VOB, Box 1, Folder 9.
6. CHM to VB, 4/22/1892; VOB, Box 1, Folder 9.
7. VB to DFAH, 4/24/1892; VOB, Box 9, Folder 6.
8. VB to DFAH, 5/1/1892; VOB, Box 9, Folder 6.
9. VB to DFAH, 5/4/1892; VOB, Box 9, Folder 6.
10. VB to DFAH, 5/15/1892; VOB, Box 9, Folder 6.
11. VB to DFAH, 5/17/1892; VOB, Box 9, Folder 6.
12. VB to DFAH, 5/22/1892; VOB, Box 9, Folder 6.
13. CHM to VB, 5/31/1892; VOB, Box 1, Folder 9.
14. CHM to VB, 6/9/1892; VOB, Box 1, Folder 9.
15. Ibid.

Chapter 26

1. VB to DFAH, 6/12/1892; VOB, Box 9, Folder 7.
2. VB to DFAH, 6/19/1892; VOB, Box 9, Folder 7.
3. The Bald Knobbers were a group of vigilantes in the Ozark region of southwestern Missouri in the late 1880s and early 1890s. The group, which for the most part had sided with the North in the Civil War, derived its name from the grassy bald knob summits of the Ozark Mountains.
4. VB to DFAH, 6/26/1892; VOB, Box 9, Folder 7.
5. VB to DFAH, 7/8/1892, VOB, Box 9, Folder 7.
6. VB to DFAH, 7/24/1892; VOB, Box 9, Folder 8.
7. VB to DFAH, 8/8/1892; VOB, Box 9, Folder 8.
8. VB to Anna & John Mills, 8/14/1892; VOB, Box 9, Folder 8.
9. VB to Anna & John Mills, 8/18/1892; VOB, Box 9, Folder 8.

10. VB to DFAH, 9/6/1892; VOB, Box 9, Folder 8.

11. VB to DFAH, 9/11/1892; VOB, Box 9, Folder 8.

12. VB to DFAH, 10/10/1892; VOB, Box 9, Folder 8.

13. VB to DFAH, 10/16/1892; VOB, Box 9, Folder 8.

14. Anna to VB, 11/1/1892; VOB, Box 9, Folder 8.

15. VB to DFAH, 11/6/1892; VOB, Box 9, Folder 8.

16. D. J. Schmidly, *Texas Natural History: A Century of Change* (Lubbock: Texas Tech University Press, 2002).

17. VB to DFAH, 11/20/1892, VOB, Box 9, Folder 8.

18. VB to EB, 12/18/1892; VOB, Box 9, Folder 8.

19. Anna to VB, 12/27/1892; VOB, Box 9, Folder 8.

Chapter 27

1. NGM to VB, 1/17/1893; VOB, Box 9, Folder 9.

2. VB to DFAH, 1/17/1893; VOB, Box 9, Folder 9.

3. VB to DFAH, 1/27/1893; VOB, Box 9, Folder 9.

4. VB to DFAH, 2/19/1893; VOB, Box 9, Folder 9.

5. VB to DFAH, 3/12/1893; VOB, Box 9, Folder 9.

6. VB to DFAH, 3/19/1893; VOB, Box 9, Folder 9.

7. CHM to VB, 4/7/1893; VOB, Box 1, Folder 10.

8. CHM to VB, 4/17/1893; VOB, Box 1, Folder 10.

9. CHM to VB, 4/26/1893; VOB, Box 1, Folder 10.

10. CHM to VB, 5/26/1893; VOB, Box 1, Folder 10.

11. VB to DFAH, 6/4/1893; VOB, Box 9, Folder 9.

12. EM to VB, 6/21/1893; VOB, Box 9, Folder 9.

Chapter 28

1. TSP to VB, 6/19/1893; VOB, Box 1, Folder 10.

2. The two women (Florence Merriam and Harriet Mann Miller) would be labeled by historian Robert Welker as among the four best women nature writers of the late nineteenth century. R. Welker. *Birds and Men: American Birds in Science, Art, Literature, and Conservation, 1800–1900* (Cambridge, MA: Harvard University Press, 1955).

3. VB to DFAH, 7/8/1893; VOB, Box 9, Folder 10.

4. VB to DFAH, 7/16/1893; VOB, Box 9, Folder 10.

5. VB to DFAH, 8/13/1893; VOB, Box 9, Folder 10.

6. EB to VB, 8/16/1893; VOB, Box 9, Folder 10.

7. HB to VB, 8/20/1893; VOB, Box 9, Folder 10.

8. VB to DFAH, 8/23/1893; VOB, Box 1, Folder 10.

9. Dyche to VB, 9/15/1893; VOB, Box 1, Folder 10.

10. VB to Anna, 9/23/1893; VOB, Box 9, Folder 10.

11. VB to DFAH, 10/10, 1893; VOB, Box 9, Folder 10.

12. Anna to VB, 10/17/1893; VOB, Box 9, Folder 10.

13. Basil Dutcher to VB, 10/29/1893; VOB, Box 1, Folder 10.

14. Ibid.

15. VB to DFAH, 11/5/1893; VOB, Box 9, Folder 10.

16. EB to VB, 12/17/1893; VOB, Box 9, Folder 10.

Chapter 29

1. CHM to F. L. Evans, 2/2/1894; McAtee papers, Box 102, Folder 2.

2. VB to Anna, 3/27/1894; VOB, Box 9, Folder 11.

3. VB to Anna, 4/8/1894; VOB, Box 9, Folder 11.

4. CHM to VB, 5/1/1894; VOB, Box 1, Folder 11.

5. CHM to VB, 6/20/1894; VOB, Box 1, Folder 11.

6. VB to DFAH, 7/1/1894; VOB, Box 9, Folder 11.

7. VB to DFAH, 7/4/1894; VOB, Box 9, Folder 11.

8. CHM to VB, 7/27/1894; VOB, Box 1, Folder 11.

9. CHM to VB, 8/23/1894; VOB, Box 1, Folder 12.

10. CHM to VB, 10/4/1894; VOB, Box 1, Folder 12.

11. CHM to VB, 10/7/1894; VOB, Box 1, Folder 12.

12. VB to Charles Bailey, 10/12/1894; Box 9, Folder 12.

13. CHM to VB, 10/21/1894; VOB, Box 1, Folder 12.

14. Anna to VB, 10/?/1894; VOB, Box 9, Folder 12.

15. T. S. Palmer to VB, 11/12/1894; VOB, Box 1, Folder 12.

16. HB to VB, 11/18/1894; VOB, Box 9, Folder 11.

17. R. E. Kohler, "From Farm and Family to Career Naturalist: The Apprenticeship of Vernon Bailey," *Isis* 99 (2008): 28–56.

Chapter 30

1. EB to VB, 2/24/1895; VOB, Box 9, Folder 12.

2. VB to DFAH, 3/3/1895; VOB, Box 9, Folder 12.

3. VB to DFAH, 3/10/1895; VOB, Box 9, Folder 12.

4. Florence A. Merriam to VB, 5/2/1895; VOB, Box 1, Folder 13.

5. Department to VB, 5/9/1895; VOB, Box 1, Folder 13.

6. CHM to VB, 5/10/1895; VOB, Box 1, Folder 13.

7. VB to George Steel, 5/15/1895; VOB, Box 1, Folder 13.

8. VB to DFAH, 6/9/1895; VOB, Box 9, Folder 13.

9. CHM to VB, 6/27/1895; VOB, Box 1, Folder 13.

10. VB to DFAH, 7/23/1895; VOB, Box 9, Folder 13.

11. CHM to VB, 8/14/1895; VOB, Box 1, Folder 13.

12. CHM to VB, 8/23/1895; VOB, Box 1, Folder 13.

13. VB to DFAH, 12/1/1895; VOB, Box 9, Folder 13.

14. V. Bailey, "List of Mammals of the District of Columbia," *Proceedings of the Biological Society of Washington* 10 (1896): 93–101.

15. CHM to VB, 5/5/1896; VOB, Box 1, Folder 14.

16. CHM to VB, 6/9/1896; VOB, Box 1, Folder 14.

17. VB to DFAH, 11/16/1896; VOB, Box 10, Folder 1.

18. W. Derring to VB, 1897; VOB, Box 2, Folder 1.

19. CHM to VB, 7/9/1897; VOB, Box 2, Folder 1.

20. VB to DFAH, 12/11/1898; VOB, Box 10, Folder 2.

21. Secretary USDA to VB, 3/20/1899; VOB, Box 2, Folder 2.

22. VB to DFAH, 10/3/1899; VOB, Box 10, Folder 2.

23. Basil Dutcher to VB, 11/2/1899; Box 10, Folder 2.

24. Newspaper announcement of wedding, 12/17/1899; FMB papers, SIA, RU 7412, Box 2.

25. H. Kofalk, *No Woman Tenderfoot* (College Station: Texas A&M University Press, 1989).

Chapter 31

1. VB to DFAH, 3/11/1900; VOB, Box 10, Folder 3.

2. H. Kofalk, *No Woman Tenderfoot* (College Station: Texas A&M University Press, 1989).

3. Ibid.

4. Program announcing lectures, 1900; VOB, Box 16, Folder 5.

5. FMB to Anna, 6/23/1901; VOB, Box 10, Folder 3.

6. Kofalk, *No Woman Tenderfoot.*

7. Stanley Castro & Horace Burke, unpublished manuscript, Sam Houston State University Natural History Archives, December 2006.

8. Ibid.

9. Ibid.

10. VB, "Recollections of Louis Agassiz Fuertes," 1901; VOB, Box 15, Folder 14.

11. VB to DFAH, 8/7/1901; VOB, Box 10, Folder 3.

12. VB to DFAH, 6/1/1902; VOB, Box 10, Folder 3.

13. Kofalk, *No Woman Tenderfoot.*

14. CHM to VB, 6/5/1902; VOB, Box 2, Folder 5.

15. CHM to VB, 6/9/1902; VOB, Box 2, Folder 5.

16. F. M. Bailey, *Handbook of Birds of the Western United States* (Boston: Houghton, Mifflin, 1902 [(eleven editions published, including four revisions to 1935)].

17. A. K. Fisher to VB, 5/13/1903; VOB, Box 2, Folder 6.

18. FMB to Anna in H. Kofalk and B. Hone, "My Game Is Mice: A Life in the Field" (unpublished and unfinished biography of Vernon Bailey, no date), copy of manuscript deposited at the Southwest Archives, Texas Tech University, Lubbock, Texas.

19. CHM to VB, 7/2/1904; VOB, Box 2, Folder 7.

20. H. H. Henshaw, "Report of the Acting Chief of the Bureau of Biological Survey for 1906," *Annual Reports, Department of Agriculture* (1906): 397–418.

21. E. W. Nelson to VB; VOB, Box 2, Folder 10.

Chapter 32

1. VB to EWN, 1/15/1906; SIA/RU7364, Box 2, Folder 3.

2. Memo from G. Pinchot to Secretary of Agriculture, 3/14/1905; OPM-VB.

3. V. Bailey, "Wolves in Their Relation to Stock and Game," *Outdoor Life* 20 (1907): 159–164.

4. T. R. Dunlap, *Saving America's Wildlife* (Princeton, NJ: Princeton University Press, 1988).

5. CHM to VB, 4/3/1906; VOB, Box 2, Folder 9.

6. H. H. Henshaw, "Report of the Acting Chief of the Bureau of Biological Survey for 1906," *Annual Reports, Department of Agriculture* (1906): 397–418.

7. Henshaw to VB, 3/31/1906; VOB, Box 2, Folder 9.

8. CHM to VB, 4/3/1906; VOB, Box 2, Folder 9.

9. CHM to J. Wilson, 1/30/1906; OPM-VB.

10. Superintendent Baker to VB, 5/4/1906; VOB, Box 2, Folder 9.

11. Henshaw to VB, 5/4/1906; VOB, Box 2, Folder 9.

12. H. Kofalk and B. Hone, "My Game Is Mice: A Life in the Field" (unpublished and unfinished biography of Vernon Bailey, no date), copy of manuscript deposited at the Southwest Archives, Texas Tech University, Lubbock, Texas.

13. Henshaw to VB, 5/15/1906; VOB, Box 2, Folder 9.

14. CHM to VB, 5/19/1906; VOB, Box 2, Folder 9.

15. Lorum Pratt to VB; 1906; VOB, Box 2, Folder 9.

16. Price to VB, 2/6/1906; VOB, Box 2, Folder 9.

17. Orders to VB, 7/30/1906; VOB, Box 2, Folder 9.

18. M. Cary to VB, 8/18/1906; VOB, Box 2, Folder 9.

19. Ibid.

20. Ibid.

21. TSP to VB, 8/21/1906; VOB, Box 2, Folder 9.

22. TSP to VB, 9/22/1906; VOB, Box 2, Folder 9.

23. Forest Supervisor to The Forester, 10/6/1906; VOB, Box 2, Folder 9.

24. W. M. L. Hall to VB, 10/15/1906; VOB, Box 2, Folder 9.

25. C. H. Barney to VB, 12/6/1906; VOB, Box 2, Folder 9.

26. Kofalk and Hone, "My Game Is Mice."

Chapter 33

1. V. Bailey, "Wolves in Relation to Stock, Game, and the National Forest Reserves," *U.S. Department of Agriculture, Forest Service Bulletin* 72 (1907): 1–31

2. M. J. Robinson, *Predatory Bureaucracy: The Extermination of Wolves and the Transformation of the West* (Boulder: University of Press Colorado, 2005).

3. Utah Forest Service to VB, 3/5/1907; VOB, Box 2, Folder 10.

4. CHM to VB, 3/22/1907; VOB, Box 2, Folder 10.

5. VB to Anna, 3/25/1907; VOB, Box 10, Folder 4.

6. CHM to VB, 5/24/1907; VOB, Box 2, Folder 10.

7. VB to Anna, 6/7/1907; VOB, Box 10, Folder 4.

8. Henshaw to VB, 6/18/1907; VOB, Box 2, Folder 10.

9. CHM to VB, 8/27/1907; VOB, Box 2, Folder 10.

10. Henshaw to VB, 10/16/1907; VOB, Box 2, Folder 10.

11. Henshaw to VB, 11/19/1907; VOB, Box 2, Folder 10.

12. VB to Henshaw, 11/7/1907; McAtee Papers, LOC, Box 93, Folder 1.

Chapter 34

1. V. Bailey, "Directions for the Destruction of Wolves and Coyotes," *U.S. Department of Agriculture Bureau of Biological Survey Circular* 55 (1907): 1–6.

2. M. J. Robinson, *Predatory Bureaucracy: The Extermination of Wolves and the Transformation of the West* (Boulder: University Press of Colorado, 2005).

3. C. C. Young, *In the Absence of Predators: Conservation and Controversy on the Kaibab Plateau* (Lincoln: University of Nebraska Press, 2002).

4. Bailey, "Directions for the Destruction of Wolves."

5. Young, *In the Absence of Predators.*

6. Pam Nelson, "Shadow Catcher: Laura Ethel Mills," *Annual Journal of the Churchill County Museum Association* 11 (1997–1998): 3–4.

7. VB to family, 9/25/1908; VOB, Box 10, Folder 4.

8. VB to Anna, 9/26/1908; VOB, Box 10, Folder 4.

9. Anna to VB, 2/15/1909; VOB, Box 10, Folder 4.

10. VB to Anna, 7/29/1909; VOB, Box 10, Folder 4.

11. VB to Anna, 4/24/1910; VOB, Box 10, Folder 5.

12. VB to Anna, 7/31/1910; VOB, Box 10, Folder 5.

13. VB to Anna, 9/29/1910; VOB, Box 10, Folder 5.

14. VB to Anna, 10/15/1910; VOB, Box 10, Folder 5.

15. VB to Anna, 10/23/1910; VOB, Box 10, Folder 5.

16. Ibid.

17. VB to Flo & Chet Hill, 10/30/1910; VOB, Box 10, Folder 1.

18. E. L. Cabot, *Ethics for Children* (Boston: Houghton Mifflin, 1910).

19. FMB to Anna, 12/15/1910; VOB, Box 13, Folder 1.

20. H. Kofalk, *No Woman Tenderfoot: Florence Merriam Bailey, Pioneer Naturalist* (College Station: Texas A&M University Press, 1989).

21. Robinson, *Predatory Bureaucracy.*

22. CHM to J. Wilson, Secretary of Agriculture, 5/30/1910; OPM-VB.

Section IV

1. K. B. Sterling, *Last of the Naturalists: The Career of C. Hart Merriam* (New York: Arno Press, 1977).

2. L. S. Mastroni, "The Conflicted Mission of the United States Bureau of Biological Survey, 1885–1940: Wildlife Uncertainty, and Ambivalence" (PhD diss., University of Oklahoma, 2012).

3. M. J. Robinson, *Predatory Bureaucracy: The Extermination of Wolves and the Transformation of the West* (Boulder: University Press of Colorado, 2005).

Chapter 35

1. FMB to Flo, 1/21/1911; VOB, Box 13, Folder 1.
2. VB to Mills family, 2/10/1911; VOB, Box 10, Folder 6.
3. EB to VB, 7/24/1911; VOB, Box 10, Folder 6.
4. HB to Mills Family, 3/31/1911; VOB, Box 13, Folder 1.
5. FMB to Flo, 4/8/1911; VOB, Box 13, Folder 1.
6. VB to Flo, 4/22/1911; VOB, Box 13, Folder 1.
7. Department to VB, 6/1/1911; OPM-VB.
8. FMB to Anna, 6/9/1911; VOB, Box 13, Folder 1.
9. FMB to Anna, 6/11/1911; VOB, Box 13, Folder 2.
10. VB to family, 7/3/1911; VOB, Box 13, Folder 2.
11. EB to relatives, 7/24/1911; VOB, Box 10, Folder 6.
12. VB to relatives, 7/28/1911; VOB, Box 10, Folder 6.
13. VB to family, 8/6/1911; VOB, Box 13, Folder 2.
14. EB to relatives, 8/8/1911; VOB, Box 13, Folder 2.
15. VB to family, 11/5/1911; VOB, Box 13, Folder 2.
16. VB to parents, 11/13/1911; VOB, Box 13, Folder 2.
17. H. Kofalk and B. Hone, "My Game Is Mice: A Life in the Field" (unpublished and unfinished biography of Vernon Bailey, no date), copy of manuscript deposited at the Southwest Archives, Texas Tech University, Lubbock, Texas.
18. W. S. Hall, *From Youth into Manhood* (New York: Young Men's Christian Association Press, 1909).
19. VB to Anna, 12/19/1911; VOB, Box 13, Folder 2.
20. HB & EB to relatives, 2/4/1912; VOB, Box 13, Folder 3.
21. Flo to EB, 3/3/1912; VOB, Box 13, Folder 3.
22. VB to Anna, 6/6/1912; VOB, Box 10, Folder 7.
23. VB to Anna, 12/6/1912; VOB, Box 10, Folder 7.

Chapter 36

1. VB to Anna, 1/26/1913; VOB, Box 13, Folder 3.
2. OPM-VB.
3. Henshaw to VB, 7/1/1913; VOB, Box 2, Folder 16.
4. EWN to VB, 7/22/1913; VOB, Box 2, Folder 16.
5. EWN to VB, 8/8/1913; VOB, Box 2, Folder 16.
6. TSP to VB, 10/11/1913; VOB, Box 2, Folder 16.
7. Survey Clerk to VB, 8/12/1913, VOB, Box 2, Folder 16.
8. EWN to VB, 9/3/913; VOB, Box 2, Folder 16.
9. FMB to VB, 10/15/1913; VOB, Box 10, Folder 8.
10. FMB to VB, 10/16/1913; VOB, Box 10, Folder 8.

11. H. Kofalk, *No Woman Tenderfoot* (College Station: Texas A&M University Press, 1989).

12. FMB to VB, 10/18/1913; VOB, Box 10, Folder 8.

13. FMB to Anna, 10/16/1913; VOB, Box 10, Folder 9.

14. Ibid.

15. Ibid.

16. Poem written by V. Bailey, SIA/RU 7267, Box 1.

17. EWN to VB, 5/22/1914; VOB, Box 2, Folder 17.

18. Ibid.

19. EWN to VB, 6/22/1914; VOB, Box 2, Folder 17.

20. EWN to VB, 8/-/1914; VOB, Box 2, Folder 17.

Chapter 37

1. D. E. Brown, *The Grizzly in the Southwest* (Norman: University of Oklahoma Press, 1985).

2. T. R. Dunlap, *Saving America's Wildlife* (Princeton, NJ: Princeton University Press, 1988).

3. EWN to VB, 7/4/1915; VOB, Box 2, Folder 18.

4. Superintendent of Yellowstone National Park to VB, 7/10/1915; VOB, Box 2, Folder 19.

5. EWN to VB, 2/18/1916; VOB, Box 2, Folder 19.

6. EWN to VB, 8/3/1917; VOB, Box 3, Folder 1.

7. Memorandum from EWN, 6/12/1917; VOB, Box 3, Folder 1.

8. EWN to VB, 3/11/1918; VOB, Box 3, Folder 2.

9. Memorandum from Secretary of Agriculture, 9/25/1918; OPM-VB.

10. Scout Commissioner to VB, February 1918; VOB, Box 14, Folder 12.

11. Ibid.

12. Henderson to VB, 7/1/1919; VOB, Box 3, Folder 3.

13. Henderson to VB, 9/22/1919; VOB, Box 3, Folder 3.

14. VB to Anna, 11/26/1919; VOB, Box 10, Folder 14.

Chapter 38

1. *The Survey, Newsletter of the Biological Survey*, Vol. 1, No. 1, 1/2/1920; Nelson & Goldman Papers, SIA/RU-7364.

2. V. Bailey, "Identity of the Bean Mouse of Lewis and Clark," *Journal of Mammalogy* 1 (1920): 70–72.

3. Henderson to VB, 6/22/1920; VOB, Box 3, Folder 4.

4. OPM-VB, 6/22/1920.

5. EWN to VB, 6/25/1920; VOB, Box 3, Folder 4.

6. OPM-VB, 6/29/1920.

7. E. A. Goldman to VB, 11/19/1920; VOB, Box 3, Folder 4.

8. VB to Anna, 3/29/1921; VOB, Box 10, Folder 16.

9. EWN to VB, 2/20/1921; VOB, Box 3, Folder 5.

10. FMB to EWN, Dec. 1920; SIA/RU-7374; Nelson & Goldman Papers, Box 2, Folder 2.

11. EWN to VB, 3/7/1921; VOB, Box 3, Folder 5.

12. A. K. Fisher to VB, 3/25/1921; VOB, Box 3, Folder 5.

13. *The Survey, Newsletter of the Biological Survey*, Vol. 2, No. 6, 1921; Nelson & Goldman Papers, SIA/RU-7364.

14. EAG to VB, 6/23/1921; VOB, Box 3, Folder 5.

15. Vernon Bailey papers, SIA/RU-7267.

16. VB to family, 3/9/1922; VOB, Box 10, Folder 17.

17. Pack to VB, 9/23/1922; VOB, Box 3, Folder 6.

18. Pack to VB, 10/2/1922; VOB, Box 3, Folder 6.

19. VB to Anna, 9/4/1922; VOB, Box 10, Folder 17.

20. OPM-VB, 4/25/1923.

21. EWN to VB, 6/6/1923; VOB, Box 3, Folder 7.

22. EWN to VB, 6/7/1923; VOB, Box 3, Folder 7.

23. EWN to VB, 8/4/1923; VOB, Box 3, Folder 7.

24. VB to Anna, 9/7/1923; VOB, Box 11, Folder 1.

25. E. D. Shaw (Scout Executive, Boy Scouts of America, DC Council) to VB, 10/10/1923; VOB, Box 3, Folder 7.

26. A. Townsend to VB, 10/10/1923; VOB, Box 3, Folder 7.

27. Columbia University to VB, 1/9/1924; VOB, Box 3, Folder 8.

28. Anna to VB, 12/23/1923; VOB, Box 11, Folder 1.

29. Travel Instructions, 3/1/1924; VOB, Box 3, Folder 8.

30. Ibid.

31. VB to Charles Knight, 3/23/1924; VOB, Box 3, Folder 8

32. Knight, a well-known wildlife artist, was a longtime friend who had created a mural of two tigers when the Baileys first moved into their Washington house at the turn of the century. His depictions of dinosaurs in their natural habitat are museum "regulars" to this day, including large murals of the LaBrea tar pits in Los Angeles.

33. EAG to VB, 4/5/1924; VOB, Box 3, Folder 8.

34. EAG to VB, 4/23/1924; VOB, Box 3, Folder 8.

35. CHM to VB, 5/12/1924; VOB, Box 3, Folder 8.

36. Travel instructions, 7/10/1924; VOB, Box 3, Folder 8.

37. Llewellyn Legge (Chief, New York Division of Fish & Game) to VB, 9/2/1924; VOB, Box 3, Folder 8.

38. EAG to VB, 9/10/1924; VOB, Box 3, Folder 8.

39. J. B. Trefethen, *An American Crusade for Wildlife* (New York: Winchester Press, 1985).

40. J. Grinnell to VB, 9/10/1924; VOB, Box 3, Folder 8.

41. M. R. VanCleve (President, American Nature Study Society), 9/20/1924; VOB, Box 3, Folder 8.

42. VanCleve to VB, 10/18/1924; VOB, Box 3, Folder 8.

43. Handwritten talk by VB on mammals of Glacier National Parks, 10/25/1924; VOB, Box 3, Folder 8.

44. T. R. Dunlap, *Saving America's Wildlife* (Princeton, NJ: Princeton University Press, 1988).

45. M. J. Robinson, *Predatory Bureaucracy: The Extermination of Wolves and the Transformation of the West* (Boulder: University Press of Colorado, 2005).

46. Dunlap, *Saving America's Wildlife.*

Chapter 39

1. VB to Anna, 1/4/1925; VOB, Box 11, Folder 3.

2. Travel instructions, 4/13/1925; VOB, Box 3, Folder 9.

3. *Dailey Mining Journal*, "U.S. Ideal for Beaver Farming, Experts Views," 8/26/1925; VOB, Box 15, Folder 10.

4. Edward Break to VB, 5/25/1925; VOB. Box 3, Folder 9.

5. Edward Break to VB, 6/3/1925; VOB, Box 3, Folder 9.

6. W. E. Sanderson to VB, 1/30/1925; VOB, Box 4, Folder 6.

7. Anna to VB, 7/12/1925; VOB, Box 11, Folder 3.

8. VB to Anna, 8/2/1925; VOB, Box 11, Folder 3.

9. VB to Anna, 11/22/1925; VOB, Box 11, Folder 3.

10. VB to Anna, 12/27/1925; VOB, Box 11, Folder 3.

11. VB to Anna, no date/1925; VOB, Box 11, Folder 3.

12. Newspaper article, 1925; VOB, Box 15, Folder 8.

13. V. Bailey, "Biological Survey of North Dakota," *North American Fauna* 49 (1926): 1–229.

14. V. Bailey, "Mammals of the Vicinity of Washington," *Journal of the Washington Academy of Science* 16 (1926): 441–445.

15. V. Bailey, "Construction and Operation of Biological Survey Beaver Trap," *U.S. Department of Agriculture Miscellaneous Circular* 69 (1926): 1–4.

16. VB to Anna, 12/25/1926; VOB, Box 11, Folder 3.

17. VB to ?, no date/1927; VOB, Box 4, Folder 1.

18. VB to Anna, no date/1927; VOB, Box 4, Folder 2.

19. T. R. Dunlap, *Saving America's Wildlife* (Princeton, NJ: Princeton University Press, 1988).

20. Statement released by Biological Survey, 2/23/1927; SIA/RU-7364, Nelson and Goldman Papers, Box 25, Folder 2.

21. L. S. Mastroni, "The Conflicted Mission of the United States Bureau of Biological Survey, 1885–1940: Wildlife Uncertainty, and Ambivalence" (PhD diss., University of Oklahoma, 2012).

Chapter 40

1. VB to Laura Mills, 1/17/1928; VOB, Box 11, Folder 6.

2. Correspondence between John Doelle and VB; VOB, Box 15, Folder 15.

3. VB to J. Doelle, 3/5/1928; VOB, Box 15, Folder 15.

4. VB to J. Doelle, no date/1928; VOB, Box 15, Folder 16.

5. J. B. Trefethen, *An American Crusade for Wildlife* (New York: Winchester Press, 1975).

6. V. Bailey, "Pennsylvania to Kill Does and Protect Bucks," *American Game* 17 (1928): 55–56, 66–67.

7. V. Bailey, "Deer Investigations in Pennsylvania," *Game Breeder* 32 (1928): 163–165, 180–184.

8. OPM-VB, 7/19/1928.

9. OPM-VB, 7/23/1928.

10. For a thorough discussion of the Kaibab deer herd controversy, including Bailey's role, see C. C. Young, *In the Absence of Predators: Conservation and Controversy on the Kaibab Plateau* (Lincoln: University of Nebraska Press, 2002).

11. Vernon Bailey, "Mammals of the Grand Canyon, Arizona," unpublished manuscript, January 16, 1929, Box 2, KNF.

12. OPM-VB, 1/28/1929.

13. VB to Anna, 3/1/1929; VOB, Box 11, Folder 7.

14. VB to P. Redington, 3/20/1929; Vernon Bailey papers, SIA-RU 7267.

15. VB to Laura Mills, 3/1/1929; VOB, Box 11, Folder 7. Barbara Hastings was a young, aspiring botanist who, in addition to driving the Baileys to the Grand Canyon, also assisted Vernon Bailey with the fieldwork.

16. F. M. Bailey and V. Bailey, *Among the Birds in the Grand Canyon Country,* (Washington, DC: Government Printing Office, 1939).

17. VB to Laura Mills, 3/29/1929; VOB, Box 11, Folder 7.

18. VB to Laura Mills, 6/1/1929; VOB, Box 11, Folder 7.

19. FMB to Laura Mills, 8/19/1929; VOB, Box 11, Folder 7.

20. Ibid.

21. VB to Anna, 9/13/1929; VOB, Box 11, Folder 7.

Chapter 41

1. T. R. Dunlap, *Saving America's Wildlife* (Princeton, NJ: Princeton University Press, 1988).

2. Announcement in *Science*, 74 (1916): 288–290.

3. A. B. Howell to VB, 5/7/1930; VOB, Box 4, Folder 7.

4. C. C. Young, *In the Absence of Predators: Conservation and Controversy on the Kaibab Plateau* (Lincoln: University of Nebraska Press, 2002). Vernon Bailey, "The Rocky Mountain Mule Deer: A Preliminary Report on the Mule Deer of the Grand Canyon Region of Arizona," unpublished manuscript, April 8, 1930, 1, Box 2, KNF.

5. VB handwritten report to C. C. Adams, SIA-ASM Archives, Box 126, Folder 3.

6. VB trip report; VOB, Box 14, Folder 9.

7. Bayard Christy to VB, 1/28/1931; VOB, Box 4, Folder 10.

8. Christy to VB, 2/11/1931; VOB, Box 4, Folder 10.

9. Christy to VB, 2/25/1931; VOB, Box 4, Folder 10.

10. Frederic Walcott to VB, 9/12/1930; VOB, Box 4, Folder 8.

11. D. J. Schmidly, "Vernon Bailey (1864–1942): Chief Field Naturalist of the Biological Survey," in *United States Biological Survey: A Compendium of Its History, Personalities, Impacts, and Conflicts*, ed. D. J. Schmidly, W. E. Tydeman, and A. L. Gardner (Lubbock: Texas Tech University, The Museum, Special Publication Number 64, 2016), 25–53.

12. H H. Kofalk, *No Woman Tenderfoot: Florence Merriam Bailey, Pioneer Naturalist* (College Station: Texas A&M University Press, 1989), 186.

13. VB to Anna, 3/22/1931; VOB, Box 11, Folder 9.

14. Travel instructions, 6/27/1931; VOB, Box 4, Folder 10.

15. Christy to VB, 4/16/1931; VOB, Box 4, Folder 10.

16. SIA-ASM archives.

17. Christy to VB, 4/28/1931; VOB, Box 4, Folder 10.

18. Foster to VB, 7/16/1931; VOB, Box 4, Folder 11.

19. Christy to VB, 9/2/1931; VOB, Box 4, Folder 11.

20. Foster to VB, 9/14/1931; VOB, Box 4, Folder 11.

21. VB to Laura Mills, 10/30/1931; VOB, Box 11, Folder 9.

22. H. Kofalk and B. Hone, "My Game is Mice: A Life in the Field" (unpublished and unfinished biography of Vernon Bailey, no date), copy of manuscript deposited at the Southwest Archives, Texas Tech University, Lubbock, Texas.

23. Foster to VB, 11/9/1931; VOB, Box 4, Folder 11.

24. Foster to VB, 11/21/1931; VOB, Box 4, Folder 11.

25. V. Bailey, "Mammals of New Mexico," *North American Fauna 53* (1931): 1–412.

26. "The Official Record, U.S. Department of Agriculture," VOB, Box 14, Folder 1.

27. W. E. Sanderson to VB, 12/9/1931; VOB, Box 4, Folder 11.

28. Foster to VB, 12/22/1931; VOB, Box 4, Folder 11.

29. VB handwritten document, 6/15/1931; VOB, Box 4, Folder 7.

Chapter 42

1. Foster to VB, 1/24/1932; VOB, Box 5, Folder 1.

2. Foster to VB, 3/5/1932; VOB, Box 5, Folder 1.

3. Christy to VB, 3/29/1932; VOB, Box 5, Folder 1.

4. Christy to VB, 4/1/1932; VOB, Box 5, Folder 2.

5. VB to Christy, 4/11/1932; VOB, Box 5, Folder 2.

6. VB to Foster, 1/10/1932; VOB, Box 5, Folder 2.

7. Bell to VB, 5/26/1932; VOB, Box 5, Folder 2.

8. VB to Anna, 8/2/1932; VOB, Box 11, Folder 10.

9. "The National Humane Review," July 1932; VOB, Box 16, Folder 1.

10. Frederic Winthropp to Bernard Bailey, 10/nd/1932;VOB, Box 5, Folder 3.

11. VB to Laura Mills, 1/30/1933; VOB, Box 11, Folder 11.

12. Jane Deland (Cornell University Rural Education Department) to VB, 3/25/1933; VOB, Box 5, Folder 4.

13. Henry Bailey to VB, 3/16/1933; VOB, Box 11, Folder 11.

14. Notes of the Recording Secretary, American Society of Mammalogists, 5/11/1933; SIA-ASM archives RU 7357, Box 85, Folder 2.

15. Murie to VB, 6/9/1933; VOB, Box 5, Folder 4.

16. SIA-ASM archives, 5/12/1933; RU 7457, Box 126, Folder 6.

17. Chief, Division of Appointments to VB 6/27/1933; VOB, Box 5, Folder 4.

18. Redington to VB, 7/3/1933; VOB, Box 5, Folder 5.

19. Redington to VB, 7/5/1933; VOB, Box 5, Folder 5.

20. VB to Redington, 7/7/1933; OPM-VB.

21. Hornaday to VB, 7/21/1933; VOB, Box 5, Folder 5.

22. Albright to VB, 8/7/1933; VOB, Box 5, Folder 5.

23. EWN to VB, 8/2/1933; VOB, Box 5, Folder 5.

24. Henry Wallace, Secretary of Agriculture, to VB, 9/1/1933; OPM-VB.

25. VB to Henry Wallace, 9/14/1933; OPM-VB.

26. Encomium presented at retirement celebration; OPM-VB.

27. VB to Henderson, 8/30/1033; OPM-VB.

28. Reconstructed from personnel records; OMB-VB.

Section V

1. M. J. Robinson, *Predatory Bureaucracy: The Extermination of Wolves and the Transformation of the West* (Boulder: University Press of Colorado, 2005).

Chapter 43

1. VB to Anna, 7/23/1933; VOB, Box 11, Folder 11.

2. Grosvenor (President of National Geographic Society) to VB, 5/22/1934; VOB, Box 5, Folder 7.

3. Calendar diary entry, VB personal papers, SIA-RU 7267.

4. Letter of invitation to 50th anniversary of Biological Survey, 2/21/1935; VOB, Box 5, Folder 8.

5. Acting Chief to VB, 8/3/1935 and 8/6/1935; VOB, Box 5, Folder 9.

6. VB to Bell, 12/19/1935; OPM-VB.

7. CHM to VB, no date/1935; VOB, Box 5, Folder 9.

8. CHM to VB, 8/30/1935; VOB, Box 5, Folder 9.

9. CHM to VB, 5/1/1936; VOB, Box 6, Folder 9.

10. D. Hoffmeister, *Mammals of Arizona* (Tucson: University of Arizona Press, 1986).

11. W. E. Sanderson to VB, 6/8/1936; VOB, Box 6, Folder 2.

12. T. R. Dunlap, *Saving America's Wildlife* (Princeton, NJ: Princeton University Press, 1988).

13. Betty Hone, Florence's grandniece, was one of two granddaughters of Charles Collins Merriam. Collie, as he was known, was Florence's oldest brother, thirteen years her senior. Betty Hone collected all of Bailey's papers and materials from various sources and donated them to the University of Wyoming in 1958. She also coauthored with Harriet Kofalk, an unfinished and unpublished biography about Bailey.

14. VB to Laura Mills, no specific date; VOB, Box 12, Folder 3.

15. V. Bailey, "The Mammals and Life Zones of Oregon," *North American Fauna* 55 (1936): 1–416.

16. VB to R. S. Oaks, 1/4/1937; VOB, Box 6, Folder 4.

17. VB to R. S. Oaks, 2/8/1937; VOB, Box 6, Folder 4.

18. VOB, Box 6, Folder 4.

19. A. Day to VB, 5/19/1937; VOB, Box 6, Folder 5.

20. *The Sunday Star*, Washington, DC, 12/13/1936; VOB, Box 16, Folder 1.

21. VB to Stejneger, 10/13/1937; VOB, Box 6, Folder 6.

22. *National Nature News* 11/29/1937; VOB, Box 16, Folder 1.

23. See VOB, Box 16, Folder 1.

24. VB to Douglas Hays, 12/22/1937; VOB, Box 6, Folder 6.

25. VB to Spigelmyre, 1/11/1938; VOB, Box 6, Folder 7.

26. VB to Lucy Furman, 2/16/1938; VOB, Box 7, Folder 1.

27. W. E. Sanderson to VB, 2/24/1938; VOB, Box 7, Folder 1.

28. Douglas Hays to ATC, 3/5/1938; VOB, Box 7, Folder 1.

29. VB to Anna, 12/10/1938; VOB, Box 7, Folder 4.

30. V. Bailey handwritten document, 1939; VOB, Box 17, Folder 17.

Chapter 44

1. Letter of invitation to speak in Toronto, February 1940: VOB, Box 7, Folder 8.

2. Invitation to speak at ASM meetings in Denver, 1940; VOB, Box 7, Folder 10.

3. Newspaper article; VOB, Box 7, Folder 9.

4. Lucy Furman to VB, 4/20 & 4/29/1940; VOB, Box 7, Folder 9.

5. VB to TenBroeck, 5/3/1940; VOB, Box 7, Folder 10.

6. Form letter to VB, 6/27/1940; VOB, Box 7, Folder 10.

7. Walter Taylor to VB, VOB, Box 7, Folder 11.

8. 1928 Bailey Family History, VOB, Box 11.

9. Prairie Trek letters, in H. Kofalk and B. Hone, "My Game Is Mice: A Life in the Field" (unpublished and unfinished biography of Vernon Bailey, no date), copy of manuscript deposited at the Southwest Archives, Texas Tech University, Lubbock, Texas.

10. Newspaper article, *Toronto Telegram*, December 1940; VOB, Box 7, Folder 9.

11. Zimmerman (President of UNM) to Sam G. Bratton, 6/6/1940; VOB, Box 8, Folder 2.

12. US Predatory Control Office to VB, 6/23/1941; VOB, Box 8, Folder 2.

13. VB to Kermit Roosevelt, 6/9/1941; VOB, Box 8, Folder 2.

14. Walter Taylor to VB, 11/19/1941; VOB, Box 8, Folder 2.

15. Walter Taylor to Bell, 12/23/1941; VOB, Box 8, Folder 2.

16. Anna to VB, 10/21/1941; VOB, Box 8, Folder 2.

17. Article in the *Fallon Standard News*, Fallon, Nevada.

18. Vernon Mills to VB, 1/12/1942, 2/9/1942, 2/11/1942; VOB, Box 8, Folder 3.

19. Charles Bailey to VB, no specific date/1942; VOB, Box 8, Folder 3.

Chapter 45

1. H. Kofalk and B. Hone, "My Game Is Mice: A Life in the Field" (unpublished and unfinished biography of Vernon Bailey, no date), copy of manuscript deposited at the Southwest Archives, Texas Tech University, Lubbock, Texas.

2. Laura Mills to May Mills, 4/26/1942; VOB, Box 12, Folder 8.

3. Harry Mills to family, 4/22/1942; VOB, Box 12, Folder 8.

4. Kofalk and Hone, "My Game Is Mice."

5. Ira Gabrielson (Chief, US Biological Survey) to FMB, 4/24/1942; OPM-VB.

6. H. Kofalk, *No Woman Tenderfoot: Florence Merriam Bailey, Pioneer Naturalist* (College Station: Texas A&M University Press, 1989), 186.

7. H. Zahniser, "Orbituary Vernon Orlando Bailey 1864–142," *Science* 96 (1942): 6–7.

8. T. S. Palmer, "Vernon Orlando Bailey," *The Auk* 64 (1947): 502–503.

9. Pam Nelson, "Shadow Catcher: Laura Ethel Mills," *Annual Journal of the Churchill County Museum Association* (1997–1998): 3–4.

Bailey in Perspective

1. R. E. Kohler, "From Farm and Family to Career Naturalist: The Apprenticeship of Vernon Bailey," *Isis* 99 (2008): 28–56.

2. Ibid.

3. Ibid.

4. H. Kofalk, *No Woman Tenderfoot: Florence Merriam Bailey, Pioneer Naturalist* (College Station: Texas A&M University Press, 1989), 186.

5. R. E. Kohler, *All Creatures, Naturalists, Collectors, and Biodiversity, 1850–1950* (Princeton, NJ: Princeton University Press, 2006).

6. Ibid.

7. L. S. Mastroni, "The Conflicted Mission of the United States Bureau of Biological Survey, 1885–1940: Wildlife Uncertainty, and Ambivalence" (PhD diss., University of Oklahoma, 2012).

8. Ibid.

9. Ibid.

10. VB to Hubbs, 10/21/1936; and Hubbs to VB, 10/23/1936; VB papers, SIA-RU 7267, Box 5.

11. Mastroni, "Conflicted Mission."

12. VB memorandum to Biological Survey, 1936; VOB, Box 8, Folder 5.

13. V. Bailey, "Review: Wilderness Warriors," *Journal of Mammalogy* 18 (1937): 104.

14. H. Zahniser, "Orbituary Vernon Orlando Bailey 1864–142," *Science* 96 (1942): 6–7.

15. VB list of publications, VOB, Box 16, Folder 10.

16. D. J. Schmidly, "Vernon Bailey (1864–1942): Chief Field Naturalist of the Biological Survey," in *United States Biological Survey: A Compendium of Its History, Personalities, Impacts, and Conflicts*, ed. D. J. Schmidly, W. E. Tydeman, and A. L. Gardner (Lubbock: Texas Tech University, The Museum, Special Publication Number 64, 2016), 25–53.

17. Ibid.

18. A. Chestnut, "Vernon Bailey a Nature Nobleman," *Nature Magazine 14* (1929): 229–232.

19. Written comments about VB by Walter McAtee; McAtee Papers, LOC, Box 95.

20. Reconstructed from papers in OPM-VB.

21. McAtee Papers, LOC, Box 95.

22. Albert K. Fisher Papers, LOC, Box 40, Folder 11.

23. Jackson Papers, SIA-RU 7172, Box 17.

24. A. K. Fisher Papers, LOC, Box 40, Folder 12.

25. C. Phillips and C. Jones, eds., *Going Afield* (Lubbock: Museum of Texas Tech University, 2005)

26. Rollin Baker unpublished autobiography, Sam Houston State University Natural History Archives.

27. 1903 poem by Edmund Vance Cooke; VOB, Box 17, Folder 16.

Index